The Romance of
NORTH AMERICA

Edited by HARDWICK MOSELEY

With an Introduction by
PRESTON E. JAMES

Illustrated with maps and photographs

CONTRIBUTING AUTHORS

Donald G. Creighton	Stewart Holbrook
Marshall B. Davidson	William Weber Johnson
Bernard De Voto	Philip A. Knowlton
Waldo Frank	Ralph McGill
Ernest Gruening	Scott O'Dell
Walter Havighurst	Jack Schaefer

Wallace Stegner

HOUGHTON MIFFLIN COMPANY • BOSTON
1958

Contents

Maps & Pictures

Preface

There are many excellent books available on the three major political units of North America north of Guatemala—Canada, the United States, and Mexico. They range in intellectual content from picture books with attenuated text to esoteric books of research.

Most public libraries and bookstores can offer the student, or the merely curious reader, countless books on Canada, Mexico, and the United States including Alaska, but strangely enough there are few, if any, books available on the North American continent which are not written from a single national point of view.

The Mexican, the Canadian, and the resident of the United States, is, and always was, a North American. It was the land, the climate, the geography of the continent that first shaped his character; his political loyalties developed later out of character already formed by the land. It is thus no accident that Democracy is everywhere on the North American continent. National character is of course unique, but our national character is molded and influenced by our neighbors. Who can visualize the Mexican, the Canadian, or a citizen of the United States out of context with his neighbors? Each of the countries of North America has made cultural, agricultural, economic, and political contributions to the others that have profoundly influenced the national character of all, and it is certain that the cultural give and take between the countries will go on indefinitely to the enrichment of all.

Preface

North America is the most successful and favored continent of historical times. It provides a better life, more personal freedom, more opportunity for individual self-expression than any other continent. The peoples who live in the major political units of North America live in a kind of unity of understanding that negates fear of neighbors—a confidence not known in other continents. There is a continental unity which has grown out of common experience and a sense of mutuality of destination which is shared by people from Alaska to Guatemala. Serious conflicts between the citizens of the four political governments are unthinkable. Our quarrels will always be family quarrels to be resolved amicably as is seemly between people who live under one roof.

I wish to thank the fourteen writers who have contributed to *The Romance of North America*, most of whom interrupted important projects to write for this book, and I want especially to thank Philip A. Knowlton for his excellent chapter on the Central East and his contribution to the chapter on New England by the late Bernard De Voto, and for his skillful and experienced editorial advice.

HARDWICK MOSELEY

INTRODUCTION:

The Nations of North America

BY PRESTON E. JAMES

North America is a remarkable continent. Almost everyone is familiar with the statistics that show how extraordinary the economic development has been. The United States and Canada together produce each year more than half of the world's wealth, and the income per person in these countries is the world's highest. But beyond the statistics there is a quality to life never before experienced by any large groups of mankind. There is more personal freedom, more security, more self-determination, more access to knowledge, more freedom from the arbitrary acts of those in authority, more equality before the law— more of many things that make life for large numbers of people at once exciting, challenging, and rewarding. Except for the grim threat of another war that could wipe out all our gains, most North Americans would still share the optimistic belief, by no means common in other parts of the world, that in the decades ahead things will be even better than they are now. How did all this come about? Why is North America so favored? Is it because of a rich endowment of natural resources? Is it because of the peculiar qualities of the people?

There is no doubt that North America has an unusual endowment of the things people call "natural resources." The United States (including Alaska) and Canada together have more than half of all the coal in the world. From the arctic tundra of Canada to the tropical coastlands of eastern Mexico, both the United States and its neighbors on the north and south have fabulous supplies of petroleum. And there is an enormous supply of other useful minerals and plants. From varied soils and climates come many different kinds of products ranging from sugar cane to potatoes, from alligator hides to furs.

But history makes clear that the possession of so-called natural resources does not guarantee a high material standard of living, nor does the lack of resources make such a standard impossible. The materials that are listed as resources change from one period to another. The coal in North America was not a natural resource for the Indians, nor even for the white settlers until quite recently. In 1804 two enterprising brothers dug up some of the black rocks of eastern Pennsylvania and floated them on barges down the Susquehanna River. The people of Lancaster County had never seen coal before and had no idea how to use it. Four years later a blacksmith made a special grate for Judge Jesse Fell of Wilkes-Barre, and the judge tried out some of the black rocks. He found coal would heat his home more easily and more cheaply than wood. Judge Fell's grate, or one like it, was used to demonstrate how coal could be used. Little by little a market was created for a new natural resource. It was not until after 1859 that coal, made into coke, was used in steel manufacture. Most people do not realize that half of all the coal that has been burned throughout human history has been burned in the United States in the last thirty years. Coal has only recently been considered a major resource. It became a resource through human ingenuity.

Human ingenuity does not always result in adding to the list of resources. In some cases materials are crossed off the list of resources. Many of the iron furnaces of early times were supplied from such low-grade ores that they would be worthless today. In other cases human ingenuity has found ways to use up a resource so fast that no more of it remains. It is already predicted that lead, zinc, and tin will be rare and therefore precious metals by 1980, copper by 2000.

So it is with all the features of the land. What the land means to the people inhabiting it at any one time depends on the way these people live—their attitudes, objectives, and technical skills. To the early British settlers in eastern North America the densely forested Appalachians were a natural barrier difficult to cross. The present-day motorist driving over the Pennsylvania Turnpike is conscious of no barrier. Slopes have different meaning for men on foot, for men with horses, for men with railroads, and for men with automobiles—and little or no meaning for men with airplanes. To the Spanish explorers of western North America, familiar with open landscapes, the dense forests of the east and north were "unfriendly." But to the French fur trappers it was the open, unwooded prairies that were unfriendly.

A nation is forged from the intimate union of land and people. A mere change in the meaning of the land factor is no reason for overlooking it. If we are to understand what people are doing in any particular place at any one time, we cannot neglect the nature of the climate, the slopes, the soils, the water, the vegetation, the animals, the minerals, and the other features included in the general word "land"; but we must know what meaning the people attach to these features. Sometimes history is presented to us as if people lived out their lives quite separately from the hills and valleys, the rivers and coasts, or the forests and prairies that make up the habitat—like a play with no scenery. To understand why North America is such a remarkable continent we must try to see each country, and each region or section, as a result of human action in a particular setting, of people creating a man-made landscape out of the earth materials at hand.

When the European explorers first came upon the continent of North America, it had already been occupied for thousands of years by so-called Indians. They were a Mongoloid people who, many thousands of years earlier, had crossed Bering Strait from Asia and had spread south and east, even to the tip end of South America. These native Americans were at first simple hunters and fishers, for whom the basic natural resource was the population of game animals. After a time, however, they learned how to plant crops. The Indians of Guatemala may have been the first ones to make use of the distinctive American grain, maize, which we call corn. The Indians of Peru first cultivated the potato. Tobacco growing and the smoking of cigars came from Cuba.

The only part of North America where Indians were concentrated was in central and southern Mexico and in Guatemala. Here the original forest had been extensively cleared and the land used for farming. Elsewhere a very thin population of Indians managed to make great changes in the original cover of plants through the use of fire. It is thought that fires, lighted by prehistoric man in the process of hunting wild animals, may have created the open grasslands of our Middle West through the burning of the young trees.

The Europeans found the whole eastern side of North America clothed in forest. In many ways eastern North America was remarkably similar to western Europe. The forests contained many trees familiar to Europeans. On both sides of the Atlantic there were rainy climates with variable weather. To be sure, the winters of North America were colder and the summers hotter than those of western Europe, but not enough so to raise very serious new problems of living for the colonists. The "many-harbored" coast of North America offered landing places for men with small sailing ships, and the abundant fish off New England provided a familiar kind of food. The crops that the Europeans had been accustomed to raising did well in the new land, and in addition there was the Indian grain, maize or corn. Inland from the coast, well-worn Indian trails through the forest marked the easiest routes for men on foot or with horses.

For all its harbors and its Indian trails, eastern North America did not offer many easy ways westward. North of New York the granite-ribbed hills of New England pointed rocky fingers toward the sea. South of New York it was possible to sail for short distances up the rivers. But on the inner margin of the coastal plain the rivers, descending from the rolling piedmont, were interrupted by falls and rapids. The colonists had found what geographers now call the Fall Line. A whole string of settlements were located along this line: Trenton, Philadelphia, Wilmington, Baltimore, Washington, Richmond, Raleigh, Columbia, Augusta. Beyond the piedmont were the forested ridges of the Appalachians, running from northeast to southwest from the Hudson Valley to Alabama. Passage parallel to the ridges was easy, but to cross them was not at all easy except where the rivers had cut gaps. Farther west the imposing and almost unbroken edge of the Appalachian Plateaus—the Cumberland Front in the south and the Allegheny Front in the north—set a major obstacle athwart the paths that led westward.

The French settlers along the St. Lawrence River, on the other hand, found an open route to the west. Carrying their canoes around the rapids, they launched them again in the Great Lakes; and from the Lakes, by easy portages, they reached the heads of the Mississippi system or of the rivers flowing northward to Hudson Bay and the Arctic.

Only a little west of Lake Michigan the first European explorers came upon the edge of the grasslands. The climate, they found, was still humid. Long ribbons of forest ran along the valley bottoms toward the west. But in between, the plains were covered by grass which grew taller than a man's head. These were the prairies. As the explorers traveled still farther westward they reached country that was not so rainy, where very few trees could be found and where the grass grew less than a foot in height at maturity. These were the Great Plains.

At the western edge of the Great Plains the explorers came upon the first of the ranges of high, rugged mountains, the Rockies. Crossing them through passes, those who still pushed on westward came upon the Great Basin. From the middle part of Colorado and Montana as far as the Sierra Nevada and Cascade Mountains, they found a mixture of wet, forest-clad mountains, their tops often snow-covered in winter, interspersed with dry basins covered with scattered desert shrubs. Wherever the explorers went, all the way from near what is now the Canadian border southward to Mexico City and beyond, they found this same kind of basin and range country. Even the Pacific coast was dry in northern Mexico and southern California. Only to the north of San Francisco Bay did the explorers come upon rainy country, with luxuriant forests growing to the water's edge.

Those who turned northward from the Great Lakes soon came upon lands of long, severe winters and short summers. Here they found forests made up chiefly of spruce, fir, and larch rather than the more familiar deciduous broadleaf trees and pines of the lands farther south. The outlines of the great Northern Forests as they are known to us today are shown on the appropriate map in this book.

Beyond the forests are the tundras and the barren lands of the Far North, facing the frozen Arctic Ocean. Here the Eskimos used to live in precarious balance with the seals on which they depended for food. When white men brought them the rifle, the Eskimos killed seals so rapidly that soon their traditional way of living was no longer possible, for the resource on which it was based had been destroyed. Now, along the shores of Greenland, northern Canada, and Alaska the Eskimos are again increasing in number, adjusting themselves to a new way of life around the mission stations, trading posts, airfields, and radar stations. We know today that the puffs of cold air which pour southward to bring cold waves and changeable weather to North America come from the icecap of Greenland and from the snow-covered lands of northern Canada in winter. These puffs are called "northers" when they cross Texas to the Gulf or when they bring freezing weather to California and Florida.

The United States, Canada, and Mexico were all created by men working on these varied landscapes, reacting to them, changing them. *The Romance of North America* is the record of what men have done with the land they found. But it is important to remember that the land at any one historical period is not the original natural earth. Rather it is the earth as modified by earlier human action. The man-made features of the present—roads, buildings, farms—are superimposed on relict features from the past. It is possible to find out what the landscapes of the past were like by reading books or looking at old pictures; but it is also possible to find in present landscapes many of the features of the past. All through the woods of present-day New England, for example, one can see the old stone walls which, more than a century ago, marked the boundaries of fields and farms. In the Middle West, where the rectangular survey of roads and properties set a uniform stamp over wide areas, the arrangement of wood lots nevertheless reflects the difference between a landscape carved out of a forest and one created on an open grassland.

To understand all this, and to grasp the motives that led people to treat the resources of the earth as they have done at different periods, we must go back to origins. The first settlements in North America differed not only in the character of the landscapes that formed the habitats, but also in the social, political, and economic institutions and purposes of the settlers. The colonists themselves came from different backgrounds bringing with them a variety of attitudes, skills, and even religious faiths. At the beginning of settlement, therefore, different ways of living or cultures were implanted on the land. Each area of distinctive settlement became a *culture hearth*, where new ways of living were forged or old ways preserved.

The nations of North America derived their characteristic ways of living from five major culture hearths. Streams of pioneers spreading from each of these hearths met and mingled. The mingling process took some traits from one hearth, some from another; and this process of mixture went on in the midst of different physical conditions of the land, depending on the place where the streams of settlement met. The five major culture hearths were: (1) Spanish-Indian Mexico; (2) French Canada; (3) New England; (4) the South; and (5) the Middle Colonies—the last three all predominantly British. There was, also, a distinctive culture hearth, but not a major one, in the Dutch colonies of the Hudson Valley.

The culture hearth of Spanish-Indian Mexico was different from any of the others. It is more closely related to the story of Latin America to the south than to that of Anglo-America; yet its impress on the United States has been important, for almost the whole of the continent south and west of the dense forests was first explored and then thinly settled by people from the central area of Mexico.

When the Spaniards came to Mexico, they had two fundamental purposes: (1) to spread the Catholic faith for the salvation of the pagan Indians of America, and (2) to acquire wealth by the quickest possible means and then to return to Spain, or, with or without wealth, to achieve a position of prestige and power in America by becoming landowners.

With these ends in mind the Spaniards were attracted first to those places in America where there were large concentrations of native Indians. In central and southern Mexico and Guatemala the newcomers found one of the two native civilizations of America. The Mayas of Guatemala had built a society with organized government in which many notable advances in the arts of living had been made. Their astronomer-priests had a better calendar than that of the Spaniards. They could point out that Columbus discovered America on October 21st rather than on October 12th as the Spaniards figured it. They had learned how to cultivate the maize plant. But they had no domestic animals other than the dog. In contrast to the Spaniards they thought of land as a natural resource, like air, that could not be claimed as private property.

Before the coming of the Spaniards the Mayas had been conquered by the Toltecs, and the Toltecs by the Aztecs. Both conquests came from the arid north. For the lean, warlike desert hunters, the well-watered green fields and forests around Mexico City and south of it seemed like paradise. The Spaniards found the Aztec Empire well established, but at war with its neighbors.

The Spaniards taught the natives Christianity and set them to work in the mines of gold and silver. Many new settlements were established at the mines—among many those of Zacatecas, Pachuca, and Taxco. The land in the central area of dense Indian settlement was soon divided into large private estates, on each of which there were many of the native Indian communities. The total number of Spaniards who came to Mexico was small in proportion to the Indian inhabitants.

North of the central area of Mexico the land was arid or semiarid, and the Indians were few. Except where mining could be carried on, there was little to attract settlement in this direction. To be sure, the mines had to be supplied with food. The nearest wet grasslands were in Texas, and here the Spaniards pastured cattle on the open ranges around San Antonio. A string of ranches ran up the valley of the Rio Grande to the Spanish outpost of Santa Fe. Farther west, settlement was left at first to the missionaries. The Jesuits, the Franciscans, and the Dominicans established missions, and around each mission the Indians were gathered together from a wide area. They were taught Christianity and also agriculture. The Fathers introduced oranges, grapes, wheat, and barley, as well as cattle and horses. A few Spanish settlers came northward to this remote frontier to pasture cattle. Their chief products were hides and tallow. Almost all of what is now western United States was given Spanish place names; but actual settlement was thinly spread, and administrative control was weak.

The second of the five major culture hearths was that of French Canada. In 1608 the French established a colony at Quebec. French missionaries spread rapidly inland, also looking for Indians to Christianize. They found no such concentrations of Indians as the Spaniards found in Mexico, but they did explore a vast area of inner North America north and east of the Spanish area. They found wealth in the form of fur-bearing animals in the forests. French trading posts were set up at strategic places such as Detroit, Chicago, and St. Louis. Like the Spaniards, the French held a vast area in a loose grip.

There were other French settlers, however, who came as farmers rather than missionaries and traders. These established themselves firmly along the lower St. Lawrence River downstream from Montreal.

Here they formed a self-sufficient, strongly conservative, Catholic community, perpetuating the way of living of rural France in these new surroundings.

Present-day United States and to a considerable extent present-day Canada derived their ways of living from the three British culture hearths of eastern North America. The northernmost of these was in New England, to which the Pilgrims came in 1620 by accident—for they were intending to settle in the northern part of the already established colony of Virginia. The early New England settlers left Europe at a time when an entirely new idea in human relations was being formulated—an idea that had no precedent in the whole previous history of mankind. The idea was that the individual should have equal rights before the law, that law should not be applied differently to people of different social status, that government should be with the consent of the governed. This was the beginning of the Democratic Revolution. The Plymouth Compact of 1620 is the world's first written expression of this basic idea: that

. . . We whose names are under-written . . . having undertaken a voyage to plant the first colony in the northern part of Virginia, do by these presents, solemnly and mutually in the presence of God, and one another, covenant and combine ourselves together into a civil body politic, for the better ordering and preservation and furtherance of the ends aforesaid; and by virtue hereof to enact, constitute, and frame such just and equal laws, ordinances, acts, constitutions, and offices, from time to time, as shall be thought most meet and convenient for the general good of the colony, unto which we promise all due submission and obedience.

This was a clear and simple statement of the basic purpose of the New England colonies. This was the first time in the whole history of man that such an attitude toward individual rights and responsibilities had formed the basic idea of a community, free from all resistance from those who might be opposed to it. In Great Britain and Holland, where this new concept of human dignity had been brewing, those who held positions of power under the old, traditional Law of Status naturally resisted the new movement, often with force. But in New England the basic ideas of the Democratic Revolution were developed in the freedom of an almost unoccupied habitat. The Indians were few, and simple in their way of living. Beyond adopting the Indian grain, maize, and certain other Indian crops and farming methods, the New England settlers received little from native sources.

The culture hearth of New England developed a number of institutions of great importance to the future development of the continent. One was the town meeting. This was easy in the compact villages where whole communities could come together to take part in the discussions of political questions. Decisions were based on the majority opinion, and the idea of a veto or the use of force by the minority was discarded. Furthermore, the New Englanders appreciated the importance of knowledge, and placed much emphasis on schools and colleges for public education. But the Spaniards had already, in Mexico City and in Lima, Peru, established universities that antedated Harvard by 85 years.

New England, however, was a harsh habitat for the early colonists. Its stony soils, its long winters, its many unnavigable rivers made farming difficult. An agricultural economy could not prosper in such a land. But the sea was rich in fish, the forests unequaled for ship timber and masts. New Englanders turned little by little to trading and seafaring and found this the most profitable way of building their economy.

Very different indeed were the ideas developed in the culture hearth of the South. The first settlements were in Virginia, but before long colonies had been established along the inner margin of the coastal plain all the way from Maryland southward to the Carolinas. Here large manorial estates were laid out, each with a lord of the manor. At about this same time tobacco, and the ways of smoking it in cigars and pipes—all derived from the native Indians of America, especially those of Cuba—was becoming very popular in England. There was a demand for tobacco. When the tobacco plant was introduced into Virginia, it was found to grow excellently there. The colonies of the South, unlike those of New England, found a commercial product on which to build an agricultural and rural economy. The work of cultivation, harvesting, packing, and shipping was done at first by indentured servants from England, later by Negro slaves. A New Englander could find little use for a slave; a Virginian could scarcely get along without slaves. In some places the planters experimented with rice, indigo, and cotton.

In the South the landowners lived very well indeed. They usually hired tutors to educate their children. Those who lived in the "Great

Houses" of the landowners could enjoy music, art and literature, dancing, and other pleasant features of a cultivated and polished society. They, too, could talk about freedom and democracy, but they usually meant freedom from interference by overseas authorities, the right to do their own governing. The idea that the slaves might have equal rights before the law was disturbing and subversive.

In between New England and the South was the culture hearth of the Middle Colonies of New Jersey and Pennsylvania and inner Maryland. These settlements were on land unsuited to tobacco or cotton, but more productive by far than the stony lands of New England. To this culture hearth came people from many sources. First were the Dutch and the Swedes, but soon there was a strong incoming tide of English, Scottish, and Irish. There were many Germans, who became known as the Pennsylvania Dutch. All established themselves on the land as small farmers, each family building a home on its own farm. Several different kinds of religious beliefs were introduced. There were the Dutch Reformed and Lutheran churches, then the Roman Catholics and Quakers, the Presbyterians from Scotland, and the Anglicans from England. All learned to live together in mutual tolerance. Because most of them lived on separate farms rather than in compact communities, education was carried on by the family. The children learned from their parents to read the Bible, to write, and to do simple arithmetic. The immediate family, grouped around the hearthside, was the basic unit, and it was usually a self-sufficient one.

From this mixture of peoples of different origins came an amazing series of innovations. These were the farmers who first put together the Indian grain, corn, and the European domestic animal, the hog, forming the now widespread corn-hog type of farming. Corn was raised as a feed rather than as a food, and the products for sale were bacon and ham. These people first built the sturdy four-wheeled wagons drawn by teams of horses or oxen, which later were known as "prairie schooners." These people invented the long rifle. These people adapted the Scandinavian log cabin to American conditions. These people invented the potbellied stove that heated the cabins much more efficiently than open fireplaces. Here there was also democracy. The self-educated frontiersmen were not so much interested in ideas as were the Southerners, nor in methods as were the New Englanders; but they did learn how to practice a system of equality and tolerance among their neighbors and equals. From this culture hearth came the restless pioneers who were most vigorous in pushing westward across the Appalachians, and later across mountains and deserts to the Pacific coast.

For a time in the 17th century another culture hearth was being established. This was the Dutch colony along the Hudson Valley. The Dutch colonists made an amazing impress on America, considering that in 1667 they agreed to exchange their colony in New York for Surinam in the Guianas, where sugar cane could be grown.

Anglo-America has been formed by the mingling of people from these source regions. Each of the culture hearths has provided certain characteristic ingredients of our ways of living—ideas, institutions, attitudes and purposes, skills and tools. But these things have not come unchanged from the source regions, nor have the culture hearths themselves remained unchanged. And underlying all this great tapestry of human development there is the earth itself which forms the setting or the stage. The earth has in no sense directed the course of the play, for at each period the meaning of the earth has changed, depending on how the actor looked at it.

The most important fact about the spread of people and ideas from these culture hearths has been the preponderant importance of the three British hearths. The culture hearths of Spanish-Indian Mexico and French Canada have retained major importance chiefly in their original areas.

In the 18th century there occurred significant changes in the extent of settlement of eastern North America. In 1700 there was a whole series of isolated clusters of people along the North American east coast, and between the settled areas there were tracts of wilderness crossed only by Indian trails. This is still the characteristic pattern of population in parts of Latin America. But by 1760 there was an almost continuous band of settlement from north of Portland in Maine to south of Savannah in Georgia, and pioneers from the Middle Colonies had already started to move westward. From settlements in eastern Pennsylvania they moved up the Susquehanna and Juniata Rivers. At the head of the Juniata near present Altoona, they climbed steeply up the Allegheny Front. Then they descended the winding headwaters of the Ohio River to Pittsburgh. By 1790 not only had the New Englanders moved into what are now New Hampshire and Vermont, but settlers from the Middle Colonies had made a major advance to the southwest. The frontiersmen found the going easy along the Shenandoah and Tennessee Valleys, where they were sep- arated from the culture hearth of the South by the Blue Ridge. It was Daniel Boone who led the way through the Cumberland Front at the Cumberland Gap and found a winding route into the Blue Grass Basin of Kentucky. A stream of settlers followed him into Kentucky and on into the Nashville Basin of Tennessee. By 1790 both of these basins were well occupied, and pioneers from the Middle Colonies had settled along both sides of the Ohio River. From Maryland and Virginia these people brought tobacco westward into Kentucky. But when they settled across the Appalachians, they found that getting their products back to the markets in the east was too expensive. From the new colonies in the west the pioneers floated lumber, bacon, and tobacco downriver to New Orleans. They had to walk home again by way of the Natchez Trace.

In 1785 the government of the new nation passed an ordinance that prescribed the method of land division in all the new and pre- viously unsettled areas, then called the Northwest. Instead of the ir- regular shapes of land properties and the winding roads of the older settled parts of the country, all the new national territory was to be divided into a system of squares with boundaries running north-south and east-west. Around the margin of each square mile roads were to be built, and rectangular farm properties were to be marked off as fractions of the square miles. Each group of 36 square miles was or- ganized as a township. All over the United States, except in Texas, this system has been applied with modifications to the land settled after 1785. It makes a very different landscape when seen from the air from that of the older parts of the United States.

The people of the culture hearth of the South were also on the move. In addition to tobacco they now found another commercial crop. In 1785 the steam engine was first used to run the machinery of a textile mill in England (at Papplewick near Nottingham). The re- sult was a rapid increase in the demand for raw cotton from America. The Southerners found that cotton did very well in the hot, wet sum- mers of the southeastern piedmont. Cotton growing was tried even as far north as Rhode Island, but it was found that without at least

200 days between the last frost of spring and the first frost of fall, yields were so low that the crop could not be grown profitably. The map shows the line of the 200-day growing season, which was little by little recognized as the northern limit of profitable cotton planting. However, Eli Whitney's invention of the cotton gin in 1793 (patented in 1794) made it possible for one man to do the work of 200 in removing seeds from the fibers, and definitely established this region as the world's cheapest source of cotton. As population increased rapidly in the older cotton-growing area on the piedmont of Carolina and Georgia, and as the demand for raw cotton increased, it became necessary to seek new cotton lands. New cotton plantations were carved out of the forest to the west. Since the Appalachian system comes to an end in the middle part of Alabama, the way was open to the west without barrier. Cotton planting swept to the Mississippi and beyond into the humid eastern part of Texas, and as far northward as the 200-day growing season permitted.

The spread from the New England culture hearth took place more slowly than that from the other hearths. It was not until the opening of the Erie Canal in 1825 that the New Englanders joined in the general westward movement in any large numbers. After that date they spread along the Great Lakes into southern Michigan, northern Illinois, and southern Wisconsin. Here they met the stream of settlers from the Middle Colonies and adopted many of their ways of living. But they brought with them their own ideas regarding the importance of public education, and it was no accident that the University of Michigan came to be known as the "Harvard of the West."

Meanwhile great changes were taking place in the original area of the New England culture hearth. This region was the first part of America to develop manufacturing industry. Of course there had been small iron furnaces in many parts of the country, not only in New England; and there had long been an interest in shipbuilding. But the cotton-textile industry opened a new era. A young industrial worker named Samuel Slater came to America with the plans for one of England's new textile machines memorized—for the export of the plans had been prohibited. Slater tried to interest the people of Philadelphia in backing the construction of a new factory. If the businessmen of Philadelphia had been willing to risk their capital on such a venture, there might never have been any New England textile industry. As it was, however, they refused. Slater then tried Rhode Island, where he found men with capital who were accustomed to risking money on more or less speculative ventures. The first textile mill in America was built at Pawtucket in 1790. In the next few decades small textile mills were built throughout southern New England.

The dotting of interior New England with small mill towns, which persist to the present day, is a result of the interaction of technology and land resources more than a century ago. In 1790 the steam engine had only just been applied to the English textile mills, and there were no such engines in America. Power was supplied by falling water, and New England was abundantly endowed with small water-power sites. Seizing upon this resource, small mill towns were developed all along the valleys of interior New England. Some thirty years later the steam engine was introduced and water power became obsolete. Steam engines required the use of coal, and coal was brought by barge from Pennsylvania. This gave an immediate advantage to the few mills that were near the ports. In fact, if Slater had brought the steam engine to America as well as the textile machinery, there might never have been any mill towns in the interior of New England at all. But as it was, the inland mills were by that time firmly enough established so that they could pay the cost of building railroads. The pattern of manufacturing, thus developed during the very short period when water power was the critical resource, has persisted and can still be observed all these many years later.

Other industries were built in New England too. Along the Merrimac Valley woolen textiles were concentrated. Shoe factories were grouped in the eastern part of Massachusetts south of Boston. Early in the 19th century, New England and central New York had become the main center of manufacturing in the United States.

The first half of the 19th century was also marked by the expansion of the national territory westward to the Pacific. In 1803 the Louisiana Purchase brought within the United States the whole drainage basin of the Mississippi and Missouri Rivers. In 1818 the 49th parallel was accepted as the border between Canada and the United States west of the Lake of the Woods. Restless frontiersmen, feeling hemmed in by the rapid advance of settlement in Kentucky and Tennessee and the country north of the Ohio River, moved on westward to new lands, and moved again as others followed behind them. When they came to the edge of the open prairies they hesitated, for they had had no experience with this kind of land. Beyond the prairies and the Great Plains was the wide zone of mountains and deserts, and beyond that California. The Mormons, attacked in New York and Illinois for their beliefs, sought refuge in the midst of this wilderness at Great Salt Lake. But the main stream of the westward movement was directed southwestward from the bend of the Missouri River at Independence, toward Santa Fe. Beyond Santa Fe the only route across the arid lands that was supplied with water followed the valley of the Gila River to the Colorado, and thence, by a short desert crossing, to San Diego.

No effective border stopped the pioneers from moving on into Mexican territory. Conflict began almost at once, for the ideas brought from the Middle Colonies were not at all compatible with those of the culture hearth of Spanish-Indian Mexico. The English-speaking settlers in Texas declared and won their independence as a sovereign state, and in 1845 voted to join the United States. Continued friction with the Mexican authorities led to war, and as a result of the war Mexico, in 1848, ceded the vast area of thinly occupied land to the north of the Gila River, and everything on the Pacific coast from San Diego northward. Almost at once the discovery of gold in California was announced, and the gold rush of 1849 rapidly filled in this previously almost empty country. In 1846 the Pacific Northwest as far as the 49th parallel became a part of the United States by agreement with Great Britain. Finally in 1853 the Gadsden Purchase took a little more from northern Mexico in order to include the easiest rail route to the west coast within the border of the United States.

As the national territory was expanded, it gradually became divided into distinct sections. The original culture hearths were the first sections, but as settlers spread from these hearths, and as they came face to face with new problems of living, new sections were created. Each section had a distinctive physical character; the people in it developed a kind of economic life that differed from that of other sections; and they began to take their own particular sectional stand on political issues. Early in the 19th century the settled part of the new United States was divided into three clearly defined sections: There was the South, with its cotton economy, its aristocracy of planters and its Negro slaves, its political concern with the preservation of slavery and with unrestricted foreign trade so that its major product could flow freely to the British market; there was the Northeast, including now not only New England but also New York, Pennsylvania, and New Jersey, with its new, struggling industries, its traders and manufacturers, its free white workers, and its political interest in trade restrictions that would protect the local industries; and there was the Northwest, west of the Appalachians and north of the 200-day growing season that made cotton profitable, with its isolated pioneer farmers, anxious to find a market down the Mississippi, politically interested in the expansion of the national territory to the west.

An important feature of the changing political geography of this period was the parallel establishment of slave and free states. After 1800 it became the custom to admit new states to the Union in pairs, so that the balance of power in the Senate would not be disturbed. When the land included in the Louisiana Purchase was available for division into states, it was clear that this would greatly increase the number of free states since most of it was north of the 200-day growing season. Enthusiasm for the admission of Texas was a result, in part, of the desire to balance all this new country to the north. But it was soon found that another climatic limit to profitable cotton planting was the line between humid and semiarid climates. In the dry areas cotton and slavery found an "unfriendly" habitat. The time had come when it was no longer possible to admit free and slave states in pairs. California as a free state completed the overturn of the balance.

By mid-century, moreover, there had come a major change in the transportation system, especially in the north. The first break in the isolation of the Northwest from the Northeast came with the construction of the Erie Canal in 1825. Other canals were started but were never so important as this one. It supported the rise of New York City to primacy over all its east-coast rivals. A turnpike was built from Washington and Baltimore in the east, across the Appalachians to Ohio and Indiana. This was the National Road, over which great four-wheeled wagons drawn by teams of six horses carried the frontier products back east to a market. It is now followed almost exactly by U. S. Highway 40. But finally it was the building of the railroads that reoriented the economic life of the great middle part of North America from north-south lines to east-west lines across the grain of the country (as determined by the arrangement of surface features and rivers). The two sections of early 19th-century United States, the Northeast and the Northwest, were now tied together. Food products moved eastward and manufactured products moved westward. These two sections began to function politically as one, especially in regard to the issue of slavery. Now, for the first time, the United States was sharply divided along geographical lines into one area where people favored slavery and the rest of the country where they did not. Whenever political differences of this sort are associated with sharply separated areas, there is danger of conflict. The stage was set for the War Between the States.

By 1865 the issue of slavery had been settled by violence. While the South was left to face the bitter problems of reconstruction, the North was ready to advance rapidly to the next step of economic development. The Industrial Revolution, which can be said to have started in Britain with James Watt's steam engine in 1769, was gathering momentum in America. During the last half of the 19th century three related developments appeared, starting in the North. One was the great expansion of the railroads, which, for the first time in all history, made possible the rapid, low-cost shipment of bulky products overland. The second was the rapid increase in the size of cities, based on new kinds of employment in manufacturing and commerce. City people in North America, and elsewhere in the world at the same time, constituted a vastly increased market for manufactured goods and foods shipped from a distance. New York reached a population of a million about 1870, Philadelphia and Chicago about 1890. Without railroads such large concentrations of city people could not have been supplied with food. And the third development was the advance of settlement onto new lands. After the Civil War the essentially twofold division into North and South was gradually transformed into six major sections.

No change during the second half of the 19th century was more spectacular than the change in the economic significance of the grasslands. When the European explorers first came upon these great, almost treeless plains they found a small Indian population supported from the hunting of bison. When European horses and firearms were introduced, the Indians and the white men together killed so many bison that soon this resource was exhausted. The Europeans brought in long-horned cattle, and soon vast herds were wandering freely over the open range. This was the land and the time of the cowboy heroes, the masked robbers and desperadoes, the rangers and sheriffs, the bands of Indians still trying desperately to hold out against the invaders. But the grasslands were not good for farming, for no instrument had been found to do the hard work of turning the thick prairie sod.

Within a few decades all this was changed. About 1837 came the steel plow, which made it possible without enormous labor to uncover the rich black prairie soils that nature had long been building. The plowing of the prairie brought the farmers and the cattlemen into conflict, for in this land of few trees there was no inexpensive way of building fences—no fence rails, not enough fence posts. It was difficult to keep the cattle out of the growing crops. Then, in 1873, Joseph A. Glidden of DeKalb, Illinois, invented barbed wire. Barbed wire and an adequate plow were the two inventions that all over the world made the soils of middle-latitude humid grasslands a major natural resource. Now animals and crops could be kept apart at low cost; corn could be raised to fatten hogs and cattle; wheat could be raised, along with other grains and hay in a system of rotation. Three strands of barbed wire, with fence posts spaced well apart, spelled the difference between thinly peopled open-range country and closely settled farmland.

At once a whole set of new problems appeared. Before the fields were fenced, the herds of cattle could move freely about from grass to water and back again to grass. But very few of the 160-acre farms had surface water on them. To dig a well with a shovel was laborious, and after the well had been dug there was no easy way to raise the water to the surface in volume sufficient for the needs of a herd of animals. In the absence of wood the building of a windmill was not easy. Two inventions solved this difficulty in the late 1800's. One was a machine for boring a deep well; the other was the standard metal windmill, low in price because it was built and sold in large quantities. About the same time huge harvesting machines were invented, which made possible the economical harvesting of grain on a large area where the yield per acre was low. Still, none of these things would have made farming successful on the western grasslands unless there had been a rapidly growing demand for meat and grain in the big cities and unless the railroads had provided fast, low-cost transportation for bulky products.

Here, indeed, was a unique experience in human history. At just the moment when new markets and new machines were changing the possibilities of producing food from the earth, the people of the United States were standing on the margins of the world's largest area of rich, black grassland soils, an area essentially unoccupied or only thinly occupied by native peoples, and an area which constituted an undisputed part of the national territory. Only in Argentina and Australia was there a similar fortunate situation.

Farm settlement advanced rapidly onto the prairies. Land was divided in advance into square-mile sections, and the Homestead Act of 1862 offered a 160-acre site almost free of charge to anyone who would settle on it and develop it as a farm. Land values went up rapidly. Whoever owned the land, whether an individual pioneer, a railroad company, or a bank, prospered, if only through the "unearned increment," the increased value that property acquired even when it was not actively developed. The tradition of the small farmer, living on his own farm, was inherited from the culture hearth of the Middle Colonies. The unearned increment, therefore, was shared widely among many people, not concentrated in a few hands as it was in Argentina. Unique in all the world and in all periods of history are the multitudes of retired small farmers living now, on income from investments, in the small towns of the farming region or in the warm sunshine of California and Florida.

Of course not everything was smooth and happy. There were business depressions, there were recurring droughts, there were invasions of insect pests, there were tornadoes and hailstorms. Sometimes agricultural disaster brought the whole system of paper values tumbling down, setting off what the politicians called financial readjustments to worry the men of Wall Street. But still the general trend was toward more and more prosperity, based not so much on the profits from the sale of farm products as on the continued increase in the value of the land resource itself.

The grasslands, however, cross the line between humid and semiarid climates. No sharp difference in the landscape made this important boundary visible. Furthermore there were cycles of wetter and drier years. After the wetter years the land companies did a huge business selling to unwary easterners. Then came the inevitable cycle of dry years with its attendant disaster and land abandonment. In one county in western Kansas in a 20-year period the farmers lost money in 19 out of the 20 years; but in one year they made $20,000 per square mile of land because in that one year there was a lucky combination of good rains and high wheat prices. As settlement moved west onto the Great Plains, the size of a farm that could support a family was increased from 160 acres to 1280 acres. But in a land deficient in moisture no kind of farming can be really secure without irrigation.

The whole great expanse of land farther to the west was also made accessible to eastern markets by the railroads. This was a land made up of towering ranges of forest-clad mountains standing above arid or semiarid basins. There was a long argument concerning the extent to which the basin lands could be irrigated. The geographer John Wesley Powell urged caution in the settlement of these lands; the land companies, the cattle companies, and the lumbermen argued that the government should permit unrestricted development. But irrigation is dependent on rain- and snow-fed streams from the mountains. When the lumbermen cut the fine stands of timber, this greatly increased the extent of the high pastures useful for summer grazing. But from the denuded slopes the water came off in torrents rather than in a steady flow. Between the torrents, and especially in late summer when water was most needed for irrigation, the streams were dry. Not enough hay could be raised on the irrigated fields in summer to feed the cattle and sheep during the winter. The Federal Government has stepped in to set aside certain scenic areas as National Parks, and other areas as National Forests in which timber cutting and grazing are regulated by the Forest Service. But the conflict of interests continues between those who want to control the resources of the area for private use and those who insist that the government should regulate use for the benefit of all the people. In some states where more than half of the area is in Federal land, the conflict becomes bitter.

Still another, and very important, section developed on the Pacific coast. There was a time after the Civil War when the Californians were finding themselves so remote from the eastern part of the country that there was even talk of separation. The railroad connection

with the east came just in time. The sharply contrasted climates and
soils of the Pacific coast offered a great variety of kinds of use. On
the remote Spanish and Mexican frontier none of these local differences was of any great significance. Most of the land was used for
pasture to produce hides and tallow. But after the transportation to
eastern markets made economic specialization possible, many distinctive kinds of land use appeared. The raisin industry was for a time
localized at Fresno. Even today about 80 percent of all the lettuce of
the United States comes from the Salinas Valley. West-coast oranges,
vineyards, and various vegetables are now concentrated in certain
small areas, making California a state noted for its many contrasting
landscapes within short distances. To the north lumbering, fish
canning, fruit raising, and other localized economies have also appeared.

In 1876 the United States purchased Alaska from the Russians. For
a long time very little was done to develop this great territory. The
discovery of gold within and just east of Alaska brought the usual rush
of miners and adventurers. But Alaska has much more enduring resources as a basis for its future development. Pioneer farmers have
occupied a few spots, as in the Matanuska Valley and in the Tanana
Valley around Fairbanks. In southeastern Alaska fish and timber are
important resources. By no means as restricted by climate as some
people seem to think, there are many who look forward to Alaska as
another frontier awaiting the technological and economic conditions
that will lead to its rapid development. The trebling of Alaska's population between 1940 and 1955 and its admission as the 49th state in
1958 indicate that this optimism is justified.

All this expansion across the breadth of North America was accompanied by equally profound changes in the east with its older settlements. Before World War I there had been a steady and powerful
flow of immigrants into the United States. Most of these came from
the various parts of Europe. There were some years when a million
newcomers arrived in the United States. Most of the railroads were
built by Irishmen; Irishmen and Swedes cut most of the forests; Italians became industrial workers, or settled in such specialized agricultural communities as those devoted to the cultivation of vineyards
or orchards or vegetable crops. Germans were especially active in
southern Michigan and Wisconsin; Scandinavians went to northern

Michigan and Minnesota. Mexicans, too, were entering the Southwest. Throughout the country there were great numbers who came directly from England, Scotland, and Wales. And before Asians were excluded, great numbers of Chinese scattered throughout the United States, and Japanese were concentrated in California and Hawaii.

These immigrants helped to swell the increasing number of city people in the United States. Jobs in the new manufacturing industries were plentiful. The same factors of cheap transportation and large markets that led to crop specialization also encouraged the growth of specialized manufacturing areas. Those in early New England persisted and grew. There were notable specializations elsewhere, such as the glove factories of Gloversville, New York, the men's shirt factories of Troy, the ladies' garment shops on Manhattan Island. A large-scale steel industry first appeared at Pittsburgh, where there was a supply of coal, iron, and limestone immediately at hand. Later, steel plants appeared at Cleveland and Gary where they could be supplied with coal from nearby fields to the south and with iron ore by lake steamer from the Mesabi Range northwest of Duluth. Before World War I manufacturing industry had spread from the Northeast into what had become the Middle West, concentrating in the rapidly growing cities such as Cleveland, Detroit, Chicago, St. Louis, and Minneapolis-St. Paul. At that time the South, still struggling with reconstruction problems, had its steel industry at Birmingham and the beginnings of industrial development along the piedmont of Virginia and North Carolina. And all these economic patterns were reflected in new political alignments.

While the United States was in the process of formation, another great nation also was developing along the northern border. As we have seen, one of the five major culture hearths of North America was French Canada. From this original culture hearth there had been very little spread—only a little to the west into Ontario, only a little southeastward into New Brunswick, and a little to the south into the mill towns of northern New England. Within the area of the original culture hearth the population remains almost pure French, Roman Catholic and politically conservative. The Canadian nation has developed around this French core which has become a distinctive part of the national structure.

During the latter part of the 18th century many English-speaking settlers moved into Canada from the south. People in New England who wished to remain loyal to the king migrated in large numbers to Nova Scotia. People from the culture hearth of the Middle Colonies migrated northward into the country north of Lake Ontario and Lake Erie, forming there the colony and later the province of Upper Canada (Ontario). In 1876 Canada was set up as an independent federation of Nova Scotia, New Brunswick, Quebec, and Ontario.

Many of the people of Canada, however, have come as immigrants in the present century. Between 1901 and 1913 pioneer farmers moved onto the grasslands west of Winnipeg, south of Edmonton, and east of the Rocky Mountains. Quite a number came from the United States, as a part of the movement onto the grasslands which, at that date, had reached Canada. Others came directly from Great Britain, from Ireland, and from many of the countries of continental Europe. Immigration into Canada continues at a rapid rate.

The settled area of Canada still forms a narrow band north of the United States border. The settled zone is quite narrow in the east, and all but broken north of Lake Superior. It is widest in the prairie provinces. In the mountains of British Columbia the settled areas are broken into narrow ribbons and spots of farming and ranching along the valley bottoms. To the north settled areas are only in little patches where there are favorable soils or where there are mines.

Canada has both a French and a British tradition. The problem of finding a compromise between the political purposes of the two quite different groups remains one of the country's perennial difficulties. At mid-century there was a rapidly increasing development of manufacturing industry, especially in Ontario, a considerable part being financed by capital investments from the United States. Canada was not only supplying nickel to the world, but also many other important minerals and wood for paper pulp. New oil fields near Edmonton gave promise of development. In many respects Canada forms an important bridge between ideas characteristic of the United States and traditions inherited directly from Great Britain.

To the south lies Latin America. In spite of certain common experiences shared throughout the Americas, such as the conquest of what the Europeans called a New World and such as the struggle for independence, still the contrasts between Anglo-America and Latin America are more significant than the similarities.

The culture hearth of Spanish-Indian Mexico differed from those of eastern North America not only in the character of the physical setting, but also in the fact that the land was already occupied by an advanced Indian society. Even today only some 10 percent of the Mexican people have no Indian blood. The Spanish agrarian tradition was strong: The ownership of land was the surest road to a position of power and prestige. Sharing power and prestige with the landed aristocracy were the officers of the army and the priests of the Church.

In the course of time only two social classes existed in Mexico. There was a small minority living in a cosmopolitan society, well-educated, traveled, well-to-do; and there was a vast majority living in poverty, illiteracy, ill-health, and with inadequate diet. Most of the land was held in large private estates called *haciendas*, and on these properties the best land was used for pasture or feed crops. But the chief food crop of the people was corn (maize). It was grown on the poorer lands, the steeper slopes, the places that could not be irrigated. Between the poverty of the many and the elegance of the few there was an enormous gulf. The independence movement did include a few cases of popular uprisings against the system—such as those led by Father Hidalgo and Father Morelos. But independence actually meant no change in the system—only that the politically powerful minority in Mexico had gained the right to govern free from interference from Spain. Liberals there were, interested in spreading the ideas of democracy; but they made little impression on the established system.

Little impression, that is, until 1910. Between 1910 and 1915 the Mexican Revolution set the stage for profound changes. The constitution of 1917 included a section on land ownership: It set forth the concept that the right to own land was based on "socially harmonious use." This meant that the private owner could be prohibited from leaving the best land in pasture. Vast private estates were to be expropriated. But it was not until the 1930's that these new ideas regarding land were put into force. By 1940 not only had the large private properties been broken up and a large area of land redistributed among the Indians of the rural communities (known as *ejidos*), but also the landowning aristocracy had been wiped out as a politically

powerful class. In 1938 the foreign-owned oil properties were expropriated.

It is too much to expect such a revolutionary change to lead to
democracy where no democracy existed before. This would require
still another revolution. But in the village communities the seeds of
democracy are being nurtured. The percentage of illiteracy has been
enormously decreased. At the local level the feeling of apathy and
hopelessness has been succeeded by one of satisfaction and optimism.
Yet no opposition political party of any importance has yet arisen to
challenge the Party of the Mexican Revolution, and the control of
national and state politics is still in the hands of a small minority.

The Revolution has brought economic changes. Any impartial observer can see that the ejido is a less efficient unit of production than
was the hacienda. And, as everywhere in the world where land is taken
from the few and distributed among the many, there is not nearly
enough good land to go around. There has been an overall decrease
in the production of the basic foods. But government farm specialists
have brought about a considerable diversification of crops, and the
drinking of milk is being promoted. In and around Mexico City there
has been a very rapid increase of manufacturing industry, largely supported by investments from the United States. Gasoline from the
national refineries is not of such high quality as that of the United
States, but it costs much less. And there has been a very great increase
in the tourist business. Mexico City has been transformed since 1940.
The old port of Acapulco, where the Spanish galleons used to sail
for the Philippines, is now a thriving winter resort where wealthy
vacationers from the United States spend millions every year. The
ways of living developed in Anglo-America have been brought into
Mexico over the new highways, by rail, by steamer, and by air. The
result is to change Mexico into something perhaps a little less authentically Spanish and a little less artistically pure. Visitors can still
find many thrilling sights, such as the volcano Popocatepetl coming
out of the clouds; but there is still enough that is primitive for lovers
of the picturesque.

Anglo-America has had a considerable impact on other parts of
northern Latin America. Venezuela has become one of the world's
chief suppliers of oil, and is becoming also a major supplier of iron
ore. Colombia's contacts with North America have been less happy.

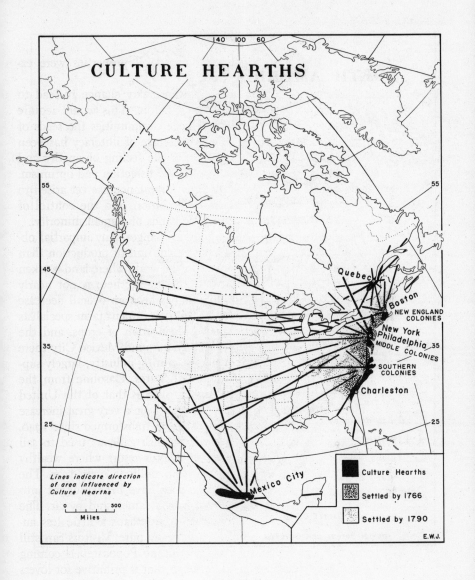

CULTURE HEARTHS

Quebec

Boston

NEW ENGLAND COLONIES

New York
Philadelphia
MIDDLE COLONIES

SOUTHERN COLONIES

Charleston

Mexico City

Lines indicate direction
of area influenced by
Culture Hearths

0   500
Miles

■ Culture Hearths

▦ Settled by 1766

▦ Settled by 1790

E.W.J.

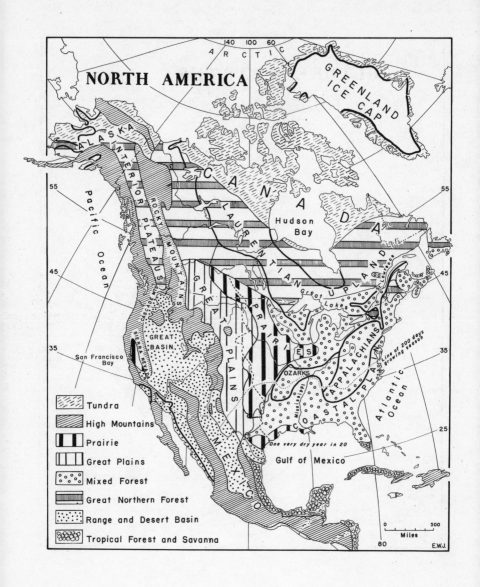

NORTH AMERICA

ARCTIC

GREENLAND ICE CAP

ALASKA

CANADA

Hudson Bay

Pacific Ocean

INTERIOR PLATEAUS

ROCKY MOUNTAINS

LAURENTIAN UPLAND

GREAT PLAINS

Great Lakes

PRAIRIES

GREAT BASIN

SIERRA NEVADA

San Francisco Bay

APPALACHIANS

OZARKS

Mississippi

Line of 200 days growing season

Atlantic Ocean

COASTAL PLAIN

One very dry year in 20

Gulf of Mexico

MEXICO

	Tundra
	High Mountains
	Prairie
	Great Plains
	Mixed Forest
	Great Northern Forest
	Range and Desert Basin
	Tropical Forest and Savanna

0   500
Miles

E.W.J.

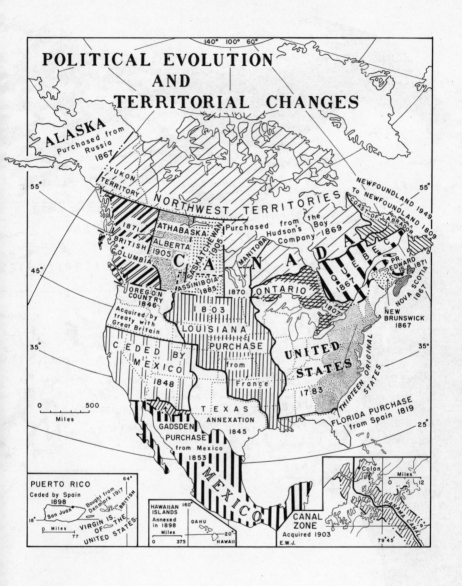

POLITICAL EVOLUTION AND TERRITORIAL CHANGES

ALASKA Purchased from Russia 1867

YUKON TERRITORY

NORTHWEST TERRITORIES

NEWFOUNDLAND 1949 To NEWFOUNDLAND 1809 COAST OF LABRADOR

ATHABASKA

ALBERTA 1905

BRITISH COLUMBIA 1871

SASKATCHEWAN 1905

Purchased from the Hudson's Bay Company 1869

MANITOBA 1870

C A N A D A

QUEBEC 1867

PR. EDWARD 1871

NOVA SCOTIA 1867

NEW BRUNSWICK 1867

ASSINIBOIA 1885

ONTARIO 1867

OREGON COUNTRY 1846 Acquired by treaty with Great Britain

1803 LOUISIANA PURCHASE from France

UNITED STATES

THIRTEEN ORIGINAL STATES

CEDED BY MEXICO 1848

T E X A S ANNEXATION 1845

1783

FLORIDA PURCHASE from Spain 1819

0   500
Miles

GADSDEN PURCHASE from Mexico 1853

M E X I C O

PUERTO RICO
Ceded by Spain 1898

San Juan

Bought from Denmark 1917

VIRGIN IS. OF THE UNITED STATES

0   Miles
18°   77°   64°

HAWAIIAN ISLANDS
Annexed in 1898
Miles
0   375

OAHU
HAWAII
160°
20°

CANAL ZONE
Acquired 1903
E.W.J.

Colon   Miles
0   12

PANAMA CANAL

79°45'

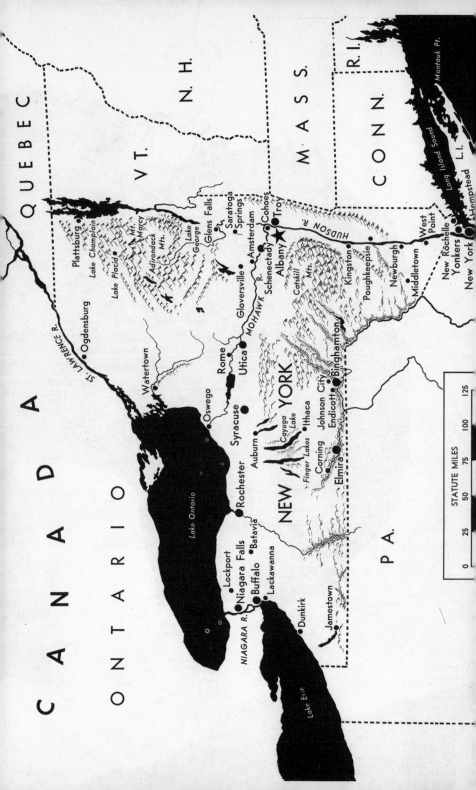

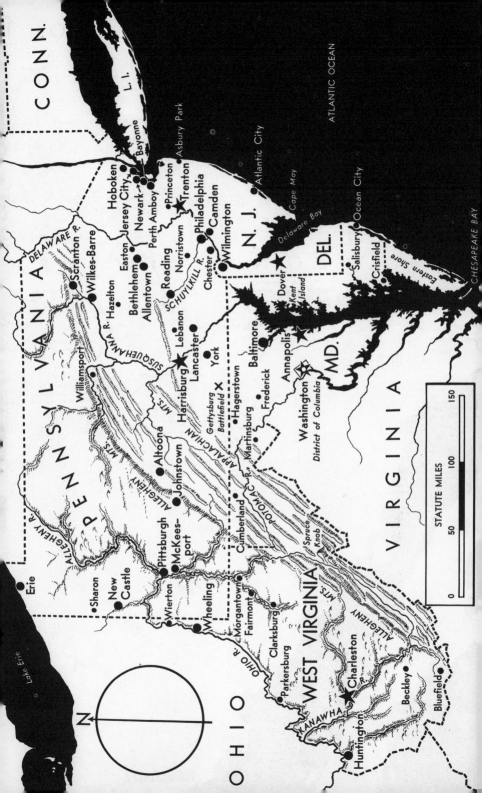

UTAH
COL
NEV.
Lake Mead
Hoover Dam
GRAND CANYON NATIONAL PARK
Painted Desert
LITTLE COLORADO R.
PETRIFIED FOREST NATIONAL MONUMENT
Farmington
Taos
Los Alamos
Santa Fe
Sangre de Christo
Gallup
Kingman
San Francisco Peaks
Flagstaff
Winslow
Prescott
CAL.
Albuquerque
COLORADO R.
ARIZONA
NEW MEX
Roosevelt Dam
Tempe
Phoenix
Mesa
Globe
RIO GRANDE
Sacramento Mts.
Ros
Morenci
Elephant Butte Dam
Yuma
Coolidge Dam
Alamogordo
Art
Ajo
Tucson
WHITE SANDS NATIONAL MONUMENT
Lordsburg
Las Cruces
Carl
Tombstone
Bisbee
Douglas
El Paso
Juarez
Gulf of California
MEXI

Quebec ★

ST. LAWRENCE R.

Q U E B E C

ST. JOHN R.

ALLAGASH R.

Chesuncook
Lake

Rangeley
Lakes

Moosehead
Lake

Mt. Katahdin

Houlton

Greenville

Millinocket

NDROSCOGGIN

KENNEBEC R.

M A I N E

PENOBSCOT R.

ST. CROIX R.

N E W   B R U N S W I C K

Waterville

Bangor

burn Lewiston

Augusta ★

Bath

Rockland

Calais

Eastport

nd

Bar Harbor

N

STATUTE MILES

0   25   50   100

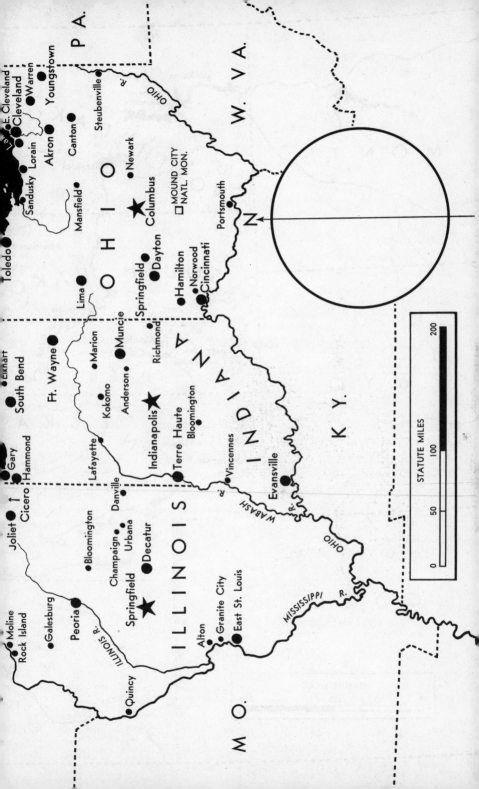

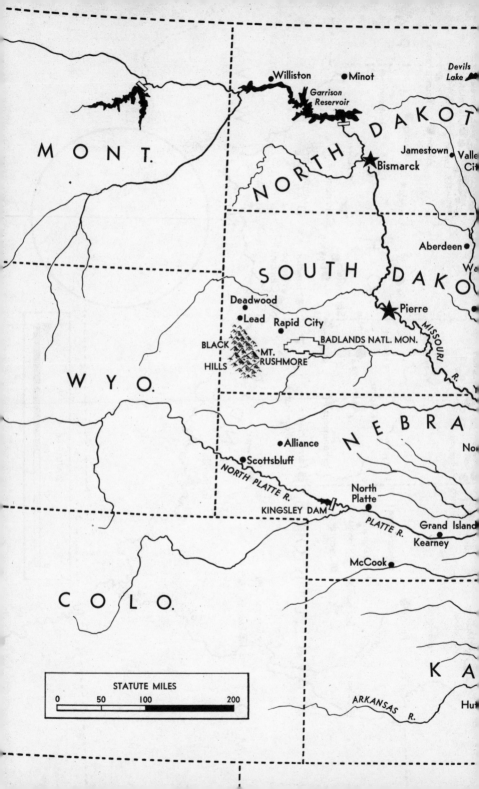

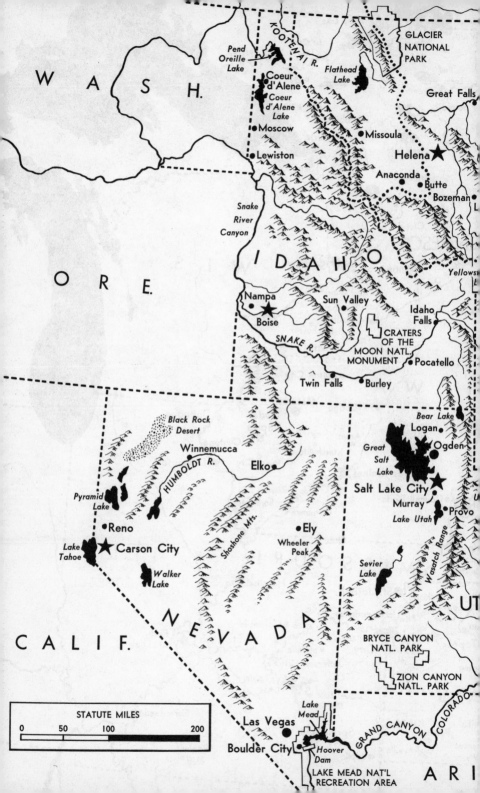

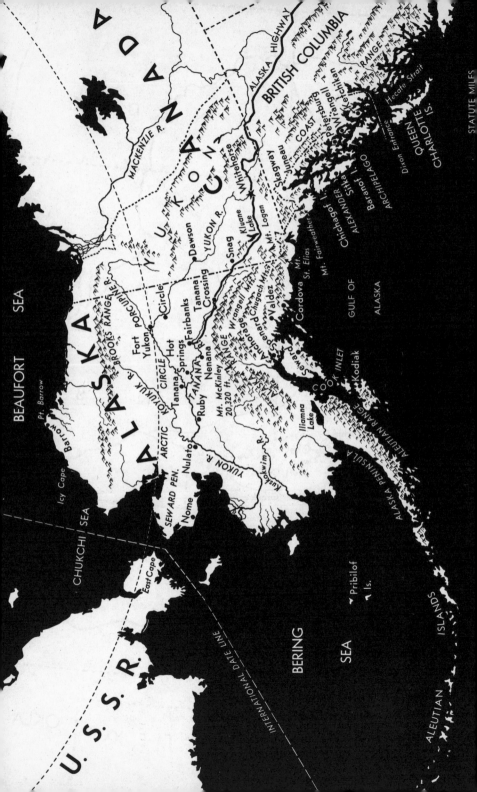

In 1903 when Colombia was hesitating about signing away the rights to build a canal in its isthmian province of Panama, the people of that strategic spot revolted from the mother country and declared their independence. Colombia was prevented by the United States Navy from sending forces to put down the revolt. So Panama became independent and granted the rights to build the canal. When it was completed in 1914, it was not only of vital concern to all the world's trading nations because of the distance it saved in shipping, but it was also a vital part of the system of defense of the United States. In recent times, however, the airplane has greatly reduced the significance of the canal in the strategy of the United States.

Of much greater importance today are the relations that have developed between the United States and Puerto Rico. This little island came into the possession of the United States as a result of the Spanish-American War in 1898. For many years it stood as a conspicuous example of the bad effects of colonialism. The United States administrators did set up medical services and schools and did build roads, but they also permitted the best third of the island to become the property of four sugar-refining companies. On the best 300,000 acres, only 76,000 acres were actually planted with sugar cane. The remainder was held in reserve and used for pasture. But meanwhile the population of the island, with the death rate considerably lowered by improved sanitation, had increased alarmingly. There was so much poverty and unemployment, in spite of extensive emigration, that it was said during the 1930's that Puerto Rico had the largest number of destitute people under the flag of the United States.

Since 1940 this situation has been changed, not violently, as in Mexico, but by political means—which is most unusual in Latin America. Under the leadership of Luis Muñoz Marín, the Puerto Ricans have formulated and carried out a balanced program of economic development. The vital truth was recognized that to lower the death rate of a densely populated area without providing for an increase of the food supply is to ask for trouble. To set up manufacturing industries and pay more wages than ever before, means that the people who receive these wages will want to make purchases of more food and more goods of all sorts. If goods are not available, inflation is the result and the economic gains are wiped out. Also the introduction of scientific agriculture inevitably results in a decrease of the number of farmers, for whom jobs in cities must be provided. A balanced program of economic development looks at the economy as a whole rather than bit by bit. In Puerto Rico one of the first steps was a mapped survey of the quality of the land and the existing use of the land. From this survey, carried out under the direction of professional geographers in Puerto Rico and the United States, a plan for the better use of the land was worked out. The government offered inducements for the investment of capital in new industries. The large sugar companies have restricted their activities to sugar refining, and the cane lands have been divided into small holdings.

Puerto Rico is still overcrowded. Only a steady current of emigration to the United States can keep down unemployment. But the income per capita has gone up so much that Puerto Rico is now one of the most prosperous parts of all Latin America.

The Puerto Ricans are overwhelmingly in favor of their new political status. The island is now a Commonwealth, freely associated with the United States. It elects its own governor and its own congress. Its defense and its foreign relations are carried on by the United States, but otherwise it enjoys complete autonomy. Its people are citizens of the United States but pay no Federal income tax on money earned in Puerto Rico.

Changes in the United States, in Canada, and in Latin America are still going on. In the United States the contrast between the sections comprising the arid west and the sections of the humid east remains strong, as it was at the beginning of the century. Water is a resource that is becoming more and more critical, even in the humid areas; but nowhere is it so fundamentally necessary to conserve water and utilize it efficiently as in those parts of the country that are deficient in rainfall. Because of the interstate courses of rivers, drainage control is clearly a field of responsibility for the Federal Government. But drainage control is more than a matter of engineering and dam building; it involves forestry, range management, and other techniques of land use. The results may be felt in a distant place, perhaps in another state or even in another country. No community is more aware of the nature of the water problem than is Los Angeles, which gets its water from a source clear across the State of California.

At the beginning of this century the Pacific coast had already emerged as a distinctive section of the United States. By mid-century numerous areas of localized crop production had become established. Some, like the Fresno raisin area, had shifted to other products (in the case of Fresno, other vineyard products) as a result of changes in the market. But most striking of all has been the development of manufacturing industries during and since World War II. Los Angeles has become a major manufacturing center, utilizing the oil of which it has an abundant local supply. On the shores of San Francisco Bay a great variety of manufactures have appeared around a center of basic steel production. Large quantities of electric power now available in the Northwest as a result of the Columbia River power development have supported a burst of industrial activity in that area.

The greatest changes of all, however, are to be observed in the humid east. The distinction between South and North is gradually becoming less important, even politically. As late as 1903 the income per capita of 19 states in the Northeast was $733, whereas the income per capita of 12 southeastern states was $312. But all this is changing. In fact the South, as a homogeneous section of the country, may before long disappear. The economic life of the Tennessee Valley has been transformed. Rural people have been resettled from lands flooded behind the big dams. Electric power gives support to a great new manufacturing development. Low-cost consumer goods made locally with machinery run by electricity are now widely used in places that half a century ago were part of the "backwoods." Between 1931 and 1953 the South increased its electric power-generating capacity more than threefold. The number of people employed in farming decreased by almost a third, while the number employed in manufacturing almost doubled. The per capita income has increased at a rate one and one-half times that of the United States as a whole.

One of the major changes in the South has been the emergence of a new section, the Gulf-Southwest. The mineral resources of this area, now made available by technological development, are vastly more valuable than were the rich, black cotton soils. This is one of the world's major oil and gas regions. Natural gas distributed by pipelines can now be utilized in distant parts of the country. The combination of oil, gas, sulfur, salt, potash, and other minerals, together with ample space for industrial buildings, provides an excellent situation for the development of new chemical industries. Such large new commercial and industrial cities as Houston and Dallas are the visible signs of this great change that is in process of breaking up the unity of the old South.

Meanwhile the Northeast also has been going through a process of economic change. Many manufacturing industries, such as those of cotton textiles, have moved away to the South or to Puerto Rico. The shoe industry is no longer concentrated near Boston, but a great variety of other industries requiring skilled labor and a nearby market have moved in.

Similarly the Middle West has changed in its economic life. Manufacturing industries, freed from the need to be close to sources of fuel by the new development of electric power, are now widely scattered in small communities around the great cities. Actually, from an economic point of view, most of the Corn Belt is now more properly designated as a manufacturing region than as an agricultural region. In fact, the typical industrial region of today represents a nice balance of farm and factory activity.

Looking at North America and especially at Anglo-America in mid-century, we see extraordinary advances in economic production and in the material level of living. Less than 8 percent of the world's people are enjoying half of all the world's production of goods and services. Not only in manufacturing but also in agriculture, there is an unprecedented increase in production per capita. Before World War II, for instance, a farm worker could produce enough food to feed himself and 10 others. But by 1955 a farm worker in the United States could feed himself and 19 others. The total production of food had been increased by about a third, while the number of persons employed in farming had decreased by about a third.

Yet industrial North America, as a result of all this, has not become more self-sufficient in its economy. Rather the opposite. In fact even the goal of economic self-sufficiency is no longer widely advocated. Modern industrial life means interdependence and thrives on widespread commerce. Though this is perhaps not generally appreciated, the kind of steel that can be used in modern machinery requires the use of some 40 different raw materials supplied from 57 different countries. Some 300 raw materials are used in the manufacture of an automobile, many of them not available at low cost on this continent. Even a can of shoe polish contains 8 imported ingredients. The high level of material well-being enjoyed in North America is based on interdependence, not isolation.

While North America was becoming more and more industrialized all the way from southeastern Alaska to Puerto Rico and from Quebec to central Mexico, certain new industrial products were both the means and the result of increased industrialization. These include modern means of transportation and communication and labor-saving household appliances. Unfortunately, they include also ultra-modern weapons more deadly than ever before. For good and for ill, these fruits of 20th-century ingenuity have transformed human life, not only in North America where most of them originated but in every inhabited part of the world, so completely that there can be no turning back.

In the early 1900's passenger automobiles were expensive toys of the wealthy. Within a quarter-century North American methods of mass production made the automobile the vehicle of the masses, carrying most Anglo-Americans and increasingly many Latin Americans everywhere from their first ride to the hospital delivery room to their last, slower trip. Every year Anglo-America makes about 6 million cars, 70 percent of the world's total. Trucks, 1½ million new ones annually, offer the railroads serious competition. Superhighways are fast replacing dirt roads. Airplanes, a mere visionary's dream at the turn of the century, each year carry the average inhabitant of North America 110 miles; the railroads still carry him 175 miles, but only a fourth or a fifth as fast.

A half-century ago telephone books were pamphlets; today they are huge volumes listing in the aggregate more than 57 million North American names. Forty years ago there were no household radio or television sets; today in North America there are twice as many radios and more than half as many television sets as there are telephones. And the typical middle-income-bracket family has in its home at least a half-dozen labor-saving or comfort-increasing electrical appliances.

Twenty years ago atomic energy was a mere theoretical possibility. Today in the United States alone we spend $250 per capita for national defense, chiefly to discourage potential enemies from using against us the weapon we first used over Hiroshima—and its still more dreadful successors. But if the world survives the threat of atomic destruction, life everywhere can be greatly eased by peaceful uses of atomic power.

Meanwhile the peoples of North America are being knit more closely together. Each retains much of its cultural integrity, but there is far greater exchange both of ideas and of products than ever before. Since one can travel from the Arctic all the way to southern Mexico without a passport and with a minimum of restrictions at the two international boundaries, tourist traffic is booming. The Alaska and Pan American Highways are traversed each year by thousands of motorists. Public sanitation and control of diseases of men and of farm animals and even of plants are carried on on a continental scale. The United States (including our virtually independent protégé Puerto Rico), Canada, and Mexico are among one another's best customers in international trade. Each has its pictorial and plastic arts, its literature, and its music, which in some respects are being slowly welded into a continental mode. Not only is there peace on this continent— there is international sympathy and understanding.

Why, then, should so many people be concerned about their security? Is it because of the rapidity of internal change and readjustment? Is it because of the shattering of the illusion of isolation and self-sufficiency? Is it because of a deep-seated and perhaps justified fear of atomic warfare?

If the whole story were to be summed up only in terms of production, income, and level of living, there might well be grounds for uncertainty and confusion. For security in an insecure world must rest on something beyond economic production. To be sure, economic and military power is based on production or on the capacity to produce. But as any military man will explain, power rests also on something else, on something intangible but none the less real. Military men call it morale, the will to victory. In a nation in peacetime, morale can be measured by the degree to which the people understand and support the ideals and purposes for which they form themselves into a "body politic" and consent to be governed.

What ideas and purposes have directed all the efforts that have been made to build the modern United States? Surely not just the search for profit. A rereading of the Declaration of Independence and of the Constitution with its amendments suggests that there are other purposes in mind. What factors have made Canada and Mexico great nations? Surely these are not exclusively, perhaps not even primarily, economic.

The people of North America are also engaged in developing and promoting some of the most revolutionary new ideas in the field of human relations that mankind has ever seen. The Democratic Revolution, the attack on the Law of Status which gave power and prestige on the basis of position in society already achieved, the demand for equality before the law, the demand for government by consent, the demand for "free access to knowledge and the use thereof"—these are ideas about human relations rarely or never before conceived. They had their beginnings in Great Britain, and they spread to many parts of western and northern Europe. But they have developed most rapidly in the relative freedom of North America, Australia, and New Zealand. The communists represent a reaction against the most advanced new idea in the field of human relations to be formulated in thousands of years.

Yes, North America is a remarkable continent. But it is not remarkable solely because of its endowment of resources or its high level of economic development. The unprecedented freedom enjoyed by the individual has given impetus to science and engineering. Throughout North America, teachers are free to pass on to students the findings of scholars. Technological advance is not accidental. One major stimulus to development has been the mixture of ideas from various and diverse culture hearths. This could only have been accomplished in an atmosphere of tolerance, never by force or by police action. The people of this remarkable continent are the custodians of the ideas of the Democratic Revolution, of the concept of the dignity of the individual here on earth. Anything in modern life, whether it be economic poverty or surfeit, or political short-sightedness, or moral insensitivity, that obscures our vision of these great purposes, by no means yet completely fulfilled, constitutes a threat to our security and a menace to the hopes of mankind.

Canada

BY D. G. CREIGHTON

The French navigators and chroniclers of the sixteenth and early seventeenth centuries often called it "the River of Canada." Obviously there was a special modern significance in the name which was hidden from them. They could not have foreseen that the St. Lawrence would, in truth, become "the River of Canada"—the river without which all the other rivers of Canada would hardly have been Canadian at all. They could not have anticipated the day when the third largest country in the world would make the St. Lawrence its east-west axis. But, from the first, the river's grandeur impressed them deeply; and Jacques Cartier, the sixteenth-century Breton navigator who was the first European to ascend the St. Lawrence, was obviously excited by the vast potentialities of the country through which he passed. His first two voyages, made in 1534 and 1535, provide a curiously significant forecast of the way in which the river was to shape the course and character of French enterprise in North America. In 1534, he sailed around Newfoundland, which was already fairly well known to fishermen and probably to Cartier himself, and found his way through the Strait of Belle Isle into the Gulf. The next year he returned, discovered the entrance which he had missed in 1534, and ventured up the river as far as the Island of Montreal. In one short sailing season he had penetrated hundreds of miles into the interior of the continent; and if he had not yet found the short northern route to the Far East, he had discovered an enormous waterway which would lead him or his successors indefinitely onward. One prophetic autumn day in 1535 he climbed the river island's high hill—Mount Royal he called it—and gazed westward through the reddening trees and over the yellowing fields of Indian corn into the future of Canada. The river—"grand, large, et spacieulx" came flowing in from the southwest. It was, the Indians assured Cartier gravely, navigable "for more than three moons"; and "one could make one's way so far up the river that they had never heard of anyone reaching the head of it."

In effect, Cartier had plotted the course of a French Empire in North America. He had vaguely anticipated the nature of the next few stages in French colonial development. But he had hopelessly outrun the outpost islands, Newfoundland and Cape Breton Island, which were the first known and solid bases for the European exploration of the northeastern part of North America; and when the curtain had finally descended upon his official exploring and colonizing expeditions, the advance into the interior was resumed much more deliberately from the islands and the coastline of the Gulf. It was a somber, inhospitable region. There was no hope here of those easy riches which Spain had looted from the sophisticated Indian kingdoms of South and Central America. There was no prospect either of those tropical and subtropical products—spices, dyes, sugar, and tobacco—which Europe became so eager to obtain from overseas plantations and trade. Great forests, it was true, covered the islands; minerals were hidden in the recesses of their rocky terrain. But it would be a very long time before Europe needed North America's timber, and a still longer time before the advance of technology would make the mining of the metals possible.

Fish was the first "crop" of northeastern North America; and the fishery was Canada's first great staple industry and trade. There were obvious reasons for its importance as a basis for commercial enterprise in the new world during the sixteenth and seventeenth centuries. Fish was a sustaining energy food, with a high protein value. The regularly recurring fast days of Roman Catholic Europe made it a frequently necessary article of diet; and the fact that, when cured with salt or sunshine, it could be preserved for lengthy periods of time, gave it a real advantage in an age which knew little about refrigeration and had to contend with the rapid deterioration of fresh meat. Above all, fish could be caught easily, cheaply, and in very large quantities by men with little ships and small amounts of capital. For generations and centuries, their catch had found a ready market in Europe; and by degrees the fishing industry in northern waters had extended westward across the Atlantic from Iceland towards the new world.

John Cabot, who landed on the northeastern coast of North America in 1497, had almost certainly been preceded by venturous fishermen; and his first great North American "fish story," that off Newfoundland one could lower a basket into the sea and bring it up full of fish, served merely to publicize what up to that time had been a well-kept fisherman's secret. The explorers had, in fact, stumbled upon what, for important geological reasons, was one of the greatest fishing grounds in the world. Ages before, a great land mass which had once been part of the continent had subsided into the sea. The peninsulas and islands which are such a characteristic feature of the northeastern coast of North America are the surviving plateaus of this lost country; but it had other plateaus, which had sunk only a short distance below the ocean and which extended out from the mainland as a submerged continental shelf. These marine uplands stretched in a great arc all the way up the ragged coastline from the future New England to the Grand Bank southeast of Newfoundland; and here were the favorite breeding grounds of a great variety of fish, including that "beef of the ocean," the prolific cod.

It was fish which had brought Europeans to the northeastern edges of the North American continent. It was fish—and the changing methods of curing it for its long haul back across the ocean—which led them into their first lengthy occupations of the soil of the new world. By the original technique, the technique of the "green fishery," the wet fresh fish were salted down as soon as they were caught; and the salt used in lavish quantities during the process was solar salt produced along the coasts of Europe by the evaporation of sea water. Obviously, countries with a dry, sunny climate, such as France, Spain, and Portugal, enjoyed a great initial advantage in the production of salt, just as fog-bound England labored under a terrible handicap; and it was the English, spurred on by their sharp necessity, who led the way in the development of a new technique, the "dry fishery."

In the dry fishery, the fish were spread out, only lightly salted, on flakes or stages on the beach to dry, and the sun and wind played a large part in the preserving process. The result was a dry hard cure which could stand the long voyages in the small ships of the age and which enabled the English to force their way into the markets of southern Europe. There were excellent profits in the new technique; but it had other consequences as well. It required the choice of suitable harbors and beaches, a prolonged stay on shore, and the erection of lodgings for the fishermen and flakes for the fish. Along the coast of the Avalon peninsula in Newfoundland, the English established the semipermanent bases for the dry fishery which were to become the centers of the island's future settlements. The French were second in the field; and when they began to vary their extensive green fishery with the new dry fishing technique, they found that many of the suitable areas in Newfoundland had already been occupied by their rivals, the English. They were driven outward, towards what was then thought of as the industry's marginal area, the mainland of the continent; and there, on the shores of the Gulf of St. Lawrence and its islands, they came into contact with the continent's native inhabitants, the Indians.

Jacques Cartier, on his voyage into the Canadian future, marked for all time the beginning of this next all-important stage in the penetration of the northern half of North America. On July 6, 1534, in a great bay of the Gulf of St. Lawrence which the thick heat of northern summer had led him to call Chaleur Bay, he saw "a large number of Indians, who set up a great clamour and made frequent signs to us to come on shore, holding up to us some furs on sticks." It was the first recorded instance of the North American advertising ballyhoo; but the barter between Europeans and natives which followed had quite evidently been preceded by other similar exchanges in the past. The Indians knew already that the mysterious white men could be induced to purchase their furs; and Cartier had brought with him the iron tools and the gaudy garments which only experience could have taught the French that the Indians desired.

For a while the fur trade remained a sporadic, unimportant enterprise, strictly ancillary to the fishery; but in the last half of the sixteenth century two circumstances gave it a vastly increased value and scope. One of these favorable circumstances was the new popularity of high-crowned, broad-brimmed beaver hats in Europe; the other was the victory of the Algonquins—the great family of hunting Indian tribes in northeastern North America—over the sedentary, agricultural Iroquoian Indians who had occupied the lower St. Lawrence in Cartier's time. On the one hand, the expansion of the felting and hat-making industries created a wealthy, somewhat capricious luxury market for furs in France; and, on the other, the retreat of the Iroquois to their historic habitat in northern New York State and the domination of the Gulf and the lower St. Lawrence by hunting Indians ensured a more copious and reliable supply of furs. The enterprisers who now sailed into the Gulf took more and more advantage of these opportunities; and there came a moment, towards the end of the sixteenth century, when some of them ceased to be fishermen and became fur traders. In 1608, Samuel de Champlain, one of the principal associates in the main fur-trading syndicate, built a trading post at Quebec—the "narrows" of the St. Lawrence; and at once the river began to play the first phase of its role in the continental expansion of the French Empire.

The landscape in which the French had established themselves and in which their main effort in North America was to be made, had its own distinctive challenges, difficulties, and rewards. Quebec stood at the narrow entrance to the St. Lawrence lowlands, which extended southwestward, broadening gradually into the great interior lowlands of the continent. Behind Quebec, to the southeast, lay the Appalachian Highland, a barrier which was to impede and delay the advance into the interior of the continent from the Atlantic seaboard. To the northwest was the Precambrian or Canadian Shield, an enormous plateau of ancient, battered rocks which surrounded Hudson Bay in a huge lopsided triangle. Up from the southwest, through the center of the landscape, came the St. Lawrence, a great but youthful, willful, turbulent river, with a series of violent rapids and the spectacular falls of Niagara as all too obvious evidences of the novelty of its course. It was, beyond all comparison, the greatest river draining to the Atlantic coast of the continent. With the Great Lakes, it formed a stupendous inland waterway which extended nearly two thousand miles into the heart of North America.

By it, the French sought furs. They particularly wanted beaver fur. And for an astonishingly long period of over two hundred years, the fur trade dominated the economic life of the St. Lawrence. The region, with its thick cover of forest, its relatively cool north-temperate climate, its elaborate, intricate drainage system of lakes, lakelets, rivers, streams, falls, and rapids, was the natural dominion of fur-bearing animals. It produced those luxuriant, pliable pelts which the trade called "castor gras d'hiver" and rated highest. It produced them in larger numbers than most other parts of the continent. But the supply of beaver was very far from being inexhaustible as the supply of cod quite literally was; and the French had not been very long established at Quebec and Montreal before several circumstances began to force them to look further and further afield for furs. From the first, the Indians revealed an insatiable appetite for the iron tools and equipment, the brightly colored cloth, and the brandy which the French were ready to exchange for pelts. They had a more insistent reason for hunting the sedentary, defenceless beaver than they had ever had before; and the possession of the white man's metal weapons —his knives, hatchets, and guns—made them increasingly expert in the business of destruction. Rapidly the region of the lower St. Lawrence became depleted. The fur trade began its inevitable journey west; and it traveled easily by the great rivers which invited it into the interior of the continent.

There was another important circumstance which helped equally to impel the French onward in their western journey. The St. Lawrence, though it was the greatest of the eastern rivers, was not the only Atlantic entrance to the continent. There were two other gateways to the interior, Hudson Bay and the Hudson River, to both of which the English navigator Henry Hudson had given his name; and these soon became the approaches and avenues of commercial rivalry and military aggression. The Hudson River, with the Dutch and then the English at its mouth and the fighting Iroquois dominating its headwaters, was the source of violent competition from almost the beginning of the seventeenth century; and the Bay was like a great breach in the northern defences of the continent through which, after 1670, the Hudson's Bay Company began slowly but successfully to invade the rich fur-bearing areas of the Precambrian Shield. The French had to do battle on both northern and southern fronts. Their purpose was, if possible, to intercept and divert their rivals' supplies of furs. They could hope to accomplish it only by outmarching and outflanking their enemies. And once again they were committed inescapably to a policy of westward expansion.

At first the French had relied upon the trade of the Indians who could make the journey down to the annual fur fairs at Quebec and Montreal. Then, with the help of those invaluable middlemen, the Hurons of the Georgian Bay region, the range of the business was vastly extended westward. It was the annihilation of the Hurons by the Iroquois, together with the constant pressure of Iroquois attacks on the settlements on the lower St. Lawrence, which brought about a radical reorganization of the fur-trading colony. New France, which up to then had simply been the commercial monopoly of a succession of fur-trade companies, became in 1663 a royal province of the French Crown. Trained administrators from the great state organization at Versailles were sent out to govern the colony; regular soldiers were dispatched to protect its boundaries from Indian assaults. And on the basis of this new-found strength and security, New France entered upon an even more active phase in its career of western expansion. Up to that time, Indian agents had carried the main burden of the inland trade; now, with a mixture of political, commercial, and religious motives, the French themselves assumed leadership in the task of opening up the west. The movement of exploration, discovery, commercial exploitation, and missionary enterprise, which had begun with the coming of Champlain, reached its climax in the last three decades of the seventeenth century. Men like Radisson, Groseilliers, Dulhut, Joliet, La Salle, and Iberville pushed French trade and empire north to the shores of Hudson Bay, west to the head of the Great Lakes, and south to the Gulf of Mexico.

It was an enormous empire. But it was also a commercial empire, facile, primitive, unsubstantial and transitory. The fur trade had made it. The fur trade had stamped New France with its characteristic marks of strength and weakness. It had given the colony its vast geographical extent and political grandeur. It had left it with a small population and a narrow, precarious economic base. Fundamentally the fur trade was hostile to settlement. Hunting Indians and beavers were the human and animal population which a fur-trading province required. European colonists, farms, villages, and towns were not only unnecessary, but—after a certain point—positively injurious to its interest. All the fur-trading companies had realized that settlement meant the annihilation of the forests, the destruction of the fur-bearing animals, and the westward flight of the fur trade. All the fur-trading companies with no exceptions, though their charters formally required them to bring out settlers, had persistently evaded their obligations. After New France became a royal province in 1663, the government of Louis XIV for a time actively encouraged and promoted settlement; but there were few strong natural incentives for emigration from a great, self-sufficient, continental country such as France; and once the official efforts declined with the passing of Louis XIV's interest, the movement of peoples to the colony on the St. Lawrence virtually ceased. The colony grew, but it grew slowly, mainly from its own natural increase. A hundred years later, when New France was formally transferred by treaty to the British Crown, the population of the province numbered only about sixty-five thousand; and it was largely strung on a narrow band of settlements on the lower St. Lawrence between Quebec and Montreal. Down in Nova Scotia, a few thousand more Frenchmen, the Acadians, had settled along the shores of the Bay of Fundy.

New France was woefully deficient in the solid and enduring stuff of settlement. It lacked a substantial agricultural base and healthy related trades and industries. It utterly failed to develop a vigorous and diversified Atlantic trade. In the first few decades after the establishment of the royal province, the French imperial planners at Paris and Quebec had earnestly but vainly attempted to check the colony's perilous concentration upon the single luxury staple, fur. They had sought to develop agriculture. They had tried to encourage mining, shipbuilding, and other domestic industries. They had dared to hope that New France, along with the fishing regions of Acadia and the French sugar-producing colonies of the West Indies, could be combined in a single, great, mutually supporting economic integration. They dreamed great dreams for the future. But, in the end, New France disappointed them all. It never became a prosperous agricultural or commercial center. The valley of the St. Lawrence led into the interior lowlands of the continent, the best agricultural land in the whole of North America; but the fur-trading colony never succeeded in occupying more than a small fraction of it. And it was New England, not New France, which supplied the French forts and fishing stations in Acadia, and which shipped salt fish, lumber, and provisions to the sugar-producing French West Indian Islands. In the center of the continent, the fur trade spread out in a radiating network of trade routes; but, on the ocean, the commerce of New France ploughed a single, undeviating course from the Gulf of St. Lawrence to the ports of the Motherland.

The colony grew, though slowly; and it grew in a fashion which neither the Paris planners, nor the bureaucrats at Quebec and Montreal, nor even the settlers themselves had entirely expected. Like all the others—Spaniards, Portuguese, Dutch, and English—who had anything to do with the seventeenth-century colonization of the Americas, the French were citizens of a mature, highly developed civilization. The political institutions, social organizations, religions, philosophies, literatures, and art forms of West European culture had all attained an advanced state of growth at a time when the earliest settlements were being founded in the new world. This cultural inheritance was by all odds the most important of the settlers' effects which the migrants carried with them across the ocean; and their first instinct was to preserve it. Their greatest hope was to reproduce, with only the relatively minor modifications which they considered necessary or desirable, the way of life which they had known so well and loved so much in the old world. Many of the material things which were required to preserve their culture from depreciation would have to be imported from Western Europe for some time to come at least, and they could be paid for by the sale of North American staple products. But there were other immaterial but equally important elements in their civilization—institutions, social hierarchies, laws, conventions, and values—which could be freely transported merely by being established, obeyed, and honored in the new world. The first impulse of all those who founded the colony on the St. Lawrence was to make it literally what its name implied, a New France overseas. They established the political institutions of the efficient, centralized, and absolute French monarchy. They set up the landholding system and social order which they, like all other West Europeans, had inherited from the Middle Ages.

Yet the Seignorial System, as it came to be called in New France, differed radically from the social feudalism which still existed in Old

France; and some of the most important of these differences were the work of the French colonial administrators themselves. They sensibly realized that in the new world they would have to soften some of the harsh rigidities of the Old Régime of France. The *habitant* of New France—he was significantly never given the humble title of *paysan* —was not called upon to labor under the heavy burden of taxes and services which his counterpart carried in the old land. The seigneurs or landlords of the St. Lawrence valley, who were often ex-officers and sons of good but untitled families, had nothing like the wealth, the power, or the arrogant social pretensions of their prototypes back in the Mother Country. In effect, their main function was to act as government agents in the settlement of the province. Their obligations were at least as substantial as their benefits and privileges; and both were regulated by the colonial administration with a careful eye on the general progress and welfare of the colony.

All this was done officially. The French imperial planners had wisely sought to adapt an ancient institution to new conditions; but the changes which they had introduced were not the only modifications of the old French social order which the environment of the fur-trading colony required. The Seignorial System, like the feudalism from which it was historically derived, was based upon the ownership of land; and land, in the fur-trading colony of the St. Lawrence, was not economically strong enough to bear the weight of the social relationships which the French sought to place upon it. If New France had been successful in developing a staple product, such as sugar and tobacco, which was well adapted to production on a large scale in manors or plantations, then the fortunes of feudalism in the St. Lawrence valley might have been very different. But agriculture in the long ribbon-like farms between Quebec and Montreal was mainly a subsistence business, which barely succeeded in supplying the small local urban market; and the seigneurs were landlords, economically dependent upon the rents and profits of land, in a colony where the only real source of riches was the fur trade. If, in some way, they were unable to associate themselves with this main commercial enterprise of New France, their social position became inevitably depressed. Their political powers had already been taken over by the centralized state; their honors and privileges became increasingly meaningless. They failed to maintain the positions of economic importance and social leadership which everybody had instinctively assumed would be theirs.

Their places were soon taken by others, and naturally enough the others were people who were identified, not with the drab life of subsistence agriculture on the lower St. Lawrence, but with that impulsive western expansion which became the dominant pattern, the main style, of the affairs of New France. The colony had begun, and for a long time continued, as a simple combination of fur-trading outpost and mission station; and the prominence which the clergy on the one hand and the fur-traders or *coureurs-de-bois* on the other had acquired was traceable finally to the key parts they had in the opening of the west. After 1663, when the secular-minded efficiency experts of Louis XIV's centralized monarchy arrived at Quebec, they tried their best to change this state of affairs. They succeeded, to some extent, in reducing the influence of the clergy in the politics of the colony; but they utterly failed to diversify the economy of the St. Lawrence valley and to prevent the fur trade from draining away the colony's best manpower into the west. They tried to suppress the fur traders, the *coureurs-de-bois*; but the *coureurs-de-bois* resisted all their efforts. Jaunty, reckless, impatient of authority, inured to hardship and cunningly resourceful in danger, they were the men who made their own and the colony's living through travel in far, savage countries and traffic with wild and alien peoples. They were the distinctive social creation of New France, its real though raffish leaders, its unacknowledged nobility. They supplied the fur-trading province with its economic drive, just as the priests and the members of the religious orders imposed its social standards and maintained its spiritual values. And to the end, these two social groups—the fur traders, grown increasingly solid and respectable in character, and the clergy—remained the two poles around which the active life of the province revolved.

To the end, also, the fur trade dominated the whole French effort in North America. The fur trade had inspired that continental strategy which from the first captured the imagination of the rulers of the St. Lawrence. It led even the soberest of the French colonial administrators to nurse those grandiose dreams of conquest which in the end proved impossible of realization. The vast, facile territorial acquisitions in the west, which had been won so easily through the St. Lawrence River system, were too great for a small but heroic colony to hold; and yet the continual enlargement of this western domain

was at once its first impulse and the fundamental necessity of its being. The growing competition from Hudson Bay and the Atlantic Seaboard, which was creeping slowly but steadily inland, could only be
met and hurled back by a more effective French occupation of the
interior. The men of the St. Lawrence redoubled their effort to protect their continental empire. They undertook the increasingly hazardous and desperate forced marches by which alone their enemies
could be outflanked and the long, tenuous lines of their communications protected. In the northwest, in order to meet the competition
of the Hudson's Bay Company, they crossed the height of land beyond
Lake Superior and pushed their trade in the valleys of the Red and
Saskatchewan Rivers. To the southwest, on the eve of the Seven
Years' War, they were busy occupying and defending the headwaters
of the Ohio. These defiant efforts helped to bring about their own
nemesis; and New France, the incredible little colony that had won
half a continent, collapsed under the dead weight of its own ambitions and conquests.

What would the British conquest mean for Acadia and Canada?
Would the colonies which the French had tried in vain to hold in
northern North America experience a real alteration in character and a
decisive change in growth as a result? Up to then the scattered regions
of New France had had a distinctive and unusual history, very different from that of the sober, solidly growing communities on the
Atlantic Seaboard. Acadia had been a disputed outpost of the North
Atlantic fishery. Canada, with its dominant fur trade and its enormous
inland commercial empire, had achieved an unique record in western
expansion. Both these northern regions had formed their first patterns
of development under the direction of the French. But now, after a
prolonged conflict, their old masters had vanished. In 1713, at the
Peace of Utrecht, the French had already ceded the peninsula of Nova
Scotia to Great Britain; and half a century later, by the Peace of Paris
of 1763, France surrendered not only all the rest of Acadia, but the
whole of Canada as well. The conquered provinces, which were renamed Nova Scotia and Quebec, now formed part of an enormous
British American Empire, which occupied all the Atlantic side of the
continent and stretched unbroken from Hudson Bay to the Gulf of

Mexico. It was a large, lively family of self-assertive colonial children into which these strange northerners had been forcibly adopted. Who would not have expected that they would promptly acquire the family resemblance and become normal, healthy little British colonies themselves?

At first it seemed that this was exactly what was going to happen. Great Britain, after a long period of neglect, had forcibly taken Nova Scotia in hand before and during the Seven Years' War. Halifax had been founded, the Acadians deported *en masse*, and a legislative assembly called for the first time in 1758. The Royal Proclamation of 1763, which promised an assembly and English laws for the inhabitants of the St. Lawrence, seemed to foreshadow exactly the same respectable British future for the French-speaking colony of Quebec. For all of British America, settlement west of the Alleghenies was temporarily prohibited; and the Province of Quebec was severed from its inland empire by a new boundary line which was drawn just west of the Ottawa River. Western ambitions were to be held in check for a time; but, in generous compensation, immigration was encouraged to move up the Atlantic coast and into the new and largely unoccupied northern colonies. Army veterans and frontiersmen from the Atlantic Seaboard, attracted by free lands and British institutions, were to move into Quebec and Nova Scotia and remake them in their own image.

Yet it did not turn out exactly as had been expected. Natural tendencies seemed oddly at variance with official plans. New Englanders, it was true, did migrate to Nova Scotia, though not perhaps in such large numbers as the planners had hoped; and although they informed this remote, isolated peninsular province with much of their way of life, they never quite succeeded in making it a completely typical northern extension of New England. In Quebec, the other new northern colony, English immigration failed to leave any distinct new impression at all. The very few English-speaking newcomers who arrived in the St. Lawrence valley in the first two decades after the conquest were not farmers or mechanics, but merchants; and soon these capitalist immigrants had taken up the old St. Lawrence fur trade, had accepted its ancient rivalries with Hudson Bay and the Hudson River, and had begun to assert its historic claims to western dominion just as vigorously as the French had ever done. In fairly short order British colonial officials realized that their plan of anglicizing this still overwhelmingly French-speaking, Roman Catholic province was a failure. By the Quebec Act of 1774, Great Britain declared that the creation of an assembly had been postponed and that French law would henceforth be the rule for the decision of civil suits. At the same time—and this was equally a confirmation of Canada's historic character and purpose—the Act annexed the whole of New France's inland dominion, as far south as the junction of the Ohio and Mississippi Rivers, to the Province of Quebec.

The northern provinces had managed to preserve—and in the process had strengthened—their slowly developing personalities. They had resisted the first British effort to establish a political uniformity in North America; they were equally unwilling to welcome the second, American attempt. The purpose, which the Thirteen Colonies nursed, of arousing the whole continent in a united resistance to Great Britain, was impossible of realization. All hopes of a truly continental concord broke against the apathy, neutrality, dislike, and resistance of Nova Scotia and Quebec. At first blush, it might have seemed that these two conquered provinces, one of which had been acquired scarcely more than a decade before, would have welcomed the first opportunity of uniting with their rebellious fellow subjects to the south and of throwing off the rule of their new masters. In fact, at the moment when the revolutionary movement was reaching its climax in the Thirteen Colonies, a strong opposition to the local imperial governor and to imperial policy had arisen in both Quebec and Nova Scotia. Yet these provincial political struggles never became merged in a general, continental resistance; and northern public affairs, relatively unaffected by the tumult which was raging on the Atlantic Seaboard, pursued their separate distinctive way through calms and crises of their own.

It was soon obvious that if Nova Scotia and Quebec were to join the American Revolution, they could be brought to do so, not by a voluntary movement from within their boundaries, but only by armed force from without. The American invasion of Quebec in 1775–1776, which came by the traditional Hudson River-Lake Champlain route, was a dismal failure, which effectively alienated any small remaining sympathy for the revolutionary cause in the St. Lawrence valley; and the small raid on the frontier of Nova Scotia which occurred later in

1776 made even less impact upon a more favorably disposed English-speaking population. The formal parting of the ways came only in 1783, when by treaty the Thirteen Colonies were granted their independence; but long before this it was perfectly clear that the St. Lawrence and the Seaboard had set out upon increasingly divergent ways. The Seaboard gained its independence from Europe; but the St. Lawrence and its outposts kept its independence in North America.

The northern provinces had preserved their odd, detached, stand-offish personalities during the war. It was the peace which for the first time brought about a fundamental and far-reaching change in their characters. The peace, which in 1783 legalized the disruption of the first British Empire, gave the British North America which remained a separate political existence, and, in establishing the boundary between it and the new United States, prescribed the limits and effectively set the terms within which this separate political existence must henceforth be carried on. With the passage of time, this boundary has come to seem natural. But it was not natural in 1783. It cut a clean, decisive line through what up to that time had been the undivided empire of the St. Lawrence. The whole of the southwest, which had been explored and exploited from the River of Canada and which as late as 1774 had been accepted as logically a part of the Province of Quebec, was now torn away from its natural and historic connections to become territory of the United States. Nothing, of course, could really cheat the St. Lawrence of its destiny. It was, and would remain, the greatest river draining into the Atlantic Seaboard. It was to provide the inspiration and the basis of all Canadian dreams of western empire and continental expansion. But though these dreams remained as ambitious as ever, the new boundary inevitably effected a change in their character and direction. South of the Great Lakes, the empire which the St. Lawrence could now aspire to win, would be a commercial empire only. Its potential political dominion lay to the northwest beyond Lake Superior.

The Peace of 1783 not only set the stage; it also provided the actors. The American Revolution was a civil war which was followed by the separation of British peoples as well as by the division of British properties and assets. Approximately one hundred thousand emigrants—the first English-speaking "displaced persons" in history—left the United States after the recognized triumph of the Revolution.

These Loyalists—"United Empire Loyalists" was their official title—were just as good social and political democrats as the fellow citizens whom they left behind in the republic; but they preferred parliamentary government in a constitutional monarchy to republican institutions and they strongly objected to the breakup of the unity of the English-speaking people by force. Socially, they formed a good average sample of the colonial population—a fair cross section of seaboard and frontier, town and countryside, skills and trades, and professions. Between twenty-five and thirty thousand of them journeyed to Nova Scotia in one of the great migration fleets which sailed north from New York in the season of 1783; a much smaller number, not more than ten thousand in all, reached the St. Lawrence and the shores of the Lower Lakes via the headwaters of the Hudson-Mohawk system or by the Lake Champlain-Richelieu River route.

The Loyalists changed the face of British North America. They profoundly altered its probable destiny. Up to that time, the northern provinces had been relatively small, underpopulated outposts of the fur trade or the fishery. French settlement had not ventured westward beyond the confluence of the St. Lawrence and the Ottawa Rivers; the New Englanders in Nova Scotia had done little more than occupy the abandoned Acadian farms on the Bay of Fundy and set up small fishing settlements on the south shore of the peninsula. All this was now changed. The Loyalists brought solid and enduring settlement into what up to then had been silent and empty forest. From the Bay of Fundy they pushed northwestward up the St. John valley into the heart of continental Nova Scotia; they made homes for themselves on the banks of the St. Lawrence west of the Ottawa and along the north shore of Lake Ontario. In twelve months from 1783 to 1784, the population of British North America increased by approximately fifty percent. The whole outlook, political, economic, and social, of the northern provinces rapidly and drastically altered. New provinces had to be created in both the Maritime and St. Lawrence regions; and within a decade after the coming of the Loyalists, five British North American colonies—Upper Canada (Ontario), Lower Canada (Quebec), New Brunswick, Nova Scotia, and Prince Edward Island (even Cape Breton became for a while a separate province)—faced the very different conditions of a new future. The Loyalists brought commercial agriculture and its small related industries into the northern forests; they began to build up the new staple trades and to alter and diversify the first primitive fishing and fur-trading economies of British North America.

Settlement had come. Settlement was the implacable foe of the fur trade; and the St. Lawrence fur trade was doomed. Yet, for another generation, Montreal retained its old western, commercial interests; and during that last generation of the old Canadian westerners, the fur trade performed a great, an essential, service for the transcontinental Canada of the future. To the northwest, beyond Lake Superior, lay an immense region which in rich compensation for the territorial losses to the south, the St. Lawrence might one day be able to claim as its own political dominion. Four great powers—Spain, Russia, the United States, and Great Britain—had either old claims to press or new interests to assert in these territories. The urgings and the enterprise of British North Americans were necessary to spur Great Britain on to the acquisition and retention of the northwest. If the Hudson's Bay Company had enjoyed an undisturbed monopoly of the fur trade, it would probably have failed to give the necessary impetus; but in fact it was forced everywhere to meet the aggressive competition of the traders from Montreal; and it was this savage and unrelenting rivalry between the St. Lawrence and the Bay—between the Hudson's Bay Company and the North West Company of Montreal—which made the restless western advance of the fur trade inevitable. The Nor'westers attempted, as La Vérendrye and his sons had attempted a generation before, to intercept and divert their rivals' fur supplies. They reached the headwaters of the rivers flowing eastward into Hudson Bay. They pushed beyond into the drainage systems of the western Arctic and the Pacific. It was a famous trio of North West Company explorers—Alexander Mackenzie, Simon Fraser, and David Thompson—who solved the main geographical puzzles of the northwestern quarter of the continent and ensured their own immortality in the names of the great rivers which they discovered and explored. They made good British North America's claim to its northwestern empire. They established the boundaries of the future Dominion of Canada. And when, in the nineteenth century, the North West Company was finally absorbed in its rival's organization, their work had been done; and the Hudson's Bay Company had merely to guard an acquired inheritance.

It was, of course, an inheritance which could not be transmitted for a long time yet. Rapid transcontinental expansion, except for purposes of the fur trade, was quite beyond the capacities or the ambitions of the British North Americans in the late eighteenth and early nineteenth centuries. The settlements which the Loyalists and their successors had established on the shores of the lakes and rivers of eastern and central North America faced a long, slow, painful period of adjustment and growth. The settlers had first to come to terms with their immediate landscape, overcome its obstacles, exploit its possibilities, and use its riches to support and ameliorate their way of life. The good land which they occupied and the deep forests which surrounded them provided two new north-temperate staple products, timber and wheat. The northern provinces hoped and expected to sell these products principally in imperial markets; and they relied upon the tariff preferences and shipping monopolies of the Old Colonial System of Great Britain to give them a competitive advantage over their American rivals in the United Kingdom and the British West Indies. Two important new circumstances, which made Great Britain much more receptive to imports of staple products from north-temperate colonies, helped to realize their hopes. On the one hand, the Industrial Revolution was rapidly transforming England into a manufacturing community which could not produce enough wheat to feed itself; and, on the other, the French Revolutionary and Napoleonic Wars soon created a desperate scarcity of strategic raw materials.

It was an age still of wood, wind, and water. Wood was the main material of construction; wind and water the chief sources of power; river, lake, and ocean the principal avenues of transport. England's defensive walls were the wooden sailing ships which protected her islands and enforced her mastery of the seas. Timber was a vitally necessary structural material during the Napoleonic Wars; and when in 1807 Napoleon and Alexander signed the Treaty of Tilsit and attempted to extend the Continental Blockade to the Baltic, Great Britain awoke to the terrible realization that her main source of supplies was endangered. Up to that time the costs of shipping a bulky product such as timber across the Atlantic had made it quite impossible for British North America to compete with the low prices of wood from the nearby Baltic countries; but now British merchants were encouraged to risk their capital in the British American timber trade by the imposition of a colonial tariff preference high enough to protect their investment and to ensure a continuation of the business during the competitive times of peace.

With almost miraculous rapidity, the timber trade sprang into vigorous existence. Wood became the second great staple product of the new British North America; and the supplies of British North American wood were almost literally unlimited and inexhaustible. In New Brunswick, the St. John, Miramichi, and Restigouche river valleys sloped up to high plateaus bearing magnificent stands of red and white pine. In Upper and Lower Canada, the Ottawa and St. Lawrence Rivers and their northern tributaries provided easy, open avenues into the copious forest riches of the southern Precambrian Shield. The great buoyant sticks of timber, carefully and wastefully squared by cunningly wielded adzes, were lashed together in rafts and floated down the rivers; and all summer the river and ocean ports were crowded with those big, clumsy, capacious ships, the "timber droghers." A new way of life, the life of the lumbermen, hard but carefree and adventurous, came into being; and young men, tired of the dull labor of the farms and restive under the puritanical restraints of small communities, sought the uproarious companionship of the lumber camps much as the *coureurs-de-bois* before them had gladly escaped into the exciting freedom of the fur trade.

The end of the War of 1812 marked the beginning of a new and very different period in the development of British North America. For over half a century, through a long and agitating series of wars, revolutions, migrations, and invasions, it had managed, with increasing assurance and conviction, to preserve its separateness and its character. It had survived several attempts, made by both Great Britain and the United States and backed either by legislative enactments or armed force, to unify and standardize the continent; and the complete defeat of all the American attempts at invasion and conquest during the War of 1812 had ended in a peace which solemnly confirmed the existing political division of North America. At long last, the tiny communities of British North America could draw a breath of relief.

They had survived. Their roots had clutched fairly deeply into the soil. They had come to terms with their environment, discovered its most obvious commercial possibilities, and learnt to pay their way with new staple products. In the long, slow, back-breaking process of settlement, their numbers had grown steadily, both by new immigration and by natural increase. The movement up the coast into Nova Scotia and New Brunswick had virtually ceased with the coming of the Loyalists; but pioneers from the New England states, New York, New Jersey, and Pennsylvania pushed northward into the Eastern Townships of Lower Canada and found their way westward to the north shore of Lake Erie in Upper Canada. At the opening of the War of 1812 the population of British North America numbered nearly five hundred thousand. It had come almost exclusively from native, North American stocks. It had come either from the long-established French-speaking population base on the lower St. Lawrence or from the two English-speaking bases of New England and the Middle Colonies.

At this point there came an abrupt change. The War of 1812 had severed the connections with the United States; but the peace brought a renewal of British North America's direct contact with Europe. The steady column of American frontiersmen, which had been coming for decades along the natural inland migration routes into Upper and Lower Canada, was deflected after the War into the new western American states; and, in compensation, a great army of immigrants began to push westward up the St. Lawrence from overseas. The long upheaval of the Industrial Revolution, the economic depression and social unsettlement which recurred periodically in the decades following Waterloo, were potent inducements which helped to set the British peoples on the march again; and, for the first time, it was British North America, and particularly the inland Province of Upper Canada, which caught the imaginations and fired the hopes of the intending migrants. They came from all over the British Isles—from every part of England, from the Scottish Lowlands, from the Highlands and the Western Islands, from Ulster and Southern Ireland. They filled in the empty spaces of Nova Scotia and Cape Breton Island, pushed up the green river valleys of New Brunswick, swelled the urban populations of Quebec and Montreal and, journeying westward up the St. Lawrence and the Lower Lakes, spread their settlements over the great triangular peninsula between Lakes Ontario, Erie, and Huron.

The turmoil of the great migration lasted for about a quarter of a century. It was most severe in the Canadas, where small-scale, abortive revolts occurred; but gradually the vast, painful confusion of the settlement period subsided and out of the chaos small, solid, prosperous provincial societies began to emerge. Economically as well as politically, they were still colonies, for, in the main, they produced staple raw materials for export, and imported manufactures; and their small but growing native industries—flour milling, lumber milling, and shipbuilding—were all fairly closely related to the fishery or the basic staple trades of timber and wheat. In Newfoundland, which was the last colony to receive representative institutions, the fishery was the be-all and end-all of existence. In tiny Prince Edward Island, men were already beginning to desert the sea for the cultivation of the island's rich agricultural resources. Nova Scotia, with its fishing, its shipbuilding, its cattle-raising, and its rapidly growing ocean commerce, had a more diversified provincial economy. The forest and its varied industries dominated the economic life of New Brunswick; and timber and shipbuilding made work and brought prosperity for the ports and settlements along the lower St. Lawrence and up the Ottawa River as far as Bytown. Southwest of the Ottawa, in Upper Canada, the lowlands of the St. Lawrence broadened out into more smiling, fertile amplitudes; and here, in the rich peninsular country, lay Canada's first wheat-growing "west."

Despite the enormous disparity in size of the two political associations, British North America was forced at every point to compete with the United States. The northern provinces and the republic occupied the same continent, shared common resources, produced many similar products, and fought for the same markets. The unequal rivalry which the French had once sustained was taken over by their successors; and both Canadians and Maritimers strove to defend their economic riches and to maximize their every natural advantage for the struggle. The Maritime Provinces, whose obvious rival was New England, built up a large and efficient provincial marine and sought to protect their fisheries and to monopolize the British markets in the Atlantic. The Canadas, whose historic competitors were New York and the northern seaboard ports, attempted to make the St. Lawrence the dominating transport route for the new agricultural society which was growing up around the Great Lakes on each side of the international boundary.

The St. Lawrence was an unique natural advantage; but the falls at Niagara and the rapids on the upper river were serious flaws in its magnificence; and the completion of the Erie Canal in New York State dramatically revealed these weaknesses and quickened the Canadians' impulse to remedy them. The Lachine Canal, at the south side of the Island of Montreal, was completed in 1824, and the Welland Canal, around the obstruction at Niagara, five years later; but the huge task of constructing the canals on the upper St. Lawrence was spread over another twenty years as a result largely of the division of responsibility between the two provinces of Upper and Lower Canada. The long, cheap inland waterway was Montreal's greatest asset; but the river city, which was not an ice-free port like its great competitors, suffered an annual and prolonged interruption of its navigation and labored also under higher rates for freight and insurance on its northern ocean route. The Canadians struggled to offset these added costs by tariff advantages in their chosen markets. They had long possessed a substantial timber preference in Great Britain; the complex British Corn Laws gave their breadstuffs a preferred but variable tariff rate. And they now sought to convert this into a stable token duty on their wheat and flour.

The northern provinces had retained their old imperial connection as the essence of their being and the condition of their survival. They had grown up inside the protection, political and economic, of the Old Colonial System of Great Britain; and they were now reaching towards their first maturity. A satisfactory degree of economic well-being and social security had been attained. The countryside was a tranquil, ordered landscape in which the rough work of settlement had long been done. The little ports and towns—Halifax, St. John, Quebec, Montreal, Kingston, and Toronto—were soberly active commercial centers. There was time now for the cultivation of the mind and the spirit and money for public school systems and provincial universities. A half dozen little colonial societies were rapidly coming of age. They had their own rights to protect, their own purposes to fulfil, their own interests to attend to, and their own values to safeguard. They were outgrowing the protection which had once supported and limited their action; they wanted a larger measure of control over their own course and destiny. A potential nation was ready to emerge from colonialism; and the old and tragic American problem—the problem of reconciling the demands of emerging nationalism with the requirements of imperial control—appeared once more, impatiently demanding solution.

The first attempt had ended disastrously in the breakup of the first British Empire. The British North American colonies had no desire to assist in the dissolution of the second. They preferred monarchical to republican institutions, and parliamentary to congressional government; and it was through a reforming rather than revolutionary technique that they sought to make colonial government a more sensitive instrument of their will. Representative institutions they had had, of course, for generations now; in the newer colonies, such as New Brunswick and Upper Canada, the local parliaments dated their beginnings from the founding of the provinces themselves. What they had not had, and what they now demanded in substance, was greater executive control and direction over their internal affairs. The radical leaders of the 1830's had argued that this greater self-determination could be most effectively achieved through elected governors and elected councils in the American fashion; but these proposals were discredited in the defeat of the Rebellion of 1837 and the colonial reformers returned to the British parliamentary tradition for inspiration. The first Earl of Durham, in his famous *Report on the Affairs of British North America,* recommended that provincial executive government should be placed in the hands of a cabinet which enjoyed the confidence of the majority of the assembly and hence of the electorate as a whole. A radical Whig peer thus gave the weight of his authority to the idea of "responsible government," or cabinet government, for colonies. But it was a Canadian, Robert Baldwin, who first stated the principle; it was a Nova Scotian, Joseph Howe, who gave it its most eloquent defence; and it was organized political parties in Nova Scotia and Canada which in 1847–48 secured the first truly "responsible governments" in the second British Empire.

This radical change in the political structure of the Empire did not come alone. It was accompanied by an equally profound and far-reaching alteration in the Empire's economic organization. The colonies had taken the initiative in political reform; but the main pressure for economic change came from Great Britain herself. In the great upheaval of the Industrial Revolution, the Mother Country was rapidly revising her whole commercial policy in general and her attitude to colonies in particular. To this first great industrial power, with its new determination to cut costs and enlarge markets, the British Empire had most definitely declined in commercial value. Colonial raw materials were not worth the costly system of tariffs and preferences which encouraged their production. Colonial markets were nothing in comparison with the vast international markets which the British manufacturers had set their hopes upon. The first workshop of the world was moving rapidly away from mercantilism and towards free trade; and the revolution in British commercial policy had its dramatic beginnings in 1846 with the repeal of the Corn Laws. By 1850, both the timber duties and the navigation laws had also been abolished. Great Britain was a free-trade nation, open on equal terms to the staple products of all countries; and all the commercial advantages— the tariff preferences and shipping monopolies—which British North America had hitherto enjoyed in British markets had vanished utterly.

It was these two great events—the British adoption of free trade and the colonial acquisition of responsible government—which completely altered the structure of the second British Empire. The combination of economic change and political reform constituted a major revolution in the life of British North America. Henceforth the northern provinces would have the opportunity of making most of their own political decisions; henceforth also they would be under the necessity of relying upon their own unaided material resources and commercial policies. It was true, of course—to the infinite satisfaction of British North America—that the imperial connection remained and that Great Britain would continue to extend her military assistance and diplomatic support. But the old governance and the old mercantilism had vanished. Partly at her own request, partly against her agonized protests, British North America had escaped, and had been ejected from, colonialism. To a positively alarming extent, she was now mistress of her own destiny. What destiny would she embrace? What would she do with the freedom which had been won and thrust upon her?

One road into the future lay open and invitingly easy. The northern provinces could simply refuse to accept the anxious and heavy burdens of their new-found maturity. The old British Empire, political and

1. The sparse Eskimo population of northern and northeastern Canada
has a fusion of cultures. Here the child is carried in primitive manner
in a fold of the mother's garment, the fabric of which is manifestly
machine-made.

2. Within an Eskimo tent home on Baffin Island.

3. Undeveloped water power in the remote wilderness of western Labrador.

Galloway

4. The harbor of St. John's, Newfoundland, at the eastern extremity of Anglo-America.

5. Quebec, where students don't frown on gentlemanly attire.

6. In the hills of British Columbia.

7. Downtown Toronto. More than any other Canadian city, Toronto's skyline follows a pattern familiar to its neighbors across the border.

Galloway

8. Stock judging in a pavilion in Toronto.

9. At Montreal, several hundred miles from its mouth, the St. Lawrence is still a mighty river.

10. Contour plowing preserves the soil on prairie farms in Saskatchewan.

11. Small timber — but lots of it — is given its springtime push into a stream that will float it to distant mills.

12.   Fiord, forest, and vast power generated beyond the mountains combine to make Kitimat, B. C., one of the world's most impressive scenes of industrial installations. End product: aluminum.

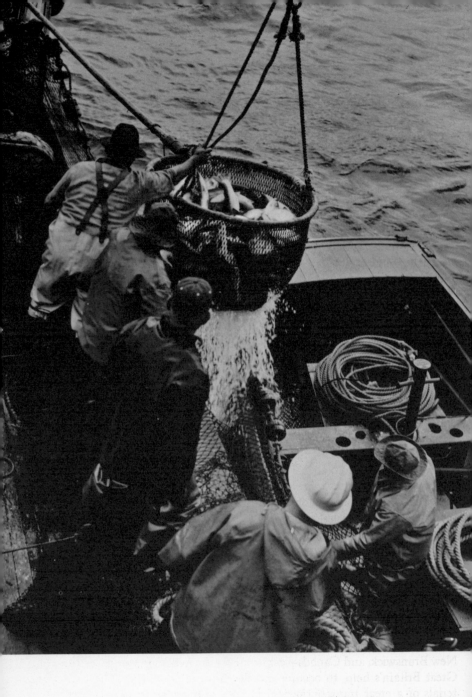

13. Commercial seine fishing on the west coast of Vancouver Island

economic, had ceased to exist; but the United States was engaged in erecting a new and rival empire in North America; and British North America, yielding to its colonial impulse to attach itself to a larger metropolitan power, might simply seek a refuge in this new continental organization. In 1849, when British free trade was just going into operation and when it seemed to many British North Americans that the end of the world had come, a group of Montreal merchants surveyed the difficult situation of the colonies and came to the conclusion that the only real solution was annexation to the United States. The Annexation Manifesto was backed by some of Montreal's best commercial leadership; but it won extraordinarily little public support. British North America was doing a good deal more trade with the United States than she had done in the past. Canada still hoped to make the St. Lawrence the major east-west transport route for the whole of North America. And when, in 1854, the United States was persuaded to accept a broad reciprocal trade agreement, there was fairly general satisfaction throughout the northern colonies. But the Reciprocity Treaty was concerned only with natural products, not manufactures. It did not prejudice British North America's fiscal freedom. It had no continental political implications. And it was in these important considerations that a considerable part of the attraction of the Treaty undeniably lay.

If retreat into the old British Empire were impossible and surrender to the new American continental empire were unthinkable, then there was only one effective course of action that lay open to British North America. The northern colonies could embrace the most difficult, hazardous, and exciting destiny of all. They could unite their fortunes in a new, separate British North American nation of truly continental proportions. The southwest sector of the old empire of the St. Lawrence had been lost politically to the United States by the Treaty of 1783; but northwest, beyond Lake Superior, lay an equally vast dominion, which had been won by the Montreal fur traders, carefully preserved by treaties, and held in trust for the future by the Hudson's Bay Company. A union of the Maritime and St. Lawrence Provinces —a federation of Newfoundland, Nova Scotia, Prince Edward Island, New Brunswick, and Canada—would surely prove strong enough, with Great Britain's help, to occupy and develop the northwest. The materials of a great transcontinental nation were available; and in the new age that was then beginning, the means of its successful integration lay also ready at hand. An intercolonial railway could link the Maritime Provinces with the St. Lawrence valley; a Pacific railway could connect the St. Lawrence with the Pacific coast.

It was this ambitious design for the future which, in the decade 1857–1867, won both the intellectual acceptance and the emotional conviction of the British North Americas. The rapid internal development of the colonies was driving them towards the mature enterprise of nation building; the pressure of external circumstances, which, for the northern provinces, was chiefly felt through the United Kingdom and the United States, was hastening the beginning of their transcontinental adventure. On the one hand, Great Britain was obviously anxious to transfer most of her territorial obligations in North America to a colonial state strong enough to accept them; and on the other hand, if the British colonial state were not created soon, the territories themselves might slip rapidly into the control of the United States. Already the advancing western American frontier was drawing ominously close to the undefended and almost unoccupied boundaries of British North America. The danger of penetration, occupation, and eventual annexation was great even in times of peace; and the American Civil War, which brought acrimonious disputes with Great Britain and British North America over the question of their neutrality, added the further peril of American armed might and diplomatic pressure.

The compulsive force of these inward urges and outward pressures was felt by all of British North America; but it was felt with a peculiar intensity by the Province of Canada. Canada, the province of the St. Lawrence, the "empire province" which had inherited all the old continental ambitions of the River of Canada, had been formed in 1840 by the union of the two earlier, smaller provinces of Upper and Lower Canada. Upper and Lower Canada had found it economically impossible to live apart; but since 1841 they had discovered that it was almost equally difficult to live together. The river system united all those who had come to live upon its northern banks; but the two cultural traditions, French and English, which were established in the St. Lawrence valley, divided its inhabitants. For years, sectional disputes and rivalries distracted the province and paralyzed its public affairs; and finally in June 1864, a new government, formed by a coalition of the Conservative and Reform parties, took office pledged to end the political deadlock by constitutional change.

From then on events moved rapidly. In September 1864, in Charlottetown, Prince Edward Island, at a conference summoned ostensibly to consider a legislative union of the Maritime Provinces, the Canadians first presented their plan of a general federation of the whole of British North America; and at a second conference, called at Quebec in the following month and attended by delegates from all the northern provinces including Newfoundland, a detailed federal scheme was worked out and embodied in the Seventy-Two or Quebec Resolutions. Two and a half years later, in March 1867, the British North America Act, uniting the provinces, was passed by the imperial Parliament; and on July 1, 1867—the first "Dominion Day"—the union went into operation. A new nation had been born—a nation which, by its own choice, remained a Kingdom of the British Crown. A new federation had come into existence—a federation which had been deliberately designed to preserve the centralized political strength, as well as the political institutions, of the British parliamentary system.

The Canada which began its political career on the first of July 1867 was only a small fragment of the ambitious continental nation of which the British North Americans had dreamed. Only three provinces—Nova Scotia, New Brunswick, and Canada, now divided, by the British North America Act, into Ontario and Quebec—had joined the original union. The two island provinces had remained aloof; the western dominion—Rupert's Land and the Northwest Territories—was still under the jurisdiction of the Hudson's Bay Company. Obviously the first task which faced Sir John A. Macdonald, Canada's first Prime Minister, was to attain his country's projected continental boundaries and to secure British North America's political inheritance. It was a delicate and dangerous business, this acquisition of an unoccupied quarter of the North American continent; but Macdonald completed it in the record period of six years. The Hudson's Bay Company's territories were acquired and Manitoba became the first western province of the Dominion in 1870. British Columbia, the Pacific coast province, entered the union in 1871; and two years later, Prince Edward Island, reversing its previous stand, finally decided to join the federation. Newfoundland, the rocky sentinel island at the northeast corner of the Gulf of St. Lawrence, still remained unresponsively detached; but, apart from this, the original design of united British North America had been completed six years after Confederation itself.

Yet this was only a beginning. In 1873, when Prince Edward Island entered Confederation, the transcontinental union was little more than the political framework of a nation. Before the dreams of the Fathers of Confederation could be realized, this embryonic form would have to be developed and filled in, and given substance and vitality. The whole base of the national economy would have to be broadened to continental dimensions; the new Canada would have to achieve a far greater economic diversification and maturity than staple-producing British North America had ever enjoyed in the old days of wood, wind, and water. And finally the eastern and western divisions of this transcontinental system would have to be linked together and integrated on the solid basis of an east-west axis, which was the logical extension of the St. Lawrence River. It was a tremendous, threefold task which confronted this small country of a few million people. The Canadians must settle and develop the virtually unoccupied northwest; they must build up in the east an industrial machine sufficiently diversified and strong to support the tasks of western settlement and nation building; and they must bind the whole together with gleaming iron bands of railways. The Appalachian Highland, which stretched between New Brunswick and Quebec, would have to be bridged by tracks. So also would the endless Precambrian Shield which separated Ontario from Manitoba. So also would the towering masses of the Rockies and Selkirks which shut off British Columbia from the prairies.

In the summer of 1869, the Dominion surveyors drew the principal meridian northwards from the international boundary through what was to become the city of Winnipeg. And with the establishment of the Winnipeg meridian, the people of Canada set about the giant task of opening the northwest for the army of migrants which could alone exploit its possibilities. More than two generations before, in the days of the Loyalists and their followers, when the United States had been selling its public domain, the Province of Upper Canada had been granting Crown land free to intending settlers; and now that the republic had abandoned sales and itself introduced the free homestead system, there was all the more reason for the new Canada to revert to the original British North American practice. The Canadian northwest would be made available to a new generation of frontiersmen on terms which were competitively just as good as those offered by the United States; and it was to be surveyed on the familiar North American rectangular pattern, in sections of six hundred and forty acres, with a quarter section of one hundred and sixty acres as the typical "free homestead" farm. For over ten years, with scientific accuracy and at headlong speed, this survey of the northwest quarter of the North American continent proceeded. There was some local opposition, mainly from the half-breeds, the children of the fur trade, and partly from the Indians with whom, in the past, the fur-trading colonies of the St. Lawrence had always had amicable relations. But the Northwest Rebellion of 1885, in which only a few small bands of Indians joined the half-breeds, was fairly easily crushed; and, with the collapse of this last frail resistance, the northwest stood open and waiting for the people who would exact its promises and reap its rewards.

In the meantime, while the west was being made ready for its first occupants, a different but equally important chapter in the national development was being recorded in the east. The nation would still continue to be dependent upon the sale abroad of its staple raw materials—including the vast quantities of wheat which were expected from the new prairie west; but this dependence was no longer nearly so simple and unqualified as it had been in the days of the old commercialism of wood, wind, and water. The railways, which were being built so vigorously during the 1850's, had brought the techniques of steam and steel to British North America; and throughout the provinces, small local blacksmiths', tailors', carpenters', and shoemakers' establishments were growing steadily into foundries, clothing mills, and manufacturers of furniture, agricultural implements, and boots and shoes.

For the first six promising years after Confederation, their prosperity continued; and then in 1873 came a serious, world-wide depression. It arrested progress everywhere. Its effects were so grave that it aroused a general anxious debate about the whole future of Canadian commercial policy. In the past Canada, like British North America before it, had relied upon the reasonably low duties of a tariff for revenue.

Could it afford to do so any longer? The manufacturers clamored for more protection; the state, which had a big railway construction program under way, badly needed more revenue. And beyond all these particular demands and necessities was a vague but powerful general conviction that Canada could fit itself for the continental tasks that lay ahead only through a greater industrial diversification and maturity. In the general election of 1878, the "national policy" of protection was the main issue; and in the next year a boldly protective tariff was adopted by Parliament.

An occupied west and an industrialized east were the two inseparable halves of a national economy which could be integrated only by the means of a transcontinental, all-Canadian railway. The Intercolonial Railway, which linked Halifax and St. John with Quebec and Montreal, was completed in the first years after the union. It was an important undertaking pledged at Confederation in the interest of the Maritime Provinces; but the section of the national transport route which remained to be constructed—the vast span between the St. Lawrence valley and the Pacific Ocean—was a more difficult and onerous enterprise. The first attempt to build the Pacific railway, through a company in which American capital was heavily represented, ended ingloriously in failure and political scandal; and it was not until the autumn of 1880, after a frustrating and costly delay of seven years, that a new syndicate came to terms with the government for the contract to construct the railway. This time the enterprise was much more definitely nationalistic in character than it had been in 1872–1873. It became more emphatically nationalistic still as the work progressed and its agonizing difficulties mounted.

From the first, direction and control were in the hands of Canadians. The line was to run through Canadian soil from end to end; and George Stephen, the company's first president, and his fellow directors, in order to defend their western territories from American competition, decided to adopt a southerly route, using the Kicking Horse Pass and Rogers Pass through the mountains, instead of the more northerly route which had originally been planned. It was a Canadian design, a Canadian company, and in the end the undertaking was carried through to a successful conclusion only by the collective effort of the Canadian people. Even at the beginning there was little financial support for the venture outside Canada. The money markets of Lon-

don and New York were indifferent or coldly hostile; and after the
depression returned in 1883 and the bottom dropped out of North
American railway enterprises, the Canadian Pacific Railway, having
exhausted all possible sources of funds, turned back in desperation
to the nation which had given it existence. With two government
loans, made in 1884-1885 and repaid in full only a few years later, the
company escaped the bankruptcy which, for a time, George Stephen
hourly anticipated. The line was completed by the autumn of 1885, in
less than half the time that it had been expected to take. And a small
nation, of fewer than five million people, through sheer determination,
had finished a huge work which was essential to their destiny as they
conceived it.

Yet the future for which they hoped still receded before them. Plans
had been made, sacrifices had been made, effort and energy had been
expended without limit; but the goal of successful national integration
still lay unattainably far ahead. Canada was like a half-built edifice
which threatened to become dilapidated before it was ever effectively
occupied. Economic depression, which returned at frequent and
lengthy intervals during the last quarter of the nineteenth century,
worked persistently and powerfully against Canadian plans. Its effects
were harshly unfavorable and infinitely discouraging; but they were
not alone responsible for the frustration of Canada's national enterprise. The fact quite literally was that the Dominion's hour had not
yet struck. It had not yet captured the world's interest and imagination. For the whole of Western Europe, the United States still remained, above all others, the land of opportunity and hope; and the
tumultuous western expansion of the republic, which continued irre-
pressibly despite the paralyzing effects of the depression, monopolized
the people and the energy which might have gone into the creation of
transcontinental Canada.

Transcontinental Canada seemed a dream which had become stuck
in frustration and disappointment. In 1891, nearly a quarter century
after Confederation, the Dominion had not yet attained a population
of five million people. The prairie west was still largely unsettled; in
some eastern provinces the population was almost stationary. And to
many Canadians, the tariff and the railway, in failing to attain the ends
which had been set for them, had come to seem extravagantly costly
burdens which ought never to have been incurred. The great prosper-

ous national economy had failed to materialize. For a while even the political structure of Confederation seemed in jeopardy. Most of the provinces were leagued in an angry revolt against the centralizing policies of the Dominion; and English-speaking and French-speaking Canadians were quarreling over language, schools, and the relations of church and state with a vehemence which everybody had hoped the Confederation settlement would prevent forever. To not a few people, in the black depths of the slump, the whole scheme of a separate, economically viable Canadian nation began to seem a gigantic mistake; and in 1888, when the Liberal party adopted the plank of commercial union or unrestricted reciprocity with the United States, continentalism emerged once more as a direct threat to Canadian nationality.

The election of 1891, which was followed by the death of Sir John A. Macdonald, the principal architect of the union and its national development policies, was perhaps the most important general election in Canadian history. In it, the electorate of the Dominion rejected the continentalism which the Liberals had proffered once again and decided to stick to their conception of a separate viable Canadian nation. For five more years the long attrition of the slump continued. For five more years the Canadians endured frustration of their hopes; and then, coinciding almost exactly with the return of the Liberals to power and the appearance of a new Prime Minister, Sir Wilfrid Laurier, a great, an almost miraculous change occurred. For thirty years, world circumstances had been persistently hostile to the Canadian national adventure. Now, almost at a stroke, they became benignantly favorable. And amid all the lavish blessings of good fortune with which those wonderful fifteen years from 1896 to 1911 were crowded, one stupendous piece of luck arrested everyone's attention and captured the imaginations of all. At long last, the world's immigration army had turned sharply northwest into Canada. The frontier in the United States had ended. But the frontier in Canada lay open. And it was Canada's hour.

Beyond the Ontario-Manitoba boundary, the harsh, rocky uplands of the Precambrian Shield dwindled and disappeared, and the landscape spread out in the wide rolling spaces of the great central continental plains. As it extended monotonously westward, the prairie plateau rose gently through three distinct levels of altitude, from the Red River valley of Manitoba to the high plains of the future Province of Alberta. To the north, the rich black soils and patches of woodland of the "park belt" were excellent for dairying and mixed farming. The dark-brown earth of the second, more southerly soil zone was ideal for the mass production of wheat. And below this, in southwestern Saskatchewan and southeastern Alberta, lay a great triangle of semi-arid, short-grass country which savage experience was to teach the Canadians could be safely used only for cattle and sheep. Into this vast, unoccupied, repetitive but varied, country the migrants swarmed. They came in huge but not unequal numbers from eastern Canada, the United States, and Great Britain. They came also—and this was relatively new in Canadian settlement—from central, eastern, and southern Europe. In the decade 1901–1911, the population of Canada as a whole rose from five million three hundred thousand to seven million two hundred thousand; and of this total national increase of nearly two million people, well over a million were distributed in the three prairie provinces and British Columbia.

Everything seemed to favor their ventures and prosper their efforts. The migrants could draw upon the experience which many of them had already had under very similar conditions in the United States. The machinery and equipment necessary for the production and transport of wheat and flour on a grand scale—reapers, steel-roller mills, elevators, boxcars—were all available; and the special and urgent necessity of the Canadian northwest—the need for a spring wheat which would mature safely within a short growing period—was dramatically supplied in 1908, when Charles E. Saunders, the Dominion Cerealist, succeeded in producing Marquis wheat, a new variety which had all the fine-milling qualities of Canada's first hardy, prolific northern wheat, Red Fife, and which also matured about a week earlier and with a higher yield. In an incredibly short space of time, the new Canadian west was ready to go into full production; and at the same moment, the markets of Great Britain and Western Europe, enlarged now by the great and increasing masses of industrial workers, opened capaciously for the import of Canadian cereals. The price of wheat went steadily up. The cost of ocean freight and insurance drifted persistently lower. And all the while, capital and immigrants were pouring into the country from overseas.

Wheat was the King of the Golden River which was transforming Canada's valley of despair into a garden of successful achievement. Wheat was pouring out of the west in a golden torrent which roused the whole country into a great, unified burst of productivity. Swiftly and with astonishing ease after the long years of struggle and waiting, the national objectives were attained. The west was occupied and settled at headlong speed; in the east a revolution of comparable magnitude was taking place in industry; and despite the enormous growth in the value of agricultural production, the value of manufactured goods provided for the home market increased at an even more rapid rate. The mature, diversified national economy, based on an east-west axis and united by east-west, all-Canadian transport, had suddenly become a triumphant reality. The Pacific railway, which had been attacked less than two decades before as an appalling financial burden upon the community, was now found to be inadequate for the task of carrying the vast quantities of western produce to the eastern seaboard; and the protective tariff, which only a short while ago had been the subject of so much bitter criticism, was now tacitly accepted as one of the foundations of national prosperity.

The creation of the two final prairie provinces, Alberta and Saskatchewan, in 1905 was a public, formal announcement that the task of nation building had been done. The political structure of responsible provincial governments, like the national network of economic activities, now extended from ocean to ocean. The difficult, long-sought object of the Fathers of Confederation had been attained; and with its achievement there came inevitably a distinct and important change in the mental outlook of the Canadian people. For decades, for generations now, they had been preoccupied, almost obsessed, with the staggering problems of their own internal development; but now, with a strange new sense of self-realization and maturity, they could lift their eyes from the immediate task and look over the oceans and continents about them. Their interests grew more complex; their mental horizons perceptibly widened. It was true, of course, that Canada, unlike the republics of North and South America, had never broken its historic ties with Europe; it had remained a member of a much larger political organization, the British Empire. But its membership had been that of a junior partner who had little concern and less responsibility for the Empire's global affairs. It was this position, and the mental outlook appropriate to it, which now began to change. Canada was emerging from North American isolationism and from colonial tutelage. She was an adult confronted with the increasingly agitated and dangerous world of the twentieth century. She wanted to play her appropriate part in that world, to accept her proper responsibilities, and to exert her proper influence. And how, as a member of the British Empire-Commonwealth, could she best carry out the task?

Changes would be necessary, for the evolution of the British Empire-Commonwealth rested ambiguously in mid-passage. The responsible government which British North America had won half a century before had given it effective control over its own domestic concerns. The ambit of national self-determination in Sir Wilfrid Laurier's day was very great; but it had not yet attained the dimensions of sovereignty, for it did not completely include foreign policy and defence. These ultimate sovereign powers had remained, formally at least, in imperial control, not so much at Great Britain's as at Canada's request. Canada's greatest and most difficult task in the nineteenth century had been to maintain its economic and political independence in a continent dominated by the United States; and for this, which was the basic condition of its being, the military and diplomatic support of Great Britain had been absolutely essential. This Anglo-Canadian alliance, which was the political reality underlying the formal imperial connection, had enabled Canada to survive and develop; and now the very fact of her growth to maturity had made a revision of the original terms of the alliance natural and indeed inevitable. The Canadian people were no longer either attracted or frightened by the thought of annexation to the United States; they had complete confidence in the independent success of their own national experiment. In the past, during the last three decades of the nineteenth century, they would have given much for a good reciprocal trade treaty with the United States; but in 1911, when the Laurier government in fact negotiated a Reciprocity Treaty with the republic, the nation, giving free rein to its new mood of exuberant self-reliance, rejected the agreement and turned out the government which had made it.

The time had come for a new imperial relationship and a new status in the world at large. Canada was prepared to pay the price for it. Increasingly her statesmen wanted to exercise some influence upon the international affairs in which their nation was inextricably involved; but at the same time they were equally prepared to accept the responsibilities and to perform the functions of national maturity. The first two decades of the twentieth century witnessed a steady enlargement of Canada's activities, and an equally steady enhancement of its position in both the British Commonwealth and the society of nations as a whole. The change began in the last year of the old century when the Dominion dispatched a contingent to the South African War; it continued when, in the face of the ominous armaments race in Europe, the Canadian Parliament accepted the burden of providing for the nation's own naval defence. And its impressive culmination came in the First World War which Canada entered, not as a submissive dependency, but as a voluntary principal, and to which she contributed armed forces totalling over six hundred thousand.

These services and sacrifices required, and received, their appropriate recognition. During the course of the war, Sir Robert Borden, the new Conservative Prime Minister, became a member of the Imperial War Cabinet, which controlled and directed the entire Commonwealth war effort; and when the fighting ended, he and his Canadian colleagues were determined that the Dominion should have an equally effective voice in the making and keeping of the peace. The great conference of the powers in Paris and the establishment of the first international organization, the League of Nations, gave the Canadians an exceptional chance of winning international recognition and securing international status; and, with an almost naive eagerness, they took all possible advantage of the opportunity. Canada played its part in the work of the conference both in its own right and as an important member of the British Empire delegation. Along with the other British Dominions, it was recognized as an original member of the League of Nations, with separate representation in the assembly and the International Labor Organization, and the right to election for the Council. Canada's delegates signed the peace treaties separately and the Canadian Parliament solemnly ratified them in due course.

This formal achievement of international status at the Paris Peace Conference was followed within the next decade by the public recognition of the principle of equality in the British Commonwealth. It was a foregone conclusion that, after the war, the last formal vestiges of imperial suzerainty would disappear and that a nation which had put an army of over half a million men in the field would henceforth formulate and implement its own foreign policy as far as it desired. The Imperial Conference of 1923 began the work of reorganizing the structure of the British Commonwealth; and the Imperial Conference of 1926 laid down the principles and established the main lines on which the task was to be completed. "They are autonomous Communities within the British Empire," declared the *Report* of the Conference in defining the position of Great Britain and the Dominions, "equal in status, in no way subordinate one to another in any aspect of their domestic or external affairs, though united by a common allegiance to the Crown, and freely associated as members of the British Commonwealth of Nations." It was an eloquent general declaration, the full consequences of which followed easily and rapidly in the next few years. Almost immediately, with the establishment of diplomatic missions at Washington, Paris, and Tokyo, the Canadian government began to set up the machinery for the conduct of its own external relations; and in 1931 the Statute of Westminster, passed by the British Parliament, removed the last, slight, formal limitations on the legislative sovereignty of the Parliament of Canada.

The great depression of the twentieth century, which began with the stock-market collapse of 1929, brought the long Canadian boom to a close. It did more than this. It served also as a tragic conclusion to one whole phase of Canadian development. The slump lay like a dead weight upon the entire nation; but its pressure was particularly paralyzing in the west, for in the west the economic misfortunes of falling prices and contracting markets were accompanied by the natural calamities of drought, soil drifting, wheat rust, and repeated crop failures. The prostration of the wheat-growing prairies was the greatest disaster of the depression; and, in its somber fashion, it marked the relative decline of agriculture in the Canadian economy as a whole. For three decades an enormous expansion had been taking place in all sectors of the nation's business. The sources, like the manifestations, of this great economic advance had been many and varied; but unquestionably the greatest single factor in the whole development had been wheat.

Wheat was the last of a great quartet of staple products—fish, furs, timber, and wheat—which for generations Canadians had been exporting to more mature industrial markets. This dependence upon a basic export specialty had been the distinguishing economic feature of the period of colonialism, of the age of wood, wind, and water. It had continued during the first phase of Canadian nationalism, during the long ascendancy of coal and iron, and steam and steel. The growth of industry and the economic diversification which had taken place since Confederation had been very great; but these developments had not sufficed to rob wheat of its central economic importance. Wheat was the greatest—and also the last—of the great single export specialties. And with the disappearance of wheat's primacy, the country passed from the old industrialism of the nineteenth century to the new industrialism of the twentieth. Canada was ceasing to be an economic satellite of other powers; she was becoming a junior industrial power in her own right.

Twentieth-century industrialism, with its new metals and new sources of fuel and power, suited Canada and its capacities far better than nineteenth-century industrialism had done. Yet even with respect to coal and iron, the main sinews of the old industrial strength, the Dominion was obviously better equipped than it had seemed likely to be a generation before. It was true that many of the country's enormous coal deposits were situated in the western provinces of Saskatchewan, Alberta, and British Columbia, far away from the industrial concentrations in central Canada. Industry in the St. Lawrence valley still continued to rely upon American coal; but its old dependence upon American iron ore was rapidly disappearing as the twentieth century neared its middle point. The discovery and exploitation of huge deposits of ore at Steep Rock in northwestern Ontario and on the Quebec-Labrador border enabled the country to become in a few years a large exporter of iron and will probably make it by 1960 the world's third largest producer, outranked only by the United States and Russia.

In the meantime, through one revelation after another, the nation was realizing the richness of its endowment of the twentieth-century sources of heat and energy. Every Canadian region, and almost every

Canadian province, had its satisfying share of the newly discovered wealth. The St. Lawrence River and the drainage systems of the Precambrian Shield and of British Columbia contributed enormous quantities of hydroelectric power. The amazing series of petroleum discoveries, which began in Alberta with the find of the Leduc oil field in 1947, rapidly transformed the western plains into the major source of the nation's supplies of oil and natural gas; and the deposits of uranium which were found in the far north by Great Bear Lake and Lake Athabasca have helped to make Canada one of the principal producers of atomic energy in the Western World. The new sources of heat and power were present in virtually unlimited quantities. The Precambrian Shield and British Columbia were almost inexhaustible storehouses of metals, both base and precious, old and new; and twentieth-century technological advances made it possible to exploit Canada's manifold resources more quickly and successfully than ever before. The country shot up to industrial maturity; the complex, diversified strength of its economic foundations steadily increased. By the middle of the twentieth century, the simple staple-producing Canada of the past had become an industrial power whose manufacturers contributed fifty percent of the total value of national production.

It was the Second World War which both fostered and revealed the development of this latent strength. Canada entered the conflict as an independent principal, by the decision of her own Parliament, on September 10, 1939, a week after the British declaration of war. From the start she was one of the major powers on the side of the United Nations; and the triumphant German offensives of the spring of 1940 and the collapse of France served merely to enhance her industrial and military prominence. For a whole year, from June 1940 to June 1941, while the British Commonwealth alone sustained the burden of the great struggle against Hitler's Germany, Canada remained Great Britain's first and principal ally. The continuing neutrality of the United States and the United Kingdom's desperate preoccupation with her own problems of procurement and armament gave Canada the opportunity—and imposed on her the obligation—of providing the strategic materials, the mechanized equipment, and the manpower of a major belligerent.

The entrance of Russia and the United States on the side of the

Allies during the course of 1941 profoundly altered the character and control of the war; but it did not affect the importance or the variety of the contribution which Canada was to make to the ultimate success of the allied arms. The country labored to arm itself, to exploit its resources, to realize its full industrial potential, and to defend the communications and fight the battles of total war. Through the Permanent Joint Board on Defence and other agencies of military and economic co-operation with the United States, the Canadians sought to strengthen the defences of fortress North America and to protect the transport routes between their own continent and the overseas theaters of conflict. They contributed four-fifths of the trainees to the large-scale Commonwealth Air Training Plan for which over a hundred and forty training centers and stations were built throughout Canada. Their fleet of swift and agile ships—destroyers, corvettes, frigates, motor torpedo boats, and mine sweepers—rapidly took over the major part of the anxious and dangerous task of guarding the convoys on their journey across the Atlantic from North America to Great Britain.

In the field, an overseas Canadian Army, of two army corps, one of which was armored, had been created by the time the Allies resumed the offensive in the autumn of 1942. The Canadians bore the brunt of the desperate experimental raid on Dieppe. They shared the fortunes of the gallant Eighth Army all the way from the Sicilian Coast to the plains of Lombardy. They were carried in over the tumbling breakers towards the shores of Normandy on the morning of June 6, 1944; they fought all through the long and varied campaigns that followed; and, as the proud German armies broke in pieces, they joined in the pursuit that streamed eastward across Europe in the spring of 1945. All this large and varied effort—men, supplies, armaments, and money—had been made at the sole charge and sacrifice of the Canadian people. Canada had accepted no American lend-lease; and through loans, outright gifts, and mutual aid legislation, she had given material and financial help to the United Kingdom and Europe on a scale proportionately larger than that of the United States.

The First World War had given Canada international recognition and status. The Second World War had raised her to a place of power and usefulness which, in the eyes of Canadian statesmen, was a "middle" position, immediately below that of the great powers. Her stake in the post-war world was huge. As a large-scale trading nation, with close European affiliations as well as North American interests, she was vitally concerned in the rehabilitation and security of international society. She was prepared to give financial aid to the work of recovery on a scale equal to that of her wartime contribution; and she was also ready to accept, with a new and sober conviction, the political obligations which international security seemed to require. Unlike the United States, Canada had from the first been a member of the old League of Nations; but she had instinctively distrusted and feared its extensive commitments and relied, as time went on, more and more upon her Commonwealth associations and her North American security. Now, when the lessons of isolation and unpreparedness had been driven home by six terrible years of war, the Canadians were far more willing than they had ever been before to put their trust in a general security system. They wished to assert the claims of "middle powers" such as their own in the United Nations organization and to place some limitations upon the exclusive powers of the Security Council; but, apart from this, they were prepared, at the San Francisco Conference, to accept the leadership and the preponderant authority which the great powers had carefully arrogated to themselves.

The post-war program of economic rehabilitation and political security depended upon the concord of the great powers; and the hopes of mankind were soon frustrated by their strife. The world began to divide into two camps, which soon became armed camps, of incomprehension, distrust, and hatred; and over these two frightened divisions of humanity, the two super-powers, the United States and Russia, assumed a large measure of influence or control. As early as the winter of 1947, Canada renewed her wartime defensive association with the United States. A continental system for the defence of fortress North America was an obvious first response to the threat of Soviet aggression; but, in the eyes of the Canadians, it was in itself an unsatisfactory response, for it left unprotected the nation's overseas interests and British and European associations. Canada much preferred to be a member of a union of nations on both sides of the Atlantic rather than a solitary North American protectorate of the United States. The North Atlantic Treaty Organization suited the country's historic loyalties and existing position very satisfactorily; and

Canadian statesmen took an active part in the negotiations which
ended in the creation of NATO in the spring of 1949.

The international world was clouded with portentous uncertainties;
but in Canada the winds of good fortune were blowing steadily across
clear skies. The depression whose coming everybody had feared in the
first post-war years had not materialized; and, as the century reached
its middle point, the Canadian people began to look with increasing
confidence into the future. They were certainly experiencing a remarkable burst of prosperity. But perhaps something even greater and
more exciting than a burst of prosperity lay in store for them. The
first half of the century had opened in a period of unparalleled growth
and national expansion. Would the commencement of the century's
second half see a return of this remarkable success? In 1949 Newfoundland had at last joined Confederation. The dream of a united
British North America which the Fathers of Confederation had conceived over eighty years before had finally been fulfilled; and the new
sense of national achievement and maturity had been given its most
appropriate political expression. The entrance of Newfoundland was
a symbol of Canadian fulfilment. Would the years that followed 1949
see that fulfilment become a reality?

In the first years of the 1950's everything seemed to promise the
realization of good fortune. All the indices were favorable. Each successive year seemed to add some new discovery to the long list of
Canada's material riches. Obviously, the nation's natural resources
were enormous. Obviously they were still not completely known. And
yet it was not simply in natural resources—in western fuels, northern
metals, hydroelectric power, and atomic energy—that the hope and
promise of the future lay. It lay, above all, in the Canadian people;
and once again, after an interval of nearly thirty years, Canada's population was growing with a new and confident rapidity. The rise in the
domestic marriage rate and birth rate, the influx of immigrants which
mounted steadily as the decade of the 1950's went on, demonstrated
both that Canada had won the unquestioning trust of its own citizens
and had aroused the interest of the rest of the world. The population
was increasing at a rate of nearly half a million people a year. The
decennial census of 1951 revealed a total of slightly over fourteen million Canadians; and it was expected that they would become seventeen millions sometime in 1958.

In 1952, a new Queen, Elizabeth II, ascended the throne of Great Britain, Canada, and the other Realms of the Commonwealth. Canada had never come under the rule of the first Elizabeth. The first Elizabeth had died in the very year that Champlain, the founder of New France, first ventured up the St. Lawrence River. The great efflorescence of the first Elizabethan age had been no part of Canada's experience; but might not "Elizabeth the Second, by the Grace of God of the United Kingdom, Canada, and her other Realms and Territories, Queen, Head of the Commonwealth, Defender of the Faith" come to watch over a comparable period of restless energy and creative achievement in the greatest of her Realms overseas? The Canadians were fast growing out of their cultural colonialism just as they had already outgrown their political dependence and economic insecurity; and the sustained burst of activity in literature, scholarship, music, painting, and the arts of the theater, with which the second half of the century opened, was at least some indication that the energy and endeavor of the next generation would be put into mental and spiritual as well as material things. The future which opened with the accession of the young Queen seemed more richly diversified than ever before; and no one of her peoples looked forward to the second Elizabethan age with greater confidence or more eager anticipation than the Canadians.

Alaska:
"The Last Frontier"

BY ERNEST GRUENING

So it is called, affectionately, by Alaskans. And so indeed it is, in North America. It was the last considerable area on earth to be "discovered," when Vitus Bering, sailing for the Tsars of Russia, sighted Mount St. Elias in 1741 and completed the outlines of the hemispheric land mass on the previously blank maps of the North Pacific. It was also the last region on our continent reached in the westward pioneering that, in part, motivated this book. Historically—and geographically—Alaska was and is "the last frontier" of the New World.

As Alaska passed its ninetieth year under the Stars and Stripes, the decennium ahead that would complete the century of United States rule loomed up as a decade of destiny. Statehood for Alaska had at last been won!

The Alaskans' quest for it was inextricably bound up in their history. After the great vision of William H. Seward, Secretary of State under Presidents Lincoln and Johnson, brought the acquisition of "Russian America" from Tsar Alexander II, the purchase suffered the scorn of distant and uninformed men in public office and press. When the Congress, in 1868, the year following the Treaty of Cession, was required to appropriate the $7,200,000 sale price, Alaska was called many harsh names—"Seward's Folly," "Icebergia," "Walrussia" —and pictured as an uninhabitable waste whose acquisition was a reckless squandering of taxpayers' dollars.

But before following Alaska history which has been so adversely affected by this misconception, let us discover what the climates of Alaska really are. And it is climates, *plural*. It is no more possible to refer to *the* climate of Alaska than to *the* climate of the United States. For Alaska, too, is a vast area. To say that it measures 586,000 square miles, one-fifth as large as the other 48 States, only hints at its extent. That is better revealed by an oft-reproduced map of Alaska superimposed on the map of the United States on which Alaska touches the Pacific and Atlantic Oceans, the Canadian and Mexican boundaries. In other words, in its total spread it is as wide and deep as the United States—2700 miles from Ketchikan to Attu, westernmost island of the Aleutian chain, and actually in the Eastern Hemisphere, and 1400 miles from south to north, where Point Barrow, Alaska's northern tip, lies well within the Arctic Circle just above the 72nd parallel. With numerous lesser variations there are at least three principal climatic zones: coastal, interior, and northern.

Along Alaska's Pacific or southern coast dwell the majority of Alaskans. Here are all but two of Alaska's principal cities: Ketchikan, Wrangell, Petersburg, Sitka, Juneau the capital, Douglas, Haines, Skagway, Cordova, Valdez, Seward, and Anchorage, the metropolis. Concerning this zone the U. S. Weather Bureau reports:

"Warm winters and cool summers are the rule. . . . To those whose conception of Alaska is that of a desolate waste of perennial ice and snow it will come as a surprise to know that the mean temperature of January at Sitka is nearly a degree higher than the mean for that month in St. Louis." And Juneau, one thousand miles north of the U.S.-Canada boundary, "experiences on the average only about one day a year with minimum readings below zero."

Thus the majority of Alaskans live in a climate warmer in winter than that of most of New England, New York, Ohio, Illinois, and much warmer than that of Maine, Michigan, Wisconsin, Minnesota, the Dakotas—and cooler in summers, whose temperatures seldom exceed 80°.

The Kuru Siwo, the warm Japan current along the coast, a "Pacific

Ocean Gulf Stream," is in part responsible for this phenomenon. The tepid moisture it generates, blown against the colder mountain slopes, accounts also for a greater annual precipitation in southeastern Alaska than is received anywhere in continental United States. Some 150 inches of rain fall annually at Ketchikan at the southern end of the Panhandle, diminishing northward to some 84 inches at Sitka and Juneau and tapering off to a mere 25 inches at Skagway at the northern end of the Inside Passage.

As one moves inland, winters are colder, summers hotter, precipitation less and less. Anchorage, on an arm of the sea yet with the land mass of the Kenai Peninsula and the towering Chugach Range between it and the ocean, partakes of both coastal and interior climates, experiencing a very occasional –30° cold and a rare +90° heat, and a rainfall of only 15 inches.

But it is north of the Alaska Range, prolongation in Alaska of the continental Sierra, which bisects Alaska from east to west in a great curve and is apexed by 20,320 foot Mount McKinley, that one finds the extremely low temperatures that Jack London's fiction publicized. Fairbanks, "Golden Heart of Alaska," may experience minus sixties and plus nineties with only a dozen inches of rainfall a year. But the winter cold is dry, and when the mercury occasionally drops below the minus forties, not a breath of wind stirs. Snow stays on the telephone wires for a week, so still is the air. The greatest range of temperature under the Flag is found at Fort Yukon where the mighty Yukon River skirts the Arctic Circle, with a record of –78° in winter and +100° in summer.

The fact is that Alaska climates find almost their equivalents in the other States and are no less habitable by reason of cold, heat, rain, or snowfall. Moreover, Alaska does not experience the disasters of hurricanes such as ravage the Atlantic and Gulf coasts or of the tornadoes that afflict the Middle West and South. More striking is the contrast wrought by length of day and night. Fairbanks celebrates the summer solstice every year with a midnight baseball game. Even in southern Alaska the late spring and summer have only a few hours of dusk between sunset and sunrise—a happy circumstance for those who commune—as all Alaskans do—with the great outdoors. And the short winter days and long nights give Alaskans the opportunity to be as well-read as their fellow Americans "down below."

Now we return to Alaska's introduction to U.S. rule.

The United States was gaining an area of three hundred and seventy-five million acres at a cost of less than two cents an acre. It was indeed "the Great Land," as its name in the unwritten Aleut language, uttered to the first Russian fur hunters (A-lak-shak, Al-ash-ka, A-la-as-ka) signified. But there was scant recognition in the federal seat of power of Alaska's value and potentialities.

For, having annexed Alaska, the authorities promptly forgot it. One would suppose that some curiosity might arise in federal legislative and executive circles as to what this vast terrain contained, some thought given to its future integration into the national scheme. But although the Treaty of Cession provided that "the inhabitants . . . shall be admitted to the enjoyment of all the rights, advantages, and immunities of citizens of the United States," few attempts were made to validate that pledge and little concern shown for said inhabitants.

During the first seventeen years, the Congress enacted just two laws dealing specifically with Alaska. One extended the commerce and navigation laws to Alaska, making it a customs district. The other vested the control of the fur-seal fisheries of the Pribilof Islands in the Secretary of the Treasury, who leased them for twenty years as a private monopoly to a San Francisco company. No government was established. For seventeen years it was impossible for a prospector to stake a claim, for a settler to acquire title to land, for property to be sold or deeded, for the lovelorn to be married, for an aggrieved party to secure legal redress, for crime to be punished.

Authority was exercised *de facto* and without legal sanction by the General commanding the United States troops stationed at Sitka, the old Russian capital. And when, in 1877, the General and his men were removed to Idaho to put down an uprising of the Nez Percé Indians, not even that semblance of authority remained. For the next two years the Collector of Customs was the ranking federal official in Alaska.

The idea of an Indian uprising, likewise feared throughout the West in the 1870's, was contagious. Alarm spread among the white newcomers to Alaska. So they requested Washington to send a war vessel to Alaska waters to overawe any possible uprisers and to furnish a measure of protection. The federal authorities paid no heed. Finally, in desperation, the Alaskans appealed to their neighbors, the Canadians, who promptly dispatched one of Her Majesty's ships, which performed the service that had been vainly requested of Uncle Sam. When, at last, an American warship arrived, its commander and his successors were, for the next four years, Alaska's rulers, also with no legal authority whatever.

Seventeen years may not be long in the pageant of history. Yet it represents four Presidential administrations. It spans eight Congresses, which in those days averaged three sessions per Congress. Yet over a score of sessions came and went without a single additional piece of legislation or executive action to validate the pledge in the Treaty of Cession. This period is known, quite naturally, in Alaska, as "the era of no government."

In 1884, in response to the proddings of five successive Presidential messages, Congress passed an Organic Act for the "District of Alaska," for Alaska was not yet deemed worthy of being called a "Territory."

The new Organic Act created the offices of Governor and Federal District Judge, to be appointed by the President, and four lesser court judges. It extended the United States mining laws to Alaska but specifically excluded the general land laws, making acquisition of real estate still impossible. It forbade the creation of a legislature and of a delegate to Congress. It prohibited the establishment of counties. It provided $25,000 for education. It applied the legal code of the State of Oregon to Alaska.

The Act proved unworkable. The Oregon Code's provisions for county officials and county functions were inapplicable to a District forbidden to have counties. The Oregon Code likewise provided that to be a juror—grand or petit—one had to be a taxpayer, but as the Congress had provided no taxes in Alaska, legal juries—and hence jurisprudence in accord with the American system—was impossible.

For the next fourteen years the annual reports and communications of five successive governors embodied urgent pleas to the federal authorities to give Alaska some workable body of law. Nothing was done, however, until the discovery of gold in the Klondike in the late nineties brought some 60,000 gold-rushers from the States. While "the Klondike" was across the border in Canada, the routes to it lay through Alaska. Within a year or two, other gold strikes in Alaska, near Nome and in the Tanana Valley, transformed the gold rush into an Alaskan episode. When the newcomers from the States discovered the total inadequacy of existing legislation to meet their needs they wrote caustic letters to their Senators and Representatives, and still being voters back home, their pleas registered with the national lawmakers. Then, at the turn of the century, came the beginning of legislation for Alaska.

But as this well-intentioned legislation, drafted by men thousands of miles from the scene and with no first-hand knowledge of Alaska, proved unsatisfactory, there arose a demand for someone who could speak officially and informedly for Alaska—a voteless Delegate—such as every American Territory had had from its beginnings. A Delegate had been sought by Alaskans since 1881, when a convention in Juneau elected the Collector of Customs, Mottrom D. Ball, to go to Washington and request that Congress create the office and seat him. Not until 1906 was this concession made.

By this time, Alaskans, their numbers augmented to some 60,000 by the gold-rushers who stayed on, demanded an equivalent of the home rule which every Territory had enjoyed—a legislature. Six years later Congress complied. It had taken 45 years to grant the American citizens of Alaska that minimal amount of self-government to which every American community feels itself rightfully entitled. As in many remote and thinly settled colonial areas the world over, from Canada's Northwest Territories to Argentina's Patagonia and from Russia's Siberia to Britain's Australia, political progress in the first half-century of occupation had been slow; but of direct, overt oppression there had been none. With too little government, there was plenty of liberty. Men strong enough to brave the rigors of a new land could "make their stake" with little molestation except from the occasional outlaws among them.

While the Organic Act of 1912 was a great improvement on the Act of 1884, it was still more restrictive than any Act enacted for any other American Territory. It was notable chiefly for what it forbade Alaskans to do. It prohibited any legislation affecting the primary disposal of the soil—thus preventing Alaskans from acquiring land in an area one hundred percent in the public domain. It again forbade the creation of counties. It retained federal control of Alaska's principal resources, the fisheries and wildlife. It maintained the judiciary under federal control. There were numerous other restrictions.

When the first legislators in 1913 had created the framework of a territorial structure, they memorialized Congress to legislate in the fields where they had been forbidden to tread. They asked the Congress:

To enact land laws suitable to Alaska and to stop making reservations and withdrawals which already were erecting further obstacles to settlement.

To provide roads—a natural request in a Territory all public domain.

To transfer management of the fisheries to the Territory.

To pay the lower court federal judges (called U. S. Commissioners) a salary rather than making them dependent on fees.

To lower maritime transportation rates.

To correct defects in the mining laws.

These and other requests were repeated by legislature after legislature. Responses were few and meager.

No sooner had the limitations of the Organic Act become clear to Alaskans than a cry for "full Territorial government" arose from them. But through the next 43 years Congress rejected almost every attempt of Alaska's voteless Delegates to enlarge Territorial powers. One exception came in 1956, with an Act permitting Alaska to provide for its mentally ill.

In 1916, the Congress enacted a highly important piece of legislation—the Federal Aid Highway Act. It coincided with the development of the automobile as a practical vehicle. The Congress realized that if this new instrument of locomotion were to be put to wide use, a national system of highways of a uniform, and reasonably high, standard was essential; that to achieve this objective joint federal and state enterprise was required, because, if left wholly to the States, wide disparities would be inevitable between highways constructed by progressive or prosperous states and those built by others less so. So the Act provided a matching of federal and state funds on condition that a federally approved standard be maintained. Every state receives at least one dollar of federal funds for every dollar of state money. But the Western States, where substantial areas remain in public domain from which no tax revenues can be derived, receive a larger federal participation calculated on a complicated formula which figures total area, proportion of public domain, population, and existing post-road mileage. Alaska was excluded from this Act (except within National Forests) although it was extended to Hawaii, annexed 31 years after Alaska, and to Puerto Rico, which pays no federal taxes whatever. (Alaska came under the provisions of the federal income tax when it was enacted in 1913 and pays all federal taxes.) For the next 40 years, Alaska's voteless Delegates would, in every session of Congress, vainly introduce bills to include Alaska in federal highway legislation.

Because of these exclusions, Alaska has only some 3,500 miles of highway, in an area one-fifth as large as the rest of the United States, and such highways as it has were built as a result of military necessity, and not to take care of civilian needs, although, needless to say, all highways are useful. The first highway constructed by the War Department is termed the Richardson, which runs from the Pacific coast port of Valdez north to Fairbanks. This was the first important piece of road construction. It was begun in 1905 for the Alaska Road Commission, then an agency of the War Department, and was completed some 10 years later, as a low-grade wagon road. There was no appreciable new highway construction in Alaska until World War II when, in response to military demands, a road called the Glenn was built connecting Anchorage with the Richardson Highway and was further extended to connect with the so-called Alcan Highway—the road from the United States to Alaska. It likewise was begun after the United States entered World War II, and completed by the Army Engineers in the incredibly short time of one year. Its name has since been changed to Alaska Highway. It is an unpaved road, and the Canadians have not yet seen fit to pave it. One other major road extends from Anchorage southward into the Kenai Peninsula; one branch going to Seward, the other to Homer.

There is one principal railroad in Alaska—the Alaska Railroad—some 470 miles in length, extending from Seward through Anchorage to Fairbanks. It was constructed by the Government and is operated by it. It is now considered principally an adjunct to defense. A British-owned railway extends from the port of Skagway to White Horse and

Yukon Territory. It is known as the White Pass and Yukon Railway. The first 20 miles are in Alaska.

Other minor railways which existed in the past have been abandoned. One of them, the Copper River and Northwestern, which connected the port of Cordova with the famous Kennecott Copper Mine, ceased to operate in 1938, when the mine was no longer productive.

In 1954 President Eisenhower proposed an additional super-program both for defense—to enable urban populations to evacuate in case of atomic attack—and to improve the national highway system. The original estimate of $101 billion was to be secured by long-term bonding. While approving the project, Congress differed as to the method of financing, preferring "pay-as-you-go" with additional taxes on trucks, trailers, tires, and gas. But in one respect President and Congress agreed: Alaska was to be *ex*cluded from the benefits of the legislation, but *in*cluded in the taxation. And so the Act provided. Every time an Alaskan filled his gas tank he paid an extra cent a gallon to build roads in every state from Alabama to Wyoming, but not in Alaska. He likewise paid the extra three cents a pound tax on tires.

Eventually an amendment was proposed to include Alaska in the regular federal program, but on the reduced basis of reckoning only half of Alaska's huge area in the formula. Alaska's potential share was eventually limited to an amount based on one-third of its area. In exchange Alaska would be permitted to use its own and federal matching funds for maintenance as well as for new construction.

Alaska has fared no better in the federal regulations governing maritime transportation. The Merchant Marine Act of 1920 permitted the use, interchangeably, of domestic and foreign carriers for transportation of goods across the continent and the oceans beyond, "foreign" meaning chiefly Canadian. Alaska was specifically excluded from the benefits of this Act.

The economic consequences of this exclusion were immediate. Several budding Alaska industries were obliged to forego the nearer and less costly port of Vancouver and to ship through Seattle. So much higher were its costs that they could no longer operate at a profit, and were forced to suspend. Other industries have been prevented from starting.

Efforts made by the Alaska Legislature to have Alaska's exclusion from the benefits of the "Jones Act" (the Merchant Marine Act of 1920) reversed brought the matter to the Supreme Court of the United States, which sustained the exclusion.

There is similar discrimination in railroad rates—discrimination which federal agencies have failed to correct when appealed to. Any rail-freight shipment to or from Alaska through Seattle, Alaska's port of exit and entry, is subject to a much higher rate than applies to any other area in the Pacific, including Mexico, Australasia, and the Orient. For instance, on household appliances shipped from the Midwest to destinations in the Orient, or anywhere in the Pacific but Alaska, the rate to Seattle was $1.58 per hundredweight. If consigned to Alaska, the rate was $3.80, or 140 percent more!

The federal government itself is adversely affected by this differential. In a recent year it paid $2 million more freight charges on defense construction materials and other government supplies consigned to Alaska than it would have paid if one of its agencies had not denied the appeal of Alaskan businessmen for rates comparable with those paid elsewhere.

Alaska today leads the world in its per-capita use of the airplane; Canada is second, continental United States third. Such preëminence —and in an air age it is something to brag about—was achieved by the "bush pilots" who were proudly independent of government subsidies or restrictions. That Alaska's leadership has continued into a jet age, and that Alaska has two airports that would be shown on the smallest toy globe, is a tribute partly to Alaska's strategic position, which is terrific both in the literal and in the slang sense, and partly to the fact that millions of federal dollars have been spent in defense installations. For until intercontinental missiles render bombers obsolete—if they ever do—Alaska is a key part of America's far-flung line of defense. Yet even the development of Alaskan aviation was long retarded by bureaucratic insensibility to the needs of the local population.

Alaska's greatest natural resource has been the Pacific salmon, which has been likewise one of the nation's greatest fisheries. Salmon canning began in Alaska in 1878, carried on by enterprises headquartered first in San Francisco and later on Puget Sound. This abundant resource was early menaced by overfishing. Beginning in 1889, Congress enacted conservation measures. These have never been adequately enforced and have been generally resisted by those harvesting this bonanza. Alaskans ascribe the depletion to the "fish-trap," a sizeable structure anchored in the path of the salmon returning from the high seas to spawn in the rivers. The fish-trap has been abolished in all other Pacific salmon areas—British Columbia, Washington, and Oregon—where the fishery is under local control and has been conserved despite the handicaps of industrial waste pollution which Alaska has lacked.

Depletion was already a danger when the first Alaska Legislature met in 1913. It and every one of its twenty-two successors memorialized the Congress to transfer control of the fisheries to the Territory. In session after session, Alaska's voteless Delegates introduced bills to that end. In vain. The combination of federal bureau and absentee industry control continued to thwart the incessant pleas of Alaskans.

The result has been a steadily diminishing supply of salmon which had shrunk from a pack of 8,454,948 cases in 1936 to less than a third of that amount, 2,447,448 cases, in 1957. So serious was the depletion, that in the first three years of his administration, President Eisenhower felt obliged to declare Alaska fishing villages to be "disaster areas"—disaster caused not by so-called "acts of God" but by acts of men.

For all such handicaps, statehood was the obvious remedy. The 1945 Legislature provided for a referendum on statehood, which recorded a favorable sentiment among Alaskans by a vote of three to two. Statehood bills were promptly introduced in Washington (the first one had been introduced as early as 1916), but bill after bill failed to pass both Houses during the same Congress.

Impatient at the delay, and with statehood sentiment mounting in Alaska, the 1955 Territorial Legislature provided for a constitutional convention that would draft a constitution for the *State* of Alaska. At a subsequent election, Alaska voters ratified the Constitution. Political scientists declare it to rank high among such documents. The voters likewise approved an ordinance authorizing the election of the two United States Senators and a Representative, to go to Washington and seek Alaska's admission as a State. This action followed well-established precedents, begun by Tennessee in 1796 and continued by Michigan, Iowa, California, Minnesota, Oregon, and Kansas. Alaska's "Tennessee-Plan" Delegation was soon at work in the national capital, securing favorable committee reports in both Houses for statehood bills in the First Session of the 85th Congress, and finally achieving success in the Second Session in 1958.

Who are these inhabitants of Alaska who waited so long for validation of the 91-year-old pledge that they be "admitted to the enjoyment of all the rights, advantages, and immunities of citizens of the United States"?

Six-sevenths of their population of some 225,000 came from the older States—either they, or their parents or grandparents. They came to Alaska, following the oldest American practice, which antedates even the founding of the Republic, the westward quest for greater freedom and greater opportunity. They struggled with and overcame the hardships of America's northernmost and westernmost and most rugged frontier. One-seventh of the population are the descendants of the aboriginal inhabitants—Eskimo, Aleut, and Indian, friendly peoples all—who have become assimilated into the twentieth-century culture which the newcomers brought.

What has been their livelihood?

Furs were the motivation which first brought Americans to Alaska, as they had been the Russians' more than a century earlier. Furs were followed shortly in the 1870's by fishing and mining. The once-abundant Pacific salmon and plentiful gold have been the chief economic mainstays of Alaska during the American occupancy. Now both have declined but continue. To them have been added pulp manufacture and the logging incidental thereto. The first important utilization of Alaska's vast virgin forests began in 1954 with the building of a 500-ton-a-day pulp mill at Ketchikan. A second mill is under construction at Sitka. Two more are in prospect at Wrangell and Juneau.

The first oil well in the course of extensive exploration "came in" in 1957 on the Kenai Peninsula. Agriculture, given an impetus by the Matanuska colonization project in 1935, has become a steadily growing

14.   A typical Alaska cabin in the old days, rude but strong and weather-proof. This picture was taken at Eagle on the Alaska-Canada boundary in 1912.

15.   A pioneer homesteader at Palmer in the Matanuska Valley.

16. Along the Alaska Highway. Views like this delight the traveler at many points along this 1600-mile scenic route through an unspoiled wilderness, which becomes more and more interesting as one approaches the northwestern terminus.

17.   An Eskimo couple goes shopping in Nome.

18. Fairbanks' waterfront in 1913. River traffic with stern-wheelers long ago gave way to the railroad, the automobile, the truck, and the airplane.

19. Here again we see a blending of cultures — Eskimo women equipped with gasoline-powered washing machines.

20. The old Russian church in Sitka (Greek Orthodox) antedates the Alaska Purchase. The weather — typical!

1., 22. "Before and after." Fairbanks in 1912 (above) and as it looks today (below). In each case the camera faced approximately north. That a pity, for in the south would be seen the Alaska Range, culminating in Mt. McKinley 160 miles to the southwest.

Galloway

Galloway

23. Juneau, Alaska's capital city on the Inside Passage. For many years Juneau was the biggest Alaskan settlement. In recent years it has been surpassed in size by Anchorage.

24. Ketchikan, near Alaska's southeastern tip, thrives on fisheries and timber products.

economic asset. Farm activity consists chiefly of dairying, though production thus far has been wholly for Alaska consumption.

Development of the baser metals is foreshadowed with iron mining, initiated in southeastern Alaska, and an intensified search for strategic minerals known to exist in Alaska is under way. National defense has recently become enormously important economically with military bases at Anchorage, Fairbanks, Big Delta, Eielson, naval bases at Kodiak and Adak, and the DEW line installations in the far north. Missile bases are in prospect. A tourist industry—as nearly everywhere outside Iron Curtain countries—is rapidly developing. The Alaska Visitors Association, created by the 1951 Legislature and supported both by Territorial funds and by popular subscription, beckoned the world to Alaska's matchless scenery.

Alaskans have provided themselves, except in the remoter areas, with every up-to-date facility. Their Territorial services included those of any state save those Congress had prohibited. To their educational system, they point with justifiable pride. Alaskans led the way in appreciating the importance of the teacher, translating their belief practically by salaries which long exceeded and still exceed those paid in most of the states. (They surely need to, in view of current living costs!) Before statehood, a federal educational system for the "natives" (Alaskans of aboriginal descent) was being absorbed into the Territorial system. The federal government was still conducting two boarding schools which emphasized vocational training.

The newcomers from the States, whose arrival in substantial numbers began with the gold rush of sixty years ago, brought with them the tradition and training in self-government that is integral in the American heritage. They are hard-working, independent-minded individualists and pioneers by inclination and circumstance.

Their First Legislature, in 1913, enfranchised women—by its very first Act—anticipating the Nineteenth Amendment by seven years. The Second Legislature, in 1915, established old-age pensions, thus antedating nation-wide Social Security by a generation. A special legislative session in 1946 passed the first World War II Veterans Act adopted anywhere under the Flag. Recognized as one of the best of such Acts, it has enabled Alaska veterans, through loans, to acquire homes, farms, and fishing boats and to engage in businesses. Financed originally by a sales tax in effect for three years, the fund is now operated, at no cost to the people of Alaska, from the proceeds of repaid principal and interest of loans. While the abolition or drastic control of billboards within the States was defeated in the national Congress, Alaskans rejoiced in the action of their 1949 Legislature in banning billboards along the Territory's highways.

Social life in Alaska is much as it is in the States, with such adaptations to the geographic setting as might be expected. Frontier people love to organize. Principal centers of one kind of social activity in Alaska towns are the fraternal organizations, whose headquarters, usually among the largest and best-kept-up buildings in town, are available for community functions of various kinds.

The service clubs, just as "down below," hold their luncheons on different days, listen to local or visiting speakers, and hold their annual picnics in midsummer at some nearby beach or other resort, and their Christmas parties in one of the hostelries. The local Chamber of Commerce foregathers at noon on one of the weekdays when it would not compete with a service club for attendance. Veterans' organizations have their "dugout," clubhouse, or rooms and hold regular evening meetings.

The local Women's Club is affiliated with the world-wide General Federation of Women's Clubs. The Four-H Clubs for the younger generation are active in the agricultural areas of central Alaska. Boy Scouts and Girl Scouts are thriving organizations, and nature and man have combined to provide them with as fine camp sites for their annual outings as may be found anywhere in America.

There is in Alaska, as often in the West and indeed anywhere, considerable pride in priority of arrival. Reminiscent of the forty-niners of California, but banded together in a uniquely Alaskan organization which originated in the early days, are the Pioneers of Alaska. Its locals are designated as "igloos," although contrary to popular misconception there never were any igloos in the sense of snow houses in the areas occupied by the Alaskan Eskimos. (*Igloo* is the Eskimo word for "house" regardless of the material with which it is constructed.) The first members of this territory-wide organization were, as the name implies, pioneers who came to Alaska in the late nineties and earlier, chiefly in search of gold. Since with the passing years the number of surviving gold-rushers steadily diminishes, the date of arrival which qualified one for membership in the Pioneers of Alaska has been repeatedly advanced. Thirty years' residence in Alaska is now the requirement.

In a recent campaign for a seat in the Territorial Legislature, one candidate—a woman—proclaimed in her political advertising that she was "an 1887 pioneer" (she had crossed the Chilkoot Pass as a child with her parents) and therefore, sentimentally at least, a notch above the far more numerous gold-rushers of '98. For there were occasional and unpublicized prospectors who came to Alaska years before "the Klondike," lured northward by the hope of repeating the gold strikes of the far West. They came particularly after the finds in the Canadian Cassiar at the Headwaters of the Stikine River, which furnished them a swift downstream entry into southeastern Alaska, and then gave to Wrangell, the Indian village near its mouth which the Russians had converted into a "fort" and which the American troops briefly occupied after the purchase, a temporary importance greater than it ever achieved thereafter. Juneau, a hundred miles further north, and vanished Treadwell, now Douglas, on opposite sides of the Gastineau Channel, owed their founding, and for over half a century their economic mainstay, to the discovery of the precious metal on Gold Creek in 1880.

However, the earliest Alaskan pioneers were those who established trading posts along the Yukon and elsewhere in the remote Interior. Here they bartered with the natives for furs, giving them in exchange manufactured goods such as canned foods, ready-made clothing, and tools and gadgets and thus introducing the primitive inhabitants to the white man's ways. Some of these trading posts survive as individual enterprises in the remoter villages. Others have been taken over by the Northern Commercial Company, an Alaska chain of retail department stores which (with their predecessors) antedate the cession of Alaska. This is the oldest business enterprise in the Territory and is the Alaska counterpart of the Hudson's Bay Company of Canada.

Pride in priority of arrival has faded a bit since the initial period of adventure and hardship in "opening up Alaska." But emphasis upon early or at least long residence in Alaska was greater than it might otherwise have been because of the practice of the federal government of choosing its officials for service in Alaska from outside. Alaskans borrowed from pioneers from the South the opprobrious designation "carpetbagger" for members of the federal bureaucracy sent in to rule them. That feeling persists to a degree. It was evidenced the first time Alaskans had a chance to elect their own officials, when the members of the first Territorial House of Representatives proudly listed in their official biographies the number of years each had been a bona fide resident of Alaska; and 'way back then, in 1913, the average was fifteen years, which synchronized their arrival with the '98 Gold Rush.

But lest it be thought that there is in Alaska an elite, based on either who came first or on wealth or other yardsticks that do not always measure, it should be made clear that nowhere in America is there so nearly a total absence of class or caste; nowhere a more genuinely democratic feeling. The Alaskan frontier is little concerned with what you were or whence you came; rather it is interested in what you are and do in Alaska now.

The only distinction between the old-timers and the newcomers is found in the Alaskan appellations of "sourdough" and "cheechako." The former is derived from the practice of early Alaskan prospectors of making bread or flapjacks with flour and water fermented without yeast. The latter, pronounced *cheechawker*, the equivalent of "tenderfoot" in the old West, is derived from a word in the Chinook dialect meaning "newly arrived." That, and *skookum* meaning "good," "strong," "very"; and *tillicum*, which has come to mean "pal" or "friend," are among the few words that Alaskans have adopted from the aboriginal frontier dialect. It is pertinent that in Alaska (unlike Hawaii which retains some Polynesian words in everyday speech and preserves the more picturesque customs to the enhancement of local color) the pre-annexation cultures—Eskimo, Athabaskan, Tlingit, or Russian—have left almost no trace linguistically or otherwise in contemporary Alaskan culture.

From the Russian occupancy, to be sure, many place names survive: Baranof, Chichagof, Kruzof and Kupreanof Islands, Lake Resanof, in southeastern Alaska; and, to the westward, Shelikof and Isanofski Straits; Cape Sarichef; the villages of Belkofski, Chernofski, and Nikolski; Chirikof and Semeonof Islands, Mount Veniaminof—to name only a few. Also a few material vestiges are preserved in the Russian Orthodox churches, now little attended, in Juneau, Kodiak, Ninilchik, Unalaska, and on the Pribilof Islands of St. Paul and St. George. The finest is at Sitka, where the Cathedral of the Archangel Michael, a beautiful example of the Russian variant of Byzantine architecture, lifts its bulbous steeple and dome, each surmounted by the two-barred Greek cross, above the town. Within is housed one of the world's finest collections of icons.

Of the Indian culture, the chief material survivals are in southeastern Alaska, the Tlingit and Haida totem poles. Restored from damaging exposure to the elements, they are found chiefly in communities formerly and now in part Indian villages—Ketchikan and neighboring Saxman, Klawock, Hydaburg, Wrangell, Sitka, Juneau, and Klukwan, the last of which has a unique and priceless collection of house totems preserved within their owners' homes.

But save these, and excepting also the 30,000 Eskimo, Aleut, and Indian population, Alaskans, being transplanted Americans—transplanted of their own free will from the other States—together with a few born in the Old World, brought their culture with them. One hears all kinds of accents in Alaska—of Maine and Massachusetts, the various Southern drawls, the Hoosier twang, and among those recognizably "foreign," chiefly those of Scandinavia.

Norsemen have found Alaska, resembling their home land, to their liking. The prosperous and tidy fishing community of Petersburg, dependent largely on the halibut and shrimp fisheries (which have not been depleted), is peopled chiefly by former Norwegians. As in the northwestern states where most of the Governors and not a few Senators and Congressmen have Scandinavian names, so too in Alaska these north Europeans, whose concepts of freedom parallel ours, have made their mark. Of such was Andrew Nerland, born in Norway, who came by way of Minnesota to Fairbanks when the town was born of a gold strike made by Felix Pedro, an Italian, early in the century. A carpenter and painter by training, Nerland helped build the new community, founded what has become the North's leading home-furnishing store; served eleven terms in the Legislature, was President of the Senate, a Regent of the University of Alaska—a respected and beloved embodiment of the American dream.

Prominent in Fairbanks society are folks with Yugoslav names. Alaskan-born John Butrovich, a graduate of the University of Alaska, who founded his own insurance agency, has served for over a decade in the Territorial Senate. President Eisenhower's second gubernatorial appointment went to Michael Stepovich, lawyer and legislator, likewise Alaskan-born, son of an immigrant who had the foresight to invest the proceeds of his placer gold mining in Fairbanks real estate.

Despite man-made handicaps which Alaskans hope will end with statehood, many have found "the last frontier" an outpost of opportunity. Many more will find it so.

One reason is to be found in Alaska's resources, largely untapped. Another lies in the sparseness of its population. Here the individual is not lost in the mass as in the older, more densely populated parts of America. Whatever ability, energy, determination he possesses are more evident, count for more than in the crowded, urban "Stateside" centers. Alaska's spaciousness means elbowroom for each and everyone. It will be increasingly appreciated as soaring population begins to crowd the other States. Independence of mind and action are stimulated in the wide vistas and limitless expanse of a relatively empty land. And, being younger, its ways of life are not yet cast in rigid molds. Participation in their shaping is therefore easier. Thus was all America "only yesterday." Alaska's is merely a later chapter in the American epic.

A scant score of years ago, before World War II, any one of the hundreds of Alaskans who made frequent, perhaps annual, trips to and from the States was likely to be acquainted with most of the others of that group, whatever their place or places of residence. The only mode of travel was maritime. (Scheduled airplane service between Alaska and the States was not initiated till 1940; the Alaska Highway, completed in 1942, was opened to civilian traffic in 1946.) The voyager leaving Seattle would enjoy 48 hours of scenic beauty along the Inside Passage before landing at Ketchikan, appropriately named "the first city." Succeeding stops were at Wrangell and Petersburg, then Juneau. Side trips either on the northward or on the southward journey would take in Sitka, Haines, and Skagway. Then the vessel, leaving the protected waters and rounding a range of mountains that rise directly out of the water to heights greater than those of any mountain in the other 48 States, would cross the Gulf of Alaska to Seward. On the way, stops would be made at Yakutat, Cordova, and Valdez. At Seward the traveler would debark and, if he were headed for the Interior, the Alaska Railroad would carry him inland to Anchorage and Fairbanks.

The trip lasted a week. Many acquaintances were made and friendships formed aboard. Contacts established while traveling in one di-

rection were renewed, afloat and ashore, while traveling in the other
direction or on subsequent voyages. Travelers to and from Bering Sea
ports, including Nome, followed different routes but had similar experiences.

The many-hour stops at each port to load and unload freight furnished ample opportunities for social visits and for business transac-
tions ashore. Or the passenger might leave his ship for a week's stay
and proceed northward or southward by the next sailing. Thus Alaskans came to know each other. Perhaps nowhere else on earth, and
certainly nowhere else under the American Flag, were so widely scattered people so well acquainted with each other. The highly seasonal
factors of Alaskan activity—for placer mining and fishing are summer
occupations—made these outward and inward trips as rhythmic and
unvarying as the migration of the birds. And it was not uncommon,
as the exhaustion of mineral or other resources blighted the economy
of one Alaskan community, for a professional man or a businessman
or a laborer to transfer his home and occupation from one Alaskan
town to another. But the Alaskan migrating within Alaska would not
come to his new home as a total stranger.

The airplane and World War II changed all this considerably.
Constellations and *D.C.7's* of four different airlines now fly passengers
directly from Seattle to Anchorage and Fairbanks and back, "over-
heading" or bypassing the intervening towns or stopping but a few
minutes in their airports. Passenger service on the Alaska Steamship
Line was suspended in 1954. It now carries freight only. The leisurely
coastal journey on American boats through the beautiful Inside Passage, with the visiting in every port, seemed destined to be no more,
although a Canadian Pacific Company and a Canadian National vessel make the trip through southeastern Alaska weekly. But fortunately,
an enterprising Alaskan, a pioneer in the Alaskan tourist industry,
Charles B. West, has acquired two fine passenger ships—the S.S.
Chilcotin and the S.S. *Glacier Queen*—which now travel the Inside
Passage from Vancouver to Skagway in the summer months, with
stops at Prince Rupert, Ketchikan, and Juneau, and with a side trip to
Glacier Bay National Monument, a unique scenic wonderland. Their
objective is to carry tourists.

War, the great destroyer, is sometimes also a great constructor.
World War II, for all its heartaches and bereavements, contributed

greatly to Alaska's development. It brought to Alaska the first substantial aids to aviation—airfields and radio-range stations previously nonexistent. It brought the highways the military needed, including the Alaska Highway. It brought new economic props to Kodiak, Anchorage, and Fairbanks. It left a naval base in Sitka harbor which was usefully converted into a vocational boarding school for native youngsters. It brought additional population, not merely in the military and civilian personnel stationed in Alaska during the War and in the sequent Cold War, but in the thousands of G.I.'s who returned with their brides to make their homes there.

Modern inventions, whose wider use is accelerated by war, particularly the airplane and radio, have had a greater impact on Alaska than elsewhere, and have done much to diminish its former isolation.

In the years following the Wright brothers' demonstration at Kitty Hawk, Alaskans became the "flyingest" of all Americans. Their pioneering spirit gave them the urge to explore the newly penetrated third dimension. Besides, with no roads to speak of and only one 470-mile railroad, flying was the only way to get around. The Alaskan "bush pilot" had no airports, beacons, or radio beams to help him. He would merely hold up a moistened finger to the breeze and take off. His landings were in tiny clearings, on beaches, on sand bars in rivers, on lakes and coastal waterways on floats, or in winter in the north on the snow-covered tundra on skis. And so intra-Alaskan aviation was developed almost wholly by Alaskan daring, initiative, and financing. Today Alaskans fly some thirty times as much as other Americans—measured either in number of flights or passenger miles per capita. Freight of all kinds is carried by air to the remotest outposts. From these brave beginnings over half a dozen certificated carriers now function in Alaska, and two of them operate all the way to the States. In southeastern Alaska, a network of waterways which serve as landing "fields" supports the two largest commercial seaplane operations in the world, wholly the product of local enterprise.

At the edge of booming Anchorage, two small circular lakes have been connected by a canal which serves as a runway for the privately-owned seaplanes parked completely around Lake Hood. The other lake, Spenard, is reserved for bathing. From there after working hours in summertime, Anchorage people take off for their camps on the hundreds of lakes dotting the great Susitna plain which stretches a hundred miles northward to the Alaska Range. To most of these camps there are no roads. Their owners utilize these float planes as suburbanites or week-end vacationists use their automobiles in the States.

The radio too has helped to relieve these summer homes of their isolation. It has done the same for the trapper in the forest, for the miner on the creeks, for the fisherman in his boat. It brings the news of the world to those remote from daily newspaper distribution, which includes a fairly substantial proportion of all Alaskans. Nowhere else in America do people owe so much to modern invention.

Electrification of urban and rural homes, made possible to a large degree by the R.E.A., whose co-operatives are expanding rapidly in response to increased demand, has made much of Alaska a frontier with modern comforts. Automobiles in Alaska are numerous out of all proportion to the limited road mileage and population. Television too has come to the principal cities.

Little more than a stone's throw beyond the civilization and modern conveniences of the cities and towns lies the primitive beauty and mystery of the unspoiled wilderness with its virgin forests, its deep fiords, its shining glaciers, its myriad lakes, its high waterfalls, its juxtaposition of lofty mountains with the sea, its abundant wildlife. In this soul-lifting setting, Alaskans are determined to make the new State of Alaska increasingly a shining example of all that is best in the American way of life.

Mexico

BY WALDO FRANK

1. THE LAND

The first Americans came from Asia or Australasia. A generation ago
the experts were sure they had all crossed the Bering Strait, which
at the time was perhaps an isthmus or still solid with ice of the last
Glacial Age. The authorities imagined (because experts in such matters must be imaginative men) that through many centuries these
Mongoloid pioneers increased and multiplied, growing variant as they
settled in distinct climes and conditions from the frozen north to the
tropics and from the tropics to the American Antarctic. Thus, the Eskimo and the savage Red Man of our plains, the highly civilized nations of the Mexican *mesetas*, the wild human animals of the Amazon
jungle, and the subtle communist imperialists of the Peruvian Andes
who labored in vain to subdue them—all were somehow "explained"
as issuing from the solitary trickle of the Mongol men up from Eastern Asia into Alaska, and thence southward and southeastward.

Today, the experts are less certain. Many favor what may be termed
a pluralistic version of how the Americas were peopled. All are agreed
that man is a relative newcomer in the Western Hemisphere, going
back perhaps ten thousand years (the oldest trace of him yet found
is the "Tepexpam man," a Mongoloid hunter buried near the bones
of a mammoth and probably dating from 9000 B.C.). According to

this version, there were many voyages from many places and at many times, over the Pacific. The Bering Strait (or isthmus) was used, but also the islands of the broad South Seas. Primitive stone-age Asians came across and developed American cultures; but also the children of more advanced civilizations who either lapsed into savagery (the aborigines of the Amazon, for instance) or went forward in specific, specialized American ways. One theory even postulates the invasion of America by missionaries of Chinese and Indian religions, philosophers schooled in the Eastern sciences, artists with the techniques of Cambodia, Indo-China; thus to explain the similitudes which strike the eye between sculptures, glyphs, domestic arts, and basic attitudes of Asian and American, before Columbus; and such miracles as the Mayan astronomy, the Zapotec calendar—more accurate than the European before the nineteenth century, yet apparently rising fullborn from barbaric nescience.

This much is certain: The men who reached and settled what is now Mexico, whether their forebears worked their way down through a countless age from Alaska or made a vast eastward ladder of the South Pacific isles, found no easy, hospitable land. Northern Mexico was desert; the trail through California, Arizona, and New Mexico, probably taken by Nahua-Aztec tribes before they reached the lakes of the central *meseta*, led through desert. The tableland was cold, the lowlands bordering the Gulf and the Pacific were steaming cauldrons breeding malaria and yellow fever. Half the year was dry, the other half was flooded with torrential rains which turned the baked arroyos into unmanageable, unharnessed turbines. Two great mountain ranges, the Sierra Madres, mother mountains of the East and West, joined the Andes with the Rockies. Between them was a plateau, from five thousand to ten thousand feet in height, crisscrossed by mountains bare and almost perpendicular, which made each valley a fastness—and a prison. The mountain slopes were stone and arid earth, at the mercy of flood, drouth, and erosion. Rivers vanished until the months of rain, when they assaulted the land. Not one was navigable more than a few miles from its mouth. In the hot lowlands, the forest had to be cut away before the corn could be planted, the city built. And when cut back, the jungle had to be held back, a constant rising menace.

Even today, with our modern methods of agronomy, only a tenth of Mexico's 760,000 square miles of land is cultivable.* Even today, despite its relatively meager population of about 30 million, Mexico is a food-importing country. When one flies over the land, one wonders: Where is man? Height twists from rocky height, disordered as by a god with hostile hand knocking and scattering the stony structure. Valleys of deep green, revealing town or village, are shut from one another by the mountain walls that cast deep shadows. In the central plateaus, the houses look from the air like tiny stones. In the *tierra caliente*, the roofs of bamboo thatch merge in the enveloping verdure. In the soil indeed are shards of buried cultures over which a hostile earth seems to have triumphed. In the soil too are minerals; despite the Colony's haphazard and modern industry's more rational mining, Mexico's subsurface wealth has been barely scratched. With the metal, machines can be made and hostile nature overcome. For the age of science vaults mountains as if they were anthills; bridges valleys and binds them together; gathers and preserves the floods of the rainy season in reservoirs and dams, for irrigation of the desert and for power.

But all this was not within the ken or reach of the pre-industrial civilizations; and to the first men who settled in Mexico, Mexico's land was fiercely, effectively unfriendly, to a degree the dwellers of the thirteen British colonies could not imagine. For the land from New England to Georgia and west to the Appalachian wall was an open, temperate, readily responsive land. By Mexican or Andean standards, mountains were hardly more than hills and did not isolate the valleys. Rain or snow fell at all times, drouths were rare. The rivers, wide, deep, and constant, beckoned from accessible harbors into a good land. There were swamps, but the mosquito was less deadly. Winter in many parts was severe, but pre-scientific man could make an axe chop wood, and build a fire in his hearth to fight the cold, whereas only technological man can fight the heat, its drain on the body nerves and muscles, its nurture of disease-carrying insects.

The first Mexicans had a greater handicap even than this ferocity of their earth. They lacked cattle, horses, sheep, and goats; hence were barred from the pastoral stage: normal transition from the nomad hunter to the fixed farmer, by which all the known great civi-

* Seventeen percent of China's land is cultivable.

lizations of the East have risen. The hunter raided nature, but nature through its tamable beasts made an armistice with the hunter. Flock or herd kept him on the move, but not too much—until he was matured enough for the long wait in one place required by planting and reaping.

This organic gap in the early American civilizations had vast psychological results. It was as if an infant were forced to become a man without the nurturing interlude of childhood. The leap might succeed, but at what emotional and mental cost the psychologist will tell you!

The Mexican tamed only the wild dog—to eat him. He had no milch cows, no wool-bearers, no draft animals; not even the untamable bison of the north prairies, not even the unsocial and disagreeable llama, alpaca, and vicuña of the Andes. It is an error to say he did not know the wheel. He used it in his arts, in his children's toys. He did not, as in China, employ man as beast of burden to draw a wagon. All these lacks moved him perhaps by compensation into abstractions of mathematics and astronomy, and into arts expressing the experience of cosmos.

The long trek which the Aztecs are supposed to have taken from eastern California down the thousand-mile desert announced the end, not the beginning, of Mexico's great pre-Columbian cultures. But it reveals much of the nature of the amazing story. The long journey must have taken many generations. One can make it today; but even today, in a luxurious car going sixty miles per hour on a perfect highway, with maps and stopovers fully known, it is not an easy journey. What must it have been to those men with no wagons, no horses, with no more than rumors about the nearest water hole, through the hot stone and sand, through the forests of cactus! To those women bearing their babes on their backs! What could have driven these human beings to believe in their goal: a happy valley of many waters and of sacred towering cities?

They found the valley, forty miles wide, sixty miles long, a steep mile and a half above the seas, heart of a tableland fifteen hundred miles from north to south with width tapering from five hundred miles to the slim Tehuantepec isthmus where it falls to sea level. They found the Lakes: Zumpango, Xaltocan, Texcoco, Chalco, Xochimilco. And they found cities and ruins of ancient cities whose rhythm of rise and fall the Aztecs broke forever—broke before the Spaniards could come and conquer.

Here, the Aztecs built their own capital: Tenochtitlán, a gallant city, which we cannot understand unless we have some knowledge of what came before.

2. THE FIRST RESPONDERS

Above all, bear in mind the earth. It was for the most part unfriendly to man, with hostile extremes of heat and chill, of tropical spilth and waste. It was a land of fiery volcanoes, old and new.* It was a land of shut-in valleys with no navigable rivers, where communication was the work of feet—of human feet since Mexico had no beasts of burden. From the people of such a land, speaking scores of languages (in 1940 over 50 spoken languages remained), living in hundreds of isolated valleys, one would expect much of what one reads in the pages of Mexico's history: conquest by the more dynamic Spaniards; colonial servitude for the three centuries of Spain's empire; political disorders; endemic violence; military, bureaucratic, and capitalist exploitation.

Yet this is *not* Mexico's true story. It is a surface reading of partial facts that mislead, and must disqualify all our attitudes and relations based exclusively on them.

Mexico is a *mestizo* world. It is not Indian (thirty percent are "pure" Indian); it is not European (ten percent are "pure" white); and it is not mestizo merely or chiefly because sixty percent of the people are of that "mixed" blood, Indian and European, technically known as mestizo. Mexico is mestizo, not demographically but culturally, and both in its "whites" and in its Indians, two million of whom even today speak no Spanish. When the Spaniard embraced the Indian woman, there was a psychological marriage, a marriage of emotion and mind. Not an easy union. It meant creativity but also it meant war. It meant the preservation of diverse ethnic traits, but in new forms dissimilar from any of the past. Mexican and mestizo became syn-

---

* Mexico's latest volcano burst from a cornfield in Paricutín, state of Michoacán, in 1943. It reached a height of more than 1500 feet above its base before it settled.

onyms; and the pure white and the pure aborigine partook of this fusion no less than the biological mestizo.

This is why Mexico cannot be understood without some knowledge of its first great cultural articulations: the Maya, the Toltec, the Zapotec, the Mixtec, the Totanac, finally and fatally the Aztec; nor without some knowledge of the deeply Catholic culture of Spain. But the picture, to be faithful, must be even more complex. Mexico lives now within the orbit of the West. Airplane, electricity, electronics have transformed it, abolishing the conditions which fixed the Mexican nature. The U.S.A. is a potent magnetic and gravitational field upon it. The modern Mexican, with an intelligence both mobile and wire-strong, prepares eagerly to become a member of a world of atomic energy and space-moons. How will this dimension of his future affect his past values? Will it efface them or can they affect his future? And what concern is it *of ours?*

Look at a map of the North American West. Mexico, now a land of 760,000 square miles, was until 1847 a theoretical republic comprising what had been the Spanish kingdom of New Spain, an expanse of 1,650,000 square miles. But most of these huge spaces from the north boundary, the 42d degree parallel southward, including the Californias, Texas, and the present northernmost tier of Mexican States: Sonora, Chihuahua, Coahuila, Durango, Nuevo León, et al. was never under effectual control by either Spain or Mexico, nor did it produce important Indian cultures. The pious *padres* pushed a few missions into these vastitudes, whose crude churches, compared with those of Puebla or Guadalajara, reveal their distance from the cultural center. The local Indians were barbarians or, in a few cases such as the Pueblo tribes of New Mexico, dim and remote echoes of the Mexican South. Long before the Mexican-American war, pioneers from the United States to Texas far outnumbered with their slaves the handfuls of Mexican herders and ranchers. It may therefore be said that in that war Mexico lost to the United States—outside of spottily scattered settlements—no land already integral with the Mexican culture.

Now let the reader observe what lies south and east of this immense periphery. For here, in a compact narrow space, symmetrical as the two wings of a butterfly, is all historic Mexico. The west "wing" is limned roughly northwest from Vera Cruz up the Gulf to the Panuco River, site of modern Tampico; thence west to the Pacific which here bears to the east; thence southeasterly to the peninsula of Tehuante-pec, including the great Zapotec and Mixtec cities of Oaxaca. Here, the Pacific, due south from Vera Cruz, becomes the "southern sea" that it was called by the Spaniards. This is the start of the east "wing" of our radiant butterfly, which spreads north to include all Yucatán and east to embrace the Mayan cities, such as Tikal and Copan, now respectively Guatemalan and Honduran.

This concentrated land, smaller than Texas, contains what we may rightly call the Mexican complex of responses to the rigors and the mystery of nature. Here, before 500 B.C., an archaic culture, already millennial, had spread from the high Mexican *mesa* down to Vera Cruz, perhaps to Oaxaca and northward into Chiapas, Campeche, Yucatán, and Guatemala. It seems to have been fairly uniform, and closely related to archaic cultures in coastal Peru and the Andes. Perhaps it began in Vera Cruz, whose forests grow the wild rubber of the ball used in the universal Mexican game. What puzzles the experts is the seemingly sudden emergence from this archaic stone-age state of a high metaphysical and aesthetic culture.

We cannot here explore the luxuriant varieties of the pre-Columbian Mexican art. One example must serve to suggest its strength. At Teotihuacán the builders of the sacred city covered eight square miles with pyramids and painted temples that compose a contrapuntal whole as strict as a Bach fugue. The notes of the fugue in music, and the fingers of the player of the fugue, are controlled with precision. Here the individual notes are mighty blocks of stone borne by human bodies from a volcano at the north of the valley; the themes are complex structures (one of them basing the temple of the Sun over two hundred feet above earth); the inward and overall relations of the parts are exact as the tones and timbres and notes in fugal music. The master goal of this mighty plastic form is the experience of light. As one climbs the stone steps, light is there; as one passes through the painted and sculptured corridors, light is along. And the weavers of these exquisite polyphonies in stone had no modern instruments, no beasts of burden!

The arts were various; the basic theme was unity of celebrant and cosmos. And cosmos, for the Mexican, was earth and the stars, numbers, and weight: never a transcendental concept. To the Indian a beating heart was of the same substance as the radiant sun. The truncated pyramid from which the temple rose must be earth—a stylized hill. With the ages, dust and detritus made the abandoned temple heights real hills—at times big enough, as at Cholula, for the Spaniards to use the summit as the foundation of a church. Within the Mexican complex, nations and their arts rose and fell in a cycle that seemed kin to the cycles of the cosmic seasons.

The Mexican arts were supreme expressions of this sense of existence. Action and deed counted less than Being. But Being meant existence; the Mexican existentialism made a unity in the arts profounder than the distinctions. In all these early cultures, human sacrifice was practiced. But it was always carefully restricted and controlled, being a rite full of peril, whose sacred use had overtones of lust and contagious terror. There is some evidence that in the early Mayan culture, as certainly in the Peruvian culture of the Incas, human sacrifice was finally forbidden and overcome. What was the meaning in Mexico of this rite? Sacrifice to appease the gods is almost universal in an immature stage of religion, although the Pascal lamb may have long since replaced the human victim. No mystery here. But an early Mayan fresco reveals a deeper substance to the practice, a metaphysical meaning. The body of the Serpent is the universal Indian symbol for Existence (the snake is the earth, and it is feathered for flight and for freedom). In this fresco, the serpent is so spread forth that the victim lies outstretched on it, back down on the serpent's scales, arms and feet held by the priests. The head priest plunges his obsidian knife into the breast, to extract the heart still beating; and it is offered to the god through the priest's ceremonial eating. At this moment, *the face of the victim changes into the face of the god*. This transfiguration was the common event in Mayan sacrifice, and probably in all the classic Mexican rites. It is, of course, a perfect symbol of the individual transformed into the universal. By sacrificing self to the god, man partakes of the god. The great religions of the East express a similar experience, but the sacrifice is sublimated: Man gives up the lusts of his heart, not his literal beating heart. This is sublimation; the literal human sacrifice negates it.

Does this analogy mean that the Asians who crossed to America by the Bering Strait or the Bering isthmus, or who ferried across the Pacific, had been influenced by Asian philosophies? I doubt it. They came over perhaps millennia, surely centuries before the Vedas and

Upanishads were sung. The basic principle that man must "lose his life to find it," must give up the clamors of his ego in order to be part of Being, which he calls divine, is a human intuition universal as our intuitive form of space and time. From this common undifferentiated knowledge come varying forms of conduct. The Hebrews erect an elaborate ethic and method-of-living (the 613 commandments), designed to bring nation and man close to the face of God. The Brahmins and Buddhists elaborate withdrawals of the will-to-live, with complex rationalizations. The Mexican Indians reached a cruder solution: the victim's heart was actually torn from the bared breast; and in the act the victim partook of the god, the priest who partook of the victim partook of the god, and the people profited. This is the meaning of human sacrifice. It remained in the great classic Indian cultures, Maya, Olmec, Toltec, Zapotec, a rare ceremonial act. With the Aztecs, it became a monstrous, a maniacal obsession.

As one examines the rich relics of these cultures, the human evidence of their survivors living today in Mexico and Guatemala, one is struck by the deep passivity which seems to have been their common trait. They responded to nature, only to the extent of primitive need: for example, in the clearing of the jungle. The dynamic Western will for novelty for conquest's sake was alien to them—although their intelligent contemplation of nature, as for instance in their mathematics, went far beyond pragmatic need. Before the Aztecs, who transformed the whole Mexican scene, the many tribes and nations seem to have fought little against one another. Maya, Toltec, Zapotec, Mixtec . . . these were not warlike nations, once they had found a home and built their cities. Their own dwellings must have been of wood or 'dobe, for they have vanished; only the stone precincts of the gods survive. They seem to have been humble folk, readily controlled by theocrat and priest. The odor of sacrifice was pleasant to them, a contemplative people: whence a people of arts, but of arts swiftly conventionalized and hieratic.

Was this their original trait? If passive, could they have trekked the long hard way, generation after generation, from eastern Asia? The forebears of the Mexicans must have been dynamic, resourceful. And we have seen that the Mexican land is explosive, fiery, and hostile. The passivity of the Mexican appears therefore to be a compensation for the land's violence—but the violence within; for the land's hostility —but the hostility, the aggressiveness within.

The great age of the Mexican cultures was the millennium before the coming and spreading of the Aztecs (in the thirteenth and fourteenth centuries). It was a time of predominant peace. There were wars about hegemony, about valleys, dynastic disputes—but they were minor. And the arts flourished, almost without change, once the definitive form was found. There are indeed some extraordinary variants. In the sculpture of Monte Albán and the Totanec, for example, there are figures that seem Semitic, bearded; there are displays of the genitals unknown to the chaste Mexican tradition. They remain eccentric, do not *faire école*, as the French put it. The social customs also were not liquid. Invention lagged, where discovery of a harmonious way of life had been established. The grace of the Indian woman expressed this. (She still has it.) It is a grace of passivity within life, informed by a positive knowledge of one's part in it. The men have insecurities; it was they, surely, who conceived the sacrificial mystery to storm their place in cosmos. And the women permit it; self-assertion against their men is not their way of self-realization. In them is the key to the pregnant passivity of the great Indian cultures.

I think of the Tehuanas, the women of Tehuantepec, who, until the Pan American Highway recently broke their privacy, used to bathe twice daily and nude in their river. Strong, stately, indeed magnificent women! Their feet, never tortured into shoe or sandal, hold them erect, and their breasts are erect even after the nursing of many children. Their social order seems matriarchal; it is as if they had usurped men's ways. Thus, it is they, decent matrons, who are permitted to flirt in the *mercado*, not their husbands. It is they who express possessive jealousy of their men, not granting them their privilege of bathing naked in the river; they who may drink too much on festive nights, when they keep stern eyes on their husbands. But is this deeply a reversal of the Mexican's role? I think not. The women positively express the passivity of the culture.

Or I think of the town of Juchitán, a few miles to the east, which must have changed little since the Conquest. It still has the spread and sprawl of the Indian city (or the Oriental city), built like a coral colony with no articulate organic pattern beyond accumulation. Its expanse of low 'dobe houses, recessed from streets dusty or muddy within a wreath of flowering trees, seems interminable, although the town's population is barely twenty thousand. Here I stayed in the home of the *cacique*, local chieftain. The sense of the place is that the patios come first, the walls and ceilings (if any) docilely follow. And the whole is drenched in the atmosphere of women. Sure, the cacique is boss, but the women by their nature of women—wife, household servants, family, rule the boss. Do they actually outnumber the men? It seems so. There are dogs and cats, too; but the reigning household pet is a tame deer. He has the freedom of the patios, and he judges the guests. He sniffed me, as I reclined in my *chinchorro*, as a German police dog, bred to gentleness, might do. Then he squatted below me, sign that I had "passed." He was at home in the house, as the house and Juchitán are at home on the Isthmus.

Pre-Columbian Mexico is riddled with unanswered questions. Where did the great Toltecs vanish? Why did the Mayans move, abandoning their sumptuous cities in the south to build new ones in the north? Whence the seemingly Semitic beards in the sculptures of Monte Alban, the apparently Egypt-inspired woman of Chac-Mool in Chichén Itzá, the lotos blossom on Mayan friezes, the Hindu motifs, the near-replicas of Cambodia? "How come" the wild maize which, cultivated, became the Indian's staff of life, has never been found on the continent that gave us the potato, the sweet potato, the pepper, the tomato, the avocado, the squash, manioc, bean, cacao, pineapple, guava, quinine, coca, and tobacco? Where did the people come from: Were they Australoid? And their leaders? Is there a point in the guess of Harold Sterling Gladwin* that heirs of Alexander the Great in some of Alexander's ships brought the Mediterranean to peoples of far lower cultures? But if so, why did the Indians not work metals until 900 A.D., then suddenly become swift masters of metallurgy, working iron, copper, zinc, lead, tin, silver, gold and gold-lining with techniques more advanced than contemporary Europe's? Perhaps the greatest mystery of all is the grace of the Indian woman. Unanswered questions! All the more important, therefore, that we comprehend the psychology of the Mexican today. And for this we must understand the Aztec. . . .

* See his delightful book: *Men Out of Asia*, Whittlesey House, 1947.

The Aztecs emerge about 1200 A.D. into central Mexico. They had lived on the huge periphery to the north; and before their arrival Teotihuacán and Cholula are already ruins, the Zapotecs in Oaxaca are past their prime, and of the Mayan cities only a few in Yucatán survive to fight a flickering rear-guard action with inward decay and with the Aztecs.

The Aztecs are warriors and great adapters. They "collect" gods. When they defeat a tribe, they take over its divinity and take care of him, which means that they provide him with a satisfactory diet of human victims. At the time of their twilight, the Aztecs were officially sacrificing to over two thousand gods, all hungry for human hearts because the hearts of the Aztecs were anxious. The Romans "allowed" the gods of their conquered peoples. They were willing to have Jehovah, when the Jews were conquered, build his temple in Rome. What they could not tolerate was the intolerance of any god toward other gods. The Romans widened their pantheon with tolerance; the Aztecs greedily collected gods because they were worried.

Loose analogy is made between the empire of Rome and the "empire" of the Aztecs; it is legitimate only if it is clear. The Romans took over lands far beyond Rome in culture: Greece, Egypt, Judea, Persia. Likewise the Aztecs conquered ancient and superior cultures. The Romans, wherever their legions prevailed, established law and political command. The Aztecs confined themselves to some form of tribute. They did not even control the great Mexican fairs. They were not interested in an overspreading political instrument for stability and production. They were not interested in peace. Here we come to a vital difference. The Romans wanted peace—Pax Romana; and to achieve it exploited their legal genius, their genius for building, with a vast tolerance for the metaphysics of others. The Aztecs wanted only the product of their mastered tribes, and what they came to want most was bodies . . . living bodies. For this, they needed wars; restricted, systematic wars. They called them "the flowered wars," and they dominated Aztec politics, foreign and domestic, Aztec economy, Aztec mores.

The Aztecs did not equal their predecessors, not in the arts, not in science. They made no social structures comparable to Tahuantinsuyu, the communist commonwealth of the Incas in Peru. But their inferiorities have been inflated, unjustly. Their hieroglyph writing rivaled the Mixtec and Mayan from which it was derived. Their temples and palaces were impressive. In the small arts, goldsmith work, feather work, ceramics, jade carving, mosaics of jade, lignite, turquoise, they were unsurpassed. They were precisionists. Their capital city of Tenochtitlán, set on man-made land in Lake Texcoco and joined to the valley by great causeways, would have impressed the builders of Rome's aqueducts and coliseums. The Aztecs were extroverts in a consortium of introverts; they were prosemen in a community of poets. Did they feel inferior? There was a frenzy in their successful campaigns which suppressed its own meaning. We have seen how the human sacrifice, in the other cultures, was held to the rarity of an infrequent rite, to the dimensions of a symbol. The Aztecs debauched it into habit and obsession. In one campaign at the south, it was said, seventy thousand victims were led back for the obsidian knife. The first Spanish chroniclers speak of "hills of skulls," of priestly abattoirs reeking with butchery. This doubtless was a last phase. It set its stamp on the mind of the whole country.*

With wars of normal aggression set aside, wars of normal defense also became denatured. The army of Montezuma, among other reasons we shall understand, lost because it was more concerned in taking captives alive than in eliminating Spaniards. And the flowered wars had distilled in all the nations whose men were periodically "taxed" as victims a hate so firm that Cortés had only to appear on the coast to be overwhelmed with allies.

Long before the arrival of the Spaniard, the Aztecs were a neurotic people. They were abhorred by their subjugated neighbors; but even more important, they abhorred their own conduct. They bred anxieties, met these anxieties with a repulsive practice which multiplied anxieties. The face transfigured to the god's became the mirror in which they saw their own exclusion from the god. The heart devoured by their priests, before it had stopped beating, fed their appetite, fed their need to be free of their appetite, and made the need impossible of fulfillment.

There are events in history which after the fact become symbols of some vast design. Thus, the Spaniards' conquest of Mexico and Peru. In 1519, Hernán Cortés landed near what is now Vera Cruz. He had

* The use of drugs in their religious rites was common. Mescaline, which in Aztec was called *teonatacatl*, was employed to induce visions.

with him about a dozen ships, five hundred men in coats of mail, sixteen horses, and ten brass artillery guns. He had far more. His men were certain that their souls were immortal and that they were destined to possess the earth. Metaphysically, they feared no heathen. Nevertheless, Cortés made sure by burning his ships, lest they be tempted to sail back to Cuba. For in fact, the Spaniards, hugely outnumbered in an unknown land, were frightened. This made them cruel. But they were also secure as Christians convinced that their lusting egos were the chosen vessels of God's grace. This made them shrewd. What the Spaniards had above all to aid them was the confusion of the Mexicans. Beside such allies as the Totonecs, a folk of high culture, and the Tlaxcalans, Cortés had to help him the inner conflicts of the Aztec ruler. Genius of diplomacy, Cortés sensed this when Montezuma sent down ambassadors with rich gifts but forbade the Spaniard's approach to Tenochtitlán. If the visitor was welcome, why shut him out? If he was a foe, why send him gifts?

The Aztec ruler sensed his own doom. For years his soothsayers had prophesied disaster to his generation. The expectancy of the "white gods coming from the East" may have been a *post facto* addition perhaps to an ancient story. Surely the Aztecs recognized with masochist lust the downfall of their flimsy empire which was devouring its own manhood. That the Mexicans expected the white gods may not have been true; that firing guns and mounted horses impressed them superstitiously at first may well have been. But that religious terror brought the defeat is nonsense. The Spaniard, once observed, very soon convinced the observer that under his armor he was human . . . very human. He had a lust for gold which disgusted the Mexicans; an excessive sexual lust which nauseated the submissive Indian women. (There are reports of this from Mexico south to Paraguay.) Montezuma himself, who had feared them as if they were a symptom of the national neurosis, came to despise the Spaniards. Thus finally, on the *noche triste*, when the Aztecs rose to throw them out, they were already enclaved in Tenochtitlán. It was far too late. An incision had been made and the virulent spirit of Spain had entered the body of America. Factually, militarily, by his treacherous conquest of the Aztec capital, Cortés with his Spanish reinforcements commanded the central Mexican plateau. But the event was infinitely deeper. Cities have been conquered by aliens before and the victors absorbed in the spirit and body of the victims. What happened in Mexico is symbolized in the relation of Cortés with the Nahua woman, Malintzín, who became his mistress. She interpreted for him, she revealed his potential allies, she explained to him the intricate Aztec politics, the nature of the country and of its dwellers. She was intelligent. But far more vitally, she was loyal to Cortés. Perhaps as she served him, she hated him. Who can say? The crux is that she loved him.

3. NEW SPAIN

When Cortés smashed his first Mexican idol, replacing it with the cross, the people, perhaps struck by his vehemence, were not troubled; for the cross was the symbol of Tlaloc, rain god, and without rain indeed the people perish. The crude analogy between the Eucharist and the Mexican sacrifice with its ceremonial eating of the god's heart was already observed by the first chroniclers of Spain who told the Most Catholic Court in Madrid that the Indians must be Israel's Lost Tribe, for they had stumbled upon "an ignorant makeshift of the Host." The story of Spain's Mexican "kingdom" for its whole three hundred years was a tissue of such ambiguities. More rational, Spain's Mexican life would have been less living. The young organism dispenses with reason, which comes later . . . long, long later. The ambiguities of Spain in Mexico were those of a tough forming organism. Thus, the relation between the Christian and Mexican religions. Thus, the lust of the Spaniard for gold and woman; the fear of the Spaniard, making him cruel; and at the same time his tenderness, his deep human acceptance of the Indian, because the Spaniard in his values, if not deeds, was profoundly Christian.

Within this dark womb of contradictions grew the fecundity of Spain's rule in the Americas. Indians were enslaved, thrust in the mines until they died. Women also were enslaved, even when married. Yet Spain's noble labor laws to protect the Indian worker had human meaning. The theory of the *encomienda* was a holding of land by the Spaniard in paternal responsibility and trust for the spiritual and physical welfare of the Indian. Until baptized, he was "a minor" with the Spaniard for his guardian. Such men as Francisco de Victoria and Bartolomé de Las Casas went farther, allowing Spain no right in the

Americas at all, except as voluntarily accepted missionaries of the spirit! All this was made a mockery, often enough for mockery to be the rule. The Spanish Christian premise was that the Indian was an equal under Christ; the actuality was exploitation. But tenderness was never wholly absent; the Spaniard who sent the Indian to his death for gold made the Indian know he was his brother. The Spaniard who forced the Indian maid made her feel in his arms a sacrament of union. These contradictions are the murky medium of the Spanish Conquest.

Only thus can be explained the paradox of Spain's brutal but fertile marriage with Mexico. Tenochtitlán was burned, idols that were great sculpture were ground to dust, codices of history and astronomy were destroyed; temples and the mounds of pyramids that once had led the devout up toward the free air were used for the foundations of basilicas and chapels (Cholula claimed 365 churches, one for each day of the year). Within two generations, a new ethnic and cultural chaos had been born in Mexico, a chaos which was the *materia prima* for creation.

All this is revealed in Mexico's colonial arts. The Mexican had chaos within him; as man he needed the health of order and of wholeness; and he needed to construct it from the materials at hand. This is the process of the artist. He inherits chaos, within him because of his passions, outside him because he sees the external world in terms of his needs and passions. He constructs a complex unity in which he can emotionally enter . . . in which others can emotionally enter. That is art, that is the genesis of the work of the artist. A man, a nation, which had no discords, no chaos hungering to become whole, would have no art. Whether such a nation could exist is a moot question. It hardly arises in fiery, violent, extreme, and aspiring Mexico.

These colonial arts were of course directly derived from Spain. The most urgent of them were the arts of building: churches, palaces, dwellings, sculptures, frescoes, arts for domestic uses. Spain gave the rules, Spain had the methods. Yet literally, at once, the arts of Mexico were distinct from Spain's. The new church was baroque . . . Spanish in plan and in doctrine. But the baroque became Mexican; the doctrine became Mexican, in its application, also. The colonial arts of Mexico—more precisely, the arts of the "Kingdom of New Spain"—are of a splendor and a profusion, of a reckless flow of energy and resources, which cannot be even hinted within the frame of this essay. We can stress only the vital life which they revealed. And do not assume these were "upper-class arts." The designers, the models, were certainly at first Spanish, as the first priests of course were from Spain. This ceased to be long before the eighteenth century, when mestizo Mexico was able to provide its own artists and pastors. But almost at once, upon the Conquest, the cutters of stone, the actual carpenters and glaziers, the makers of the art, had been Indians . . . sons of the folk, imbued with Christian feelings, part Spanish, part Indian, wholly neither . . . therefore *mestizo*.

I must resist the temptation to discuss the great arts of Spain's Mexican "kingdom"; works that were never Spanish and yet not Mexican in the modern or the pre-Columbian sense. I think of a church such as Santo Domingo in Oaxaca: the two great tiled domes singing against the mountain behind them, lush and tender as a woman's breasts above the fortress-body; the polychrome sculptures and ornaments within, gold and purples flowing from walls to ceiling. What does such a structure mean? Vast vitality, here poured into the intricate designs of worship, as later into the almost equally complex instrument board of a modern airplane: a design of another, shallower form of flight. Or I think of a dwelling: let us say Number One of Third Avenue East in the city of Puebla. A stone portico threshold with three bas-relief compositions carved in it, soft-textured and fluid as a Bayeux tapestry, yet with a complex introverted music like the Mayan; and a simple outdoor stair which humble people mount to simple bedrooms. Sometimes the ornament is overwhelming, as in Santo Domingo or San Francisco of Puebla, reminding one of the machines of an automotive factory—but of course totally without the pragmatic purpose. Sometimes the power is in the bare basic structure, as in the convent of San Agustín Acolman (near Teotihuacán), where the plateresque carvings and warm frescoes seem to serve only to lead one into a womb of shut, saturnine, silently brooding life.

Let me note here only that these are *collective* works. The intellectual element is tied to Spain, to its monarchy and Apostolic Church, which sought to preserve the Middle Ages. This was already out of date, with a new world shaping in Europe's Northwest. The fertile in these arts was by and of the people who are never "out of date." Plangent and plaintive song, silverwork, lacquer, ceramic, the inimitable "Judases" each to be cast in the bonfire on All Saints' Day, and each an individual: They are the folk's, because the folk under Spain received a fundamental nurture. And when one bears in mind the injustices and corruptions of the King's regime, one can decide only that the nutrition was of the spirit, and that it was in spite of social-intellectual conditions. The Church in Spain has many sins on its conscience; all the more reason to record its spiritual triumph.

The economy of the Mexicans from time immemorial had been a balance of forces, low in dynamics but stable. An agricultural economy. The people grew maize, beans, pepper, chocolate; they hunted wild game; they produced handmade goods, most of them exquisite rather than enduring. All these they bartered. Trade reached as far south as the Andes of the Incas. Nobody starved or was rich, although the differing fertility of valleys made a difference between tribes. Soil exhaustion sometimes caused migration, and migration could cause a war. But a humble, static order. The Aztecs overthrew it. With the Spaniards, even the residual balance of the economy and of its state of mind vanished.

The lands had been communal, with work allotments to each family. Now they belonged to mighty *haciendados*, thousands and hundreds of thousands of acres to one master. Among the richest landowners was the Church. And of course the balance of barter was gone. Everything Spain, and with Spain as broker everything Europe valued, was sluiced out of the country; what could not be exported, the rich *terrateniente* put to his own use or (more frequently) wasted. The Indian, reduced to peonage, had barely enough frijoles, chile, tortilla to keep him alive. Under Spain, it is safe to say that ninety percent of the Mexicans suffered some form of malnutrition. The *Nuevas Leyes de Indias* (1542) were the most advanced social legislation known to the world before the nineteenth century. The attempt to enforce them cost a Viceroy in Peru his life; a Viceroy of Mexico was expelled. The "Kingdom of New Spain" went its own way, despite the Christianity of the home Court in Madrid. The Mexican landlord read the laws for the defense of the Indian, heard thundering blame of the priests against his practices, and quietly said: *Obedezco, pero no cumplo.* "I obey, but do not carry out."

On his festive day, Huitzilopochtli had required a ration of twenty thousand hearts torn pulsing from the breast. But this voracious god of war and the hot sun was also the gentle "humming-bird wizard," symbolic of the balance here on earth against earth's violence. The Spaniards shattered this organic harmony. Christianity compensated for earthly violence with unearthly peace. This deep imbalance runs like a lesion through the whole subsequent Mexican story.

Spain wielded a vast negative control. It monopolized all trade and intercourse of its American possessions, which were separate and kept isolate one from another, not only by the mountains, desert, jungles but by the strict rule forbidding intercommunication. No ship but Spain's touched a port; without special license from the King no alien visitor was admitted. A world of intellectual and social experiment was in birth, northward and across the Atlantic: social contract in lieu of caste status, free-wheeling capital, government by the governed. Spain's Americas were shut away from all this by every device of the rulers, secular and ecclesiastic. The shell of Church and State protected the inward lethargies, injustices, and corruptions of the ruling classes.

This is an accurate picture of Mexico for the three centuries of its conquest and settlement by the Spaniards. Although every point of it is fact, it is a partial and false picture. It fails to take account of the Mexican's inward life during this epoch. A merely exploited folk, a folk wholly enslaved, wholly absorbed by the inhumanity of its masters, a folk entirely malnourished and prone, could not have filled the vast hostile land with objects of beauty, with exhibits of spiritual knowledge. A people may complacently possess freedom political and economic, and be inwardly sterilized and enslaved by the drives of mechanical production. On the contrary, a people that submitted to economic peonage might retain intercourse free and creative with self, with soil, with God. Thus it was with Mexico, in the colonial era. The owners of vast ranches ground them as the *metate* ground the corn, but they were clear of the blood-cult of the Aztecs, and the love of Christ and His saints made them a community of freedom.

The arts of the colonial age, subtly or overwhelmingly Mexican despite their frequent Hispanic model, express the vital spirit of the Mexicans under their subjection. But it is revealed most poignantly in the common peasant life. The man may still be illiterate; probably he still wears ragged pajamas, a poncho against the cold, a huge hand-woven straw hat against the heat. His wife sits on the *mercado* pavement, with flowers for sale. To whom does she sell the fragile, useless blossoms? To men and women poor as she is. Here is a woman with ten centavos left over, after she has bought her corn and beans. She spends it on a gardenia which she takes home. Her home is a one-room hut of 'dobe with a thatch roof and a dirt floor. She places her blossom on the table. It is as much her daily bread as her tortilla. Next week, the same woman will buy another blossom and carry it, not to her house but to her church, a towering fortress-structure above her village, with walls and ceilings of wrought gold and *gesso* colored sculpture. You may tell this woman that the wealth of her church is the blood of the labor of the poor, like herself; that offering her flower to a Saint is wasteful superstition; and that her priest would do better to teach her how to read. But she feels that her resplendent church is her own.

I recall a small moment of my first trip to Mexico, more than a generation ago, whose meaning has never faded. With Diego Rivera, the painter, I had accompanied a "cultural mission" into the State of Guerrero southwest of the capital. These Federal "teams" consisted usually of a physician, a trained nurse, a dietitian, a teacher, and an agronomist. They visited a village for several days, made friends, tried to help solve problems. I had slept on the bare bench of the little village school, and by 5 A.M. the wood was so iron hard, the air so icy cold, that I was glad to get up. Above the village, which was itself in a valley a mile and a half above the level of the Pacific Ocean, a hill rose steeply. I climbed it to meet the rising sun. It was not yet visible, but by its iridescent forelight the trees made the folds of mountain and valley rugose like the skin of some huge hairy mammoth. The mountains eastward and northward lay terraced and staggered, and as the light grew there was a vista far beyond them of verdant plain and of dim church towers, sensed as if in a dream as they dimly tolled the hour of the day's first call to worship. Now the sun burst forth. I saw a summit snow-covered, a vast snow shadow, with the Mexican earth beneath, dynamic and swiftly warming with the sun. And then suddenly I saw that someone stood beside me.

He had his huge hat in his hand; he had come silently on bare, calloused feet, to stand beside me. When he saw that I saw him, he nodded and chuckled, and looked again at the scene we were sharing. He spoke no word, I spoke no word. His attention was at least half as much on me as on the view; and it was manifest that he was pleased. His mind, content, was clear: I was a stranger; I was looking on his Mexican land in reverence, and this pleased him. He was sharing my pleasure. No more. Still silent, we walked down the hill together.

The man who could participate in such a sacrament of recognition with a stranger, relaxed, at ease, enjoying the other's enjoyment with no need to explain, to hide or to assert . . . this was a man of culture! Such men, if common now, must have been common in the colonial era. The Aztec tension had been challenged by a new security of the spirit. This, a creative contribution of Spain, must be acknowledged. Spain, with all its sins of commission and omission, with its own blood, its own passion, created in America a new human potential.

Mark the word "potential." It is important for understanding the century and a half of revolution which began in Mexico in 1810 and is not yet finished. Man cannot live by bread alone; this axiom the Mexican never ignored. But that man cannot live without bread was the axiom Spain neglected. The truth, however, is subtler. Bread, the growing it, the spirit beyond bread in which the bread is eaten . . . are intermingled in healthy and whole man. When the making of bread wants social and psychological practices which feed the human spirit; and when the human spirit wants contact with the economic forms of the bread's distribution, there is discord. A basic fault comes in to man's social body like the fault in earth which causes earthquake. This seismic shift in Mexico began in 1810 with the movement toward independence from Spain. It continued after a century's tragic trial-and-error, in 1910, as a social revolution.

4. The Era of Revolution

Nothing in human existence is simple, but the complexity of Mexico in every phase of its life is overwhelming. The synthesis of Mexican, Spaniard, and Indian makes both war and harmony. One would think that the Mexican war of independence from Spain must have been a simple affair: on the one side the King, his bureaucrats, the landowners, the Church (the largest landowner of all), and of course their servants, legal and domestic; on the other side the peasant who owned only the rags on his back, and the urban middle class who wanted for themselves the prizes, reserved for Spaniards, of government and trade. Something comparatively simple, like the war of our Thirteen Colonies? Far from it. Imagine a jigsaw puzzle, each of whose pieces is somehow magnetized positively or negatively by others which in turn have their charges transformed by still other pieces: the ultimate picture to be entitled *Chaos!* There were Mexicans who fought Napoleon's brother, Joseph, King of Spain, because they were loyal to Fernando VII, not because they were republicans. There were liberals who accepted the Napoleonic empire because for the moment Spain had the most progressive constitution in Europe. There were fighters for independence who were reactionaries and wanted an empire in Mexico. There was a conservative Church, but also there were in it radical priests who led revolutionary armies.

Do not look for the plain battle fronts of Washington, Bolívar, San Martín. The disorders which broke forth in 1810 brought the exclusion of Spain and Mexico's independence, not as the result of specific purposeful campaigns, but because, as the turmoil deepened, it became obvious that Spain as a political factor no longer validly existed in Mexico. Politically, *Spain was not there:* this, the one clear datum in the puzzle. Mexican was fighting Mexican, each with a slogan that could mean collision with residual Spanish forces, because it was liberal or because it was nationalistic. But whatever the slogan, at the end Mexican was still fighting Mexican, and Spain was there no longer.

The one way to see Mexico's war of independence with clarity is to study its leaders. Like the characters of a play, each stands for a concrete will, clashing with others to make the story. Mexico becomes— and has remained—a drama.

The first visible person on the scene is Hidalgo: Miguel Hidalgo y Castillo, a parish priest of Dolores, a village near Querétaro. Like so many of his generation, he had read the books of the eighteenth century forbidden by his Church; indeed he had fallen into the habit of breaking Church rules in his many little efforts to help the poor of his parish. Before he knew properly what he was doing, Hidalgo was part of a conspiratorial group, and when the news came that Spanish soldiers were on their way to arrest him, he made a quick decision: rather than arrest, rebellion. With the spontaneous speed of a vision, thousands suddenly joined him and he was the head of an improvised

25. An ancient pyramid at Chichén Itzá in Yucatán.

26. In the market place at Cholula.

27. A Mexican farmer admiring his crop of hybrid corn.

28. Taxco and its cathedral. Taxco, famous for its silver mines since early in the eighteenth century, keeps its old atmosphere by restricting new building to old and appropriate architectural patterns. Tourists love it, and have not yet succeeded in spoiling it.

29. A local bus on the Pan American Highway south of Laredo. In and on vehicles like this ride Mexicans of all ages, with their possessions animate and inanimate. Noise and confusion, yes; but never grumbling, never discourtesy to strangers.

Sargent F. Collier

30.   Jogging along placidly on the road to Acapulco.

31. A United States-sponsored library in Mexico City.

2. The Library and Museum in Hermosillo. Latest reported population, about 20,000!

3. A theater building in Mexico City, showing a late major work of Diego Rivera.

Galloway

34. The Zocalo Plaza and the Cathedral, Mexico City.

35. A modern school in Mazatlán.

army . . . soon, a victorious army; and he, who had never soldiered before, was sixty! They marched on the capital. As they approached, and the Viceroy prepared to flee for his life, doubts corroded the conscience of Hidalgo. What if his soldiers looted, burned, assaulted? He gave the order to retreat; and with it his magic ended. Thousands disbanded. The Church of course condemned him, and Hidalgo suffered. It took one pitched battle, fought according to the rules of Europe, to rout him. He was captured, and before the hierarchy and officials he was clad for the last time in his sacerdotal robes, which were then ripped from his flesh, and the man stood naked. He was asked did he repent, and he affirmed that he did. Mexico, he declared over his signature, was not ripe for freedom. While the nuns, the padres, and the pious servants of the King prayed, the firing squad closed the loving life of Miguel Hidalgo.

The play's next protagonist is José María Morelos, a stronger man, an even humbler priest. He was a peon until he was twenty-five, when he worked his way through the church college of San Nicolás. Chronic malaria and malnutrition stunted his squat body (he was barely five feet in height). But the man had genius; he trained soldiers, he trained good officers. When Hidalgo was taken, Morelos captained an army of ten thousand who escaped destruction. By mid-1813, almost all Mexico was his. He had a developed social program, and he called the Congress of Chilpancingo to enact it into law.

Rousseau, Diderot, Condorcet, even Voltaire had formed his convictions; but the man who wanted to enforce them because he loved his people was a Christian, a devoted priest, who prayed and said Mass before he entered battle. Despite his piety—or because of it?—Morelos proposed to strip the land from the Church, their accumulated gold from the wealthy; half would go direct to the poor to buy them land, seed grain, and tools, half to government expenses: schools, hospitals, roads. The Colony had set up *fueros*, privileges, by which churchman and official were practically outside and above the law. Morelos wiped them away.

Here, then, in 1813, was a Mexican program, and a victorious revolutionary army, captained by an incorruptible leader, to start work. But nothing so simple and so happy could arise from the Mexico of that hour. The radical program of Morelos solidified the opposition. It had been stunned and dispersed by Hidalgo. Now it hardened . . .

State, Church, Land, and Gold . . . behind new reactionary leaders.

The first of these was Agustín de Iturbide, an upper-class mestizo who claimed to be pure-blooded creole. His rise to power was as devious as the weaving of a spider. He made a practice of having the disciples of Morelos murdered in the villages. He sold "protection" to the silver mines, taking part of the shipments of bullion as his "cut" and using the money to curry favor with the Generals. In brief, he was racketeer and gangster, but he was also charming and persuasive, particularly when he negotiated with the princes of the Church. He defeated Morelos and proclaimed a nationalist program. Morelos was taken prisoner and shot—outside the city where the folk who loved him would not know. (The turnkey wanted to help him escape. "No," said Morelos. "It would get you into trouble.") Following closely as he could the pattern of Napoleon's coronation, Iturbide had himself crowned emperor of Mexico. But he lacked the talent for his overweening ambition; got into difficulties at once with his Congress and with his money-craving Generals; and within the year he had to escape to Europe. When he returned for another try, he was captured and shot.

He already had a "republican" successor: Antonio López de Santa Anna, who got himself elected President of Mexico no less than nine times from 1833 to 1855. Santa Anna liked to be addressed as "Su Alteza Seren íssima," possibly because he was neither exalted nor serene; and because these were bitter decades for his country, he has been unjustly blamed as the architect of its disaster, whereas in truth Santa Anna architected nothing. He was a charming man; the Generals rose to his call and the peons, on command, cried *Viva!* He was short, with dark, large, velvet, brooding eyes which could flash fire, and a 'cello voice which, I'm afraid, had nothing to say. Like Iturbide, he was a sad clown, a farcical victim of his own ignorance of his country. He represented, in the play, the wrongness of Mexico's seeking to imitate the political institutions of the great Anglo-Saxon republic, as Iturbide personified Mexico's unfitness to become a European monarchy. Ignorance of Mexican reality was the keynote of their failures.

Of course, Santa Anna should not be blamed for Mexico's loss of its northern lands. By 1830 Texas had a population of 30,000 "Anglo-Saxon homesteaders" who far outnumbered the sparse Mexican ranchers and herders. These technical citizens of the Mexican State of Coahuila owned slaves, and wanted to invest the land with their own way of life. In 1829 the Mexican Republic abolished slavery, and it was already gone from all its territories except Texas. The naive Mexican legislators thought that by making slavery illegal in Texas they would discourage the "gringos" from coming in. Their strategy sealed Mexico's loss of Texas; one might say it revealed the already established fact that Texas and California had left the Mexican orbit.

Now came the turn of the successor of Hidalgo and Morelos: Benito Juárez, one of the most remarkable of modern men. Juárez came from the cold mountains near Oaxaca now named after him: the bleak Sierra de Juárez, where the Indians still live miserably upon an earth teeming with unexploited wealth. The father of Benito was of the poorest peasants. When the boy carried the farm's produce to market, he noted the splendor of the churches as he passed, bearing his burden; and resented them. He was a bright child, the kind who in Catholic countries may receive an education gratis from the Church —and perhaps become a Bishop. Juárez got his seminary training, studied law, and turned against the institution which had taught him. His rugged honesty, his clear head, and his warm heart won him friends. He was elected Governor of Oaxaca.

Mexico had not recovered from Santa Anna and the American invasion. Each valley burgeoned little local leaders who tore the land apart. There was open talk of secession; Yucatán seriously considered offering its statehood to the United States. In Europe, ambitious men such as Napoleon III were already savoring the ripe fruit of Mexico, ready to fall into their hands—and how could the riven United States prevent it? One might have truthfully said that Benito Juárez became constitutional President of Mexico by default; he was obscure, small, inconspicuous, but when he looked you in the eye and spoke, you were impressed and enlisted. In 1860, something similar was to occur in the North when the nation, rent in two, turned for leadership and salvation—blindly turned—toward a little-known minority politician named Abraham Lincoln.

As usual, Mexico's crisis was more mixed. Instead of a dominant dissenting section threatening the Union from the South, every town in Mexico had factions whose differences, perpendicular and crucial, struck at the heart of the nation. A new bourgeois leadership chal-

lenged the obsolete hegemony of the Church, the creoles (the purely
Spanish), and the mestizo landowners. But the peasants, although
with no champions and no leaders, were also present. The tensions
therefore were multiple.

More complex also was Mexico's external situation. Europe's powers, it was true, looked on the simmering "irrepressible conflict" in the
North as prelude to the breakup of the Union, but they kept hands
off, although with greedy and with ready eyes. Poor Juárez, whose sole
"capitol" was often the black coach in which he escaped from town
to town, had to face the ugly fact of British, French, and Spanish
naval vessels anchored in Vera Cruz. Their pretext was that they had
come to collect government debts. Juárez managed somehow to persuade the British and the Spaniards to take their ships away with his
promise that the money would be paid. The French army, sent by
Napoleon III, marched deep into the country and Juárez withdrew
northward. At one time, the President of Mexico was a fugitive in
Louisiana, while the French hobnobbed with the Bishops in Mexico
City. The one comfort for Juárez was that he was sure the Church
would learn the delusion of its belief that Napoleon had sent an army
to Mexico for the sake of the Church! Napoleon's plan, of course,
was to set up an empire in Mexico that would be under his thumb,
and from which he could work north and south till all the Americas
were his. Someday, Juárez was hopeful, the United States would know
this, and act.*

Meantime, to this desperate hour, so much more perilous than
Lincoln's who could keep his eye on the Southern armies as his main
objective, the amazing little Indian replied with an offensive. He issued his famous laws of *La Reforma* (1857). By them, the Church lost
its lands and all real estate except the actual church buildings; con-
vents and monasteries were abolished; the confiscated land was par-
celed in small lots for the individual peasants. Of course, it didn't
work; a poor man needs more than land to be a farmer; he needs funds
and tools and education. All too soon, the already rich had bought
out the poor, forming a new capitalist class, with the Church soon
again leading. But the moral effect of *La Reforma* endured. Most of
the illiterate Indians had known no central organism but the Church;

---

* Immediately after Appomattox, Lincoln told the French and, indirectly,
Maximilian to get out.

now they began to know the nation. Juárez' war against the French and against Maximilian, Napoleon's puppet emperor, was Mexico's true "war of independence." Its master was the little swarthy lawyer who loved his people and whose moral grandeur, they learned, was at the people's service.

Maximilian belongs with the tragic-comedians in this drama. Like Iturbide and Santa Anna, he wrought in a vast ignorance of Mexico. Archduke, brother of the Austrian emperor, he readily assumed that the "lesser continents" should wish to be ruled by Europe—and Europe of course by the Habsburgs. Therefore he believed the Plebiscite to be authentic, which showed the majority of the Mexicans to have wanted him for their ruler. He had insisted on this "evidence" and Napoleon and the Church obligingly had arranged it. He came, overflowing with good will for his dear Mexican people. He was naive, fatuous, pedantic, extravagant, and loyal. Weren't the Mexican streets paved with gold? Did he not, shortly after his arrival, write a letter to his foe, Juárez, suggesting a friendly "conference?" On his way across the Atlantic, he had compiled a Book of Etiquette for his Court. When his reception by the populace in Vera Cruz proved less than deafening, he was sure the reason was the people's ignorance, not his own. Or was it bad manners? It did not occur to Maximilian that in accepting to be the monarch of an American people at the behest of a Frenchman, it was *his* manners that were bad.

When the French forces that sustained him withdrew (Napoleon wanted no war with the United States, which, to his chagrin, seemed to have survived) Maximilian refused to resign, spending his hours collecting butterflies. When Juárez condemned him to death, he did not believe it. The European monarchs who sent messages pleading for his life did not believe it. He faced the firing squad as a gentleman faces a *malentendu* by a social inferior.

His Empress, Carlotta, had gone to Paris to plead with Napoleon III for stronger intervention in favor of her beloved husband. When the final bad news of his execution arrived, Carlotta became insane. To the end of her days, a wraith in the bright corridors of Versailles, she spoke of the emperor and herself as alive in fabulous happy Mexico. By such notes of the macabre is revealed the gap between Mexican reality and its rulers.

Again, as in the triumphal year of Morelos, Mexico seemed free of its foes, ready to begin. In 1867, Juárez was re-elected President of a united country. But even he was not guiltless of this gap between Mexico and its rulers. As if in response to the extravagant false colors of Maximilian's court, Juárez was always clad in somber black. But black was not Mexico's color. The Puritan black of Juárez expressed a limit to his knowledge of his people that would soon cause trouble.

Juárez was worried about the schools. He resolved to build them, despite the depleted treasury left by Maximilian; but what should they teach? He sent a commission of learned men to Paris to find out the latest and most scientific doctrine of Europe, and they came back with the Positivism of Auguste Comte. This was a creed to end all creeds. The world, it held, had rounded its first two stages: the religious and the metaphysical; and was ready for the third, the reign of "pure science." Reality was what could be mathematically weighed and measured; all else was nonsense. The Indian, the Spaniard, the mestizo had lived for ages in a world of mystery, intricate and beyond the steps of reason; a world whose arts were knowledge, revealing man's link with cosmos. These intuitions had been a trap for superstition, exploitation; but it was not wise of Juárez to appear to attack knowledge because of his hatred of superstition and exploitation. He gave a weapon to the obscurantists, and they have used it.

Comte's Positivism was far too simple, its European idiom was far too narrow, for the tortured, deeply intuitive and mystical Mexican mind. It said nothing to Mexicans. Unfortunately, it took the place of true communication, by rationalizing the abyss between intellectual and peasant. It was too easy for the teacher, the general, the banker, the *politico* to say: "The peasant knows nothing; we must take care of him." Juárez, great as he was, must share the blame of sustaining an attitude of ignorant arrogance in Mexico's leaders toward the people. The humble peasant, in his relation with self, earth, and cosmos, had an incipient knowledge far beyond Positivism. It would take a whole further generation before Mexico would know and build upon this.

When Juárez rode victorious into the capital in 1867, he had dismissed with a few curt words of gratitude the officers who had fought his wars. He feared the soldier, who had been the curse of his country. Among those he snubbed was a brilliant young Mixtec Indian,

Porfirio Díaz. Perhaps this was his own intuition at work, despite his Positivist doctrine.

Juárez was re-elected in 1871, with both Díaz and his old minister, Miguel Lerdo, running against him. No candidate had a majority of the popular vote (proof that Juárez was no dictator); the choice fell to Congress which elected Juárez. Díaz staged one of Mexico's interminable soldier revolts against the ballot and the law; and failed. But in 1872, Juárez died suddenly of a heart attack. Four more years, and Díaz was in power—to remain Mexico's master from 1876 to 1910.*

Mexico was inured to suffering; one might say, recalling the frenzied masochism of the Aztecs, that Mexico loved its pain. Only thus can the dolorous and yet indolent years of the Díaz dictatorship be understood. Díaz was a Positivist, and an Indian. His creed (the Positivists called themselves *los científicos*) made him despise his own people. For if the growth of man had its final peak in the manipulation of figures, each standing for a specific quantitative fact, clearly the European with his mathematical machines was superior to the Mexican; and the best the Mexican could do was to deliver himself over to this European, who could perhaps make something of him— certainly something of his lands, rich with oil and ore. If Díaz despised his fellow Mexican, sure he was serving him by turning his land over to the wild freedom of the foreign investor, it must ensue that Díaz despised himself. This, the key to the Díaz era. Its symbol was the Positivist creed with its implicit contempt for Mexican values and its exaltation of an intellectual idiom in which Mexico had hardly spoken. Its result: paternalism, servile submission to the foreign operator and speculator (British, French, German, increasingly American as the *Porfirista* decades doubled).

Díaz was an extraordinary man. He was not financially corrupt; all he lusted for was power. But he was willing to let his subordinates steal and murder; this kept them satisfied, and also held them in his hands under the constant threat of blackmail by the President. Díaz had a genius for keeping ministers and factions divided, and for using the instrument of exposure when any of them got too independent.

* He was legally elected President for each term, except the period 1880–1884, when he still wielded power.

Perhaps the most cynical and successful of his stratagems was his handling of the Church. On the books, still, were the anticlerical laws of
La Reforma. Juárez had drafted them to use them. Díaz kept them
merely as a threat—in case the Church ever forgot its master. So long
as it was "good," his lawyers showed the Church how to evade the
statutes against property and special rights. And the Church was again
among the great landowners.

What did the priests teach? Loyal submission to the State despite
its Positivist doctrine. Positivism in the schools? Of course. But there
were so few schools it hardly mattered.

The Mexican was an illiterate peon, laboring the field and mine
forever at the level of bare subsistence. Production of course lagged
in such a system. There was no incentive to improve it. And more
and more of the ore-yielding land was sold for a song to the foreign
investor. Díaz and his científicos always got their rake-off, but it was
so ridiculously low that one must conclude either that Díaz and his
crowd had no notion of industrial values or an opinion of themselves
too humble to permit them to sell their country at more than a de-
risory figure. Under the old laws of Spain, the sale of land did not
alienate the King's right to the wealth beneath the surface. Republican theory said the folk was King; but Díaz abrogated the folk's rights,
and virtually extraterritorial towns, privately policed, began to abound
in Mexico . . . producers of great wealth, most of which left the
country.

At the turn of the century, a small group of progressive Christians
protested the exploitation of the people. Díaz put the screws on the
Church leaders who suppressed the good Catholics.

Of course, Mexico took certain progressive steps. Already in the
last years of Juárez, the British had begun to build the spectacular
railway which rises from Vera Cruz on the Gulf over the sweating
jungle, ladders to the moderate zone of Orizaba, and then leaps gorge
and beetling precipice to the mesa 9000 feet above. Railroads were
also coming down through California and Texas. (Díaz did not like
the Americans, but he was too shrewd to antagonize them, recalling
how Washington had weakened his one early rival, Lerdo, when Lerdo
opposed American investments.) There were soon telephones in the
cities—at times rival telephone systems, causing much confusion.
Hotels reasonably modern arose in the capital; roads began to join

valleys that had been accessible only by horse or mule or (earlier) by the Indians' bare feet. Yet a somnolence was upon the land; not deep, dreamless sleep but stagnation.

Mexico's arts during the *Porfirista* years reveal the general state. It was a poor time for architecture in any land, with Mexico no exception; witness the wedding-cake *Palacio de Bellas Artes*, the gingerbread statue of Juárez in the Alameda. Painting was dull academy, dim France or echo of Spain.

Mexico's great voice had never been literary; it is a folk essentially of plastic expression. Now, through the influence of France (to which the nineteenth-century intellectuals turned in their hate for Spain) the modernist poets made a conquest. In the master of the movement, the Nicaraguan Rubén Darío (1867–1916), there is a dynamic surge of energies released from ancient forms for the creating of new ones: Darío is a more erudite, more cultivated Whitman, less bewildered by the new external civilization. The leading Modernists of Mexico, Manuel Gutiérrez Nájera (1859–1895) and Amado Nervo (1870–1919), were but Americans recording ultimate scenes and tinctures of Europe. The Mexican folk arts went on, the basic work in silver, copper, lacquer, straw, and clay—not improved, not visibly failing: gracious, humorous, luminous arts of a gifted, submissive people. Mexico is not primarily a musical nation, although its folk song (particularly that of the State of Jalisco) is poignant and rich. Its bands of singing troubadors, the *marriachi*, so named because they used to play at weddings, kept wandering, with fiddle and guitar, over the paths of the Republic with their *corridos*, up-to-date and ancient spot-news in the shape of ballads. But no great composers appeared to symphonize this melodious outpour.

By 1910, Porfirio Díaz was an old man and his reign as stiff-jointed as he. The revolt against him rose spontaneous, inevitable, widespread—and as programless as the revolt headed by Hidalgo an exact century before. There had been stagnation, a ferment simmering beneath the surface.

Now suddenly, from all the valleys of the nation the people overflowed. They had a slogan, *Tierra y Libertad* ("Land and Liberty"), and they had a patron saint, Francisco Madero, as pure and as unequipped a leader as Hidalgo. Madero, scion of a rich family of land and mine-owning capitalists, was the typical liberal of culture: the kind who tend to flatten economic problems into political, and to solve basic psychological problems with slogans. A new act in Mexico's drama of struggle to emerge into an adequate world of its own was being staged—with Mexico ready to supply the properly expressive actors of its unpreparedness.

Madero had been elected by a majority so immense that the people looked for a miracle, as if they had elected the Virgin of Guadalupe. And nothing happened. The peons were still peons, the Church was still the Church, the Generals were still around, and the mines were still in the arrogant hands of strangers (although Madero mildly had begun to frown on their future expansion, thereby earning the suspicion of the Government in Washington). The American Ambassador, Henry Lane Wilson, was violently opposed to Madero; but I think it doubtful that even Washington's active support could have saved the little idealist from the State of Coahuila.

Soon the Generals were rebelling. The best of them all, General Bernardo Reyes, tried to achieve peace gently by quietly walking up the steps of the Palacio Nacional, where a bullet killed him. The worst of them all, Victoriano Huerta, was the most successful. This monster of drunken sadism and treachery—in an attempt to appease the military—had been appointed Minister of Defense in Madero's Cabinet. He took the President prisoner, and on the pretext that he was trying to escape, had him shot from the rear. He declared the Revolution over, and himself successor to his old master, Díaz.

It all sounds, does it not, like a repeat performance? Superficially, it is. There is analogy, for instance, between Miguel Hidalgo, pious parish priest, and Francisco Madero, Tolstoyan, vegetarian, pacific Christian in action. No new Morelos appeared, no Iturbide, of course; but the old motifs re-asserted themselves in revolutions and counter-revolutions.

From the states south and west of the capital comes Emiliano Zapata, crude Apostolic knight of social justice, leading his peasants to take the land and—unlike Hidalgo, who feared disorder—marching his men into the capital to make law of their new possessions. In the North rises Pancho Villa, flailing and scorching like a rocket out of control and horizontally on the loose.

Villa has been over-chronicled as "the beast" of Mexico's Revolution: as bandit, insatiate lecher, butcher. He was doubtless a tough *hombre,* unschooled as Zapata but with far less interest in planting the fields he took over. His life seems to have known two gestures only: the pull of the trigger for man, the carnal embrace for woman. The North he operated in was semidesert, its Indians had been barbarian or savage. Villa represents this scene of violent nature. Why then did the young intellectuals gather about him? How could such men as José Vasconcelos, Martín Luis Guzmán, Felipe Angeles suffer this bestial sadist who shot prisoners, mingling gore and lust? Did they feel that if Mexico was ever to come into its own, the god Huitzilopochtli must be acknowledged again? That the bloodthirsty men of Villa and Zapata were more legitimate, more creative than the grocers and brokers of Díaz?

To the profound young men of 1910, Villa and Zapata stood for the volcanic land, the volcanic folk who must discover their salvation, not by imitating dead and alien orders, but by the return to their own sources, however bloody, and starting up again from there.

Meantime, the vitality of the Mexican chaos revealed itself by putting forth still another kind of leader. Zapata and Villa had a challenger in Venustiano Carranza. The governor of Coahuila was a slow-moving, homespun civilian, dry-witted and shrewd, more like the cartoons of Uncle Sam, like the cracker-barrel solons of Vermont than the conventional Mexican, although his arched moustache was Latin, his sombrero voluminous as any rancher's. The enemies of military coups all called themselves "constitutionalists," but Carranza had some claim to the title. Man of law and modest property, his small rhetoric was homely. Under him began a true military progress against the Huertas, with such gifted generals as Obregón and Calles (both later to be President). Under him, such enlightened social critics as General Francisco Mújica began to have weight (Mújica's influence was decisive on the young Lázaro Cárdenas). The Constitutional Congress of 1917, called by Carranza but guided by Mújica and other socialist-minded men, established again, this time firmly, the peasant's right to his communal land, the nation's right to the resources within the land, labor's right to organize and to improve its status. A design, under the blood and chaos, begins to assert itself. In 1917, it is still blurred and often blotted out. After all, furious men like Villa and Zapata are its first protagonists. And Mexico is sorely wounded. The railroad tracks are torn, the villages are ravaged, the cattle are dead, the oppressor factories are razed. A decade's action in Mexico has been destruction. North of the Rio Grande, Respectability (headed by such men as William Randolph Hearst whose Mexican lands and mines are threatened) shakes its head prayerfully and deplores that all this good wealth cannot be taken over by a respectable government in Washington. Despite the leaping birth rate, Mexico's population has shrunk. The design is not easy to follow or to further, but it is there; some men consciously, the people instinctively, begin to know it. There has been passivity in Mexican culture—under the Aztecs, under Spain. Now arises the sense that Mexico is destined to create an order of men and of Man, not Indian, not Spanish, not of Western Europe and the United States, but a new creation. The passion of this promise suddenly possesses the best of the men who were young in 1910. . . .

5. THE CREATORS

Early in his career, José Vasconcelos wrote a book, *La Raza Cósmica*, whose thesis was that the Hispano-American peoples, with all the human bloods of the earth's continents within them, are called to create a universal culture. The argument is doubtful. For the cosmic in man is not a quantitative measure, it is not a result of addition but of consciousness; and if there were such a specimen in the world as a "pure-blooded man" he would be no less qualified to express the universal than the most variegated human being. The reader will at once understand what I mean if he considers the experience of cosmic relation which a simple object . . . let us say a flower . . . may give him. This experience will not be enhanced with a more complex, more variegated flower. But as a symbol, the idea of a cosmic race in America was effective, and for many years Vasconcelos was the leader of hopeful youth throughout America Hispana. Psychologically, also, the thesis has value. The man of mixed bloods, if only by suggestion and training, will be aware of the values of his various forefathers and feel their conflict within him. Their existence in his mind and emotions will cause confusion. This in turn will stimulate his need to overcome the confusion, the conflict, by an integrating acceptance. And where else is the way toward cosmic consciousness, toward cosmic participation?

The Mexican folk is agrarian by culture, yet its land is a vast mine. This has opened it to the invasive influence, from the North, of a potent non-agrarian industrial civilization. Only in an economy where both agriculture and industry were transfigured could the Mexican feel deeply at home—and this is a long reach into the future. Consider the complexity of these unexampled problems, and the fact that the mestizo is still an unresolved type is not surprising.

By his European fathers, the Mexican inherits a sense of the individual as the focus of universal value; by his Indian (Asian or African) mothers, his sense is of the tribe or of the earth as focus, with the "absolute" individual as unreal. These dichotomies are deep in Mexican, in all Hispano-American life. Vasconcelos most eloquently recognized them. The young men of 1910 knew once for all the dismal farce of Positivism as a guide to Mexico's future.

When, under Obregón, Vasconcelos became Minister of Education, he set off an explosion of creativity visible round the world. Having torn down the banner of Positivism from the schools, Vasconcelos built hundreds and thousands of new ones. Profoundly religious, always Catholic at heart, he opposed the intellectual as well as the economic hegemony of the Church. The schoolmaster, he said, must replace the priest. It was Vasconcelos who sent the first missions abroad into Mexico's remote valleys. He revolutionized the curriculum, revealing to the Mexican the treasures of India and China, so apposite for the heirs of Toltec, Zapotec, Maya. But the most sensational event was the appearance, sudden as magic, of a group of painting giants. Vasconcelos recognized them, showed them the bare walls of public buildings, and said: "Paint!"

The result was an efflorescence luxuriant as a tropical forest, various as the human fauna of the contradictory land. Diego Rivera, José Clemente Orozco, Siqueiros, Rufino Tamayo, Leopoldo Méndez, Manuel Rodriguez Lozana, Julio Castellanos represented for the world the scores of young, potent artists who in a decade had begun a pictorial record of Mexico's self-possession. For this was the underlying theme of all the pictures on the walls: Rivera's peons revealing the endurance that prevails within submission; Orozco, dynamic, critical, rebellious, transforming the potential energy of Rivera's quiet groups into explosive action. We have no room here for even a glance at the versatile triumphs of Mexican painting (much of it veiled from view by the fame of a few leaders). Let us bear in mind that it was a popular uprising. It went beyond the plastic arts. Mexican music, unlike that of other Hispanic nations, had never—except at the folk source—been distinguished. Now, the musicians joined ranks with the painters: Carlos Chávez, Silvestre Revueltas, perhaps the most eminent among them, integrating aboriginal and mestizo rhythms and moods, rather than themes, into a modern music.

The writers of Mexico have been less successful in drawing the attention of the world. But a novelist, Mariano Azuela (1873–1952), in his somber pictures of revolution and of humble city life; a philosopher, José Vasconcelos (1882–   ) in his passionate autobiographical and polemic volumes; a poet, Alfonso Reyes (1889–   ) in his exquisitely balanced expressions, both verse and prose, of the intricate Mexican temperament, deserve the world's regard. The careers of these three men have been archetypical. Azuela, a practicing physician, in 1910 gave his services to the Revolution; then, as after a conversion, refusing to exploit his opportunities for profit (as if profit were beneath him), hung up his shingle in one of the poorest slums of the capital; and there he practiced and wrote his sedulous, luminous novels. Alfonso Reyes, acknowledged dean of Mexico's men of letters, was twenty-one in 1910. His father was the General Bernardo Reyes, Minister of War under Díaz, who came from exile in 1911 and was shot down as he was "peacefully taking over" to save Mexico from chaos. This tragic end had a profound effect on the son. There is an element of trauma in his stress on the classical in his country's culture: Horace, Virgil, Góngora, as an ordered offset to the native violence. But the disciplined, fine brush uses a palette of primary Mexican colors.

Relative to Reyes' fine-cut work, I think of what the new Mexican architects are doing. They have learned the modern functionalism well, but they transcend it. In their good work, the functional and classic orders are adapted to moods warm beyond those of the nations where functionalism started; one could never mistake this art for that of Italy or France, Sweden, or the United States. These men have utilized Mexico's tropical nature, which is both hot and cold, flexible and fiercely firm. In many of the buildings on the *Paseo de la Reforma*, midtown Mexico City, green vine, cactus, bamboo, flowering jacaranda suffuse the chaste and frozen structures. Something of this contrapuntal tension is in the decorous work of Alfonso Reyes.

For many years, Reyes served his country as a diplomat. And wherever he was stationed, Madrid, Paris, Rio de Janeiro, Buenos Aires, a kind of seminar of Hispano-American culture flourished under his guidance. On the fiftieth anniversary of the publication of his first poems (at the age of fifteen, in a provincial paper of his native Monterrey), the country rose in homage; the newspapers devoted pages, the magazines whole issues to his art, the universities published volumes of appreciative essays, and the appearance of the definitive edition of his complete works began. This response to a man of letters, who has never raised his voice in an inelegant shout, reveals much of Mexico.

Perhaps the career of Vasconcelos reveals most. As a young intellectual barely out of law school, Vasconcelos joined Villa. His book *Indología* recognized that if the Mexican is not European, he is also not of China or Indo-China. There is nothing Mongoloid in the Mexican's treatment of women and children. In China, the child was expendable; girl infants could be destroyed if the family chose, or sold into slavery and concubinage. Women were always minors, bound to husband, husband's father, or—if these died—to their own sons. The great Indian cultures, we have seen, sacrificed man, but not out of economic need or greed; on the contrary, their impulse (which became pathological with the Aztecs) might be called anti-economic, an irrational hostility to being moved by profit. Something of this is in Vasconcelos and his Mexican dislike of our American civilization.

He did not approve of the way the Revolution was going. Far too slowly, the peasants received their land, and even when the *ejido* was theirs again, they lacked the machinery, the funds-credit, the "knowhow" needed for modern farming. Labor was uniting in the cities— and falling into the hands of venal labor leaders, wielding their new-won powers for corrupt and vulgar ends. The Church impressed the Catholic Vasconcelos as un-Christian. And over the land, with its two basic "races" unchanged, the rich and the poor, lorded the new *caciques* such as Calles, hand in hand with the Ambassador of the United States! So Vasconcelos went into politics, ran for President, and—not having the state machinery on his side—was defeated. He was sure he had legally won, and waited in vain for the people to rise and place him in office.

The disappointment of his defeat had a profound effect on Vasconcelos. He had recognized the people's need of new methods, psychological and political, to express and to live its truth. Now, frustrated, he veered vaguely toward an authoritarian Right which betrayed the impulse and the body of all his past works. And this today is Mexico's danger. There are deep similitudes between this passionately endowed man and his country.

If José Vasconcelos is archetypical of his volcanic land in its extremes, let us hope that Lázaro Cárdenas, whose lifework has been to resolve and integrate . . . to polarize . . . Mexico's contradictions, is also archetypical. With Cárdenas, we leave the domain of letters and art; his work has been an exemplary life in action.

He became President in 1934, when he was not yet forty. Calles, the "strong man" of Mexico, chose him for the office because the fervor of the people, despite the drooping Revolution, still needed to be appeased; and Cárdenas as soldier, minister, governor of his native Michoacán, had proved his honesty and devotion. Calles was sure, once he was President, that he would settle down, like them all. The symbolic act of Cárdenas' regime came when Calles interfered and Cárdenas had him bloodlessly escorted by plane out of the country.

Cárdenas revolutionized the methods of governing. He turned governing into *learning*. We have seen how even in Juárez there was a certain ignorance of the people, resulting in the Positivist folly. Cárdenas made his office the instrument of knowing Mexico, and made the people know. "A chief executive," he said to a friend, "should leave the detailed mass of his work to his subordinates and be free . . . free to think, to explore, to listen to his own imagination." Cárdenas insisted on plenty of free time; he spent it, literally, learning to know every spot of his chaotic country. Presidents of the Republic had never traveled; they remained safe in their Palacio Nacional on the Zócalo, or in Chapultepec where both Montezuma and Maximilian had unfurled imperial banners. Cárdenas turned Chapultepec into a public park and a public museum. For his use, when he was in the capital, he reserved a subordinate villa, Los Piños. But more than half his time he was away from the city. By plane and by train and by car, he went from town to town and was accessible to every townsman. Mexico had an ominous fame for political assassination. The brilliant Obregón had been only the latest of the long list of Mexican chief magistrates to be shot by a political foe. Cárdenas took no precautions. He told a friend: "Precaution is senseless. Barring the kind of insulation achieved by a Hitler or a Stalin—unthinkable in a democracy, no President can effectually guard his life. So why sacrifice one's freedom?"

The men and women crowded to the table, when the President sat down to greet them; most of their demands were trivial; they were all carefully noted by a secretary, classified, acted on. Then Cárdenas escaped his entourage. He went alone to the village or town plaza and mingled with the people.

There are villages in Mexico inaccessible by car. Cárdenas reached them on horseback. There are hamlets, virtual eagles' aeries, beyond horses. These Cárdenas approached on foot.

To observe Cárdenas on these pilgrimages was to grow aware of a sacrament, beyond the specific problems discussed with each man or woman. The President was revealing to the people that the Government of Mexico was theirs, and as intimately—one might say as physically, as the presences of their household. This sense of ownership was new in Mexico. They had it transcendently in the Church whose lavish gold altars reminded them that this earth of tears was the threshold to Heaven. Now they could feel the presence of a caretaker, constant and attentive, in their humble problems. This was Cárdenas' theory of statehood. I do not mean that Lázaro Cárdenas figured it out as I have put it; by the intuition of genius, he sensed and lived it.

The two great acts of the Cárdenas administration are judged to have been the speeding up of the partition of *ejidos* among the peasants and the nationalization of the oil industry. More significant, more original, were these consecrated visits among the people. It was as if Cárdenas had instinctively remembered the survival in them of the blood sacrifice of the Aztecs. He was substituting life for that death. Of course, the ritual would have been a failure if its chief actor had not been wholly involved in his role, and yet detached from it. One saw him scores of times with his eyes full of tears as he listened to the pathetic story of some old man. And yet one never saw him beneath the dignity and the perspective of his office. What the long-range political result of this play will be, who can tell? As art, it was significant, a permanent contribution, revealing a potential of Mexican life. After all, perhaps Cárdenas belongs with the great Mexican artists.

I recall one occasion when he went to meet the Yaquis in the hot northern State of Sonora. This warlike nation still professes independence, owing fealty to its own chiefs and, presumably, living "by treaty" and as an equal with the Republic. When the Yaquis made trouble in the time of Díaz, he solved it by deporting a whole village to the south or drafting all the men into the army. Cárdenas wanted to persuade the Yaquis to plant wheat in alternation with corn. He and his retinue of about twenty men were formally received by the *caciques*. There were long powwows (fortunately with no pipes of peace, for Cárdenas does not smoke); then an even longer feast: wild birds and boars, chile and innumerable fruit. The orations were in the Yaqui tongue. Cárdenas stood through it all, not strained, not long-suffering, not in a hurry. He was not feigning respect, he lived it. Finally, he had his chance and made his agricultural suggestion. The wheat was planted.

The portrait of Lázaro Cárdenas should be painted against such a background as this half-circle of Yaqui elders, untamed Indians of the dry Mexican plain: the man, tall, erect, a little stiff in his brown suit, faultlessly tailored, despite the hundred-degree heat, holding his slouch hat in his hand and nodding as he listens. The face is brown (Cárdenas in large part is Tarascan). The mouth is full, sensitive, and mobile (this is not an Indian trait). The eyes look forth with a reserve which does not preclude pain. When he smiles, a certain violence is done to the stern face, as if its strength had no form for humor. And his laugh shakes the whole frame of his body, a dislocation, as if a boy were knowing that the Mexican's lot is tragic.

Six years ended his term of office, with re-election forbidden by the constitution. Cárdenas could, within the letter of the law, have imposed a successor of his choice, pleading as justification the healthy continuance of his program. The man for this was his old associate, General Francisco Mújica. "At this point of Mexico's history," he told a friend, "loyalty to law is more important than any man or any statute." He did not back Mújica; he backed no one. The man chosen by the dominant party was a conservative, colorless but honest: Manuel Ávila Camacho, who could be relied on not to press the Revolutionary program, and not to disturb Washington—or Business, which, with the world war closer to home, was booming.

In the war years, Cárdenas served as Minister of Defense. Then he went back to his native state of Michoacán in what is perhaps the most significant phase of his career. He had himself appointed chief of public works: roads, dams, hydroelectric plants to catch the waters of the torrential season which now poured wasting into the sea. This job enabled him again to be among the people. Irrigation and erosion are Mexico's first economic problems. But Cárdenas sees another as of hardly less importance: the potent magnetic field of North American expansion, industrial, commercial, cultural. It is a force ever-present, indeed atmospheric. The land's mineral wealth is now defended by law against the non-national satrapies of old. But there is this new invasion, not of industry but of commerce. The small Mexican shopkeeper is overwhelmed by huge alien bodies, such as Sears Roebuck, which can undersell him. Could the day come when Mexican curios can be manufactured more cheaply in the U.S.A. than their Indian-made originals? Such problems worry the Mexican who loves the creative potential of his land, and whose hero is still the reserved Tarascan leader from Michoacán.

There are other troublesome symptoms. The *ejido* policy depends for success on the peasant's financial credit. Without money to buy the tools of modern farming, his land becomes a burden. In parts of Mexico, rationalized farming has prospered: Lower California, for example, or the cotton-raising Laguna near Torreón in the State of Coahuila, where the successful *ejidatorios* ride around in new cars like the farmers of Iowa. But in far too many sections, the banking arm has failed or at least halted.

The problem of transforming the Mexican into an efficient farmer is infinitely complex, if his qualities as a human being are to be preserved. Mexico today still imports food, even corn! The minerals, the potential power of its harnessed waters, suggest that the Mexican should be primarily an industrial worker. But those who know the folk best are convinced that Mexico must be a nation of farmers. Mexican genius, they insist, should command the industrial plant, not surrender to it. The economic doubts of the *ejido** system must however not blind us to one inescapable fact: the psychology of the peon is waning. This victory is irreversible. The Mexican never again will be a peon.

Meanwhile the capital, which has grown in thirty years from 500,-000 to three million, is one of the dazzling cities of the world. Its broad central avenues and squares are a promenade of dynamic buildings, fusions of tropical color and functional line. A new prosperous middle class has sprung up: from banking, from the management and sales of machinery, from commerce, and of course—as always in Mexico—from political corruption.

In the provincial cities too, the new *bourgeoisie* puts up villas and plans shopping centers. There are still in Mexico the "two races" of Disraeli, the rich and the poor; but the rich are spreading, leveling down in what the statistical view of the whole economy would call a "leveling up." The Mexican rich used to be the proprietors of huge estates, the owners of mines, the officials with access to the Treasury, and the Generals. Now, they are the conductors of Mexico's commerce. In this development, the magnetic pull of American Business is manifest. Mexico's Revolution seems to have stopped running. Or rather, it has gone the classic way of economic revolution which, starting with the motive power of the people, the ideology of the intellectuals, establishes a middle class who take it over and control and suppress it.

A new tension therefore is set up in this country of tensions. There is the nature of the people, and the nature of the land which through the ages has formed the successive waves of incoming peoples. This folk does not fit the current molds: not the capitalist-bourgeois, formed in Western Europe, perfected in the United States; not the regimental mold of Communism, formed in Eastern Europe and now invading Asia. It must find its own form. That it has not yet done so, given its immense complexity, is understandable.

---

* "It may be said that his (the Mexican peasant's) economic situation has changed little. In the times of Díaz he earned 50 cents daily . . . but he was given lodgings and corn. Today the *ejidatorios* who work for the bank barely make the minimum field wage of 7 or 8 pesos: which is 50 cents gold. But they have to buy their own corn and pay interest to the bank on the credits which enabled them to plant."

(From a letter to the author.)

Its first articulations were largely of its weaknesses and morbidities. (Always the fragment is articulate before the whole.) Now, its strengths begin to find voice in mighty arts and healthy leaders. All this calls for long gestation. But the pressures on Mexico, from the North, the South, the world, create crisis and call for immediate decision. This is Mexico's dilemma.

We have looked at the magnetic field of the North; to the South also there is growing pressure. It is good, this increasing weight of America Hispana within Mexico, but it is also complex and not easily encountered. Brazil, with its large African elements and its traditions from Portugal; Argentina, whose stock is more purely European than that of the United States; Colombia, Peru, Chile, with their distinctive Indian populations—all these complicate Mexico's living experience even while they enrich it.

6. MEXICO IN AMERICA

Every year, a half-million or more Mexicans, for the most part illegally, cross to the United States. They are *braceros* (day laborers, harvest workers), called "wetbacks" by their Gringo bosses because so many have come by swimming or wading the frontier river. They do not come because they like their treatment in the United States; they come for the money. And when they have it, they usually go home.* They are hardly touched, except indirectly, by the mores of the U.S.A. But they can tell you quite specifically what is good about Gringoland. What is good is the good pay for short hours, the car you can buy on credit, the houses with running water and electric gadgets for the comfort of the *señora*, the plenty of roads and schools,** the doctor if he is needed.† And because his own country is still weak in these matters; because there is still so much poverty, so much malnutrition, so much infant death, the *bracero* will feel inferior.

While the wetbacks steal across the Rio Grande, another temporary

---

* Largely in the areas of Los Angeles and San Antonio, Texas, about two million Mexicans have permanently settled. Usually they become American citizens. They are of a higher economic class than the *braceros*.

** Illiteracy in Mexico in 1950 was 40 percent; in 1940 it was 50 percent; in the time of Díaz, it was over 90 percent.

† The statistical life expectancy of a man today in the U.S.A. is 70 years; in Mexico in 1940 it was 39, though recent estimates are much higher.

migration goes on in the opposite direction: the constant flow into Mexico of the American tourists. Some fly in, a few take the train or local bus; the vast majority glide in by car. The cars have the gleam of arrogance. The pockets full of travelers' checks suggest a magic to the Mexican, who sees these little slips of paper turn into pesos enough to buy up a whole village *mercado*. But if American tourists have to the common Mexican eye a certain hauteur, the Mexican would call it justified; for is this not a people who run their country smoothly, hygienically, for their own good? The average Mexican intelligence is high—higher, I suspect, than that of the average American tourist (not of course because of any nonsense about "racial differences" but simply because the American mind is more dazed and drugged, benumbed and bewildered by the constant regimen of electronic and printed pressure, whereas the average Mexican mind is as yet more spontaneously nourished by contact with self, earth, and cosmos). But what the Mexican, despite his sensitivity, may miss, observing the American tourist, is that these clean-clothed Gringos in their upholstered cars do not share *his* sense of *their* superiority at all.

Of course, this is not always the case. Many Americans come to Mexico as on a slumming party, a jaunt to never-never land, or to "let themselves go" as they'd never dare in Little Falls and Grand Rapids. They are the exceptions. Some Mexicans look on the invasive Gringo with resentment, with hate, with the conviction that he is an infidel and, for all his shiny gadgets, damned. They too are the exceptions. On the whole, the Mexicans have romanticized the "Yanqui." We have seen the results of this in the war of independence from Spain and in the times of Juárez, when Mexico foolishly tried to imitate our Anglo-Saxon institutions. The American invasion of 1846 caused revulsion of feeling. Theodore Roosevelt's version of what Bolívar and Colombia had destined to be an international Canal at Panama caused grave doubts. But generally, until the present generation, the Mexicans who knew of us at all have greatly admired the United States.

The attitude of the United States toward Mexicans has differed. For long, we were hardly conscious of their existence, except perhaps as a slight barrier in the irresistible path of American Destiny. The readers of Prescott's "Conquest of Mexico" did not identify the Aztecs with the living Mexicans, and quite rightly. During the long rule of Díaz, most Americans assumed that the Dictator was wise to suppress what must be an unruly, half-barbarous, superlatively unimportant people.

All this has changed. The Mexican squatting on his *petate* on the earth floor of his hut imagines the American riding past to have a life of perfect comfort, and does not suspect that he (the Mexican) is—in the judgment of the American—the more comfortable human! He does not know that although all Americans—unlike most Mexicans—sleep in beds, more than half the hospital beds in the United States are occupied by victims of nervous and mental diseases.

The American lady, leading her humble husband up the Pyramid stair at Teotihuacán, hushed before the sumptuous graves of Monte Albán at Oaxaca, overwhelmed by the carven gold of the churches in Puebla, Taxco, Guadalajara, collects silverware, ceramics, ponchos, and serapes as if she were bearing sacred symbols home. Symbols of what? The tourist would be hard pressed to explain. Of *a quality of living* that cannot be weighed or charted, but the need of it is like the body's need of vitamins. Every woman feels its presence or its lack at home, although words for it are missing; and every man who is not obsessed to madness by the treadmill of keeping up with the Joneses. This quality of living comes directly from the acknowledged relation of one's self with the mysterious Cosmos in which we are born and with which we feel a positive relation or pay the price of alienation . . . alienation for which all the world's gadgets and their power are no remedy. If the kinship is there, the body has comfort even in a cabin; if not, the whole Waldorf Astoria made into a private suite won't give it. If it is there, what the hand makes (even the humblest thing) is beauty; what the heart makes is love. If it is not there, amidst overwhelming plenty, desert! The American tourist brings home to Worcester or Seattle these trophies of loveliness and beauty, as from a "past" that he feels "present" in Mexico and lost in his own land. This may be romanticism, idealization, even sentimentalism. There is truth in it, also.

It is a basic fact in Mexico's idealization of the U.S.A. that the U.S.A. does have something Mexico needs. It is a basic fact in the American's romanticization of Mexico that Mexico does have something the Americans need.

The error and the danger come when, from the dual sense of deficiency and possession, the notions of inferiority and of superiority arise (they always rise together).

The people of the United States founded their independence in the eighteenth century *on* the eighteenth century. There was no abyss, no break of continuity between their values and the means they believed in to achieve them. That was the century of technics: technics of mechanics, technics of political democracy, technics of industrial invention and production. The explorers of steam power, the codifiers of the forces of inertia and gravitation, the architects of constitutions for the checks and balances of social powers, the champions of the rights of individual freedom, of ego-expression (called Romanticism in the fields of literature and art) were all at home in the eighteenth century; and the American nineteenth century issued from it not without the struggles that inhere in growth but within the full deep continuity of growth.

Mexico's independence as a nation was the fruit of a far more violent process. Mexico may be said not to have had an eighteenth century at all. Therefore the orderly growth which produced Newton and Locke, the inventors of power machines, Hamilton, Jefferson, Madison, and Marshall, had no equivalent in Mexico. Spain's values and concepts, most potently expressed in Queen Isabel, in the great Spanish mystics, and in Philip II, were of the Middle Ages and of the sixteenth-century Counterrevolution. If they had been established whole in "the Kingdom of New Spain," Mexico would not have been too aloof from the eighteenth century to make a relatively smooth transition; for after all the eighteenth century did spring finally from medieval Europe. But we have seen how Christian European Spain fused in Mexico with values and concepts still more alien to the West: with the cultures of Toltec, Zapotec, Maya, Aztec. This contrast of origins explains the contrast of adaptations of the United States and Mexico to the modern world.

One might say, the United States was in the direct line of succession. It had only to develop its own inner trends, which were the trends of the West, in order to "inherit" the West. Mexico required and requires a far more basic transformation. This has been Mexico's handicap, in terms of modern values; it is also Mexico's promise. For it is tragically manifest . . . increasingly each day . . . that only by a profound, organic transfiguration can the Western world hope to survive.

The priority of the Northern nation over Mexico in the realms of applied science, power, and the machine, which have made—and to-day menace—the modern world, is obvious. The argument of superiority from priority, which is perhaps instinctive, is nonsense: a nonsense which could breed for the white races a lethal poison. One or two examples will make the nonsense clear. . . .

Ancient Palestine had priority in the idea of the One God and of man's ethical relation with the Cosmos: the concept of life on which our Western world was founded. The men of Europe came late to this idea. Ancient Greece had priority in the search for order in physical nature and in the discovery of natural law. The men of the North and the West came to such inquiry centuries later. Do these priorities mean the ancient Hebrews and the ancient Greeks were superior to the Briton, the Frenchman, the German, the American? Certainly not. Then the Northern Europeans in their turn developed science and the machine of power. In the field which has revolutionized modern man, they have been obviously prior to the Russian, the Chinese, the Indian, the Spaniard. Superior? Of course not! These inconsistencies of consciousness, trend, and growth belong to the organic process of man. Conditions endow priorities, and conditions change. The Russians today are the equals of the West in mathematics and mechanics. Likewise, probably tomorrow, India and China. And the Europeans who were "laggard" in religious knowledge while the Hindus and the Jews wrote their great books, revealed in the thirteenth century and thereafter a religious genius as exalted as the Bible's. America Hispana and China may become masters of power tomorrow to challenge the European. Nothing in history precludes it.

We must be wholly free of the cloudy notion that there is a link between priority in a specific realm we happen to esteem and superiority ultimate and essential. Then we shall be ready to recognize and to profit by a reciprocity of values between Mexico and ourselves.

Emerson, prophetically speaking of the American civilization of his day, said: "The Thing is in the saddle." A hypertrophy of the develop-

ment of *means for living* has impoverished our inward experience of
life itself: a condition reflected in our shallow arts and in our neurotic
insecurities which grow as we grow "stronger." The realm of man's
basic experience of his place and part in Cosmos is the Mexican's
common ground—so instinctively possessed that he is hardly conscious
of it. This experience must be, of course, the matrix and the living
fulfillment of all aids, mechanical, political, intellectual, and economic, for living. We Americans cannot imitate the specific expressions of this consciousness in other lands. If we could, the imitation
would be sterile. But we can grow aware of this spiritual and emotional resource in our neighbors, and treasure it, and defend it, and
by a creative dialogue stimulate our own expression.

The exchanges between Mexico and the United States should become far more ample and dynamic. Our ignorance of Mexican literature is deplorable. The place, in the curriculum of our schools and
colleges, of Mexican history, archeology, and art and the Spanish
language should be far larger. We are aware of our continent's wealth
of natural resources. We are not sufficiently aware that in population
all the Americas are a minority hemisphere, making all the more urgent our qualitative human resources. We are hardly aware at all of
the immense human wealth which Mexico offers. When we grow conscious of it, like the lady tourist, we are likely to conceive it as "a past,"
whereas it is in fact a great Potential.

The remarkable genius of the Hispanic empire was its projection
of new human forms. They have not yet had time to mature. Obvious
elements in our mechanical civilization threaten their maturing. And
of course, our own deeply human values are imperiled by the same
elements. In this sense, facing a shared danger, hopeful of a shared
human future, the United States and Mexico should be brothers.

The Southwest

BY WILLIAM WEBER JOHNSON

The land lies flat, dry, and unending until the earth's gentle curvature is a subtle reality under the great arch of cloudless sky. String-straight highways thrust forward and diminish until they pierce the horizon and disappear. The landscape is so empty that its few adornments are seen, distantly, with startling clarity. A stark, sun-bleached house is suspended in space, its only companion an idle windmill. Dusty red-and-white cattle are dots in the distance, moving slowly, searching for sparse grass on the seemingly barren earth. Heat waves paint the illusion of shimmering water far away, but there is no water. Here and there a faint green patch in the dusty distance shows where some underground stream has ventured near the surface, but nothing more. Mesquite and bear grass and cactus are there. Dusty and motionless in the still, clear air, they seem only half alive. A slain coyote is impaled on the barbed-wire fence as a warning, and far overhead buzzards wheel in the sky.

This is the U. S. Southwest in its most familiar guise. Although a true likeness, it is incomplete, little more than a caricature, telling as little of the country and its people as baggy pants do of the clown or reading glasses of the scholar.

For this is a vast, ill-defined, deceptive, and contradictory land with an infinite capacity for bewildering the outsider and inspiring both love and madness among its dwellers; and an equal capacity for luring the newcomer and making of him a fiercely partisan regionalist.

A century ago Thoreau wrote that when he left his house for a walk, letting his instinct guide his steps, more times than not that instinct led him in a southwesterly direction: "My needle is slow to settle, varies a few degrees and does not always point due southwest . . . but it always settles between west and south-southwest. The future lies that way to me, and the earth seems more unexhaustible and richer on that side. Eastward I go only by force; but westward I go free . . ."

Thoreau's southwest wanderings took him no farther than a deserted field or a lonely woods; he could always return to Walden Pond by nightfall to watch the end of the sun's migration and muse on the temptation to follow it beyond the Concord hills and the Berkshires. Thoreau was sensitive to the urge in a mystical way; others, less cognizant of what it was that drove them, were already moving west in countless numbers. The two classic urges were at work—the thirst for a quick fortune in land or gold or trade, and the more profound, more selfless hope that life might somehow be better for the next generation in a new land. Or it might be a religious conviction or as simple a matter as flight from justice.

But whether as fugitives or zealots or seekers after profits or homes, westward and southwestward they went, beyond the Connecticut, across the Mississippi, and over all the strangely named rivers, each more fickle and unpredictable than the last—the Arkansas, the Red, the Brazos, the Pecos, the Rio Grande, the Salt, and the Gila.

But unlike so many tides of migration, this one did not reach the flood stage and then recede. It had been going on since the sixteenth century when Spanish soldiers in clanking armor and Spanish monks in dusty robes and shuffling sandals came looking for gold to plunder or souls to save. And in the twentieth century it continues to draw the young and adventurous in ever-increasing numbers. For the country has a great capacity to reward the diligent, the imaginative, and the lucky. But there is always the implicit promise of cruelty and punishment. Like the sea, it is correctly regarded with a mixture of love and fear; and like the sea, it has many faces.

Any definition of the U. S. Southwest can successfully be challenged and corrected. It is not a neat, compact, homogeneous package as is

New England, for instance. But if we draw a line around Texas, Oklahoma, New Mexico, and Arizona we will encompass examples of all that the Southwest is; and it is a very mixed bag.

Its people may speak in the flat drawl of the Western plains, with the nasal intonations of the Middle West, the corn-pone-magnolia accents of the deep South, the *pocho* Spanish of the border, any of the many ancient Indian dialects, or the polished diction of the Ivy League.

The bayous and pine thickets of East Texas and the thickly forested hills of Oklahoma are the Southwest just as much as the lunar landscape of the Big Bend of the Rio Grande and the gaudy geology of the Grand Canyon of the Colorado; the lonely dunes and glistening seascape of Padre Island as much as the shimmering sea of grass of the Llano Estacado.

The jarring contrasts are, paradoxically, the area's only consistent characteristic, and they abound—in the landscape, among the people, their manners, their homes, their industries.

The city dweller in Houston, Tulsa, Phoenix, or Albuquerque sits in air-conditioned comfort and stares through his picture window at lush lawns and blazing semitropical plants that water and fertilizer have wheedled from an unfriendly soil. And the pueblo Indian stands on the flat roof of his adobe house, his blanket whipping in the parching wind, staring stonily at an arid landscape that has, incredibly, nourished his people for centuries.

The brush country cowhand tends his critters with tools and workwords that are older than the nation. And the nuclear scientist, working in well-guarded laboratories on unmentionable problems, deals with abstruse equations and foresees a future that is, alternately, all bright confidence and, again, terrifyingly empty.

Offshore rigs seek oil under the waters of Mexico's Gulf and windmills creakingly draw water from secret streams beneath the dusty land. Petrochemical plants make jackstraw patterns against the stridently blue sky; and an ancient Navajo woman, seated before her hogan, weaves with wool that is dyed in earth colors, making patterns older than man's memory. The Indian sand painter works with enduring symbols for such verities as the sun, the moon, and the stars; and missilemen at White Sands or Holloman study their monstrous machines and regard the stars and outer space much as we regard the next turn in a strange road.

The oilman looks at a city skyline, astonishingly new and clean, and remembers when it was little more than oil derricks and frame shanties. The dry-land farmer curses the burning sun, the cloudless sky, the undying wind, and the dust that levels the furrows in his fields. The cattleman loves the land, come good times and bad, for the precious freedom it gives him. And the *mojado* or wetback of the border country, caught in the toils of economics and politics, wonders why the Lord God in His wisdom ever created such a bewildering country.

It is an old country and a new country and there is a great dizzying gap between the old and the new. It is a world that had a long infancy —from dim prehistory down to the memory of still living man. Then, without a proportionate adolescence, it plunged into a spectacular maturity. As with humans who have grown rapidly, there are certain weaknesses; the maturity is at times erratic and undependable. But it is still brilliant and exciting.

The Hopi Indians explain the country's history thus: Their forebears lived in a succession of dark caves. As the caves became crowded they climbed upward to larger caves and finally emerged into a world of darkness and water. A spider-web mantle became the moon, a jar full of sparks became the stars, and a deerskin shield became the sun. The tribal saints dug canals from the caves which, in draining the land, became canyons; and the vulture that had emerged from the caves with them spread and flapped his wings and the land became drier and drier. A less tidy but equally colorful history is registered in the country's geology, in the vestiges of ancient marine life, in the rings of petrified trees, in bones and fossils, stone tools and weapons and shards of pottery. Creatures who were later to be named Llano man and Folsom man roamed the region tens of thousands of years ago. Through the ages the region was subject to great and devastating droughts. One of the worst was in the thirteenth century. Game was destroyed and nomadic tribes that followed the game disappeared for a time. Primitive agriculture was wiped out. Towns and villages of the sedentary tribes were depopulated; their ruins, preserved in the dry air, exist to this day as monuments to a mysterious past. Droughts return, again and again, to scourge the land. They never quite kill it; for it has an invincible vitality.

At some time the comparatively civilized aborigines of southern Mexico, who had developed their own arts and sciences to a high degree, moved north and east across the land. And again the barbarous nomadic tribes of the region moved southward into Mexico, becoming, in time, the Aztec nation which unified and ruled the other tribes with a complicated and fearful system of taxes and tributes, only to collapse in fierce confusion before the wily Spaniard, Cortés, and his miniscule army.

The harshness and cruelty of the land first made its mark on white men when the Spanish explorers, whipped into a frenzy by the quantities of gold and silver Cortés had seized from the Aztec ruler, Montezuma, made their first tentative thrusts into the seemingly empty country, hoping for another treasure.

Between 1528 and 1536 three shipwrecked Spaniards and a Moorish slave made an incredible odyssey that took them over much of what we now know as the Southwest. By trading bits of shell and berries and performing simple medical treatments they managed to live, passing from one tribe of aborigines to another. Led by Alvar Núñez Cabeza de Vaca, a resolute and honest man, they slowly and painfully made their way from the Gulf coast of Texas across the plains, followed the course of the Rio Grande, bore westward and again southerly, until finally they encountered a party of Spanish soldiers from one of the new outposts of empire in Mexico. That they survived, naked, hungry, and thirsty, for nearly eight years was little short of a miracle of stamina and spirit. But this was not the sort of miracle that interested Spaniards. Had they found gold? Silver? Jewels?

Cabeza de Vaca gave honest answers. He had heard natives say that gold and silver could be found but that they were not highly regarded. They had been given, by the Indians, arrow points made of a polished green stone.

The Spaniards in Mexico quickly expanded these meager facts into promise of great wealth, fitted them into a legend of lost cities populated by workers of gold and silver, and soon mounted expeditions to find the wealth of Cibola and Gran Quivira. They prowled the deserts, mountains, and plains of the Southwest. They found the Grand Canyon of the Colorado. They traced the source of the Rio Grande. They marveled at the pueblos of the natives and noted that while some dwelt in peaceable and civilized fashion in these "house towns," others, nomadic by nature, ranged the plains and desert in search of game and were, generally, more warlike and dangerous. Francisco Vásquez Coronado led his men as far as the prairies of Kansas and, like the others, experienced only grief; the cities of gold were nowhere to be found.

This apparent poverty of the region was to determine the Spanish and Mexican attitude toward the Southwest for centuries to come. The men of war and politics and business had little stomach for it. Some stalwarts, such as Juan de Oñate, made serious efforts to colonize the region, and established a primitive capital at San Gabriel in 1598, little more than a century after Columbus' discovery of the New World. But for the most part efforts to settle the country were left to the priests. The holy men in gray and brown and black cassocks gradually replaced the arrogant men in clinking, shining steel and brass; their low-pitched prayers replaced the rough commands of marching men. This was not to become a proud and prosperous colony of New Spain, bustling with pomp. It remained little more than an outpost, the scene of patient missionary work on the part of the priests and bloody clashes between the Spanish soldiers and the Indians.

For the most part the Spaniards left the region alone. They established a few towns and a few more garrisons and missions. For nearly three centuries the area lay dormant. There were forays against the Indians. Rebellions were bloodily suppressed. Settlements were made. Some survived, more were abandoned. The Indians were Christianized in part. Adventurers, hunters, trappers, dealers in furs, freighters and traders of a half dozen nationalities traversed the great emptiness, slowly learning more about the country.

But it was not until the first third of the nineteenth century that the westward bulge of the young United States began to be felt. The expansive, romantic nature of the fledgling nation, the old drives of desire for better homes and/or quick wealth exerted a pressure that was to alter the entire region and, in the end, fill out the boundaries of the United States as we know them today.

In what is now Oklahoma, an unsettled land acquired in the Louisiana Purchase, there was a terminus to the "trail of tears"—the course followed by the unfortunate civilized Indians, the Cherokees,

6. An oil derrick in west Texas. Though they seem to grow like forests of steel in east Texas, oil derricks, singly or in groups, may be seen from the Gulf to the Panhandle and from Louisiana to New Mexico. This is a "workover" derrick, smaller than those used for drilling.

37, 38. Tulsa (above) and Oklahoma City (below). To a visiting European, one Anglo-American city looks much like another from the air — a
cluster of tall buildings on a checkerboard of streets, surrounded by
industrial and residential districts flattening out in the distance.

Galloway

39. Houston, largest city of the entire South, adheres to the familiar metropolitan pattern, but with greater dispersal of its chief buildings.

40. Here, in a pueblo in Taos, New Mexico, we see a truly American prototype of "setback" architecture.

41. Apache Indians with their steer entries in Arizona National Livestock Show at Phoenix.

42. A registered Hereford bull on an Arizona ranch. Here is an animal with personality!

43.   On the campus of the University of Arizona at Tucson.

44.   A cotton harvest in the Santa Cruz Valley in southern Arizona.

45.   The plaza at Santa Fe, on which faces the 350-year-old Palace of the Governors, is closed to traffic during the four-day Labor Day weekend for the annual Fiesta.

46.   The Grand Canyon, more than a vertical mile and several horizontal miles from rim to river, can be traversed by mule or shanks' mare — or in an emergency, by helicopter.

7. A Navajo Indian woman demonstrates rug-weaving at the State Fair in Albuquerque, New Mexico.

48. Through the heart of downtown San Antonio (referred to loving
by Texans as San Antone) meanders a well-bridged rivulet which flo
or trickles according to the season.

Creeks, Choctaws, Seminoles, and Chickasaws who were forced from their old homes in the southeast by the rising white flood. In the rude new country the migrant Indians sadly built new homes, cleared land, and established schools, bringing a degree of culture and gentility to the raw country that itinerant white men had never given it. And as the red man proved the land's worth, the white man again, and still again, pushed him back, violating his supposedly guaranteed boundaries.

To the west Santa Fe, one of the oldest settlements on the continent, became a busy trading center, a crossroads for ambitious and adventurous impresarios. Freighters carried manufactured goods of cloth and leather from eastern factories along the Santa Fe trail. Other traders and, in increasing numbers, settlers, thronged the Osage trace, the Texas road, El Camino Real to San Antonio and the Rio Grande beyond, or came by ship to Galveston Island, the headquarters of thieves and pirates, to work their way into the new country.

The most heavily traveled of the various routes led to Texas. Here the loose rule of Mexico left a great and desirable void—rich bottom lands in the river valleys, thick grass on the sunburned plains. Restless people poured into the vacuum.

Some like Moses Austin and his son, Stephen, came with large parties of settlers they had organized. In conscientious and businesslike fashion they accepted grants of land from the Mexican government, in return for which they pledged loyalty to their new governors.

Others came for a variety of reasons. It was a plain and widely understood fact that Mexico, at first engrossed in her struggle for independence from Spain and later staggering under the responsibilities of that independence, stunned and confused by internal political upheavals, could not long maintain even loose control over this rich land. It must, in time, become part of the United States, another phase in what men were later to describe as the manifest destiny of the Yankee nation.

Land speculators were everywhere. And so were their victims, the innocents who had bought baseless claims to land in Texas from big speculators in the East. Many such claims, the would-be settlers sadly learned, were "not deliverable in Texas but in Wall Street."

The wild, anarchic country was a natural refuge for men fleeing from justice, men accused of murder, thievery, and lesser infractions.

The phrase "gone to Texas" or simply "G.T.T." found its way into the language as a standard chapter ending for a stormy period of a man's life. So did "I'm going to Texas to fight for my rights."

An anonymous English traveler who visited Texas in those days faithfully records in his diary that in a simple inn at San Felipe de Austin "I saw at the breakfast table one morning, among those who were seated with me, four murderers who had sought safety in this country." And, with a note of sincere admiration for such one-upmanship, he added "a gentleman assured me that on one occasion he had set down with eleven."

And there were, of course, the adventurers—the Sam Houstons, the Jim Bowies, the Davy Crocketts. Some of them were heroic and significant and some were merely comic. But all were in search of fame or fortune or simply a fight, and all were eager for the new land which they all sensed would, inevitably, be up for grabs.

These ingredients could lead to nothing but war, and Mexico responded with a vigor that no one had really expected. The massacres at the Alamo and Goliad gave the rebellious but poorly organized Texans a war cry.

But the "Runaway Scrape" which followed made it appear in the United States that the Texas rebellion was over. The Texans, volunteer soldiers and settlers alike, fled in chaotic, disorderly retreat from Central Texas to Buffalo Bayou in deep East Texas. There, on the plains of San Jacinto, Sam Houston's military genius somehow converted the fleeing rabble into a masterful weapon. Singing, oddly,

> "Will you come to the bower
> I have shaded for you. . . ."

they rushed into battle against the over-confident Santa Anna and his vastly superior force and overwhelmed them in one of the most curious, improbable, and deeply significant military victories in American history.

Indirectly, since the war with Mexico and the subsequent treaty of Guadalupe Hidalgo stemmed from it, it was responsible for adding more than a quarter to what was later known as the continental United States, including most of what we now know as the Southwest.

After a short and turbulent life as a republic, Texas was annexed to the United States. Mexico had never recognized the young republic's ambitious boundary claims but had done little about it. Yet when these claims were taken over by the United States it became a more serious matter. President James K. Polk, an ardent expansionist, tried to settle peacefully, offering cash for a clear Texas boundary and a quitclaim to New Mexico and California. Mexico declined and war came again, brief but bloody.

American attitudes were ambivalent. Some dreamed of acquiring the whole of Mexico, or a federation of northern states—Tamaulipas, Nuevo León, Coahuila, and Chihuahua—that might be added to the Union. Others, weary of Texans and Texans' claims—and fearful of the addition of more slave territory to the Union—insisted: "We must whip them until they agree to take back Texas."

The treaty of Guadalupe Hidalgo firmly fixed the Texas frontier on the Rio Grande. It also added to the United States a vast area that comprises the present California, Arizona, New Mexico, Nevada, and Utah and cleared the United States title to Texas. In return for this empire the United States gave Mexico $15 million, less than three cents an acre.

In the same month of 1848 in which Mexico ratified the treaty, gold —which Spaniards and Mexicans had so long and so unsuccessfully sought in the Southwest—was discovered in California.

"We compromised," the Mexicans said with Latin fatalism. "They took everything."

The excitement over gold in California and the bitter division between the free and slaveholding territory during the Civil War obscured, for a time, just what the United States had acquired in the Southwest.

At first glance it did not appear to be too promising. Perhaps the eastern half of Texas was arable and useful. Oklahoma was somewhat more attractive, but it was reserved for Indians (a reservation the white man was not to respect for long). As for the rest, it appeared to be a desert. In the classic jape of the frontier all it needed was what hell needed—a whole lot of water and a better class of people.

Jefferson Davis, as the pre-secession Secretary of War, had regarded the Southwest as nothing but a barrier between the civilized world and the promising, rich new land of California which could be economically and strategically important if a means could be found to cross the barren vastness. His solution, sensible and logical at the time, seems grotesque in retrospect. "The camel," he wrote, "would remove an obstacle which now serves greatly to diminish the value and efficiency of our troops on the western frontier."

At great cost both camels and camel drivers were imported from the Middle East. They brought a circus air to the rough frontier towns where they were corraled and occasioned much skeptical joking. But they proved their efficiency, carrying men and supplies across the arid wastes, and at least one camel train went from San Antonio, Texas, to Bakersfield, California, substantiating the judgment of the Secretary of War. Private investors began importing camels as the coming thing for travel on the Great American Desert.

But the Civil War ended it. The camel herds were allowed to wander away. Strolling camels for years afterwards were to stampede horses and cattle, terrify women and drunkards, and provide an exotic change of diet for hungry Indians. After the war the railroads stretched out across the lonely places and the camel was relegated to a curious cul-de-sac of U.S. history.

By all that was sensible and logical, Jefferson Davis was right about the Southwest. It was an arid—or at best, a subhumid land, capable of supporting a few wild Indians and their primitive husbandry but offering little to the white man. Why did it not, then, remain a sort of geographical vacuum, a New World version of the Sahara or the Gobi?

The pat answer lies in the aggressive American spirit, the expansiveness of a vigorous new nation. And this was a tremendous factor. But the most energetic and acquisitive people in the world could have made little out of the Southwest had it not been for a series of fortuitous factors which Jefferson Davis could no more foresee than could Cabeza de Vaca.

When the Spanish expeditions had first come into the country, they had brought along extra horses for remounts and herds of cattle as an ambulatory meat supply. While the explorers were preoccupied with their fruitless search for gold, the animals would wander away. Many perished in the desert, but some survived and were joined by strays from the ranches the Spaniards established in northern Mexico.

The wild horses—*mesteños* or mustangs—were to play a dramatic part in the development of the region.

Indians captured the wild horses and quickly proved to be brilliant natural horsemen. The Indian on foot had been a wily adversary against the advance of the whites; on horseback he was far more formidable in battle. Instead of poorly armed pedestrians they became fierce, resourceful, fast-moving fighters that had to be quelled by sizable expeditions of the intruding whites. And the more whites required to subdue the Indians, the more whites settled on the land bloodily wrested from them.

Similarly, the wild cattle prospered in the new land. They adapted themselves to the arid country, grew long of limb and lean of flank, developed widespread, needle-sharp horns, were awesome in combat, and could run like horses. They ranged far and wide to find scarce water holes, and fought like demons to save their young from predators. On one occasion, early in the war with Mexico, one of them attacked and put to rout a fully armed detachment of the U. S. Army. They overspread the whole region, from the forests and hills in the east to the deep grass of the prairie, to the short grass of the plains, to the sparse feed of the desert. But the greatest wild herds developed in South Texas, from present San Antonio to the Rio Grande, with the greatest concentrations in the Nueces valley where the grass grew deep on the Gulf coast plains.

Indians bothered them little, preferring the meatier buffalo. Early settlers occasionally hunted them for food, and occasionally slaughtered them for nothing more than the hides and tallow, leaving the carcasses to the buzzards. But they made no serious inroads on the size of the herds, which seemed to increase in geometrical progression under ideal climatic conditions. In one mid-century decade the herds in the Nueces valley alone increased 1450 percent.

But as the population of the more settled regions in the east and north grew beyond the food-producing capacity of their immediate environs, a market for wild cattle came into being. There was no transportation, but the hardy longhorn could be driven, could travel great distances over rough country with a minimum of water and feed. The meat was tough and stringy, but it was meat and it could be sold.

Entrepreneurs hired men who had learned the horsemanship and cattle-handling tricks of the Mexican *vaquero* or cowman (*vaquero* in Spanish became *buckaroo* in frontier English) rounded up herds and began to drive them to market—to California, where the gold seekers were hungry and prices were high, to St. Louis, to Chicago; east and west the strange beasts went. And in the Civil War they were driven cross-country to supply Confederate troops. There is even one instance of a herd being swum across the Mississippi River.

The war in time put an end to the cattle drives, but postwar the new industry began to come into its own. Extension of the railroad made the drives shorter and more profitable, and trail herds grew larger. It was a violent, strenuous life. Men and animals were subjected to cruel weather, the horrors of the stampede, and the ever-present hazard of human avarice. The profits were high. Animals bought on the range at $5 a head could be marketed at $40 or higher —with only slight interim expense. Ownership of animals, which had once been free for the taking, became important. Quarrels over unbranded cattle and altered brands frequently reached a degree of violence worthy of the inventor of brands, Hernán Cortés, who first used the fiery irons on rebellious Aztecs and later on his own vast herds of cattle in Mexico.

As the cattle market grew (Abilene, Kansas, alone received 1,460,-000 head of cattle between 1866 and 1880), so did the ranching industry. There was increasing pressure of homesteading farmers, and a threat to the free range was inherent in the invention of barbed wire (wooden fences had been out of the question in a timberless country). Ranchers spread farther and farther, taking in more and more land, stocking more and more cattle. They began improving the quality of their herds and watched prices zoom.

The supposedly easy fortunes to be made in the cattle industry brought adventurers from all over the world. Land and cattle syndicates were formed. One such syndicate built a capitol building for the State of Texas in exchange for land extending through ten whole counties of the Texas Panhandle. It became the famed XIT (ten in Texas) ranch, a vast conglomerate of 3,050,000 acres. Ranches of a million acres or more were numerous. Some, such as the King ranch, survive intact, managed by descendants of the founders.

Promoters flooded Europe with prospectuses to lure more investors into the booming new industry. Their literature showed imaginary garden spots in the desert country, mythical steamboats plying "rivers" that in reality were alternately dry beds of gravel and gushing torrents of flood water.

Speculation spiraled; ranches and range land were overstocked, a severe drought set in, and in 1885 the whole shaky structure came tumbling down. The adventurers and suitcase cowmen were driven out. The real cowmen stayed on, completely in love with a business that could, in good times or bad, be conducted on horseback. They learned how much grazing their land could bear and stocked accordingly. They upgraded their herds by buying blooded bulls, learned how to combat the diseases to which the native cattle had been immune. Gradually the longhorns disappeared; today they can be found only in zoos and in small herds on some ranches where they are maintained solely for reasons of sentiment. Ranching became scientific. Today's large ranches breed selectively, raise and ship cattle with the precision of mass-produced machinery. Despite this the modern ranch, whether it is devoted to cattle, sheep, or goats, maintains in its daily operations a strong flavor of traditionalism. The cowman, though he may ride his fence lines in a pickup truck, will still wear boots with heels designed to keep his feet from slipping through the stirrups on a bucking horse; he will, almost instinctively, crease his hat into the "crush" that is a trademark of his ranch or his region. He will use ancient, proven methods of handling a herd at roundup time, and will show a mastery of horsemanship that exists only where the horse is still a valuable working tool. He will squat on his hunkers at the end of a chuck wagon and chew hard bread and tough bull meat that have been cooked on mesquite coals, and he will talk in a language that is an ancient but living blend of Spanish and English.

The physical vestiges of what the cattle industry once was are eclipsed by the almost overwhelming impact the cowboy and the ranching business had on American folklore and behavior. The lore and mythology of the cowboy, his struggles with nature and four-legged and two-legged creatures, are an inexhaustible source of story and song. Improbable tales of cowboys and Indians struck a more responsive chord in Europeans and were always more popular than were the more significant struggles of the founding fathers. The cinema, television, radio, and publishing industries would be vastly poorer without the elaborate mythology of the cowboy, the ranch, and the cowtown. So would the firms that manufacture cowboy boots and gaudy shirts and outsize hats for sale in the Bronx and Shaker Heights and Oak Park; and the dude-ranch business which reaches statistical dignity in the Southwest and has, incredibly, crept into such unlikely places as Pennsylvania, New York, and New England.

Agriculture has had no such glamorous history in the Southwest. The aborigines that attempted a primitive agriculture limited to corn, beans, and squash, confined such activities either to river bottoms or to the land lying east of a line that could be drawn, roughly, north from San Antonio through Oklahoma City. Their methods were simple. They burned off the grass, punched holes in the ground with a stick, put in seed, cultivated it with the shoulder blade of a buffalo, and harvested quite enough to meet their needs. This was the thirty-inch rainfall line; to the eastward agriculture was even easier; westward the Indians rarely tried it—this land was good only for hunting.

The white man observed no such restrictions. The swell of migration pushed farther and farther west. The railroads promoted the sale of "farming" land; the boll weevil drove farmers out of the cotton business and sent them westward; huge ranches were broken up and small plots sold to the hated "nesters." Sod that had been thousands of years abuilding felt the bite of the plow; rich in humus it produced, for a time, phenomenal crops.

Finally, reduced to powder, it was at the mercy of the wind. Mile-high clouds of dust—red, yellow, greenish gray, or black played over the land. Topsoil was swept thousands of miles across the continent and out to sea. Seed was alternately blown from the ground or buried in the choking drifts of dust. Farmers who had bought the promising sod land and tilled it and dreamed of a fortune literally watched their farms blow away; one of the few distractions was picking up arrow-heads that the scouring wind uncovered—a subtle reminder of the time when the land was rich in grass and the Indians had hunted the buffalo and the plains antelope. There was a mass migration out of the region, mainly toward the west and California, the route marked, they used to say, by the skins and bones of jack rabbits and the feathers of field larks that had become dietary staples.

The hardiest stayed on, learned new methods of tillage, found new crops which could withstand the rigors of the region. In some areas great underground water supplies were discovered. Snow meltage from the mountain slopes goes underground and is tapped by an elaborate system of wells and pumps. It is perhaps exemplary of the way in which man has bested nature in the Southwest that some of the areas most ravaged during the Dust Bowl days of the 1930's have been developed into one of the world's greatest and most extensive examples of irrigated farming. In Texas alone irrigated farming increased nearly fivefold in the period 1940–55, and most of it was in the normally semiarid country of the High Plains and the Trans-Pecos.

Irrigation, of course, was not new to the area. Indians had practiced a primitive sort of irrigation along the rivers long before the white man reached the country, but it remained for the white man to push irrigation to the limit with economic results that are staggering. The Southwest is thus able to produce, in tremendous quantities, the widest variety of crops, semitropical and even tropical fruits and vegetables, cotton and all the grasses and grains of a temperate climate.

Although the volume of agricultural produce continues to rise and the number of acres in cultivation shows no diminution, the number of people engaged in agriculture is dropping steadily, and so is the number of farms, thanks to mechanization, consolidation, and large-scale farming. As industry grows it siphons off more and more people from the rural areas to become industrial workers—and in the same way industrial production is rapidly minimizing the importance of agriculture in the region's total economy.

As modern farming—with its new crops and its methods of producing crops in an arid land with or without irrigation—moved west, the cattle industry has slowly been moving east. When land and cattle were cheap it was possible to devote a hundred acres to the support of a hardy cow and calf. But with the price of land rising steadily the inefficiency of such a system became self-defeating. To the east of the thirty-inch rainfall line land that had been exhausted by generations of row cropping could be put back to grass and could, in time, become lush pasture capable of supporting a large cattle population. This reversal of the familiar rural economy has been particularly true of Oklahoma and Texas.

There has also been a sharp rise in the number of part-time farmers. Men and women employed in industry—and industrial employment is rising in all of the Southwest—find they can live within easy driving distance of their work, own a few acres, and do as much or as little farming as they like.

Important as both cattle and crops have been in the region's development, both are overshadowed by the wealth and industry that have come from minerals that underlay the land in the widest variety and profusion.

The Spaniards, intent on their search for gold and silver, largely overlooked the minerals that in the long run far outweighed the stores of gold that they took from the New World. They noted the presence of copper but scorned it as unworthy. They found bubbling springs of oil and may have sniffed unhappily at seepages of gas. If the age of electricity, which placed a premium on copper, and the internal combustion engine, which gave oil tremendous economic significance, had come a century or so earlier, Spain might today be a world power and the Southwest might still be Spanish.

In 1543 a little fleet of storm-battered Spanish brigantines bearing survivors of the De Soto expedition sought shelter in a cove near Sabine Pass on the Gulf of Mexico and noted a thick scum on the surface of the water. It resembled pitch, so they gathered it and used it to calk and smear their hulls. Later explorers were to note that there were many oil springs in the area, and that Indians came there to bathe in it for the relief of rheumatism, dropsy, and boils—and also took it internally.

Three centuries later white men were gathering "rock oil" and using it to lubricate harness and wagon wheels and even dug shallow wells to increase the supply. By the 1890's the use of petroleum and petroleum derivatives as fuel and in lubricants and medicines had grown to an extent that encouraged commercial exploration for larger supplies in both Texas and Indian territory. The big oil strike at Spindletop, near Beaumont, Texas, early in 1901 brought in undreamed-of quantities of petroleum; the gushers poured out the oil faster than earthen dams could be pushed together to hold it. The vast supply speeded its industrial use. Coal-burning power plants in factories, locomotives, and steamships were quickly converted to use the new fuel. And by 1910 the gasoline motor was beginning to come into its own as a consumer of what had, only a few generations earlier, been regarded as a peculiar natural resource of doubtful value. From that time to this the discovery of oil has brought a succession of booms to the whole region. Spindletop was the first of a series of spectacular strikes—Glen Pool, Electra, Seminole, Ragtown, Oklahoma City, East Texas, Burkburnett, Desdemona, Ranger, West Texas, and the rest. The oil-boom town had the excitement and violence that fiction so often—and unjustifiably—credited to the western town in the colorful days of the cattle empire. Fortunes were made and lost overnight; spying, subterfuge, and violence were commonplace.

Oil and the things that came from or with it—natural gas, carbon black, and the whole wide field of petrochemicals—have been of prime industrial importance to Texas, Oklahoma, and more recently to New Mexico. The Southwest is, to a large extent, blossoming as an industrial region without having passed through the industrial revolution to achieve it. Much of the credit belongs to oil and its associated industries. Oil and gas and the money they brought worked a profound change in both the landscape and the people.

There was the old man, a retired bronc stomper, who watched with mounting nervousness while a wildcat crew prepared for a drill stem test on the well drilled in the middle of his barren ranch in West Texas. Neighbors were there, too, jibing at the old man, asking him what he was going to do with his millions, or what he was going to do if the hole was dry. Finally the old man said: "Look, a man don't need no goddam million dollars; all he needs is some decent circumstances."

He got his decent circumstances and a whole lot more. His children got ranches of their own, his grandchildren got college educations, and the old man moved to the city where he sits in the Petroleum Club day after day, thinking with no nostalgia about the years he spent breaking horses.

The Southwest is full of tales of the oil-rich farmer, rancher, or wildcatter who, faced with sudden wealth, took to ordering Cadillacs from room service in the Adolphus in Dallas or the Skirvin in Oklahoma City, but the most diligent researcher can never find the original. The vast majority go about their business with no more than the normal aberrations of sudden wealth. Almost all build new homes. Some of them are sentimentally reminiscent of the combined horrors of both Victorian and Edwardian periods with ranch-house overtones—a style local architects refer to as "mid-continent crude." But more, well able to retain the best of architects, build tastefully and well and in many cases become knowing collectors of art. Some, who equate oil wealth with political wisdom, fancy themselves as king-makers and at times are beguiled into spending their money to influence the outcome of elections in states a thousand miles away; but most content themselves with local politics except when legislation having to do with the regulation of their industry is pending in Washington.

Regionally, Southwesterners have always been preoccupied with education. A nineteenth-century traveler, after visiting a frontier outpost in Texas, noted in his diary that the townspeople had two saloons, a general store, a bawdyhouse, an academy, and "they have logs cut for a University." The University of Texas is one of the wealthiest institutions in the world; it owns vast stretches of land in West Texas which, worthless or nearly so when assigned to the University, turned out to overlie some of the vastest oil fields in the nation. Both the University of Texas and other institutions in the area have been the recipients of handsome gifts from wealthy supporters. That the gifts more often run to buildings and football teams, both monumental in quality, rather than to endowment, is attributed to youthful ebullience.

This same ebullience leads to an exaggerated behavior away from home. The broad-brimmed white hat, hand-painted necktie, embroidered boots, and lavish manners to match are more frequently worn abroad than at home, where a man's friends will, as often as not, describe him as "just a plain old country boy." But the masquerade has worked to the extent that "Rich Oilman" and "Wealthy Rancher" have taken their place in the language along with such stock characters as the Boston Trustee, the Philadelphia Lawyer, the New York Banker, and the International Sportsman and Financier.

Texas and Oklahoma no longer monopolize the Southwest's oil industry. New Mexico has been rising steadily in the ranks of oil- and gas-producing states. Oil was first found in the southwestern part of the state; in recent years both oil and gas have been found in the northwestern corner, particularly in the San Juan basin. Drilling equipment and drilling crews have been flown in and out of otherwise inaccessible sites, and dusty desert settlements have become dustier oil-boom towns. The Navajos, chronic sufferers from poverty, have come into wealth. In one recent year alone the Navajos were paid $30 million for oil leases. Tribal treasuries are swelling with lease and royalty money. The Indians are wisely putting the money to uses benefiting the tribe as a whole: agricultural projects and educational funds to send the tribe's brightest youngsters off to college, with the understanding that they will come back and work with and among their own people.

The fact that the bleak, isolated Navajo country, harsh and uninviting to anything but a poetic eye, should turn out to conceal great wealth in oil, natural gas and, later, uranium, is typical of the entire Southwest.

In analyzing what has happened, one must take into account not only the great historical milestones—the treaty of Guadalupe Hidalgo, the cattle empire, and the spectacular rise of the oil industry—but also the way in which man's mechanical ingenuity—and science—helped make the land habitable. The whites were not really effective in fighting the Indians until a gunsmith in New England designed and made the first six-shooter. The modern cattle industry could not have grown to its present stature if barbed wire for fencing had not come along at the right time. Some of the greatest mineral deposits might never have been touched without the modern high-speed drilling equipment which can sink a hole miles into the earth. The airplane has solved the problem of transportation over vast barren country—the problem Jefferson Davis attempted to answer with camels. And many of the Southwest's fastest-growing cities would be uninhabitable in the summer months for any but the hardiest souls without air conditioning.

World War II was a milestone for the Southwest as it was for the rest of the world; but for the Southwest it had some important overtones.

Since the frontier days the region had long been dotted with military forts, and there was always a strong military tradition. But it also had a climate that made it possible to train men in the open during most of the year and to fly aircraft with almost no hindrance from the weather. In both World Wars I and II military establishments in the Southwest grew at an exponential rate. And in a sentimental but statistically important manner this contributed materially to the growth of the Southwest. Men who trained in the area liked it, liked the friendliness of the people—and in many cases liked the pretty girls —and returned postwar to start a new life in a friendly atmosphere.

But this homely, sympathetic fact is much less cogent than the scientific impact of World War II on the Southwest.

Early in World War II an isolated multifingered plateau on the side of the Jemez mountain range in northern New Mexico was chosen— almost entirely because of its isolation—as the headquarters for secret work on the atomic bomb. Here, at Los Alamos, noted scientists and highly skilled engineers and technicians gathered to work out one of the most forbidding scientific problems of all time. Then, in the drizzling pre-dawn darkness of July 16, 1945, the bomb was taken to "Trinity site" in the desert and detonated. Again the country's emptiness was a decisive factor, affording the sort of secrecy that was vital. There in the Sierra Oscuro, or gloomy mountains, in the region the Spanish explorers had labeled the *Jornada del Muerto* or dead man's march, the history of the world was violently altered.

Entirely aside from the military and political implications of the bomb, it marked the beginning of an age of science, an age in which science was to dominate warfare to an unprecedented extent; and similarly a period in which science was to become an overriding concern of industry. The latter was in time to become a dynamic factor in changing the character of the Southwest.

The existence of Los Alamos dictated the establishment of corollary industries and military bases. At Sandia Base private industry and armed forces jointly turned out the casings, firing mechanisms, and other hardware needed for the bombs. Air bases were keyed to scientific work, some flying security cover for scientific laboratories, some devoted to training in the use of atomic devices. And around them sprang up many small industries to meet the needs of the large government installations.

The result was that New Mexico, one of the most sparsely settled regions of the nation, entered upon a period of explosive growth both in population and income—and the character of the state's economy was radically altered from pastoral to scientific in one dizzy leap. In the first decade after World War II the state's population jumped by more than 50 percent—exceeded in rate only by its next-door neighbor, Arizona. Per-capita income increased by almost the same percentage. Farm and ranch hands swarmed into the towns for industrial jobs, joining the migratory streams pouring in from the east and north. Albuquerque, for instance, tripled in size between 1940 and 1957.

Again because of the country's sparse population, New Mexico achieved primary importance in the development and testing of missiles and rockets—which may in time equal if not exceed the growth that was stimulated by nuclear research. Work done at the White Sands Proving Grounds and Holloman Air Development Center at

Alamogordo may in time rank with the historical significance of Los Alamos.

By happy coincidence the prospectors who were galvanized into activity by nuclear science's need of uranium made their greatest discoveries in New Mexico. The Four Corners region—where New Mexico, Arizona, Colorado, and Utah meet—contains the nation's greatest known beds of ore. Deposits found under the dry bed of Ambrosia Lake doubled this country's known reserves of uranium and put New Mexico in the position of having 70 percent of the U.S. supply. The town of Grants, because of the uranium finds, tripled its population, as Albuquerque had, but did it in less than a year.

The science-based boom was not confined to New Mexico. New light industries have sprung up in all states of the region. The vast petrochemical industry that now flourishes all along the Gulf coast was largely an outgrowth of World War II. The same is true throughout the area of the manufacture of aircraft and aircraft components.

Much of the new industry is of the footloose variety. Electronics is a good example. Both raw materials and finished products are low in bulk. Unlike the old heavy industries that had to be near a railroad or waterway—for the sake of coal and iron coming in and heavy machinery going out—many of the new industries can situate themselves in any place that is wired for electricity, has gas or oil piped in for fuel, and a highway for trucks. This being the case, climate becomes a major industrial concern. Engineers and technicians—of vital importance to such industry—are in short supply. The engineer or technician can pick and choose. More often than not he will choose the company that has had the foresight to locate its plant where the climate is mild and the living is easy.

Arizona has been one of the principal beneficiaries of this combination of circumstances. Both military bases and rapid industrial expansion helped boost the population by 70 percent in the decade after World War II, tripling the size of some of the cities. But of all the impressive statistics on population, industry, and income, none is more revealing or effective than Arizona's claim that it has more private swimming pools than any other state in the nation. (There are said to be 4000 in the Phoenix area alone.) The private swimming pool is a symbol of the sort of relaxed and easy living in a benign climate that is at the heart of the matter. Many of Arizona's immigrants come there solely because of the climate and stay to get a new job in industry or to start a business of their own. Perhaps they don't become customers for a private swimming pool; but they no longer have to shovel snow.

The character of the people is changing rapidly in the transition from a ranching and farming rural economy to an urban industrial and commercial economy. The native population is becoming a dwindling minority as the population flood pours in. Said one old settler, standing at a busy intersection in Albuquerque and shaking his head at the traffic: "Why, when I first came out here this was nothing but a dirt track, no traffic but jack rabbits and lizards and maybe a rattlesnake. That was two years ago last January." This sort of short-term nostalgia is quickly swallowed up in the excitement of growth.

But there are two chronic concerns.

One is that since so much of the new industry is based on national defense, much of it would collapse if an enduring peace were achieved. No one knows the answer to this.

The other is as old as the country: water, or the scarcity of it. The maximum usage of surface water is rapidly being reached. Underground water resources, put to more and more strain as both population and industry have grown, are diminishing rapidly.

But with the characteristic optimism of the region, everyone is certain that by the time the problem becomes critical a solution will have been found, either in new resources, more effective conservation and re-use of present resources, or in distillation of sea water, a thing that might become feasible with the abundant power of a truly atomic age. Or solar power might provide the answer.

Such confidence is completely in keeping with the history of the region. For the strength, the vitality springs from secret, invisible things. There were none of the classic indications of future growth and wealth; no waterfalls to turn the mills, no great harbors or deep navigable rivers to carry commerce, no great forests to provide building materials and fuel.

There were, instead, oil and gas locked deep in the earth; the power locked in uranium ores; the strong sunlight and the clear air; and above all, the empty land that always beckons to adventurous men.

The Southeast

BY RALPH McGILL

One begins with geography.

The "South," which is the more usable name for the Southeast, sweeps south and west from Virginia, to Mississippi, Arkansas, and Texas. Through it, from a beginning in New Jersey and Pennsylvania, curves the great red- and brown-soiled crescent of the Piedmont Plateau. The great, many-folded Appalachians reach south and west, creating a vast, seemingly endless wilderness of peaks, ranges, and ridges in the Carolinas and East Tennessee, and thrusting buttresses into South Carolina and Georgia. Northward beyond the mountains are highlands with bluegrass and limestone streams. To the south are prairie lands rich and lush, wire-grass regions, and pinewoods. And farther on, the bayous, the tidal swamps, and the delta lands.

The region's settlers came first to the coastal plain and put names upon it—the "Tidewater" in Virginia, the "Low Country" in South Carolina. Two-thirds of Florida is coastal plain, which runs about 300 miles inland into North Carolina, thrusts deeply into the Gulf states, and extends into East Texas.

The Appalachians were the great barrier to movement by the new settlers. Philadelphia was the first great port of entry. And from it men and their families pushed on, seeking a way through the Appalachians.

They found the great valley in Virginia and followed it into Georgia and North and South Carolina. The probing, restless men discovered Cumberland Gap and pushed into the dark and bloody ground that became Kentucky.

Geography began to do things to people.

A land so divided by mountains and rivers did not make for unity or cohesion. Cabins and clearings slowly dotted the Piedmont. Grist mills were built on its streams and along the Fall Line. They were as separated from the great coastal-plain plantations, where rice, tobacco, and indigo had brought wealth, slavery, luxury, and a cultural tie with Europe, as if they dwelt in another world. And, in a sense, they did.

The coastal aristocrats were, for the most part, self-made, though the myth says otherwise. There were few cavaliers. They were mostly vigorous, middle-class stock, for whom the wealth produced by tobacco and rice made it possible to establish themselves in the English way. Their manor houses were named after the great halls in the mother country and furnished with English goods. Some few lived like feudal barons. But the aristocrats, barons, and the white-pillared manor houses were in the minority. Ownership of slaves was the usual identifying badge of the gentry. By 1860 there were only 383,637 slaveholders in a white population of more than 8 million. Of these, only 48,566 owned 20 or more. By 1860 the great body of Southerners were of the middle class whether measured by economic or by social yardsticks.

From the beginning the planters, being more or less concentrated along the coastal plains, and possessing transportation and communication to and with Europe and its capitals, became essentially what the nobility are in England. They were able to put the stamp of the country gentleman so firmly on the South that even the rise of the cities, with their commerce and trade, did not change it. The planter pattern held until the end.

The weather, like geography and the planters, put its stamp on the customs and the people of the region. Long growing seasons, heat, and high humidity were its features. In Virginia this season of growth was six months. In the deeper South it was nine. There was plenty of rain, but it didn't always come when needed. Summer droughts were common and winter freezes sometimes reached to the

Gulf. Crops grew lush, but the soil washed easily in the often torrential rains and the fields "wore out" within a few years where slave cultivation was careless.

The heat put its stamp on architecture. Ceilings were high. There were wide porches and balconies.

And, finally, there was the Negro with his influence to add to geography, the planters, and the weather. His exact contribution cannot be dissected out of the whole. Where culture and refinement were accepted, his labor provided the necessary leisure and opportunity. If, in some places, he fostered a kindly paternalism, he provided, too, an example of loyalty and good manners which were a part of the plantation tradition. Psychologists think that, perhaps, by giving some men and women freedom from drudgery, the Negro made possible close family relationships. Fostered by security within the family came an attitude of self-assurance which somehow became a distinguishing attribute of the planter sons and daughters.

There was a trace of the Negro's inflections which found its way into the Southern tongue, and some of his laughter and superstitions found their way into the Southern personality. Exactly what the Negro gave to the sectional character and quality of the South is an inseparable part of both. Suffice it to say, he was a major factor.

There is one thing that may be defined. The presence of more than 4 million dark-skinned enslaved persons in a population of not quite 12½ million created a race problem and made the section acutely race conscious, with a nagging current of accusing guilt in that sectional consciousness.

For many years, however, there was none of this—not even a hint—but only the surging nationalism of the new and burgeoning young Republic.

As 1820 began it could be said with truth there was no sectional America. There was, to be sure, the "West," and the "East." But the "West" was the frontier, the restless, never-fixed line of settlement.

In 1820 it was a straggling line of great unevenness. It had one end at Lake Erie. It made a sort of wedge-shaped line across Ohio and southern Indiana and Illinois on into Missouri. From there it cut back to middle Tennessee and Alabama. It was drawn not too deeply back from the coastline of South Carolina and Georgia.

Wherever this line of frontier settlement ran was the "West."

There was, in 1820, neither Southeast nor a South, though there were proud Southerners. They had shared and suffered in the war for independence, the struggles of the confederation, the War of 1812, and had helped bring the Republic and its Constitution into being. There was pride in the fact that Southerners had made so positive a contribution, but in the main it was a national pride and not in the narrow regional sense. Indeed, the Southerners were, in general, satisfied with the government. They were, in 1820 as they had been since the founding of the Republic, playing a major role in the direction of national affairs. There was but one political party, the Republican (later known as the Democratic). Southerners came close to dominating it. In 1820 James Monroe of Virginia was President. Of four Presidents before him, three had been Virginians. Three of his six cabinet members were Southerners, as was the powerfully influential Speaker of the House.

The Congress of 1820, contrasted with those of the twentieth century, seems too good to be true. There was no party rivalry. There was no Southern states-rights faction, no slave-state bloc, no farm lobby, no liberal or conservative factionalisms, no pro- or anti-labor sentiment, and no regional nationalisms. The South was at peace with itself, with the nation, and with the Republican Party. Yet there were fundamental regional differences which climate, crops, and events all too soon were to bring into focus.

In the region south of the Ohio River were 10 of the 20 states making up the Republic. Five were on the Atlantic coast: Maryland, Virginia, North Carolina, South Carolina, and Georgia. Their populations thinned out a few miles back from the sea. These were the colonial states. There had been in them a strain of loyalty to the king and the mother country which had made their entry into the Revolution a slower and more cautious one than that of Massachusetts.

Five were the younger states, hacked out of the inland frontier by the more restless and discontented ones from the colonial "East." These were Kentucky, Tennessee, Louisiana, Mississippi, and Alabama. The last two had but recently come to statehood. They had been admitted in 1817 and 1819, respectively, with the Indian war whoop still in their ears. Long years of harassments, pressures, and treaties had been slowly eroding away the lands of the Creek confederation, but not until 1832 would the Indian population be removed westward.

Some 14,000 persons had pushed on into the territory of Arkansas. Florida was still a subject of bargaining with Spain. Mexico, of which Texas was a colony, was nearing victory in her war of independence with Spain.

While the Southeastern area, or the "South," had exactly half the states, there was a slow falling behind in population. The census of 1820 showed them a half-million behind. There was a feature of the region which contributed to making it unique, or "different." Of the South's 4,298,199 persons, 1,496,189 were slaves with no right of citizenship. In addition, there were 116,915 "free persons of color" in the 10 states. These, while free, were not citizens. The white population was 2,685,095, about half that of the North.

There were other population contrasts. The region had received little influx from foreign countries since colonial days. There was a smoothed-out homogeneity. In the whole South there were only a few more than 12,000 unnaturalized persons. The cities of the North had more than 40,000. The opening up of Mississippi and Alabama Indian lands was to have a further containing effect on the population. It did not push westward.

In 1820 one of every four Southerners was a Virginian. As the tobacco lands of that state, farmed since earliest colonial days, began to wear out, there was an exodus to the new cotton lands in Mississippi and Alabama. There was a like movement from other older states, especially South Carolina. The only Southern states which, in 1820, could boast of any substantial growth in the preceding decade were Mississippi, Alabama, Louisiana, Tennessee, and Georgia.

The slave population also varied. Wherever the plantation economy was best suited, the percentage of Negroes was high. But slavery was the one common trait, and as time would tell, the most meaningful. In each Southern state, save Kentucky and Tennessee, Negroes made up a third or more of the population. It ranged from 52.7 percent in South Carolina down to 19.6 in Tennessee. In Kentucky, Tennessee, Virginia, and North Carolina, the mountain regions not only contained few slaves, there was a feeling of resentment against slaveholders. This was not because of any antislavery sentiment but was rather one of class. The small freeholder yeoman of the Appalachian valleys and coves resented the ease and luxury of the great plantations. And, perhaps more, he regarded slavery as an unfair, even un-American competition.

By 1820 the South, contented and satisfied with national affairs, was thoroughly committed to an agrarian economy. And though none knew it then, this agrarianism was a road which inevitably forked off from national unity into regional nationalism.

Ninety percent of all Southerners were engaged in agriculture, as compared with 77 percent in the rest of the nation. But it was not "farming" as the North knew it. It was an intense concentration on huge money crops, and the market was the world. There were, of course, enough acres devoted to food to maintain the plantations, large and small. But it was very much a secondary operation. Cotton, tobacco, rice, and sugar were the preoccupation of planters. Each crop had its kingdom, but King Cotton's was the largest and most powerful.

Tobacco had its domain in two wide areas in the upper South. Because it is a crop which requires great and continuing personal care, it was not well suited to large plantations and large numbers of workers. It came, finally, to be the crop of small farmers with a few slaves or none. For many it was a family affair.

Here and there hemp was a rival of tobacco, but it occupied only a small domain, never an empire.

Rice ruled a region of marsh and swampland inland along the Atlantic from the lower North Carolina coast down past Georgia where the fresh-water tidal rivers ebbed and flowed. South Carolina led, with about three-fourths of the total crop. Georgia was next.

As late as 1935 old Liverpool Hazzard, who had been a slave on one of Pierce Butler's island plantations off the Georgia coast, would talk to visitors about the rice fields, the harsh, heavy work, the mosquitoes and the fevers. There was one memory which he savored. The rice birds came in great flocks, and old Liverpool would smack his toothless gums as he recalled them spitted over hot coals. The rice planters, of whom there were never more than 600-odd, were the real aristocrats, looking with a certain condescension on the vulgar mob which came clearing land to grow cotton or sweated down the tobacco rows. Some increased their wealth with Sea Island cotton, also a semiexclusive crop, suited only to the islands and coastal strips. There, the percentage of slaves was high.

Sugar ruled in the lower reaches of the Mississippi River, with Louisiana as its major territory. Here was work which great gangs of slave labor could do well.

Cotton was something else. Anyone could grow cotton. By 1820 the value of the crop was greater than all the others put together. In 1819 and 1820 the crop was around 350,000 bales. Three-fourths of it was sold abroad at 16 cents per pound.

Each decade, from then until the war began in 1861, the cotton crop just about doubled. There seemed no end to the demand for cotton. New, improved gins and better seeds and varieties at home were matched by the invention of new spinning machines in England.

Growing it did not require great capital or slaves for a beginning. But men who began small thought and dreamed big. The bales of cotton were steppingstones to the far-stretching acres, to hundreds of "hands," to the white-pillared mansions, to juleps stirred with a silver spoon.

Most of the wealth flowed overseas. The more prosperous Southern planters imported their literature, wines, furniture, rugs, and silver from England and France.

Government in the Southern states was centered in the counties. The counties sent men to the legislature. The legislature elected the United States Senators and exercised, directly and indirectly, almost complete control over all affairs of the state. The right to vote was restricted largely to freeholders. Government represented, in the main, the opinion of the slaveholding planting class. This influence was great in national affairs, and so in 1820 there was no nationalistic "South."

But there was a growing resentment against the money power. Chief creditor of the land hungry who had poured into the new lands to buy cotton was the Federal Government which had sold public lands, and the banks. The constrictions of currency and credit which began in 1818 had extended into 1819 and 1820. By this latter year, discontent had united the frontier West and the South in economic opposition to the East and the Bank of the United States and Federal policies and legislation dealing with tariff, land sales, and bankruptcy. The East began to agitate containment of slavery in the South and to argue more loudly than ever before that enslavement of human beings was a moral wrong.

The charge came to dominate the debate over the admission of Missouri to statehood. From that time on, slavery was a dark Nemesis on American development. It began to color all attitudes and slowly to crowd aside most other considerations. Symbols replaced realities. All chance of defining the role of planter and industrialist, of farmer and worker in American life was lost sight of in the fierce controversy over the extension of slavery and the deeper meaning of political control which was at the heart of it.

The three-fifths provision of the Constitution allowed a state to add to its free population three-fifths of its slave total for the purpose of determining the number of congressional representatives to which it was entitled. The faster-growing East, with a developing urbanism with its craftsmen and builders, was becoming more and more restive over the political strength of the planters in national affairs. They saw in each new slave state a strengthening of the planter influence.

Had slavery been merely a social and moral issue, it could have been met and resolved as such. But suddenly, out of nowhere it seemed, it burst on the young nation as the emotional factor of a sectional issue, linked to sectional rivalry and national expansion.

Before the expansion controversy began, there had been little difference between North and South in the vigor of expressed antislavery sentiment. Nor could the great surge of Northern moral indignation over slavery be regarded as the harvest of long years of Northern compassion for the slave.

To this day it is not entirely clear how what could have been a normal sort of sectional rivalry turned into a bitter, at times irrational, struggle between the North and South. Slavery became the symbol of the many differences between them. Soon, too, it became the symbol by which partisans were to prove "right" and "wrong," to define "progress" and "backwardness," "evil" and "good."

From 1820 there were 41 brief years before the "irrepressible conflict" began. They were swift, sweaty years of sound and fury, of astonishing growth and vitality.

Regional nationalism, or sectionalism, which was thrust seemingly full-born into being in 1820 by the debate over the slavery sections of the new state of Missouri's constitution, was one of three dominant characteristics of American life in the period from 1820 to 1860. All were related. All moved swiftly.

Growth was rapid. The line of frontier settlement was never still. People came. People moved westward.

Population doubled in nearly every decade. By 1860 there were substantial settlements on the Pacific, in Minnesota, Kansas, Arkansas, and Texas which had ceased to be a republic to become a state. In that period the people broke a hundred million acres to the plow. Wheat and corn grew on the prairies. They had built cities and fought a war, adding by the latter land enough for a small empire in the Southwest.

The four great sections emerged and took on form and substance during these four decades: the Southeast or "South," the Southwest, Northeast, and Northwest. Each had differences within itself, but regional cultures began to grow and be shaped by their economics and their history.

Of these four, no other was so distinct and so set apart as the old South. Its great staple crops, dependent on a world market, its system of plantations worked by slave labor, had produced a unique social ideology, a way of life. The presence of slaves had held to a minimum the development of an artisan and craftsman class. As its weather, too, was distinct, so was its thinking.

The South thought of itself as different. There was a certain agreement in this. The three other sections also thought of it as different. From 1820 on it became more and more self-conscious. Myths began to grow about it. To the outsiders the South seemed to possess complete unity. Actually, in the colonial years and the early days of the Republic, its leaders had acted in co-operative accord. But as the nation expanded and prospered, the South developed internal conflicts. In weather, population, and political influence, the South began to be outdistanced. All this served to emphasize sectionalism, to create a slow-growing psychology of always being on the defensive. It spread from politics to religion, and in time caused the withdrawal of the Southern Methodist and Baptist churches into regional conferences and associations of their own. In the field of economics, this defensive push to withdraw was even stronger.

Only the belief that John C. Calhoun would soon be President re-strained South Carolina from complete defiance of the protective tariff of 1827–28. Calhoun himself, seeking to avoid this revolution, came forward in 1832 with his plan of nullification or interposition. A sovereign state, he argued, could declare an act of Congress null and void and appeal to its fellow sovereigns to endorse or reflect that action. The South Carolina legislature adopted this action. President Andrew Jackson was brusque. The Union, he said, must be preserved. South Carolina failed to receive support expected from her sister states. There was a tariff compromise. But bitterness remained. And there was increased talk of state "sovereignty" and "states rights."

The Mexican War, which began in 1846, soon became the issue of sectionalism. The abolitionists, joined by economic interests damaged by the war, cried that it was an unjust war of conquest and imperialism brought on by the slave interests. It was, they said, merely a war to extend slavery. The legislature of Massachusetts went so far as officially to describe it as such a war and declared that honest men could not support it.

Sectional hostility distorted and colored every issue. All differences came to be oversimplified by describing the South as a land of slavery and the North as one of freedom.

The great compromise of 1850, defining slave territory and free, attained after two years of bitter debate, dissension, and threats of secession, revealed the lack of unity in the South. But the agreement settled nothing. The absolutists, for this word fits them even better than extremists, had not changed their attitudes nor abandoned their objectives. In the North the abolitionists scorned the compromise and also extended their efforts to nullify the fugitive slave laws. In the South, Robert Barnwell Rhett, William Lowndes Yancey, South Carolinians; and Edmund Ruffian of Virginia, were the fire-breathing absolutists who, during the 1850's, shouted down the moderates and prepared mass opinion for secession. They had many helpers, but more than any others, they pumped adrenalin into the political veins of the South.

The Southern states, driven by these men and inflamed by the abolitionist extremists, began to drive for economic self-sufficiency. It was a program too late to succeed. Failure and frustration induced a withdrawal both intellectual and spiritual. There were boycotts of Northern summer resorts, a rewriting of textbooks, the founding of Southern magazines, a glorification of all that made them and the region different. It increased in heat and volume as Northern abolitionists painted an increasingly harsh picture of a brutal and licentious slave power. Each made of the other a stereotype.

Thus was the ground prepared. There were many who sowed the seeds. Many of these seeds produced perennials which have continued to push themselves out of the soil to be reaped over and over again, long years after the deadly harvest of civil war.

Despite all this, the presidential vote of 1860 proved, without doubt, the majority of the people were still conservative. Lincoln polled 1,866,452 votes. Stephen H. Douglas, nominee of the Northern Democrats, 1,376,957; John Breckenridge, of the Southern Democratic wing, 849,781; and John Bell, candidate of the Southern states-rights conservatives, 588,879.

In 10 Southern states Lincoln did not receive a single vote—or so said the grimly gleeful men who counted the ballots and announced the results.

But even the Southern people were of a conservative mind. Breckenridge carried the South but surprisingly did not win a majority of the popular vote. He had more votes in the North than Lincoln in the South, but they were few.

A minority President had been elected.

The parties, like values, minds, and emotions, had become sectional.

There were the moderates, in the press and in person, who pointed out that though Lincoln was legally elected, he could not hurt the South. There was, they said, no need for the secession. The South would still control the Congress and its important committees.

There were some who suggested that Maryland, Virginia, Kentucky, Missouri, Arkansas, Tennessee, and North Carolina create a border confederation by which the sane people of the South could escape the extremists of both regions. But the radicals of absolutism went their irrepressible way. Most of the moderates capitulated in bitterness of spirit, many of them with praise of the Union on their lips.

By December 17, 1860, Rhett and his associates had called a convention to order in South Carolina. Three days later a state ordinance of secession was voted. Within six weeks Mississippi, Florida, Alabama, Georgia, Louisiana, and Texas had duplicated that action. The deep

South, the Cotton Kingdom, began to look toward a confederacy. In Georgia, North Carolina, and Texas there was substantial, stubborn conservative opposition which fought a delaying action.

There was a great surge of enthusiasm, but also a foreboding. There would be no war, men said reassuringly. A common saying was that a lady's thimble would hold all the blood that would be spilled. Sometimes this was varied by asserting that a handkerchief would wipe up all the blood that would be let. Many argued that reconstruction of the Union would be easier with the South out than in.

On February 4 the Montgomery convention met to form a new nation. In the elections on the 9th the fire-eaters were excluded from office. Jefferson Davis and Alexander Stephens were selected, respectively, as President and Vice-president. Both were conservatives. Stephens was, for many, a bitter pill to swallow. He had fought against secession with all his skill, was a friend of Lincoln's, and—many believed—was a Unionist at heart.

When spring and April came, impetuous South Carolina fired on Fort Sumter. Lincoln called for volunteers. In the emotional upsurge that followed, the conservatives who had controlled in Virginia, North Carolina, Arkansas, and Tennessee were swept aside. "Nobody," says an old letter of that time, "is allowed to retain and assert his reason."

An understanding of some aspects of the South of today and tomorrow may be had from that yesterday.

The Cotton Kingdom had come with a rush.

Sumter and the call for troops brought in Virginia, but the western counties which had voted Union began a new state movement. In 1863, under Federal protection, these were admitted to the Union as a state—West Virginia.

Arkansas, which before had voted not to secede, came reluctantly to secession. North Carolina and Tennessee followed, with a large minority dissenting.

Kentucky had in her political and emotional blood stream the tradition of Henry Clay. She hopefully determined on a policy of neutrality. Her strategic position made this impossible. The Confederates moved first. But Federal troops hurried across the Ohio and seized half the state. In December 1861 unoccupied Kentucky voted to secede. But the strategic area was in Federal hands, and they never relaxed the grip.

Nowhere in the Confederacy, for all the tumultuous support of se-cession, was there universal acceptance of it. The western parts of Virginia and North Carolina and the eastern areas of Tennessee and Kentucky were primarily Union. Had there been an easy military route into east Tennessee as into West Virginia, that region, too, would have been admitted as a loyal state.

Here and there about the South were islands of unionism, including two counties in Mississippi. One of these, Jones, was known as the Republic of Jones.

Where no, or few, slaves were, Union sentiment was strongest. And in the Appalachians the old legends of the Revolutionary War and pride in the mountain men at Kings Mountain held men to the Flag.

Certain Unionists, like the aristocratic intellectual James Louis Petigru of Charleston, S. C., were tolerated through the war.

The war itself was a curious one, bloody, glorious, and cruel. Any of the adjectives will fit at least a part of it. All through its four des-perate years there were times when certain amenities were observed. Pickets often traded and fraternized. When General George Pickett's baby was born, Grant's troops lighted bonfires and sent congratula-tions. When Lincoln visited Richmond, captured after so many de-lays, he visited George Pickett's house. "Just say an old friend called," he said.

Confederates cheered Meagher's Irish Brigade when it made its heroic charge up the steep slopes of Marye's Heights in the battle of Fredericksburg. The Federal army had great and undisguised admira-tion for Stonewall Jackson and for Beauty Stuart's great artilleryman, John Pelham. General William T. Sherman, for all his decisiveness, thought enough of the amenities to engage in a long, written debate with the mayor of Atlanta trying to make that unhappy man see the necessity of burning the central part of his city.

The war began with atrocity stories, but the actual atrocities were few. There were looting and vandalism. Much of this was done by ir-regulars or guerrillas, who sometimes plundered their own people. But crimes against women and civilians were so few as to provide excep-tions. There was, on occasion, vast and sometimes wanton destruction of property, but never were there crimes against the people such as the world saw in 1914–18, and on a larger scale in 1940–45. To this day there is a controversy whether Columbia, S. C., was burned deliberately. But as historians have noted, it is unusual that there should be a controversy at all.

Abraham Lincoln, who had planned to bring the Southern states back into the Union with honor, never referred to the Confederates as rebels. General Robert E. Lee had no harsh phrases for the men on the other side. To him, they were always "those people." The soldiers called each other "Johnny Reb" and "Billy Yank." There were some who felt hate and exercised it. The newspapers thundered for blood and the scalps of generals. They invented the scurrilous phrases, the rhetoric of abuse. The politicians also slandered, boasted, vilified. They, too, though failing more than any connected with the war, demanded success of the generals, many of whom were incompetents placed in commands by the influence of politicians.

It was an American war, a fact which made it unique. Even the German and Irish brigades in the Federal armies were fighting with new-country ideas in their heads. No old-country emotions stirred them. The flag they followed was theirs. In the South, soldiers thought of themselves first as being from individual states. As the idea of a national loyalty had not won a place above that of state allegiance, so the Confederacy never replaced the identity of self with state.

Even the commanding generals of the South thought of their regiments as state organizations, never as being merely soldiers sworn to a new nation. Much of the morale of the troops on both sides came from this pride in state. To fail in a charge or to retreat was to disgrace the state.

There was not much talk of states rights among Southern troops. This political obsession with states rights later was to do as much to defeat the South as the opposing regiments. All through the war the governors and the legislatures were bickering and were increasingly difficult for the central government to handle. It was a matter for cajoling, and Jefferson Davis, an austere man, was not good at it. There was never enough unity.

Because it was the last war of the individual, the unmachined man, and since it was an all-American war with a great proportion of men in arms and otherwise directly committed with it, it has remained a personal sort of thing. The officers on each side had friends on the other. It was a war of brother against brother, especially in the states of Kentucky and Tennessee. But while the editors, orators, politicians, and many civilians carried on a war of bitterness and abuse, the troops fought bitterly but held each other in real esteem.

It was at once a war of the rank amateur and the best of professionals. There was never enough discipline. Nor was there ever adequate planning for medical and hospital services, for morale or welfare of the families of soldiers or sailors. The troops might fight and perform like mobs, or with a skill and perfection never attained in previous wars. Some of the battles and campaigns were ludicrous, preposterous caricatures of war—though nonetheless bloody. Others were so perfectly contrived from the viewpoint of tactics and strategy that through the years many of the general staffs of Europe have studied and imitated them.

It was a war, too, which called for all the arts of war, and for the invention of new ones.

For the first time in history the railroad was a major factor of war. The first Battle of Manassas was turned by troops hurried there by rail. Thereafter the railroads were a prime consideration of each opponent.

The telegraph, which largely followed the rails, also made its world debut as a factor of combat.

The Civil War provided, too, the first large-scale sea blockade which in part was countered by large-scale blockade running. Submarines played a small but significant role. There was amphibious war on beaches and the banks of rivers. The South made a great sweep into Pennsylvania. Pragmatic "Crump" Sherman marched from Atlanta to the sea, wholly lost for weeks to the top command and to Washington.

Though war had been talked and blustered for almost 10 years, neither side was prepared for it. The South, of necessity, came close to marshaling all its resources. The North never did. From the administrative viewpoint the war was, North and South, a shambles. There was vast waste of human beings and materials. There was almost incredible inefficiency. Both governments suffered from the insistence of the states on playing state and local politics to the detriment of the respective national governments. In the North, Lincoln was better able to command support than was Jefferson Davis who was increasingly plagued, and destroyed, by states rights.

Despite the failure of organization and bureaucracy, both armies proved enormously resourceful. The feats of engineers, both the Blue and the Gray, sometimes test the credulity of readers of history. They spanned rivers, great and small, with bridges. They built dams, dug canals, kept the railroads running—or prevented them.

In resourcefulness the South again led, for the old reason that necessity is the mother of invention. The Southern currency became valueless in trade soon after the war began. The region was agricultural, with few factories and no backlog of skills in its people. Slavery had stood in the way of the growth of a class of artisans such as urban and industrial centers require. Yet, despite all this, so well did the Southern people fill the many voids that not a single Confederate army or navy defeat could be excused for lack of arms, ammunition, or equipment.

Both sides were, with few exceptions, led by men of great and devout religious conviction. Both armies were swept by revivals. Each prayed to the same God, and quite humanly believed this same God looked upon them with favor.

The great lack of bitterness between the armies cannot too often be noted. The meetings to agree upon terms of capitulation between Generals Robert E. Lee and U. S. Grant, and a few days later between Generals Joseph Johnston and William T. Sherman, were emotional because of their lack of it. Both were significant for their compassion, understanding, and the recognition of the great American bond between them. There was a touch of humor in the Johnston-Sherman meeting, as there was not in the momentous one between Grant and Lee. Somehow a bottle of bourbon appeared on the table in the farmhouse meeting in North Carolina. After they had talked terms over drinks, Joe Johnston proposed another. Sherman declined, saying that if he took another he might be doing the surrendering.

The supreme tragedy of Lincoln's assassination loosed the hatreds nurtured and aggravated by political and extremist ambitions for power and revenge.

But, even so, the American character, which had placed its stamp on the years of war, reasserted itself. There was no blood shed after the war. The plans and attempts to convict the leaders of the seceding states fell of their own weight.

The four years of war in the South were a time of elation and de-

9. Edward Valentine's recumbent statue of General Robert E. Lee is
n Lee Chapel on the campus of Washington and Lee University, Lex-
ington, Virginia.

50. One of the world's greatest and most modern shipbuilding and ship-repair plants, at Newport News, Virginia, along the estuary of the James River.

51. Historical settings are artfully and authentically recreated at Williamsburg, Virginia.

2. South Holston Lake, impounded behind TVA's South Holston Dam,
lies chiefly in eastern Tennessee, but extends into Virginia.

53. St. Augustine, Florida, as the oldest city in the United States, has historic sites that date back to the late-middle 1500's, two generations before the *Mayflower*. This is the Castillo de San Marcos, built more than 200 years ago.

54. Moss-draped trees beside one of the multitudinous lakes of central Florida.

55. Harvesting rice in east-central Arkansas.

6. A tobacco warehouse in eastern North Carolina, just before auction time.

57.   Miami Beach, Florida — in any season.

58.   An infrared view of a roadside canal in the Florida Everglades.

59.   Kentucky is justly proud of its horses.

0.   The Pickwick Landing Dam near the point where Tennessee, Mississippi, and Alabama come together, is but one of many in the TVA chain.

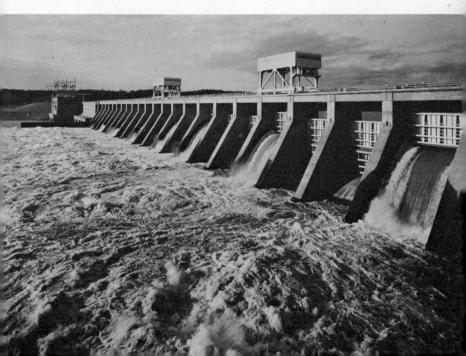

61. In the Cypress Gardens, a former reservoir near Charleston, Sout
Carolina.

spair, heroism and defection, self-sacrifice on a scale which has inspired all generations since. It was a period, too, of greed and great callousness. Defeat did not merely bring to a conclusion a society, a slave economy, an era. It had a profound effect on the United States and its future. (Since 1865 one of the South's preoccupations has been with the anatomy of that defeat.) As there had been hope of avoiding war with secession, peace movements continued throughout the war. Roughly two-thirds of the Southerners owned no slaves at all and civilian bitterness grew out of that fact as the fortunes of war declined.

It is possible to dissect from this resentment some of the political "have not" attitudes which were to become so demagogic a part of cotton-South politics after the war. A class feeling developed early in the first year of combat. It was, an increasing voice said, a rich man's war and a poor man's fight. Because of the South's desperate need for production, ownership of 20 or more slaves was made grounds for exemption from military service. This ruling was abused. While economically necessary, it was politically injurious. In the last years of the war the discontented were saying, as letters to newspapers revealed, that "if a man is poor—no matter how virtuous or intelligent he may be—his poverty as effectually excludes him from the presence of the aristocracy as if he were afflicted with the leprosy or the smallpox." There were proposals that once the war was won all soldiers who owned no land be given 50 acres and a slave as a bonus. These are but samples of many complaints, all on the same theme.

Peace movements, large and small, continued all through the war years. In 1863, Governor Zebulon B. Vance of North Carolina became so concerned over the strength of one in his state that he demanded of President Davis, in a letter of December 30 of that year, that the Confederacy make an effort to obtain an armistice.

Davis was never in any sympathy with these movements. He regarded the separation as final. Even after Johnston's surrender, to which he reluctantly agreed, he nursed the hopeless dream of somehow escaping to return with a following to fight on to victory. Time after time he refused pleas and plans proposed by Southerners as ways to end the war. Davis wanted peace, but with independence. He tried, through agents secret and public, to create a peace demand on Lincoln from the old Northwestern states of Ohio, Illinois, and Indiana whose southerly areas had largely been populated by Southerners. He failed, but he did create there the secret society—Knights of the Golden Circle—which promoted the Copperhead movement. The greatest Northern supporter of these Southern overtures was Clement L. Vallandigham, Ohio Democratic leader. For months the Union tolerated him in open defiance of the government. He was, finally, deported southward in the summer of 1863. There he was treated courteously but coolly. He at last sailed from a Southern port to exile in Canada.

In June of 1863 Vice-president Alexander Stephens, brooding on the cool veranda of his home near Washington, Georgia, wrote President Davis for permission to go to Washington ostensibly to seek ways and means to alleviate the sufferings of personnel, but really, once there, to discuss the possibility of peace. Stephens had few, if any, illusions about the permanency of the Confederacy. He informed Davis he wanted to negotiate on the basis of the sovereignty of each state and its right to "determine its own destiny."

Davis, almost certainly with cynical restraint, withheld from Stephens the news that General Lee even then was making ready to invade the North. He believed, correctly, that Stephens would not have begun his journey had he known. But the frail and crippled little man did start by boat down the James. He reached Newport along with news of the Confederate failure at Gettysburg and of Lee's retreat back into Virginia. Federal officials turned him back.

Joining with Governor Joseph E. Brown of Georgia, Stephens created a peace movement in their state which coincided with that led in North Carolina by William Holden and Congressman William W. Boyce in South Carolina. State sovereignty was their slogan, and they attacked Davis for having destroyed it. There was some sentiment for a second secession, this time from the Confederacy. In Richmond President Davis remained as aloof as possible. He was wholly uncompromising on independence for the Confederacy and knew that any peace plan based on state sovereignty would be immediately fatal to the deteriorating government he headed. He had seen what a disaster states rights, as exercised by a sovereign state, could bring to a central government. Vice-president Stephens, his dislike of Davis increasing, boldly charged that the Confederate leader wanted Lincoln elected, rather than the Northern Democratic nominee, George

McClellan, who was pledged to peace and a restoration of the Federal union.

But Atlanta fell to Sherman, and Lincoln easily was re-elected. Sherman marched through the soft autumn days to Savannah and in the South the talk grew stronger that it was a rich man's war, that the politicians had made it, not the people.

Stephens tried once more. Francis P. Blair, a political figure since the years of Andrew Jackson, obtained permission in December 1864 from Lincoln to write Jefferson Davis about negotiations looking toward peace. Stephens headed the delegation which in February 1865 met with Lincoln and William H. Seward, Secretary of State, on a ship at Hampton Roads off Fortress Monroe. The Confederates went there bound by Davis not to discuss any agreement which did not include independence.

No minutes were kept. There are many versions. One is that Lincoln did say to Stephens that if he, Stephens, would write "Union," he, Lincoln, would sign anything else. The writer has talked with two old men, close to the postwar Stephens, who said Stephens told them so. Lincoln almost certainly promised to push for congressional reimbursement of slave owners in exchange for emancipation agreement. He also pledged an honorable return to the Union and therefore asked for an end to the war, not merely an armistice. He was reasonable, even liberal, in everything save that one word "Union."

History turns often on small pivots. Had Davis accepted peace at Hampton Roads, Lincoln would hardly have had his Booth. And without Booth there would have been no radical reconstruction by Thaddeus Stevens, Charles Sumner, and Henry W. Davis.

But Jefferson Davis was adamant. If half the men absent from Lee's army would return, he said, then Grant could be defeated. He sent out speakers. Ben Hill spoke four times in his all-but-disaffected state of Georgia. "We have all we need to win but fighting spirit," he cried, closing with a brilliant whip-lash denunciation of Governor Joe Brown, "the subtle serpent which coils within our garden."

There was a last surge of patriotic effort. But Georgia and South Carolina were effectively out of the war. Only in Virginia, where Lee was, and in North Carolina was there organized strength. Even this was melting away through desertion and illness.

Appomattox came almost with a rush.

Why was the Confederacy defeated? Why had the all-consuming enthusiasm of 1861 been greatly eroded as early as 1863?

At the outset the failure to ship every possible bale of cotton to Europe left the South without financial resources. Judah P. Benjamin had urged it. A majority in government insisted it be held so that cotton-hungry Britain would be forced to intervene to rescue King Cotton. When a prisoner in Fortress Monroe, Jefferson Davis mourned this fatal mistake. He estimated that before the Federal blockade became effective three million bales could have been shipped to create a war reserve of a billion dollars in gold—enough for twice as many years of war as were fought. There were many other factors. But basic in them was the lack of unity and a general will to carry on. Arguments go around and around. "The seeds of destruction, states rights," were planted at the birth of the Confederacy, wrote able historian E. Merton Coulter. These seeds "were destined to sprout and flourish," tended by the politicians most dedicated to state sovereignty. Mrs. James Chestnut of South Carolina, whose famous diary is one of the great source books of the war, wrote, "The Confederacy has been done to death by the politicians." Secretary of the Navy Stephen R. Mallory said in bitterness he regretted he had spent four years of his life in working for a people unfit for independence. The Augusta *Constitutionalist* summed it up more accurately, "If this revolution has produced some of the meanest and most groveling of mankind, it has held an even balance by the example of some of the most exalted and aspiring souls."

There was nothing evil or immoral in the concept of one or more states seceding. To be sure, states rights had rendered impotent the old confederation of states and brought the republic and its central government into being. And it was the ambitions of politicians which caused the concept of states rights to be stretched into secession and, then, into a false weakening of the internal structure of the Confederacy.

The armies of the Confederacy fought with a bravery and a devotion which has become legendary. Their ideals, courage, and dedication were equaled by many of those at home. As there was nothing immoral or evil in belief in the right of secession, the same could be said of the determination of men and women to fight for a way of life in which they believed. It was this ideal which caused the two-thirds of nonslaveholders to stand with the third which did. The nation's great development and place in the world have ratified Lincoln's concept of Union.

General Robert E. Lee published a message to the South a few months after Appomattox:

"The war being at an end, the Southern states having laid down their arms, and the question at issue between them having been decided, I believe it to be the duty of everyone to unite in the restoration of peace and harmony. . . . I have too exalted an opinion of the American people to believe they will consent to injustice, and it is only necessary, in my opinion, that truth should be known for the rights of everyone to be secured. I know of no surer way of eliciting the truth than by burying contention with the war."

But contention was not buried—as Lincoln might have been able to do.

The South was prostrate.

Two hundred sixty thousand Confederates had died in battle, of wounds, and of disease. If to those be added the crippled and maimed, the South had lost roughly one-fourth of her white population of productive age. Most of the war had been fought in the South. The destruction of railroads, bridges, cities, towns, livestock, and general property was great. Desolation and ruin set upon her.

There was left the land, the warm weather, the long growing seasons, the rains, and the Negro. The agricultural South began to rebuild on this foundation. There were heartbreaks; toil, harsh and unrelenting; suffering and self-denial.

To this was added a period called Reconstruction. In essence it was the antithesis of all the words, wishes, and plans of Lincoln.

Andrew Johnson replaced Lincoln. He was honest. He was devoted to his country and to the Constitution. But he lacked Lincoln's strength and flexibility. He was geographically and politically vulnerable. He had been a constitutional Democrat, drafted by the National Union Convention of 1864 to appeal to the War Democrats of the North. He was a Southerner, disliked by Southern leaders and distrusted by many in the North. Had Lincoln merely died of a heart attack in the box of the Ford Theater, the chances of his successor carrying out the peaceful policies of reconstruction, with Federal assistance, would likely have been impossible. But Lincoln had been assassinated and the plot had contemplated the murder of other leaders of government. There developed an almost pathological state of public opinion.

The extremists, the absolutists, moved in. "By the gods," shouted Senator Ben Wade, Lincoln's chief radical foe, on the day Johnson was sworn in, "there will be no trouble now in running the government."

But there was. Johnson clung stubbornly to the Constitution. But a radical Congress was elected in 1866. And that Congress, on March 2, 1867, angered by a Presidential veto of the Reconstruction Act, passed it over that veto.

Military governors took over a South divided into five military districts. There was to be no civil government until the states were "remade and readmitted." All who had participated in the Confederate army or government were disfranchised. New state constitutions, granting the franchise to all other males, of whatever race, color, or previous condition of servitude, were required, as was ratification of the then pending Fourteenth Amendment. Military governors were charged with carrying out all steps of the reconstruction. Political resistance was not possible. It went underground, emerging as the disguised and secret Ku Klux Klan.

So great was the resolution of the radical Congress to allow nothing to bar its way that in February 1868 the House adopted a resolution of impeachment against President Johnson. The entire procedure is one of the most grievous blots on our history. Seven Senators, withstanding abuse and unprecedented pressure from fellow members, the Cabinet, and their home constituents, voted against impeachment and, by the margin of one vote, prevented it.

The Negro, unlettered, uninformed, landless, was, as Herbert Agar says in *The Price of Union,* "abandoned by the best men, North and South, and corrupted by the worst. . . . It was wicked to force the Negro to rule the disfranchised white man when everyone knew the position would be reversed as soon as the Northerners grew sick of governing with the sword. . . . There is a limit beyond which only mad moralists and the truly corrupt will go. It was the fate of the Negro . . . to be sacrificed to an alliance between the two. . . . But he gave them his vote—since they asked for it. . . ."

Here, not in the great war, developed the most grievous wounds, the deepest prejudices, the evil which has extended into the public and political life of our time. Antagonism of the races was carefully, energetically, ruthlessly cultivated to push through all radical candidates and measures. Out of this sprang the monstrous corruption, the incredible extravagance, the violence, the chicanery, and the mountains of debt erected by that regime. It emotionally forced most of the white people into a single party. It meant that for generations to come political demagogues would be able to poison the political wells with stories of the reconstruction and thereby create a solidly Democratic South. From this period, too, came the power of state and local extremists to exploit the race issue when it was not even remotely involved, and to do so with great and extravagant viciousness when it was. The effects of reconstruction were of long-range influence in shaping the whole political and economic life of the South.

The West, too, felt reverberations of it. National government was in the hands of commerce, finance, and industry. In *The American Epoch*, historian Arthur Lenk writes that:

"The reconstruction of national politics that began in 1861 had fully accomplished its objectives by 1877. The business classes had executed a bloodless revolution. They had . . . wrested control of the political institutions from the agrarian and changed the character, but not the forms, of representative government in the United States."

Legislation had been passed during the war and in the reconstruction years, having to do with tariffs, banking, railroads, labor, and public lands. At the end of the war the average rate on dutiable goods was 47 percent. In 1860 it had been 18.8 percent.

The National Banking Act of 1863 is a necessary piece of information for understanding why the bankrupt, postwar South clung so desperately to the one-crop economy of cotton and why it was for so many weary years a region of inertia and poverty.

The Banking Act of 1863 was not written with the needs of farmers in mind. Minimum capital of $50,000 was fixed for banks in towns with less than 6,000 population and $100,000 for larger communities. Thirty years after, there was one bank for every 16,000 Americans but only one to every 58,130 residents of the South. In 1865 a 10 percent tax was voted on bank-note circulation. Currency almost disappeared in the South. Only the merest fraction of huge Federal sums spent on internal improvements was spent in the poorest states.

Here, in the field of tariffs and the restriction of capital, was the South hurt most.

Folkways, mores, traditions, customs and prejudices—all these grow slowly like coral, requiring a special climate and condition of the sea out of which they meagerly emerge, or remain just below the surface to wreck the unwary or unknowing. Reconstruction—and the long-range effect of it—was such a climate.

Reconstruction ended in 1877 after the election of 1876, which election was almost certainly taken from the victorious Samuel J. Tilden, Democrat, and awarded to Rutherford B. Hayes, Republican. And Democrats in high places assisted in the machinations. One of those popularly believed to have played a part in the great "compromise" was Henry Watterson, the brilliant editor of the Louisville (Kentucky) *Courier-Journal*. In speaking of the reconstruction days a short time after 1877, "Marse Henry" said: "There was a time when amid the storm clouds on the Southern horizon there loomed another Poland, there lowered another Ireland, preparing to repeat upon the soil of the New World the mistakes of the old. . . . The hand of the South was in the lion's mouth, and my one hope, my only politics, was to placate the lion." The price paid for Southern assistance was an end to reconstruction and restoration of government to the Southern states. The South was given political autonomy. It could do as it pleased in matters of race policy, so long as it was done obliquely and with the appearance of legality. But what it really meant was that the North had politically abandoned the Negro. *The Nation* said as much. "The Negro," wrote that magazine, "will disappear from the field of national politics. Henceforth the nation, as a nation, will have nothing to do with him." Other Northern papers reached similar conclusions.

C. Van Woodward, one of the foremost authorities on the great compromise of 1877, wrote in *Reunion of Reaction*:

"If the compromise of 1877 revealed deep cleavages within the old party of Jackson, it also revealed the party of Radical Reconstruction in alliance with ex-Rebels and ex-Slaveholders. It revealed the party of carpetbaggery repudiating the carpetbaggers, the party of emancipation and freedom's rights abandoning the Negro to his former master—the South became, in effect and by choice, a satellite of the dominant economic region. So long as the Conservative (Southern)

'Redeemers' held control they scotched any tendency of the South to combine forces with internal enemies of the new economy—laborites, Western agrarians, reformers. The South became a bulwark instead of a menace to the new economic order."

It meant, too, that the old mutual-interest combination of West and South was ended. Political control had been given over to non-farming interests, the banking and industrial entrepreneurs—all dependent on the North for capital and political easements.

"Redeemer Democrats" began to talk of "the New South," the first of many such prophecies. But, though there was a rush of building, issuing of bonds, and much plunder, the region turned slowly back toward cotton. It became a crop of discontent. The tariffs were against the farmers. Credit was hard to come by and rates were high. Cartels rigged the prices of farm implements and jute bagging. Rail rates crippled them by having wide differentials between raw materials and fabricated goods. It was a long hard road back. It was 1878 before the region's cotton crop equaled that of 1859.

There was the further strain in the bitter postwar years, of a population drain. Thousands left to take up homesteads in the West, chiefly Texas. In 1875 some 35,000 white persons left Georgia. For a time there was a great campaign on to bring in Europeans and Chinese to become field laborers.

There was, surprisingly, little Negro migration. Negroes were hungry for land of their own and where they could they began to buy. But opportunity was small. It was this yearning to have a place of their own that gave sharecropping such an appeal. A cropper was on his own. He had his own garden, chickens, and pigs. Sometimes he had a cow. He had half the crop as his. Out of it came charges at high rates and often cruelly padded, for the seeds, tools, food, and clothing advanced him. Those lucky enough to meet with honest treatment soon came to own their own mules, wagons, plows, and tools, and could keep two-thirds of the crop. Some became owners and renters. For others the sharecropping system was little better than peonage. The breakup of the old plantations brought values down. Many of the prewar whites of the non-planter class bought land and began to grow cotton with croppers financing themselves with loans against the crop. The poorer ones became tenants, croppers. This acquisition of small farms was to have a profound effect on the economy of the South.

Shortly after the turn of the century the region included two-thirds of the nation's farms.

They were all poor—the planter, the ex-slave, the croppers, and the new landowners. Credit was provided not by banks, which were few, but by factors and supply merchants. Cotton was the only crop which made such a system possible. And cotton was the only commodity on which a man could take a chance. It was not a perishable, though crops sometimes failed. The factors and supply merchants marked up their goods and charged interest rates which frequently were 40 percent, sometimes higher. Debt and cotton came to be synonymous. Out of the discontent of the cotton growers and workers and their just grievances grew the explosive force of the Populist movement.

In those days bitter and frustrated men, with the compassion squeezed out of them by debt and disappointment, would sometimes erupt with violence between themselves or in a swift, cruel nightmare of bloodlust, not always racial, from some virus of hate and fear descended from the reconstruction excesses.

In the "redemption days" legal devices for limiting Negro suffrage were intricate registration and election laws. A law might limit the time in a voting booth to 2½ minutes—not enough for an illiterate Negro or white man. Petty larceny conviction as a disfranchising factor was another favorite. Stuffing ballot boxes was a favorite form of rather uniform corruption.

Not everyone was happy with these cynical procedures. Judge J. J. Christian, a Mississippian, in arguing a bill of disfranchisement, had the candor to say, addressing the chairman of a constitutional convention: "Sir, it is no secret that there has not been a full vote and a fair count in Mississippi since 1875—we have carried elections by fraud and violence until the whole machinery is about to rot down." In getting rid of the Negro in government, as left by the reconstruction, the white government had been corrupted by the methods used. Rationalization brought about a variety of means of disfranchisement.

The heirs of the prejudices and fears of reconstruction struggled, too, with their conscience over public education. It was all but abandoned as the states struggled to refund or disavow debts left by carpetbag governments. The rebuilding was slow and, in general, pathetic in its inadequacy. This, too, was a breeder of discontent.

Surely, and not so slowly, a political crevasse appeared between the gentry of the Black Belt farm lands and the uplands. By 1880 the Greenback-Labor Party, known also as the People's Anti-Bourbon Party, was organizing and speaking out against the conservative "Redemption" Democrats for their favoritism to railroads, banks, insurance companies, and other corporate interests.

All over the South, from the debt-ridden small farms and the struggling small businessman, there was increasing criticism of the brutally inhumane convict lease system, the lack of public schools, and "Bourbon boss rule." A Republican paper in Knoxville, Tennessee, wrote: "We call on businessmen of all parties to take warning. Communism, Socialism, Agrarianism, nihilism, and diabolism are on the increase in America."

In 1880 the estimated true valuation of property in the United States was $47,642,000,000. The South's share of this was a mere $5,725,000,000. This meant a per-capita wealth of $376 in the South as against an average of $1,086 outside. The national average was $870. The range inside the South was from $286 in Mississippi to $533 in Kentucky. The poorest state outside the South was Kansas, with per-capita wealth of $577 as against $1,567 in Massachusetts and $1,653 in California.

Poverty was another legacy of war and reconstruction. Yet, in a sense, this period, 1879–80, was the darkness before the first real dawn for the South since Appomattox. A depression of magnitude enough to have pinched both American and British centers of capital came to an end in 1879.

Economic exploitation rapidly replaced political. Suddenly released capital rushed into the vacuum. The Southern empires of timber, coal, and iron were powerful magnets. Special trains brought speculators from the North. Sales of hundreds of thousands of acres of timber and mineral lands went to syndicates and individuals. Florida, in 1881, sold four million acres of state land at 25 cents an acre to a group headed by Hamilton Disston of Philadelphia. In Louisiana alone 41 groups of Northerners bought 1,370,332 acres from private owners. All over the South vast stands of pine, cypress, and hardwoods fell to ax and saw. The rivers were crowded with rafts. Railroads pushed out their lines, the legislatures often acting corruptly to aid them. In Texas 12 railroad companies were granted a total of 32,400,000 acres, which was more than the area of Indiana. English, Scottish, and American

companies bought cheaply and heavily. Greatest of the foreign syndicates was the North American Land and Timber Company, Ltd. Organized in London in 1882, it bought more than a million and a half
acres along the Louisiana coast at from 12½ to 75 cents per acre. This
venture, largely because of the energy and vision of the man hired to
develop the land, was successful and beneficial to the region. He was
a mid-Westerner, S. A. Knapp of Iowa. He sold timber, but he also
planted rice in upland prairies and used wheat threshers to harvest it.
In five years Louisiana was a great producer of rice—and still is.

It was a time, too, of consolidations. Syndicates of Southerners,
Easterners, and Englishmen began to buy and combine coal mines,
railroads, trolley lines, infant electric and gas companies—all financed,
and almost all directed, out of New York.

It was a time, too, of crusading fervor and of expositions to show
the new machines and progress. Atlanta led with her International
Cotton Exposition in 1881. Louisville and New Orleans staged larger
ones, but Atlanta, and then Nashville, Tennessee, returned in triumph.
The latter outdid the Chicago Exposition's emphasis on things cultural with a replica of the Parthenon.

As the New South burgeoned and gloried in the swift increase in
cotton mills, new machines, and smokestacks in the sky, the Blue and
the Gray held reunions. They were great successes. The soldiers had
never disliked one another anyhow.

Voices of Southern editors began to be heard nationally. Henry W.
Grady of *The Atlanta Constitution*, Henry Watterson of the Louisville *Courier-Journal*, and Francis W. Davison of the Charleston *News
& Courier* were perhaps the most quoted. They preached the gospel
of the New South—the industrial South. And their enthusiasm and
gift for practical politics helped the new industrialists to govern.

"We are in favor," wrote the editor of the Vicksburg *Herald* in 1881,
"of the South from the Potomac to the Rio Grande being thoroughly
and permanently yankeeized."

And Henry Watterson could say, "If proselytism be the supreme
joy of mankind New England must be pre-eminently happy, for the
ambition of the South is to out-yankee the yankee."

But though industry was more varied and more widely distributed,
this New South was still agricultural. The injustices of the economic
system, geared for commerce and not for farmers, grew harsher. None

of the glitter and precious little of the profits of the New South was reaching the farmers.

There was a barrenness, too, in the arts and literature.

But there was an industrial revolution, and it was working changes in the Southern outlook, institutions and, particularly, in its concept of leadership. In England two generations passed between the establishment of factories and the Reform Act of 1832. In that period power passed from the hands of the landowners to manufacturers, merchants, and distributors. In the South this was achieved with much less industrialization and in a relatively brief period of time.

Nowhere had the farmer been redeemed.

In 1880 the size of the average farm was published as 156 acres. It had been 347 acres in 1860. This was deceptive. Each sharecropper assignment was a "farm." The plantation system was still holding on. But ownership was often absentee. In 1881, for example, the National Cotton Planters Association estimated that not one-third of the cotton plantations in the Mississippi Valley were "owned by those who held them at the end of the war." It was a plantation system, but not the old prewar plantation system. There was even less care of soil than in the inefficient days of slavery. The lien system imposed by the commission merchants was destructive. Interest rates ran as high as 70 percent. Rare, indeed, was the farmer who was a free agent. Prices dropped as rates increased. From an average of 11.1 cents per pound between the years 1874 and 1877, cotton slid down to an average of 5.8 cents between 1894 and 1897. Charges for warehousing and commissions for dealers were deducted from this low price. As the value of the farmer's crop declined, his debt, in terms of bales and bushels, deducted as payment, went steadily up.

There was discontent in the corn belt. All farmers everywhere, fighting debt, droughts, and floods with no Federal relief for the latter, grew more and more angry as they saw the Federal generosity to railroads. They became more bitter as they read the offers of their state legislatures, published in the North, offering subsidies, liberal franchises, and tax exemptions to manufacturers and railroads.

The Southern Farmers Alliance began in Texas and died of political dissension. Reorganized in 1886, it swept the South, and a major part of its strength was that it organized the Negro as well. More than 1,500,000 were associated in the Colored Alliance. Organizers

preached that the alliance was "rate conscious," and neither race nor
class conscious. In 1890 the Alliance scored "an agrarian triumph" in
most of the Southern state elections.

It was in this period of political revolution that Southerners began
to emerge who, seeking to build personal political organizations for
their own ends, knew how to exploit the thunder and the gale. The
name of Ben Tillman began to be heard outside his native South
Carolina. Thomas E. Watson of Georgia and James S. Hogg of Texas
also came to be well known as political magnets for the discontented.

Western Populism moved southward and most of the Alliance
members and many old-line Democrats joined. It was a time of great
emotions and violence. Nomination of Grover Cleveland angered
Populists and Alliance men alike. They saw him as too compliant to
the money and monopolistic interests. Ben Tillman shouted to an
angry audience he would like "to stick a pitchfork in his (Cleveland's)
guts" and thereby earned himself a picturesque nickname which was
to be of great political value—"Pitchfork Ben."

In 1895, 195 Southern newspapers, most weekly, identified themselves as Populist. Populism was native-stock radicalism, and the stalwarts of "Redemption" were never able to make "Communist" or
"Anarchist" stick. The Negro was an integral part of the movement.
He was separate, yet included. He was represented on the party executive committees in some states. In Georgia Tom Watson told the poor-
white farmers and the landless croppers, "They (the Conservative
'Redemption' Democrats) seek to divide and make you hate one
another so they can exploit and use you. You are kept apart politically
that you may be separately fleeced of your earnings."

The Populists also denounced lynch law and the hideously cruel
convict lease system. Negroes came to look upon a Populist leader
with a sort of reverence and would often try to get close enough
merely to touch his coat.

In the election of 1892 so violent were emotions that barn burnings,
attacks on speakers, and gun battles were almost commonplace. In
Texas' San Augustine County the Populist sheriff and five men were
killed. In Georgia 15 Negroes and several white men were slain. In
1894 economic depression added its complications of strikes, riots,
and misery. The Populist Party that year reached its peak. In 1896 its
leaders "fused" with the Democrats in the convention which nomi-

nated William Jennings Bryan. The rank and file were against it. "Fusion has destroyed Populism," said Watson. He was right. The "Redemptioners" or "New South Democrats" were more firmly in control.

The panic of 1893–94 had placed the South's large, sprawling railroad system almost entirely in the hands of the Northeast, and the J. P. Morgan Company was dominant in control. Purchase of the Tennessee Coal & Iron Company at Birmingham was included in the Morgan venture into "redeeming" the South.

Textile developments were accelerated by New England millowners. In 1896 they found that labor was 40 percent lower in the South than in New England, and the working day 24 percent longer. Until 1906 the lowest legal work week in any Southern state was 66 hours and a 75-hour week was not uncommon.

Coal mines, tobacco, timber—all came to be largely or entirely directed by trusts.

There were also the freight-rate differentials. Southern carriers charged higher rates per mile than did the Northern lines. Their rates and classifications were officially recognized by railroad associations. After 1887 the Interstate Commerce Commission recognized a "Southern territory." (As late as 1938 shippers of classified goods still had to pay rates which were 39 percent higher in the designated Southern territory than shippers in the "official territory" paid for the same services.)

Commodity rates for raw materials, cotton, timber, coal, etc., were lower than those for finished goods. Steel shipped from the Alabama plant had a rate called "Pittsburgh Plus." This was the price of steel at Pittsburgh plus the freight charge from Pittsburgh to the place of delivery. Later this became the "Birmingham differential." A purchaser of Alabama steel had to pay the Pittsburgh price plus a differential of $3.00 per ton, plus freight from Birmingham.

It basically was a colonial economy—with all its liabilities and its erosion of the soil, resources, and the human spirit. There also was wide disparity in the distribution of wealth. There were, of course, benefits. Some of the wealth remained. The wages were lower than paid for the same work in the North, but there were payrolls. The rail rates discriminated, but there was transportation. The living standard was raised. It can be, and is, argued there was no other way—that the widespread devastation of war, the utter lack of capital, and the desperate needs, required a crash program by the great concentration of organized capital and experience in the East.

Basic still were the old problems—the overworked soil, called upon to sustain more persons, the cut-over timber lands, the worked-out mines, the lack of opportunity for the educated.

And fundamental, too, was the problem of race. Disfranchisement laws, the poll tax, literary tests, the white primary law, property qualifications, and various other measures had eliminated the Negro from the party ballot boxes. They also barred thousands of white men in each state. But extremists proceeded from the attack on the Negro as a voter to an attack on him as a Negro. There was an upsurge of racial violence. From 1890 to 1911 Southern states busied themselves extending and elaborating their laws requiring segregation. A credo began to be formed and stated. It was built on the premise that only the Southerner understood the Negro; that political equality meant social equality, and, therefore, would not be allowed; that the South must be let alone to settle the question. The walls of both caste and segregation went higher and higher.

In 1895 Clark Howell, Sr., publisher of *The Atlanta Constitution*, pushed through, over great opposition, an invitation to Booker T. Washington of the new Tuskegee Institute for Negroes at Tuskegee, Alabama, to speak at the Atlanta Cotton States and International Exposition.

The speech became a sensation.

The eloquent Washington declared his love for the South and his faith that reforms had to come from within. He said the Negro was more interested in vocational education and job opportunity than in political rights. It was, in fact, a renunciation of active political participation by the Negro. He was especially effective in reminding the South of the fidelity and love of the Negro during the Civil War. He identified his people with the industrial hopes of the South. As he had, in effect, agreed the Negro should not seek the ballot, he seemed, also, to suggest the Negro should not be unionized. He spoke of the Negro worker who, "without strikes or labor wars," had helped build the South's industries and who would continue as a great labor force. Later he told Alabama industrialists that in the South alone, by reason of the presence of the Negro, was capital freed from the tyranny and despotism that prevents you from employing whom you please.

To his own people he preached conservatism, patience, and the rewards of material progress. The friendship of the conservative whites and wealthy Northern capitalists offered more hope for the future, he argued, than agitation and protest.

The speech came to be known as "The Atlanta Compromise." Booker T. Washington became the most effective advocate of the doctrines and attitudes of the dominant Southern forces. No white orator could match him. His position had a profound effect on subsequent disfranchisement programs. Nor is it to be overlooked that a year later the United States Supreme Court, in Plessy vs. Ferguson, handed down its "Separate but Equal" segregation decision enabling states which so legislated to segregate schools, transportation, and all public facilities. Negro labor history also reflects "The Atlanta Compromise." The young unions had not created racial discrimination, but it was widespread. When the greatest living Negro leader seemingly acquiesced, it was easier to accept and perpetuate it.

To this day, Booker T. Washington remains something of a mystery. In the East he identified himself with Northern capitalists who were, or were likely to be, interested in Southern properties, many of them large employers of Negro labor.

He, who had publicly renounced political equality for the Negro in the South, was more than once a guest aboard the yacht of H. H. Rogers of Standard Oil. He submitted many of his speeches to William H. Baldwin, Jr., vice-president of the Southern Railroad, which company employed thousands of Negroes. He was a welcome guest of Collis P. Huntington, railroad official and builder of Newport News. Andrew Carnegie invited him to Skibo Castle. These were circles open to no Southern white men of the time. To his own race he preached "patience, forbearance, and self-control in the midst of trying conditions." From 1895 to his death in 1915 his philosophy, so thoroughly in tune with that of the dominant economic and political forces of his time, determined Federal Government and national policy in matters of race relations in labor, and in education.

What he really thought, and what he really sought, none may say with assurance. His policy did make for jobs for a people untrained, uneducated, and caught in the rip tides of reaction and change. Car-

penters, brickmakers and bricklayers, blacksmiths, harnessmakers, tin-
smiths—these were trained at Tuskegee and there was work for all.

Challenge to the Washington philosophy came from W. E. B.
DuBois of Massachusetts. Educated at Fisk and Harvard and in Ber-
lin, he began teaching in Atlanta University in 1896. A brilliant writer,
able to evoke mood and image, he bitterly challenged the "Tuskegee
machine," demanding for the Negro "every single right that belongs
to a freeborn American, political, civil, and social."

But until his death in 1915, Booker T. Washington was unshaken.
In 1913, after a half-century of emancipation, he pointed to the record
as justifying his philosophy. There were, in that year, 128,557 Negro
farm owners in the South, 38,000 Negro business enterprises, and
550,000 Negro homeowners. The national wealth of the Negro was
estimated to be $700,000,000.

But DuBois was then in New York, an officer of the newly organized National Association for the Advancement of Colored People,
an organization fated not to become really well known to the average
American until after May 1954 and the Supreme Court decision of
that year which reversed the one of 1896 that had followed so closely
on the heels of Dr. Washington's great "Compromise."

In the year of 1913 all the Southern states, save North Carolina
which acted two years later, had adopted the direct primary system.
In the one-party states of the South this was equivalent to election.
The Democratic Party elected to limit these primaries to white voters.
This eliminated the Negro, but also took its toll of white voters. This
entirely frustrated the aim of those mid-Western progressives who had
urged the direct primary on the nation as a means of restoring popular
control of government.

Slowly, powerfully, full of contradictions, baffling to itself and to
the rest of the nation as well, the South moved. It was glacier-like in
its speed—but it moved. Education, assisted by the great philanthro-
pists, improved. The farmers of cotton and tobacco erupted now and
then in violence against the trusts. Sometimes it was political revolt.
Sometimes it was expressed through night-riding barn-burnings of
those who refused to join. Tenancy and sharecropping increased.

After the century was well turned, the new generation which had
grown up in the post-reconstruction years slowly began to take over.
Theirs had been a youth lived, one might say, on bread alone. There

had been neither leisure for the arts nor money for travel. But this was a generation which included those who were aware of this. The South began then its first self-examination. In literature Ellen Glasgow led the revolt against the falsely sentimental and affected style of Southern writing.

The universities, too, began to demand attention. In the scholastic year 1900–01 the Universities of Kentucky, Mississippi, and Tennessee had reported no state appropriation at all. The University of Alabama received $10,000. Of 18 American institutions with endowments of $1,500,000 or more in that year, none was in the South. Of 30 with as much as $1,000,000, two were in the South—Tulane of New Orleans and Vanderbilt of Nashville.

But for the first time there were men and women in education and politics who not merely were aware of the debased standards but were willing to proclaim them and fling the facts in the faces of the people. The old defense mechanism of fiercely defending everything Southern no longer functioned as before.

In addition to novelists, the Southern historians began to write. Young, eager sociologists examined into the ruins of the old plantation and slave economy and wrote of its effects.

It was not easy. In education the day of the "broken-down-clergyman teaching profession" was dying, but the force represented by that phrase fought back. The battle for education and educational freedom is never done, but it always is fiercest at the beginning of the fight to release the bonds of spirit and mind. The South shook with sound of combat.

By 1910 the new generation felt it had almost attained that "New South" so often prophesied three decades before. They and their fathers had suffered and endured much of humiliation, sorrow, toil, and frustration. They both had learned to take a half loaf when there was no whole one; the crumbs when there was not a half. Yet they had recovered a considerable portion of their lost agricultural and commercial power and some of the industrial.

But none of the old political glory and dominance had returned. For nearly 50 of the 72 years, beginning with Washington and continuing through Buchanan, whose term ended in the spring of 1861, Southerners had been in the White House. For 60 years Chief Justices of the Supreme Court had been Southern. In the same period an almost incredible 20 of the 35 justices of the Supreme Court had come from the South. Almost half the cabinet members, 13 of the 23 Speakers of the House, and more than half the major diplomats were from that same region. The shift of political power brought about by the War Between the States was profound in fact and effect. Nowhere in history is there a comparable shift in regional power.

When Grover Cleveland won in 1894, the first Democrat since the War Between the States, Editor Henry Grady of Atlanta rushed into the House chamber of the Georgia legislature with the news of it, seized the gavel, and declared an adjournment to celebrate. But there was no reform during the Cleveland years which alleviated the agricultural distress. By the time of his second election in 1902, Cleveland was regarded by Populists as a tool of the trusts.

It was Woodrow Wilson's victory and administration which effectively united the Democratic Party. It had been suspicious and divided through the convention which nominated Wilson. Some of the old Populists, including the then embittered leader Tom Watson, supported Teddy Roosevelt's Bull Moose Party. But even more important than unity was the fact that the stern Calvinist prophet enabled the South to regain much of its old political pride and prestige. Three of his cabinet were Southerners—Josephus Daniels, Albert S. Burleson, and David F. Houston. Walter Hines Page and Thomas Nelson Page were, respectively, ambassadors to the Court of St. James and to Italy. Colonel Edward M. House, of Texas, was Wilson's closest adviser. Thomas S. Martin of Virginia was majority leader of the Senate; Oscar W. Underwood, of Alabama, in the House. Southerners presided as chairmen over a majority of the major committees in House and Senate.

Happy days were here again.

But the problems of tenancy, of cotton, of abused soil, agricultural credit and debt were still unsettled. The boll weevil, which had left Mexico in 1892, had somehow managed to do what everyone said it could not do. It had crossed the Mississippi. And in the Balkans, events were moving toward a bridge in Sarajevo.

War came to Europe—and to the South. The 1914 cotton crop was the largest ever harvested—16,000,000 bales. That November, cotton, with the export market demoralized, was selling at 5.5 cents per pound. When America entered the war in 1917 cotton boomed with all other commodities.

The war brought boom times. The $15 silk shirts, which all shipyard workers were supposed to wear, and the $5 neckties were symbols of it. There was a surge of patriotism, and the South took great pride in the divisions which included its guards, volunteers, and draftees.

Southern shipyards boomed, too, and the training camps were bonanzas to the towns and cities nearest them.

When the Kaiser was defeated and the war done, the shipyards shut down and the barracks emptied. But in 1919 cotton went to 35 cents and some of the longer-staple varieties brought 36 and 37. It was the year of the $2 billion cotton crop. Tobacco kept it company. The cigaret had come into its own with the war, winning a place in the literature—poetry, ballads, and the stories of the men who had fought in it.

But in the delirium of those boom years not much attention was paid to the fact that some farmers had made less than half a crop of cotton. The boll weevil had arrived.

"Sometimes," said a sad, weary and beaten man, in 1922, "it seems to me the farmer is always being hammered on the anvil of bad luck."

In Louisiana the cotton crop was reduced two-thirds in two years. In Mississippi it was more than halved. All the Sea Island cotton disappeared. In Georgia, farms which had made 1,000 bales in 1919 made 200 in 1920 with the same expenditure of seed, toil, and sweat. Banks failed. There were tens of thousands of foreclosures. Bankruptcies were many. Homes, lost to mortgage holders, were abandoned. The pine trees began to grow where fields had been since the 1840's—and before.

The 1930 census reported a 10-year decline in Negro farm population and a smaller but substantial one for whites.

It was on top of this disaster that the great depression came. Old men talked of the harsh and hopeless days of the reconstruction years and those that followed.

Tariff rates went up, reaching their peak in 1930 in the Hawley-Smoot Act. The agricultural South, like all agriculture, needed markets. It got tariffs. The cotton South, which had lived largely on exports, suffered most as prices collapsed when European nations sought other cotton.

The South, already impoverished and battered by ten years and more of the boll weevil, was severely tried by the depression. Its capital reserves and savings were almost nonexistent. It had always offered the fewest jobs. In 1932 the New England States alone paid a little more than $30 million in Federal income taxes. This was about twice as much as those paid by the Southern states. The schools suffered as did the people and the land. But with a fortitude born out of so many years of the locust, with a grim humor springing from so many generations contending with austerity and trouble, they tightened their belts and lasted it out.

March 4, 1933, began the first 100 days of the New Deal and Franklin D. Roosevelt.

"So desperate was the crisis," wrote Arthur S. Link in *The American Epoch,* "and so frightened were congressmen and the people that Roosevelt possessed a power unprecedented in American peacetime history. Had he harbored imperial ambitions he probably could have attained dictatorial powers from the Congress. . . ."

By May 6, 1933, "Triple A" legislation was adopted. There began then the historic and never-solved battle to control and regulate production—to raise farm income, to conserve the soil, to cushion the farmer against the gamble of weather and crop disaster. The Southeast, with two-thirds of the nation's farms, and perhaps the sickest, turned to New Deal with an almost emotional fervor.

A President's committee, named to examine into the South's depressed status, noted the too many people on the land, the underemployment, the lack of capital and managerial skills, the abuse of some resources and the neglect of others. In its report in 1938 it referred to the South, struggling out of the great world depression which had been piled on top of the boll-weevil disaster, as the nation's "Number One Economic Problem."

The South began an amazing self-study, led by universities, newspapers, and local study and forum groups. If the region was the Number One Economic Problem, then the other side of the coin was Number One Opportunity. Results began to appear in the legislation introduced in state legislatures and in the debates therein. Out of the Congress and the White House in 1933 came the Tennessee Valley Authority. America had wasted the natural resources across all its dynamic years. But nowhere had that process gone on as thoroughly as in the South. The TVA built dams to control floods and produce electricity. Soil was reclaimed and cheaper fertilizers produced. The Tennessee Valley covers an area of 49,910 square miles. It is about four-fifths the size of New England. The river valley includes parts of seven states, Tennessee, Kentucky, Virginia, North Carolina, Georgia, Alabama, and Mississippi. The effect was immediate. The inspiration of it everywhere encouraged conservation. Phosphate fertilizers developed by the TVA program were tested and used in more than half the states of the Union. River shipping grew. The power generated provided a great national impetus to greater use of electricity and appliances. It inspired the creation of the Rural Electrification Administration of 1936 which brought power to the nation's farms. Millions of trees were planted and recreational lakes spawned fish and new business in boats and fishing.

By the time TVA had helped America out of the depression, Europe was at war, and TVA's power was a godsend in the war plants. Before that war was done, TVA was to make possible the crash program of the atomic bomb.

Farm prices went up with demand, and lend-lease defense plants were pleading for workers. The exodus from the South began to speed up. But even before the Japanese attack on Pearl Harbor, there had begun a great emigration of troops to Southern training camps and air bases, hacked out of the piney woods or spread on the coastal and wire-grass plains. This was accelerated until the South seemed almost one great base for training soldiers and pilots.

Plants came, too, as they had not in 1917–18. Bombers and fighter craft rolled off Southern assembly lines. Metal fabrication plants multiplied. Subcontractors reached into the small-town factories to find makers of parts. The timber business boomed. Service industries came into being to absorb the payroll demands. Retail shops of all kinds, dry cleaners, tailors, filling stations, drug stores, cafes—all these, and more, made the smallest towns boom. They glowed late with the splendor of neon red, green, and blue.

War had boomed life for the Negro, too. The demand for manpower was so great that thousands of Negroes found industrial jobs in their own region and demonstrated they could as quickly be trained to skills as anyone else. Stirrings of the national conscience and the need to mobilize all possible production workers brought from the

White House an executive decree against discrimination in employment because of race or religion by any employer working on Federal contracts. Out of this developed a Fair Employment Practices Commission which simply, by focusing attention on discrimination and by holding hearings in the more flagrant cases, brought about considerable reform and an improvement in attitude, even though all states in the South refused to write it into legislation.

It was a wary South which emerged from the capitulations in Europe and Japan. The prosperity of the first world war had not caught on. It had been a rich diet but it had not stuck to the economic ribs.

But by 1946 it was once again a new South. Now at last came a prosperity to match that which the prophets of bygone years had seen in their visions.

Nor was the material evidence the whole story. There was a new South, too, in the intangibles. There was a new confidence, a new and increasing enthusiasm. One of the greatest lacks of the post-Civil War South had been that of managerial skills. The World War II years had produced managers and administrators. Literally hundreds of the young and middle-aged executives who had come South to help manage war production plants stayed on to augment the local supply. Capital, too, had put down roots.

The South began to enjoy the heady wine of being able to finance sizable projects through its own banks which, in turn, did not need to obtain credit in the East to handle them. Service businesses sprang up as the GI's returned. And this time not even all the shipyards closed. Cotton consumption declined. By 1954 it was down to the 1935–39 level. But there were plants making synthetic fibers and cotton itself steadily was moving westward out of the rolling terrain of the Piedmont and the Appalachian slopes.

Mechanization needs flatter lands and fewer hands. In the West, irrigation and drier climates meant higher yields and less boll-weevil infestation. In the South beef cattle and dairy herds began to graze on new pastures where for a hundred years only cotton had grown. Small grains and hybrid corn suited to Southern climes came out of the experiment research stations. Even in the rich loam of the Mississippi Delta grain elevators began to rise out of the level landscape and by 1950 tourists were startled to see cattle grazing in pastures hard by the cotton. The commercial broiler and chicken industry boomed higher and higher.

There is water in the South, and the new industries in chemicals, synthetics, pulp, paper, and the nuclear plants are great drinkers of water. The assembly plants came, too. Furniture, metals, equipment, and machinery were all a part of the changing structure of the new industrial South.

Wages, too, were changing. In 1929 the average wage was equal to 36.6 percent of the value added per worker. By 1947 it was above 40 percent. In 1957 it was nearing 50 percent.

The industrial growth in the South that was evolving in the last half of the twentieth century could be measured in both absolute and relative terms. During the decade of depression, for example, the region barely held its own in absolute terms but made gains in relation to the rest of the country. From 1939 to 1950 the South's labor force, released from the farms being mechanized, merged, and abandoned, increased by 50 percent. This was slightly less than the increase in the rest of the nation. But in wages paid, and value added by manufacturing, the increases respectively were 274 percent and 244 percent. These were considerably higher than corresponding increases in other regions.

For the first time, too, the region began to attain an industrial structure which had balance. The textile mills had by far the smallest rate increase of production workers of any major group of manufacturers between 1939 and 1950. Other relatively low-pay groups had smaller rates of increase during and after the war years. Conversely, industry groups which employed fewest workers in 1939 and which generally paid higher workers had the highest percentage increase. There were geographic shifts, too, as the states with more hydroelectric power, water, and raw materials marshaled their resources with planning and promotion.

As 1957 drew to a close the U. S. Department of Commerce, through its Atlanta office, reported that the states of the Southeastern area had surpassed the average rate of advancement for the nation as a whole in many divisions of its economy. These included salaries, wages paid in manufacturing, gross and per-capita personal income, expenditures for new plants and equipment, electric energy produced, telephones in operation, amount of life insurance in force, retail and wholesale sales, beef cattle on farms, chickens hatched commercially, industrial and commercial firms in business, and others.

In the field of race relations the South also was in a period of accelerated transition. Because this was concerned with human beings and not with economic statistics, the action was, and is, and for sometime will be, surcharged with emotion. The South did have a way of life which made it unique among the regions. It was based on the Negro's acceptance of a secondary position in the economy and of a segregated existence in all the public life of the region. The affirmation of this status by Booker T. Washington and his long years of national dominance in the field of race relations helped fix this secondary status both in the law, customs, and tradition of the region. The nation conveniently turned its back during this period as the South created this subordinate status. The Jim Crow laws did not appear on the statute books until some 30 years after the Civil War.

But all the while the South, like the nation, was evolving, though its rate was slower. For some years after the agony of the reconstruction years, it was not well understood by the South that as the region reached eagerly for industry and the payrolls, with them would come unions, a sharing in the gain by the Negro, and an inevitable erosion of the foundation on which the so-called way of life was based.

The first great world war and the years of the boll weevil had accelerated the agricultural revolution. The great depression not merely revealed the economic and spiritual misery of the submarginal farms and their families; it exposed, too, the greater woes of the tenants and sharecroppers. And in so doing, it focused attention on the sociological features of the South and the position of the poor white and Negro.

Political and economic gains came to both out of the Roosevelt years. And out of them came, too, a slowly developing regional sense of guilt in so far as the separate but equal status of the Negro was concerned. There was a separation, rigidly enforced, but nowhere was there equality of schools, transportation, housing, parks, recreational facilities, or economic opportunity. Almost nowhere was there equality of medical and hospital care. And, worse, rare was the city where the Negro could feel confident of equality before the law in so far as police, sheriffs, deputies, and the minor courts were concerned.

By the late thirties it could be seen that the South's unique way of life, based as it was on a permanent subordinate position for the Negro, beset by moral, economic, and political forces, was doomed. The United States Supreme Court began to hand down rulings which required Southern states to admit Negroes to graduate schools where the states did not offer separate but equal classes in graduate work. It was obvious the Court was saying, when it had opportunity, that in America the Fourteenth Amendment did not permit any discrimination or second-class citizenship because of color. There began then what was a confession of guilt in the form of a building program to equalize teachers' salaries and the schools which, since 1896, had been legally separate only on the presumption they were in every respect equal. The second great world war interrupted, but by the time the 1954 Court decision declaring compulsory segregation on the basis of color to be unconstitutional, every state in the Southeast was engaged in an almost feverish building campaign and some political speeches noted these new schools were often superior to those for white children.

There was a brief lull after the Court decision of May, 1954, but resistance soon hardened. Quite inevitably it was most extreme in the deep South. The old pattern was there more deeply etched. There also was most of the Negro population, and the largest percentage of it was in agriculture in areas where there was most of the old plantation-type economy. In the deep South, too, was a long history of radical, often violent, exploitation of race for political ends. Almost all the more notorious racial demagogues had come from four deep South states.

Slowly, the South once more began to demonstrate that it is many Souths. The border state of Missouri began to obey the Court. Within three years after the Court decision, Kentucky's schools were 85 percent desegregated. Beginnings had been made, not without mass violence, participated in by outside agitators, in Arkansas and Tennessee. North Carolina alone inaugurated her program without any disorder.

In September 1957 Little Rock's school system planned to inaugurate a well-advertised ten-year program of desegregation. The governor, who had offered no opposition to the plan, suddenly, in what generally was accepted to be part of a plan for a political campaign for re-election, called out state troops on the morning the schools were to open and halted the plans.

He later asked for and received an invitation to talk with President Dwight D. Eisenhower. Emerging from this meeting the governor of Arkansas declared he accepted the Supreme decision as law and the people of his state were law-abiding. Returning home, he did not comply but maintained his troops to defy the Court. President Eisenhower, confronted with open defiance of Federal authority, had no other recourse save to federalize the State guard and send in additional troops of the regular forces to see that the Court order was carried out.

It was, of course, a historic decision. And while the immediate effect was further to harden resistance in the deep South, it had the necessary catalyst effect of demonstrating that the 1954 decision was not, as some of the wishful-thinking politicians had been saying, merely a political gesture which would never be enforced. Deep South states, joined somewhat surprisingly by Virginia, made plans for closing their public schools rather than comply. No local board was permitted any autonomy. Since all political machinery was in the hands of those pledged to abolishing schools, the deep South, not surprisingly, was facing another undeterminable period of travail and disorder such as it had known in the days of reconstruction, of Populist revolt, and of depression. Its children were certain to pay a price in the quality of their education. What the cost would be in the loss of teachers and economic progress was for the future to determine. The Supreme Court decision, while a blow to a way of life based on a subordinate economic and political position for the Negro, was merely a part of the overall panorama of change. History had moved on. Time and morality were on the side of the Negro. That the far-reaching social and economic changes going on all over the world also were at work in the South was not obvious to many. But they were. And time was at work.

But as one must look back now and then to the past to understand the future, it is plain to see that there is yet another "New South" in the making. And that South, possessing its share of great and wonderful people of both races, as well as economic assets for vast development, will not be fatefully unique in that it possesses a way of life based on a subordinate position for any of its people. It will be fully in the mainstream of American life. It will have come a long, hard road, but along the way it has never lost its best human qualities. And possessing these, and rid of the old burdens, it may very well match the dream of its most optimistic prophets.

New York

BY MARSHALL B. DAVIDSON

New York is an anomaly among the states of the Union. Its curious shape was determined as much by international wrangling, political compromise, and legal bickering as by the logic of geography or by natural boundaries. It is not large as states of America measure; in area it ranks only thirtieth among the forty-nine. But it is a land of varied circumstance, and a land that within its modest bounds accommodates a wealth of human experience out of all proportion to its size.

At its eastern limits, where the twin flukes of Long Island reach out into the Atlantic Ocean, it still retains some of the character of an early New England settlement, with salt-water habits, trim, long-weathered frame buildings, and lingering patterns of Yankee speech. Between those flukes, on a sheltered island that once served as a refuge for Quakers hounded out of Puritan Massachusetts, the warming influence of the Gulf Stream encourages the only stand of bamboo north of the Carolinas, a much earlier refugee from the southern world.

Three hundred miles to the west as the crow flies and 450 miles by commonly traveled surface routes, where the winds roar in off the Great Lakes and immigrant millworkers from central Europe learn their English with a midwestern accent, the fresh-water port of Buffalo opens onto the mass of the continent, one of the richest hinterlands in the world. Here, in 1679, Réné-Robert Cavalier, Sieur de La Salle, anchored the *Griffin*, the first sailing vessel built for these inland seas, before he hopefully sallied forth into the remote West, with barking cannons and to the chant of *Te Deums* mingled with the yelps of savages, for the greater glory of France.

The land that is New York has played an important part in the strategy of nations. It has been a coveted land, for it promised abundance and authority to those who could invest and command it. On maps of America it looks like a horn of plenty thrust down towards the sea from the north and west to receive the wealth of the continent and funnel it to the extreme limit of the land at Manhattan Island. Thus the English viewed it when they quietly and firmly took over Holland's claim from Peter Stuyvesant in 1664. And thus also did the French, who for a century and a half held a counterclaim to the largest part of the present state, as the names of some of its counties and villages—St. Lawrence and Orleans, Montcalm, Chateaugay, and Raquette—continue to remind us. If in the summer of 1609 Samuel de Champlain had chosen to follow the Indian trails that led to the south, instead of doing battle with the Iroquois beside the lake that bears his name, Henry Hudson might have found the lilies of France waving a greeting on Manhattan Island when he arrived later that same season; and the history of New York and of all North America would have been quite different.

As it happened, for most of the hundred years preceding the American Revolution the Iroquois held the balance of power between these two contending nations. In New York, as Dixon Ryan Fox has written, "the hireling tomahawk struck death on both sides." Here, too, "scarlet coats from Devonshire and Norfolk and tartan kilts from Inverness met white and brass from Béarn and Languedoc, and fell with the life within them." And here, might be added, the ground was also bloodied by the civil strife of friends and neighbors, as at the decisive and sanguine conflict at Oriskany during the Revolution—friends and neighbors who honestly differed as to whether this was rebellion or self-determination.

In later years, when the wars had subsided, New York experienced a peaceful invasion of peoples from all corners of the earth. They came by the tens of millions, from neighboring states as well as from distant

62.   A dairy farm in south-central New York. New York State, with its large urban markets, is one of the nation's leading producers of milk and milk products. Its 1½ million head of dairy cows give it third place in the Union.

63. Spooling Kodak film in Rochester, New York. For obvious reasons this picture could not be taken in ordinary daylight, and represent infrared photography.

64. Lake Placid in the Adirondacks attracts both summer and winter visitors. Right of the center of the picture is Mt. Whiteface.

55. The Thousand Islands dot the wide St. Lawrence River for nearly half the distance from the outlet of Lake Ontario to Ogdensburg. Sight-eeing boats operate from Clayton and Alexandria Bay. The islands range n size from several square miles to rocky ledges too small for even a cottage.

66. The southern tip of Manhattan Island is the world's most dramatic
bit of man-made scenery.

67. "Idlewild" — New York International Airport on Long Island in the
Borough of Queens.

. Part of the campus of Cornell University at Ithaca, overlooking
ayuga Lake. Some of the colleges or schools of this university are pub-
ly, others privately supported. New York ranks high among the states
th in the number and in the quality of its institutions for higher
education.

69. The New York Coliseum has few, if any, rivals as the world's greate[st] building for exposition purposes. At the right are the windowless expositio[n] floors; at the left, the tower used for offices.

70. The New York State Thruway crosses the Hudson River at one of i[ts] widest points on a great bridge which looks like an immense letter [S] when seen from an airplane flying over the New York metropolitan are[a.]

The Cloisters, New York. The reader may refer to the text of Mr. Davidson's chapter for specific information.

72.   Downtown Buffalo. Buffalo with its environs is one of six Great Lak
metropolitan areas with populations of a million or more. Between t
old New York Barge Canal and the new St. Lawrence Seaway, faciliti
for water transportation have had, or will have, a greater influence (
Buffalo's economy than has been true of any of the others — Milwauke
Chicago, Detroit, Cleveland, or Toronto.

nations, and they have not yet ceased to come. Compared with this epic movement of humanity the barbarian invasions of the Roman Empire were, numerically, a minor affair, and, it could be argued, hardly of greater consequence.

Yet, within its unlikely outlines and despite its miscellaneous and often tumultuous origins, the State of New York has a settled and separate character that makes it, in effect, a section of the country. It is a realm within itself, as its popular nickname, the Empire State, so plainly suggests. During the bitter struggle over the ratification of the Federal Constitution most of the people of New York believed they might in fact better go it alone as a free and independent commonwealth. No other state in the new nation knew so well the cost of freedom. Almost a third of the battles of the Revolution were fought on New York soil, as blackened ruins along its valleys and frontiers made tragically clear before the peace was won.

There were others, however, who felt as strongly that if the state did not choose to join the Union of its own accord, it would have to be brought in by force. In Albany, on the Fourth of July, 1788, a number of skulls were cracked and one person was killed in a riotous disagreement over the question. But there was also much skilled argument, some of the most brilliant and enlightened debate to come out of the revolutionary experience. And in the end it became evident that without New York the Union would be hopelessly divided and incomplete; apart from the Union New York would be isolated, incomplete.

In the year of the peace George Washington had looked out over this liberated countryside and, with a seasoned eye for its beauty and its promise, he declared that it might become "the seat of Empire." He bought a piece of it on speculation. So did Alexander Hamilton, Robert Morris, and virtually everyone else with capital to risk or a new home to build. Stolid Dutch bankers, titled Englishmen, and distinguished French émigrés vied with Yankees, Yorkers, and other native and naturalized countrymen in America's first real land rush. Mme. de Staël, daughter of Necker, author, and one of the most brilliant women of the age, speculated widely and successfully in New York real estate, following Talleyrand's report from America that here was "the best place in the world to make money fast."

Long before the present boundaries of the state were settled, restive

New Englanders had looked westward toward this promising country which in alien hands threatened to contain them within their tight little corner of the New World (with Long Island deployed along the Connecticut coast to seal off the ocean approaches). The colonists of divers origins who first spread along the Hudson Valley under Dutch rule, and who pushed their way along the Mohawk Valley into Iroquois country, eyed their neighbors to the east with reasonable suspicion. From almost the very beginnings of settlement they watched these "Johnnies" from New England (Johnny-come-latelies, we would probably call them) edging their way across disputed borders. And since the Dutch word for Johnny is *Janke*, the intrusive newcomers became known as Yankees.

Before the end of the eighteenth century this westering stream of Yankees had swollen into a torrent. In sloops and sleighs, by oxcart and shanks' mare, they flooded the valley routes into this new West. They were, as Carlyle once wrote Emerson, "tough as gutta-percha with *occult* unsubduable fire in their belly," and they were not to be denied. Early in the nineteenth century Timothy Dwight, austere president of Yale College, observed that New York was already in a fair way of becoming a Yankee "colony." He looked with solemn and pious satisfaction on the rich benefits that would thus accrue to the raw, new-born state. "I know of no physical reason," he pronounced, "why the people of New York may not be as prosperous and happy as any on the globe."

We have not yet a reliable measure for gauging human happiness. But for a century past New York has been the most populous and prosperous state in the Union. It has also been the most cosmopolitan and the leading commercial and industrial state. In spite of its many crowded and growing city areas, it remains an important agricultural state; because of their millions, and the large vote they control in the electoral college, its political influence is felt throughout the nation. And there are those who find it, winter and summer, one of the most attractive pleasuring grounds on the continent. There are even some who claim to be so sensitive to the particular character of the New York landscape that they recognize the precise moment they cross the invisible boundaries of the state. But this is a mystic view that reveals how strong a hold the countryside can have on the imagination and affection of those who have struck their roots in it. It tells, too, how intimately the nature of the land is associated with the traditions and the fortunes of its people.

No other state is, in fact, more intimately and comfortably wedded to its surrounding world. From high in the air most of New York looks to be puckered into hills and mountains, laced by waterways that seek their outlets in all directions through innumerable valleys. In the northernmost corner the Adirondacks, a spur of the Canadian highlands, provide the state's most picturesque heights. They are modest by western standards; the tallest peak is barely a mile high. But they are infinitely ancient mountains, shaped of rocks that took their place above the primordial sea scores of millions of years before the Rockies were formed; rocks that are as old as any in the world known to the geologists. Near the highest reaches of these forested uplands, from "a minute, unpretending tear of the clouds—a lovely pool shivering in the breeze of the mountains," spill the thin beginnings of the Hudson River, one of the world's most magnificent waterways.

Another province of mountains covers almost the entire southern portion of the state, rising in the Catskills to occasional lofty peaks that overlook the Hudson and leveling off into a plateau that rolls gently southward into New Jersey and Pennsylvania and extends westward to the Great Lakes. They are the product of hundreds of millions of years of erosion that has softened their contours and deepened their valleys. In one of these ample folds the water of the Schoharie Reservoir covers the oldest forests known in the world, gigantic petrified stumps of fern-trees, eleven feet in circumference, that flourished in the western Catskills far back towards the beginning of time.

Along most of its long, straight eastern border, New York is edged by still different mountains, the Taconics, which geologists tell us are but abbreviated stumps of a formation that must once have been of Alpine proportions. They are properly a margin of the New England Province, but they are a welcome intrusion into the state, for they complete the master mold in which the destiny of New York was cast.

The two broad valleys, the Hudson and the Mohawk, that cut at right angles between these separate highlands, provide a sweeping throughway from the Atlantic Ocean to the Great Lakes, the only water-level route through the coastal mountains which, from Georgia in the south to the St. Lawrence River in the north, block off the interior mass of the continent. In the late summer of 1609 Henry Hudson, searching a way to the Orient, ventured up that route as far as the present site of Albany and there turned back, frustrated, little knowing that he had reconnoitered the closest thing to the Northwest Passage that any explorer would find until three centuries later. (The States General of The Netherlands had offered a handsome purse for the discovery of a shortcut to the East, but it was never collected.)

In time these cross-country valleys came to serve as the most heavily traveled migration route in history. Long before the invasion from New England had passed its crest, fresh streams of migrants were coursing into the state, and through it, to mingle with the mixed stock of earlier arrivals. The greatest number, by far, of all the immigrants who poured into America during the last century and a half chose New York City as a port of entry, and from there the natural highway opening into the West was an irresistible temptation. The stream of immigration has laid down a rich human deposit as it flowed through the state. More than three-quarters of New York's population is clustered along this historic route, and more than half these people are still either immigrants or of immigrant parentage. The very life of New York, its economy and its culture, has been hard tried and richly benefited by the need to accommodate the numerous and motley throngs that have settled within its borders. On a larger scale than any other state, New York has known the continuous ferment and the restless excitement that attend the fusion of different peoples uprooted from their several soils and ancestries and thrown together into a common crucible.

There never has been a pause in this process of assimilation, as there was for a sensible period in New England's early history and as there long was in most of the South. As one consequence it is not easy to "type" the New Yorker. There is no caricature of him to correspond to the Yankee peddler, the Kentucky colonel, or the other stock regional figures that populate American folk art and literature. It is often said that no "immigrant" group left such a large and lasting impression on the life of New York as the Yankees—those "locusts of the West," as James Fenimore Cooper disdainfully termed them. It is as frequently remarked that contact with this more generous and tolerant western world rubbed a good deal of the asperity off the Puritan character and in good time "Yorkified" the newcomer, as ex-President McCracken of Vassar puts it. But New Yorkers are not simply transmogrified Yankees. In the end they are very much like other people, largely because so many of them *are* other people—from Italy, Poland, Ireland, Germany, Russia, New England, and way places. (As a sidelight on this point, almost 200 foreign-language newspapers and periodicals representing no less than 30 non-English tongues—including Chinese, Arabic, Welsh, Albanian, Hungarian, and Portuguese —are published in the state.)

Yet, as Aldous Huxley has observed, a countryside and its people are to a very large extent the inventions of its poets and its novelists. To the degree that this may be true, New York State is the creation of Washington Irving and James Fenimore Cooper. The whimsies of the one and the romances of the other, both culled from the lore of the land, may disturb the modern historian and anthropologist looking for measurable facts. But these legends have been indelibly stamped on New York soil and we are all the richer for them. New Yorkers, whatever their origin, are the spiritual heirs of Diedrich Knickerbocker and Natty Bumpo.

As Irving wove its magic into his stories, the Hudson River became one of the world's enchanted waterways. To this day one cannot pass the Dunderberg (Thunder Mountain) at the southern entrance to the Highlands, without harking for the voice of Mein Heer, the bulbous-bottomed Dutch goblin with his sugar-loaf hat, bawling his orders for wind and lightning. And who ever visited the Catskills without sensing the abiding presence of Rip Van Winkle and his troop of small folk?

Dutch customs and the Dutch language persisted along the Hudson Valley until well into the last century. Dutch words, such as *cruller* and *cooky*, *boss* and *scow*, *stoop* and *dope*, have found a fixed place in everyday American speech. Dutch place names—Kinderhook, Cobleskill, Spuyten Duyvil, and the like—are scattered all over the map of eastern New York. Occasionally, as in the Leendert Bronck House in Albany County and the Hendrick Bried House in Rensselaer County, one can spot a rare survival of true Dutch architecture. But in the end, the Dutch, who founded New York and held their tenure during the formative years of its development, left their most enduring impress in the tall tales with which the son of an English-born merchant so securely caught the imagination of his own and later generations.

As his province Cooper took the land beyond the Knickerbocker legends, the wide-angle segment of the upper state that centers on the Mohawk Valley and stretches northward to Lake George and Lake Champlain and westward to the Great Lakes. This, too, was enchanted ground. There is reason to believe the ancient legend that the Great Spirit regarded it with special favor. The imprint of the hand he once laid upon it in benediction may still be traced in the tapered outlines of the Finger Lakes. It was almost within the span of those clear-watered valleys, according to the Dekanawidah story, that Hiawatha dreamed and spoke of a peaceful brotherhood of men. And round about, covering practically all the present state from Lake Erie to the Hudson River, the Iroquois did in fact establish the league of Five Nations, the remarkably statesmanlike and democratic confederation of aboriginal tribes that was the most powerful combination of Indians on the North American continent.

Out of his love for this forested land Cooper spun the tales that have been called America's own "Arabian Nights of the frontier." His descriptions of the heroic life of the forest, its tawny denizens and its white pathfinders, cast a spell over readers throughout the western world that lasted for a century and more. His works were widely translated abroad (Franz Schubert called from his deathbed for more of Cooper's novels to read) and it is likely that more than a few immigrants came to the New World with vivid misconceptions of what awaited them from having read the *Leatherstocking Tales*. New York, indeed, still remains the land of the Iroquois. The Indians themselves have long since been dispossessed of their lands, but they have survived, thanks in good measure to Cooper's peculiar talent, as folk heroes celebrated in the histories and pageants of the state and lastingly recalled by more than five hundred place names.

In a land so steeped in heroic legends almost anything came to seem possible, even the final redemption of man. The book of golden pages that was the Book of Mormon was left on a New York hill for Joseph Smith to find and to translate with the aid of the diamond-lensed spectacles that lay beside it. On another New York hill, in 1844, William Miller gathered his faithful followers to be carried up to heaven when doom cracked, as he promised it would that very night. A few years later the first convention in history to argue the question of woman's rights was held in Seneca Falls. In New York, especially during the nineteenth century, doors to salvation have opened in all directions; and out of the ferment of aspiration a fresh strain of legend developed.

A good bit of the stuff that legends are made of went into New York's first great corporate effort, the building of the Erie Canal. The idea of cutting such a water passage three hundred and sixty-odd miles through a wilderness of forest and swamp seemed at the time, even to such a far-seeking mind as Thomas Jefferson's, "little short of madness." It did take vision and determination just short of madness to realize the job. But it was finished in good season, in the fall of 1825, and the Irish bogtrotters whose brawn had dug the way—whose very presence in these parts blazed a trail for millions of compatriots and co-religionists—were free for other heavy work that now needed doing.

Nothing before or since has so dramatically emphasized New York's vital place in the Union. The "mighty ditch" was only four feet deep but it quickly floated a tremendous burden of traffic. Within barely a score of years the canal business concentrating at Albany was greater than that derived by New Orleans from the trade of the whole Mississippi River basin. The original canal has long since been replaced by broader and quicker channels of communication. From a passing car you can still spot sections of the old cut, its abandoned bed choked with cattails, its towpaths run to weeds. But if you pause to listen or to read, you will soon learn that its sluggish waters still wind their way through the hearts of Yorkers. The legends of the canal grow richer with time (especially in the hands of such engaging storytellers as Samuel Hopkins Adams, Carl Carmer, Walter Edmonds, and Harold Thompson). The fact remains that it left an imperishable impress on the land. Most of the major cities of the state have grown from frontier villages that sprang to sudden life at the magic touch of the canal. Rochester, Syracuse, Utica, and Buffalo sprouted out of the wilderness at a giddy rate to feed and to feed upon the passing commerce along this golden trade route. Each is now the center of a spreading metropolitan area with the oscillating rhythm of industrial concentration and suburban expansion so common to a large part of the American scene today. More than a million people, including one of the largest Polish populations in the world, have congregated within thirty miles of Buffalo's steel furnaces, grain elevators, and other plants. Across the state to the east, the General Electric Company's major headquarters in Schenectady is virtually a city in itself, with its miles of streets, its scores of buildings, and its many thousand employees. Along the whole "Erie" valley the pattern of industrial and urban development has been worked into an almost solid wide belt.

The new Thruway—"the world's greatest highway"—closely parallels the old Erie Canal; as, indeed, does the not-so-new New York Central which, with the other railroads that were thrown across the state to exploit its bounty, involved such scandalous buccaneering as the nation has not often witnessed. Yet in these days of superhighways and airways the great natural thoroughfares do not hold the exclusive tight command over a countryside they once did. New York mines no gold or silver or coal and it drills little oil, but it has other riches that lay scattered all about its varied landscape, and people, industries, roads, and airports have converged to form important productive clusters at points far from the route of the canal. Hardly more than fifty years ago Theodore Dreiser, encased in dust coat and goggles on his long way to Indiana, drove over unfrequented roads through the Southern Tier of the state in his "handsome sixty-horsepower Pathfinder," a novel adventure he recounted in *Hoosier Holiday*. Today that route crosses one of the heavily industrialized sections of New York. The International Business Machine Corporation at Endicott in this area, like other industries in the state, sends heavy air freight to all parts of the country, bypassing the problems of topography altogether. Along the northern margin of the state, the most drastic surgery ever performed on the North American continent, the St. Lawrence Seaway, promises to bring the Aluminum Company's great plant at Massena—and the industries of Rochester and Buffalo, not to mention others in the Middle West—closer by direct sea route to major European ports than either New York or Philadelphia, with consequences yet to be calculated.

New Yorkers practice virtually every kind of manufacture listed by the United States Census Bureau, a range of industrial activity that gives the state a fair measure of its economic stability. More people are engaged in manufacturing than in any other state, and more money is involved in payrolls. It is, as already remarked, the leading industrial and commercial state in the nation. But it is a great deal more than that and such statements make it difficult for strangers to visualize the pleasant hillside pastures and flowered meadows that are a large and important part of the New York countryside. These millions of picturesque acres, with their grazing kine and ample barns, constitute one of the most productive dairy lands in America. Great rivers of fluid milk flow incessantly, by tank car and truck, from all parts of the state to the large consuming markets of its cities. Even New York City boasts of its dairies whose cows, fed on boughten fodder, blink wonderingly at their urban surroundings.

A sharp spur to the Yankee invasion of New York came, it has been said, from the tall stalks of corn and grain and the jumbo-sized onions and potatoes sent "back home" by pioneering farmers from New England. A land that could yield such prodigies was a land that in good Puritan conscience must not be neglected. Within a generation, the Genesee Valley was transformed from an unrelieved wilderness into "the granary of the nation." In the center stood Rochester, America's first boom town, already a flourishing "New England" city whose massive granite mills poured forth more flour than it seemed the world could need.

The principal wheat fields of the nation have long since moved into the farther West (although the modern Barge Canal continues to carry a good share of the produce through New York) and Rochester is now the "Kodak City" with a bent for cosmopolitan culture that is by no means discouraged by the many Italians and Germans who have settled there. But New York soil still provides abundant harvests around the seasons. No one who has traveled through the state during the March and April thaws will forget the pleasant and ubiquitous sight of maple trees draining their sap into the waiting buckets. A century and a half ago a lot of people dreamed of supplying the wide world with sweets from these groves. (The sugar maple has since been chosen the state tree.) Today, however, the bulk of their large yield goes just beyond the state border to be sold as "good old" Vermont maple sugar and syrup.

In May the great clouds of blossoms along the Hudson and Champlain valleys and in the Great Lakes plain foretell a harvest of apples that will probably be second only to that of the state of Washington. In the summer close-gardening Polish and Italian farmers take from the rich mucklands of the central state—land reclaimed from swamps by persistent immigrants—the nation's largest onion crop, along with other produce that, come harvest time, may be seen in towering piles of crates amid the level fields of vegetables. Also during the summer months, not far from Long Island's abundant potato fields, ducks in the millions cover the shores and coves of Suffolk County with a solid but restless white blanket while they are nurtured for their ultimate select place on dinner menus throughout the country. And around the calendar, in cool cellars dug deep into the hills that cradle Pleasant Valley, Concord, Catawba, Niagara, and Delaware, grapes from neighboring vineyards are transmuted into wines that bear proud labels.

As Timothy Dwight long ago said they might, the people of New York have come to happy terms with the land they live on. They have at times abused its welcome, as did the lumbering gangs that in the last century threatened to skin the Adirondacks and other forested regions of their covering of virgin timber, and that did, in fact, make New York for a time the foremost lumbering state in the Union. There are still lumbermen in the Adirondacks and the mountains are ringed about with mills that turn out prodigious quantities of paper and paper board. But today much of the pulpwood comes from across the border or from overseas. More than 5 million acres of this highland country, including all or parts of 12 counties, have long since been set aside to be "forever kept as wild forest lands." The old scars are healing and these mountains, with their glinting lakes and dashing streams, have become one of the great natural preserves and vacation areas of the nation.

The most spectacular natural feature of the state is, of course, Niagara Falls. Father Louis Hennepin, a fellow traveler with La Salle on his epic voyage down the Mississippi, first described the majesty of this imperial cataract in a book that ran to 35 editions in four languages before it went out of print. H. G. Wells, who visited the falls some two hundred years later, admired them less for their sheer beauty than for their almost infinite potential as a source of power. A good portion of that power has long since been harnessed to practical service, and more in abundance will soon be forthcoming, but the state years ago carefully preserved the beauty of the site (with the cooperation of Canada) by setting it apart as a sight-seeing reservation, a departure, new at the time, that was significant for park policy throughout the nation.

Many visitors over the years have subscribed to New Yorkers' solid conviction that the Hudson is the world's most beautiful river. Something over a century ago, Captain Marryat pronounced it "incomparably more beautiful than the Rhine." It was as he imagined the Rhine to have been in Caesar's day. For all that has happened in the meantime, there are passages along the river where it is easy enough to follow Marryat in his imagination. Indeed, since timber cutting was stopped years ago and large areas flanking the river have been preserved from exploitation, parts of the countryside have been growing ever more wild. In portions of the Hudson Highlands this wilderness is within view from the towering piles of New York City—the most extensive wild area in the world so close to a major metropolis.

Here we must face the implausible but stubborn fact that half the people who live in New York are crowded into a minute fraction of the total area of the state, at the extreme pointed limit of the land in New York City. This metropolitan concentrate is politically integrated with the rest of the state's population, although its representatives are restricted by law to a minority vote in the state legislature. It provides nearly three quarters of the state's revenue, and receives a considerably smaller proportion in return. It contributes abundantly to most of the statistics that give the state such an impressive rating in atlases and almanacs. But by New Yorkers who live beyond its tight confines, the metropolis is commonly regarded as a foreign entity, albeit one with which they obviously manage to coexist on favorable terms.

Dr. John Finley, a sage editor of *The New York Times* among other things, once referred to this strange alliance of city and "upstate" as the United States of New York, a phrase that aptly suggests the relationship of the two disparate elements. Each has a population that in itself is larger than those of all but a few other states. With more regard for logical theory than for constitutional practice the city has often been called the forty-ninth state. It has become the center of a "metropolitan region" that includes parts of four states, almost three hundred other communities, and the rural regions that lie between— a super-community whose people read the same newspapers, frequent or are dependent upon the same principal trading and distributing center, face common problems of public concern, but who maintain separate governments for approaching their shared interests.

No accurate up-to-date likeness of New York City will probably ever be put into print. The metropolis changes too swiftly for the slow business of publishing to keep pace. Even the most recent almanac has a nostalgic flavor as one reads of outstanding "monuments" already half-forgotten and since replaced by new adventures in construction. New York is the greatest city to develop since the late Middle Ages, but unlike Rome, Paris, London (even after the bombings of World War II), and other historic urban centers, it has left practically no trace of its origins or of the stages of its spectacular growth. No other city since creation has so enthusiastically dedicated itself to constant change as a positive guiding principle. No city in history has shown such indifference to the monuments of its past. There is far less left standing of colonial New York than there is of Periclean Athens; and before these words are printed, it seems likely, there will be even less standing of the Park and Madison Avenues of this author's own childhood.

There is affirmation in all this. To discard the past has become in itself an act of faith in an illimitable tomorrow. It might be said that New York's nostalgia is not for what has been but for what is yet to come. Without straining common sense we can find in this spirit of incessant change an ultimate projection of the "frontier idealism" described by the late Carl Becker in one of his brilliant essays. For the frontier, as he wrote, whether geographical or intellectual, offers little hope to those who see things as they are. To venture into any wilderness, one must see it not as it is, but as it will be. It is the promised land to be entered only by those with faith.

The form may mask the spirit. The first skyscraper in any town is nothing in itself, but it is much as a token of achievement, a conspicuous marker on the road to things hoped for. The skyline of New York, that chaotic, jagged, and preposterously beautiful outline of the city's towering buildings, is far more than an evidence of engineering skills and "engineered" real-estate values; it is the dominant symbol of our New World civilization, the shifting graph of modern man's busiest dreams.

There are some solid and unchanging reasons for New York's appearance, as there are for its consequence. The city's skyscrapers are anchored in a substantial bed of rock as old and as resistant to time as the rocks that form the Adirondack Mountains (a bed of rock, incidentally, that is generously and colorfully studded with semiprecious stones of extraordinary variety). In uptown regions, as occasionally in Central Park, this tough crystalline spine thrusts through the soil in picturesque outcroppings that are the delight of clambering youngsters from the leveled pavements of surrounding neighborhoods. Beyond the park's preserves worried contractors have to blast through it to provide cellars for their lofty structures or tubes for subway trains. Or, elsewhere, to probe through some pocket of glacial drift to reach its basic substance. But at every point this unyielding bedrock firmly supports the massive weight that is piled upon it and makes possible the city's fantastic profile.

This is to speak of Manhattan, once known to the Indians as the Island of the Hills. One can still find hills on the island, but they are almost everywhere reshaped and dwarfed by the man-made superstructure. By a strangely poetic circumstance when a steel frame is needed for some skyscraping addition to the city's architectural pile, contractors prefer to call in the Indians to raise it for them. For several generations Mohawks, descendants of Hiawatha and men who for no obvious reason excel at such work, have "walked steel" high above the city streets. Their latter-day handiwork carries the walls of the Woolworth Building, the Empire State Building, the Chrysler Building, and other giant structures on Manhattan Island.

Manhattan is the nub of the city and the smallest of its five boroughs. Within its tight confines buildings must go skyward if they go anywhere. It is possible to live on this narrow island, hemmed in and buffered by brick and mortar, and remain unaware of the lick of the tide at the ends of the short cross-town streets, not to realize the immensity of the ocean traffic that on every tide swarms about its fringe of docks. But it is also possible, and infinitely more rewarding, to view from the tops of its taller buildings one of the largest natural harbors in the world and to note how the tip of lower Manhattan reaches into the upper end of the harbor like a beckoning finger to the commerce of the world; a summons, it might be added, that is heeded by more than twelve thousand ocean-going vessels in any one year.

New York is a seaborne city, split into islands and parts of islands by salty currents that run in all directions, sometimes contradicting one another in angry patches of water, as they do at Hell Gate where the tides meet in a sort of syncopated rhythm. Here is where the ocean finds its way to the city through a separate back entrance, approached by a hundred miles of sheltered water between Long Island and the

New England coast. It is a route that was long favored by trans-Atlantic mariners wary of heavy weather, or marauding ships, on the open sea outside New York harbor. (In the shadow of one of the giant spans of the Triborough Bridge that now vaults over Hell Gate, there is the sunken wreck of a British frigate, the *Hussar*, with, it is said, several million dollars in gold that had been intended to pay off the redcoats stationed in New York during the Revolution.)

The waters of the harbor push on far past the city through the channel of the Hudson River, forming the greatest tidal estuary in the western hemisphere between the Plata and the St. Lawrence. At the head of navigation, one hundred and fifty miles inland from the metropolis, far from any trace of salt water and close to its junction with the Mohawk, the Hudson still rises and falls in cadence with the Atlantic tides.

Its solid position within that web of far-reaching waterways, in command of the most enticing natural entrance to the New World, was the city's unique birthright. From its earliest days New York has been a sailor's town and a trading place, polyglot at every level, and quickened by the constant traffic of people from the world at large. New York has never abandoned the traditions and manners of New Amsterdam, a hamlet born in the tiny image of old Amsterdam when that city was crashing the barriers of world trade. The quickness of tempo, the spirit of tolerance, the intellectual curiosity, and the preoccupation with the present that Amsterdam automatically bequeathed to her distant little namesake even survived the long period of English dominion and the genial slanders of Washington Irving to add to the modern city's inheritance.

New York is older than Boston or Philadelphia, but for more than half its history it did not enjoy the consequence of one or the other of those towns. Before the Revolution, Philadelphia was already the second largest city in the British Empire. At the time of Washington's inauguration on the balcony of Federal Hall overlooking Wall Street in 1789, New York was still a second-rate contender. By then it was larger than Boston, to be sure, but its hopes were dominated by the princely estates of the descendants of the Dutch patroons and the favorites of the Duke of York, that for a while yet closed off its hinterland to normal growth. The little city had twice been burnt over during the long British occupation of the Revolution; and, with the evacuation of the redcoats, it had also been deserted by thousands of substantial Loyalists, leaving the population smaller than it had been before the war. Federal Hall itself was but New York's old and shabby city hall, hastily if expensively remodeled for the first inaugural by Pierre Charles L'Enfant, the French veteran of the Revolutionary army who subsequently laid out the permanent capital city of Washington. L'Enfant's own estimate of New York as a future cosmopolis was probably best expressed by his refusal of ten acres of Manhattan real estate, offered him for his services by grateful citizens, since, as he said, he was above such "petty emoluments."

In less than a generation after the capital had moved, via Philadelphia, to the swamplands of the Federal District, New York was already fast becoming in both spirit and fact what old Amsterdam had set out to be and might ultimately have been, had not Pepys and Colbert intervened. In our own time it has become the busiest seaport in the world and a major crossroads of the world, more cosmopolitan than most of the cities of Europe have been in the modern age. And, above all, because it is a matchless port and "a great open window to the world," New York has become the metropolis of the nation. In most countries of the world the largest city is the national capital; or, in more precise causal relation, the national capital is normally the largest city. It is an American legend that no city can be to this nation what Paris, London, and Rome are to their respective countries—the center, not only of government, but of wealth, fashion, intellectual power, and population. There are more than half a dozen American cities that are larger than Washington, each one of which claims to have true national distinction (and, usually, the prettiest women in the land). But New York has become so indisputably the most consequential and largest city in the United States that, as Denis Brogan observes, it alone among all the striving big cities of America can afford to call itself both *little* and *old*. And, one might ask, where else do the women—housewives and actresses, models and secretaries, showgirls and shopgirls—whatever their God-given pulchritude, put on such an attractive performance of sophistication and chic?

Almost everything that constitutes "little old New York" as a popular image—Broadway and Wall Street, Park Avenue and Radio City, Chinatown and Coney Island—might be sensibly explained in terms of what has happened on the city's waterfront. Professor Albion has in fact gone a long way towards doing it in his several eloquent books on the maritime history of the port. But it has taken prodigious human effort to convert those natural advantages into the epitome of modern urban civilization that New York has come to be. The restless energies of people who have come to the city, hopefully, by the many millions and from everywhere, have been built into a community that has no precedent and no parallel. They have raised a superstructure that, almost at the same moment in time and with utmost irony, has developed into both the first capital of the world and the shining target of the missile age.

New York is a house of many mansions, each one teeming with life. There are just about the same number of different national and racial groups among its citizens as are represented by the delegates to the United Nations. Even after a generation of restricted immigration, more than two and a half millions of the city's population are foreign-born, and another two millions, roughly, of foreign-born parentage. Over a million non-whites live in the five boroughs, in addition to more than a half million Americans from Puerto Rico, most of whom speak little or no English when they arrive, as they continue to do in large numbers. But the citizens, on the whole, get along together better than the delegates do (officially, in any case). As E. B. White has remarked, New Yorkers are tolerant not only from disposition but from necessity. If they were otherwise, as he says, the city would explode in a flash of hate and rancor and bigotry.

Chinese New Year, Hanukkah, St. Olav's Day, St. Patrick's Day, Sun Yat-sen's birthday, the independence days of a score of different nations (some no longer independent), Russian Easter, the feast days of a variety of saints beloved by Italians and others, are all celebrated with uninhibited loyalty and reverence, at times with a lusty indiscrimination. Jews, Orientals, Negroes, Germans, and a host of other non-Irishmen help to make the annual St. Patrick's Day parade one of the most variegated and noisy spectacles of the city's spring season. Here in New York one may best see how, as an English journalist reports, America has lifted the curse of the Tower of Babel. The Oriental plane trees and ailanthus (the tree that grows in Brooklyn), the "English" sparrows and starlings, the rats, and mice, and alley cats of Eurasian origin have also found their flourishing places in the life of the city.

The municipal government that watches over this permanent and peaceable international congress is larger and more complex than many of those heard from in the United Nations building. In solving, among a multitude of other problems, those constantly generated by the influx of restless strangers, so often unprepared for the demanding disciplines of life in this city, New York has become what may very well be the most thoroughgoing welfare state in the world. "Real New Yorkers," those who have by chance arrived somewhat earlier than others and have established themselves, have not always welcomed the intrusions of these "gross little foreigners," as Henry James—himself an expatriate—called them, and the burdens they have imposed on the city's administration and its society. However, such recruits have filled myriad jobs in the city's laboring force left vacant by those who had moved on up the social and economic ladder. In the present day, New York's vast garment industry, as well as its hotels and restaurants, could not operate without the services of the Puerto Ricans and Negroes who have filled the gaps opened by the restriction of European immigrants.

In some lines of work skilled craftsmen from Europe are still being recruited, by involved legal procedures, to replace the aging practitioners from earlier and freer days of immigration, whose sons have become too Americanized to want to learn their fathers' patient craftsmanship. The highly diversified manufacturing operations of the city alone—there are forty-two thousand separate plants representing about three hundred different lines of activity—require a working crew larger than the combined manufacturing labor forces of Chicago, Detroit, Pittsburgh, Cleveland, and Los Angeles.

By an accepted convention there are no resident native-born New Yorkers, except the occasional rarity who is welcomed as a conversation piece at ceremonies and at cocktail parties. The truth this whimsical misstatement underscores is that the spirit and the accomplishments of the city have been determined to a great degree by people of every stripe who were born someplace else and who came here in quest of something. As Captain R. H. Macy did when he came from Nantucket as an industrial pioneer to open his little store; and Junius Spencer Morgan from Hartford to learn the banking business; or William Cullen Bryant from Great Barrington to escape the factiousness of village life and to pursue literary adventures.

The Yankees were only the first in a long line of settlers from other sections of the nation to come to the Big City to better their prospects. They were only the first, also, to form a society (The New England Society in the City of New York) dedicated to the fond memory of someplace else in the nation that could all too easily be forgotten amid the compelling interests and opportunities of the metropolis. In later days even favored states like Florida and Texas have been represented by such "emigrant" clubs, whose self-conscious nostalgias suggest how little disposed their memberships are to return homeward. The towers of New York's skyline stop well short of heaven, but for a lot of people they point the way upwards in more than one sense, and in the aggregate they reach about as far as men have a right to expect. A dozen years ago *The New York Times* reported that all together, the elevators of the city traveled half the distance to the moon every day in their ceaseless vertical shuttle, a figure no doubt long since raised to a more spectacular range. Thus even the bare statistics of New York tempt the imagination.

The city could never have been raised to its present heights, of course, without the elevator—nor without the telephone. Aside from the continuous noise of traffic—the tumult that in pre-auto days Walt Whitman likened to a "heavy, low, musical roar, hardly ever intermitted"—the most characteristic sound of the metropolis is the ringing of telephones, a sound the poet was mercifully spared. Almost nineteen million calls a day are placed through the city's exchanges, representing an increasing traffic in words that, like the automobile traffic on the city streets, seems to recognize no law of diminishing returns and that suggests a different context for the saying, so often quoted, that "it is what New York says that counts."

Before they could spread into a solid copper canopy over the main streets, about seventy-five years ago, telephone wires went underground to join the multitudinous other conduits necessary to the city's operations and its survival—water mains, gas and steam pipes, sewers, and electrical cables for highly miscellaneous purposes that must snake their ways between and into the subways and the foundations of buildings. To view the incredibly tangled subterranean world on which New York vitally depends—and it is constantly being opened up for repair and inspection and for all to look into—is reason enough to recall how large a part faith plays in the existence of the people of the city.

Some 15,000,000 miles of telephone wires play their part in integrating the city's myriad functions. Steam raised to a heat of 1000 degrees is pushed through concrete-reinforced pipes at nearly 300 miles an hour. The current that streams through 19,000 miles of electrical cables is boosted to 69,000 volts. And so on in an endless flow of energy this complex arterial skein feeds one of the most awesome concentrations of power on the face of the globe. A serious malfunction at any point beyond quick reach of the repairman could reduce the city to a state of paralysis—or widespread destruction—in short order. On his first view of the New York skyline H. G. Wells is said to have remarked, "What a magnificent ruins it will make!" At every level the city is vulnerable, and miraculously resilient.

As slightly confused visitors continue to insist, New York is not typical of America. It is not typical of anything, for there is nothing like it in the world. But with its all-American population and the extreme diversity of its activities and interests, the city does reflect the attitudes and the economy of the nation at large (and vice versa, it must quickly be added). More truly than Washington, it is the nerve center of the United States, energized by people and impulses from all over the land and feeding back its synthesis of America. John Adams once tartly remarked that there was not a cultured person to be found in all New York, an observation that did that wise statesman little credit. Today for better or for worse, the metropolis projects the dominant cultural standards of the country. It is the principal market place for culture as it is for virtually everything else. Most of the books America reads are produced and published, and what is quite as important, critically reviewed in New York; and they are often conceived and written in the almost inviolable privacy which, by another of its miracles, the city makes possible for its residents. Willa Cather wrote her sympathetic and knowing classics of the Nebraska plains in the sanctuary of a New York apartment, and John Steinbeck has fondly written of California's San Fernando Valley from the security of an East Side brownstone.

Talent in every field converges upon the city to compete for acceptance by audiences that Cecil Beaton has called "the most enthusiastic and critical in the world." Over a wide range of performance, from serious drama to popular phonograph recordings, New York determines what the entertainment program of the country will be. It is no accident that this pre-eminence in musical and theatrical activity—in the arts generally—was established about the time the city became the financial capital of the world; nor is it a reflection on the brand of the city's cultural interests and tastes that they are powered by opulence. According to the English author Cyril Connoly, New York has very nearly attained that "ideal of humanist society, where the best of which an artist is capable is desired by the greatest number."

The economy of a community and the direction of its culture are, after all, inseparably related. Wealthy patrons have brought together and paid for and deposited in the museums and libraries of New York such an incomparable collection of treasures that one French visitor was led to call the city the refuge of Western culture, alone possessed of that profusion that is "mother of the arts." By the happiest of paradoxes this city, which has so unremittingly removed all traces of its own development, has also assiduously, lovingly, and expensively rescued from neglect and destruction the monuments of medieval Europe that are so attractively incorporated in The Cloisters, with Rockefeller funds administered by the Metropolitan Museum. As a footnote to the history of philanthropy and culture it should be remarked that almost a million people a year make a pilgrimage to this shrine at the northernmost tip of Manhattan in Fort Tryon Park, whence it overlooks the Hudson and the Palisades. The Palisades do not belong to New York, they are New Jersey's. But as a further footnote, Rockefeller funds also paid for the preservation of a crucial section of the Palisades landscape now part of an interstate park, and for time to come New Yorkers will look across at that unchanging natural wonder.

Throughout the year New York plays host to an enormous floating population that comes to see the shows on Broadway, to shop on Fifth and Madison Avenues, to do business almost anywhere in the city, to study at its universities and other schools, or just to sample its varied excitements. Among other things, as Simeon Strunsky pointed out some years ago, it is a bigger summer resort than Atlantic City and a bigger winter resort than Miami. Every working day of the year the city also accommodates hundreds of thousands of commuters who by morning descend upon its shops and offices to earn their bread and profit, and who at evening flee to more-or-less domestic comforts in the suburbs. Those gigantic daily pulsations have been growing more violent by the year as the suburbs, still firmly within the city's orbit, have themselves mushroomed into prosperous urban areas, while New York's own resident population has finally stopped growing.

History, particularly over the last century, has made us thoroughly familiar with the metropolis grown large by absorbing its suburbs, as New York swallowed Greenwich Village, Harlem, and (in 1898) even such an independent entity as Brooklyn. But it has not prepared us for the prospect of suburbs taking over the city. If that should happen to New York, however, it would be just another episode in the story of one of the world's most unpredictable communities. One always leaves New York with a measure of sadness, knowing it will never be quite the same when he returns.

The
Central East

BY PHILIP A. KNOWLTON

"I abhor two principles in religion, and pity them that own them; the first is obedience upon authority without conviction; and the other, destroying them that differ from me for God's sake."

Surprisingly modern except in phraseology, this is a pronouncement of William Penn made two and three-quarters centuries ago, shortly after the famous Quaker's first visit to America. It was so far ahead of its time as to classify Penn as a dangerous radical.

Europe was becoming surfeited with the mocking of a gentle, compassionate religion by self-styled Christians who sought to "destroy for God's sake" other Christians with whom they disagreed on details of dogma. Though the burnings that made the 1400's and 1500's hideous had been largely replaced by political disabilities and economic sanctions, it still required courage to be a self-confessed member of a religious minority. Freedom of worship for the benefit of the particular group agitating for it was, of course, no new ideal; but to hold the umbrella of toleration over persons regarded as heretics was carrying ideological hospitality pretty far!

A desire for religious freedom—preferably for one's own church or sect—was by no means the sole motive, and in many cases not even the major motive, for the settlement of the English colonies that later became our thirteen original states. It was chiefly lust for adventure and hope for sudden wealth that brought the first boatloads of Englishmen into the New World at Roanoke Island in the late 1500's and at Jamestown in the early 1600's. Both of these bonanza bubbles burst, as such bubbles always do except when natural resources are unusually rich and easy to extract, transport, and market. Thereafter, through decade after decade, the colonies owed their steady growth in large part to the craving of the landless in England and other European countries for homesteads of their own.

Sometimes, as in the case of the Dutch and the Swedes who settled at and near the mouths of the Hudson and Delaware Rivers, this lure of the land operated quite independently of religious considerations and continued to be a stabilizing influence throughout colonial times. But, unlike immigrants from countries where religious minorities were not severely discriminated against, the first English settlers of New England came as refugees. And the Roman Catholic settlers of early Maryland and the Quaker settlers of Pennsylvania had just as much reason as did the Separatists and Puritans who emigrated to New England, to put an ocean between themselves and the established Church of England.

Before attempting to unravel the tangled strands of the story of European migration to the area with which we are now concerned, let us take a look at the land to which the newcomers came. In terms of today's political units, this area includes, in addition to the District of Columbia, the group of states between New York on the north and Virginia on the south. Prior to the War Between the States, these were four: Pennsylvania, New Jersey, Maryland, and Delaware. As we shall see, West Virginia, which we treat as a part of what we have chosen to call the central east, separated itself from Virginia in 1861 and came into the Union as the thirty-fifth state in 1863.

On a 12-inch globe you can cover with the tip of your thumb the five states that we have just named. Manifestly, differences in latitude within this area are too small to have a marked effect on climate.

Crocuses blossom just a little earlier and leaves fall just a little later in Bluefield, West Virginia, than in Erie, Pennsylvania; but both enjoy —and "enjoy" is the word for it except for a few weeks each year—a humid continental climate with temperatures characteristic of lower-middle latitudes.

A continental climate on a seacoast is of course no anomaly, pro-vided it be on the *east* coast of a continent in the belt of prevailing westerly winds; for in an area where the wind usually blows from over the interior of a continent, temperatures are comparatively little in-fluenced by the ocean. The usual annual temperature range along the Atlantic littoral is about ninety degrees, half again what it is along the shore line of the Pacific in the same latitudes. The rainfall of 42–46 inches, quite sufficient for ordinary farming, is well distributed through the twelve months and is noted for its regularity from year to year despite occasional droughts. There are also occasional floods, for the destructive effects of which man himself is chiefly to blame when he changes the face of nature in ways that are detrimental, or fails to alter nature when he could do so to his advantage, or builds his houses and factories in wanton disregard of the ultimate probability, indeed virtual certainty, of high water.* Day-to-day weather changes are fre-quent and invigorating.

In contrast to artificial political boundaries, which in most cases run due north-south or east-west the world over, the physical features of any region have no respect for the points of the compass, an instru-ment that was invented eons after most of them had taken definite form. The natural regions of this group of states extend from south-west to northeast. To emphasize either the north-south or the east-west trend at the expense of the other is to oversimplify. This is most ap-parent in the case of the corrugated roof of this area—the parallel ranges of mountains and stream-dissected plateaus that with occa-sional interruptions follow such a line for 2000 miles from Alabama to the Gaspé Peninsula. If, at any point, you want more of the same kind of landscape, you follow this diagonal course; if you want variety, you travel crosswise in a northwest-southeast direction. That is what

* In river control, costly pork-barrel politics is being replaced by more legitimate (and costly) programs of survival. In 1958 it appears likely that de-velopment of the valley of the Delaware River will soon be a smaller-scale northern equivalent of the TVA.

the chief rivers do, though with many a long detour on their oft-contested courses to the Father of Waters or to the Atlantic.

This is an area of old, worn-down mountains, mere vestiges of super-Himalayas of past geological ages. No point in these five states is as much as 5000 feet above sea level, and the highest point in Pennsylvania, where the uplands are widest, has an altitude of only a little more than 3200 feet. Yet the Poconos of that state are among the world's oldest mountains and may once have been its highest.

Long ages of erosion bring complexity of terrain. In the extreme northwest, Pennsylvania's corridor to Lake Erie is a low plain that lies within the glaciated region of North America whose southern extremity determined the course of the Ohio River. East of that river and west of the Allegheny Mountains in West Virginia is a wrinkled, undulating landscape of foothills and rich bottom lands with never a mountain in sight—and rarely a square mile that is flat. As one travels southeastward along the Kanawha River, foothills give way to a medley of wooded knobs and ridges of unpredictable shapes, heights, and directional trends. Once over the range into old Virginia, however, the traveler looks backward at an impressive mountain wall and is reminded of the much higher Sierra Nevada of California: a long ramp when approached from the west, an abrupt rampart when viewed from the east.

As mere scenery, the Appalachians in these states, where not defaced by man, are attractive but seldom superlative. It is no reflection upon their scenic charm that nowhere in this area is there a National Park or Monument set aside for the enjoyment of nature rather than for the contemplation of great moments in our past; for our public playgrounds are as likely to feature the bizarre as the beautiful. Nevertheless, disregarding as unfair competition the big-league vistas that abound in the western third of our continent from McKinley to Orizaba, a lover of mountain contours is likely to prefer Chocorua or Monadnock to Horseshoe Curve or Delaware Water Gap; and of course the rolling farm land between Baltimore and York is gentler and more ingratiating. But along with the charm of outdoorness which all natural scenery possesses if not defiled by billboards and other works of man, in these mountains, or if you please in this eroded plateau, lies mineral wealth that has helped mightily to catapult the United States into world leadership and will give it primacy until atomic fission replaces coal and petroleum; for in these relatively commonplace highlands lies fuel for fifty centuries.

First discovered and long disregarded was coal. Its properties known to, and sparingly used by, peoples of Eurasia more than three thousand years ago, bituminous, or soft, coal was not mined extensively in America for commercial use until the era of railroad building, nor was the value of the hard, or anthracite, coal of which northwestern Pennsylvania possesses almost a hemispheric monopoly generally appreciated until even later. Today West Virginia and Pennsylvania, our two leading coal states, together mine more than a ton and a half of coal each year for every man, woman, and child in the United States.

Petroleum, which now rivals coal as a fuel for industry and has largely replaced coal as a fuel for transportation, was until the mid-1800's little more than a harmless ingredient in nostrums with fancy labels peddled to a credulous public for the cure of real or imaginary ailments. The first oil well was drilled near Titusville, Pennsylvania, in 1859. The story of the growth of the petroleum industry in the century that followed is a fit sequel to *The Arabian Nights*, the locale of which, with an adherence to fiction seldom achieved by reality, has in recent years been the scene of many of the oil industry's most colorful episodes.

Far less dramatic, yet impressive in its production figures, is a third fuel in the development of which Pennsylvania and West Virginia pioneered—natural gas. Seeping out of cracks of the earth here and there over thousands of square miles of the surface of the latter state, the gas is piped to compression plants and repiped to city and countryside alike for domestic and industrial uses. Outdoor gas meters are as common a sight along West Virginia highways as are the back-porch washing machines which, like electric refrigerators in the Philippines, are the badge of economic status.

East of the highlands in Maryland and Pennsylvania is the Piedmont, or foot-of-the-mountain, region. This crosses central Maryland and includes much of southeastern Pennsylvania and northwestern New Jersey. The Piedmont, like the coastal plain, is well adapted for farming. The Piedmont has more soil with a limestone base than has the sandy and clayey coastal plain. The latter pioneered in tobacco three hundred years ago, whereas today tobacco is a leading crop in Lancaster and adjacent counties in the heart of the Pennsylvania Piedmont. In and near densely populated areas, crops for man's basic sustenance tend to replace crops pandering to his minor vices; and modern man's increasing ability to use his fields as mixing trays gives him the power, within reasonable limits, to adapt his soil to the needs of the crop he chooses to grow.

The transition from the Piedmont to the coastal plain is abrupt. Where the harder bedrock of the former meets the softer bedrock of the latter, falls or rapids occur in the streams all the way from New England to the Deep South. In the old days when power was normally transmitted by belts, wheels, and gears rather than via copper wires, a substantial year-round waterfall that kept going even in times of low water was an important industrial asset. Because of dependable water power from falls either of major streams or of their tributaries, Passaic, Trenton, Philadelphia, Wilmington (Delaware), and Baltimore were at some time in their development materially aided by the fact that they were Fall Line cities. Some of the larger falls are still used to generate electric power for local plant consumption, as at Passaic; but for the most part the Fall Line has ceased to be important.

One geological fact about the coastal plain has had an incalculable effect upon the history of this region: It sank. Not very much—only a few fathoms—but sufficiently to submerge a strip of land on both sides of all the streams flowing into the ocean. In one way, this was a disaster, for it put millions of tons of fine soil forever out of man's reach on the sea bottom, in contrast to the opposite process of building up projecting deltas where coasts are rising or at least not being submerged. But it produced New York, Delaware, and Chesapeake Bays. All three are, or have on their peripheries, inviting harbors. The last named has harbors-within-harbors, and harbors within those. As a result, little Maryland claims a water frontage longer than that of Florida or Texas or California, all because of the intricate bowel-like foldings and counterfoldings of the shore line of Chesapeake Bay. These vast areas of sheltered water were havens to forerunners of the *Mayflower*, and with a bit of dredging and careful navigation some of them are still used by large ships. Quays (or their more modern replacements) along the banks of the shallower headwaters of the affluent streams, once the front-yard marine approach to tobacco farms, are now moss-grown back-yard relics of bygone days. The farms, long ago converted to the raising of perishable fruits and vegetables for sale in the almost continuously urban area from Baltimore to New Haven, are reoriented to a less glamorous age of trucks speeding day and night on paved highways.

Much of the farming that we have just mentioned so badly out of its chronological context takes place on the peninsula that lies between Delaware Bay and Chesapeake Bay—a peninsula divided among the three States of Delaware, Maryland, and Virginia. Doubtless because it doesn't jut out into the sea as one expects a peninsula to do, being formed instead by the encroachment of the sea upon what used to be the land on both sides of it, it doesn't even *seem* like a peninsula. Thought of quite correctly as a part of the mainland that you have to cross water to get to if you are motoring southward from Atlantic City or northward from Norfolk, it even lacked a name until it became plagued with a plethora of names. As a peninsula, it is nameless still on atlases and road maps. Informally it is commonly referred to as the Eastern Shore. Eastern Shore of what, depends on where you live. Occasionally a gazetteer calls it the Delaware Peninsula, which seems eminently reasonable; at least two otherwise excellent handbooks tag it with the synthetic name Delmarva, formed from the abbreviations (actual or perverted) of the names of the states among which it is divided! With ramified coves on one side and with beaches, lagoons, and tidal marshes on the other and everywhere the tang of the sea, the Eastern Shore is a shore indeed, where land and water not only meet but intermingle. No metropolis disturbs its tranquillity, for Wilmington, the only city of any considerable size, is off limits—too far north to be regarded as a part of the peninsula itself. Even so, the density of population is nearly twice the national average. Youth does not have to emigrate to make a living.

This, in brief, is the land to which the European immigrants came in the 1600's. Most of it was heavily forested here with conifers and there with deciduous trees, or a mixture of both, even the sand-and-pine belt of central New Jersey where tree growth is slow. The land was sparsely inhabited by primitive tribes, misnamed Indians as a result of Columbus' pathetic inability to comprehend the fact that he had reached not the Indies of south or southeast Asia but a New World. That the Indians along the coast were friendlier to newcomers than those farther inland gave immigration its first great boost. Had the hunting grounds of the Iroquois and the Leni-Lenapes been reversed, who knows what the course of history might have been?

In the 1500's, hazardous coastal voyages along various sectors of the southeastern front of the North American continent between Labrador and Florida gradually replaced conjecture with solid fact. On navigators' charts, Long Island became less chubby, Cape Cod more hooklike. Late in that century the British made their abortive effort to establish a settlement on Roanoke Island. Otherwise, European activity in America prior to Christopher Newport's founding of Jamestown in 1607 and Champlain's founding of Quebec in 1608 was confined largely to Spanish exploration and exploitation of Middle America and Peru.

In 1609 Henry Hudson, an Englishman working for Holland, which had become colony-minded since its successes in the East Indies, entered Delaware Bay and subsequently sailed up the Hudson River in a fruitless search for a Northwest Passage—a search that only a year later was to result in his death somewhere on the bleak surface or lonely shore of the great bay that bears his name. Hudson's activities at the mouths of the Delaware and Hudson Rivers gave the Netherlands a plausible claim to the drainage basins of both rivers and to the land between them. To be sure, the English claimed the entire continent by right of the Cabots' discoveries, and Spain had even prior, though less specific, claims of the same sort based on the voyages of Columbus. But a finders-keepers philosophy generally yields to the more easily asserted principle that "possession is eleven points in the law." Five years after Hudson's visit, Cornelius May, a Dutch navigator, explored the lower Delaware River itself, and four years after that his countrymen established a settlement at Bergen on the site of present-day Jersey City. An outpost was established across the river on Manhattan Island in 1623, three years after the landing of the Pilgrims at Plymouth. In 1626 Peter Minuit, in what turned out to be history's most famous bargain, "bought" the entire island from the Indians for approximately one-billionth of its present worth.

Meanwhile the English were entrenching themselves in Virginia and in New England and were beginning to suspect that if they did not colonize the land between, other European nations with even more tenuous claims to it would forestall them. So the Crown was predisposed in favor of any reasonable plea for land or for colonizing privileges in North America. Naturally, then as now, an influential candidate for favors had a distinct advantage over a casual adventurer or a nobody.

Manifestly eligible was any member of the Calvert family. George Calvert had been a high-ranking official under Charles I, and had served his king and his country well. Such was his rectitude that in 1625, having been converted to the Catholic faith, he confessed his heresy to the Protestant king. Instead of the dire penalty he would have paid a century earlier, he was permitted to sell his job for £6000 —they were franker about such matters in those days—and was kicked upstairs into the Irish peerage. Awarded a manor known as Baltimore in central Ireland (*not* the Baltimore we see on maps at the southern tip of the island), he became the first Lord Baltimore in accordance with the feudal and postfeudal custom of naming noblemen after their estates.

George devoted the rest of his life to establishing in America a refuge for persecuted Catholics. In 1623 he acquired for that purpose the southeastern extremity of Newfoundland, but the climate and the French were too much for him. Six years later he made a reconnaisance trip to sunnier Virginia, from which he was politely expelled because of his religion; but not before he had learned that good land lay north of the Potomac, uninhabited except by Indians and therefore in the European view awaiting settlement. Application for this was made to the king, but before a patent could be granted George died. So it was his son Cecil, the second Lord Baltimore, who became the founder of Maryland, with a closer approach to regal powers over his domain than any other British proprietor had ever enjoyed or would ever again be granted.

In this charter of 1632, the only references to religion were mildly restrictive: No laws were to be passed that were prejudicial to "God's holy and true Christian religion." Though Maryland pioneered among the colonies in providing religious liberty for its inhabitants, it but transplanted to the New World a toleration that had already taken slender root in England's royal circles—a strange hothouse indeed for mercy in view of the ghastly reign of Mary I less than a century before!

Maryland's first proprietor took possession of the colony in 1634, founding St. Mary's on the long-fingered peninsula between Chesapeake Bay and the Potomac River. Baltimore was not founded until 1661, nor did it become a city until 1729.

What Preston James in his Introduction to this book refers to as the "culture hearth" of the middle colonies was, as he agrees, unlike those farther north and south in that it recruited its immigrants from three European countries each having its own national culture or composite of cultures. Here, therefore, three stories interlock. To tell them separately, even in briefest summary, would obscure their many interrelationships. In such a case, to stick fairly closely to chronology is the narrator's sole salvation. So, having (we hope) made it clear that the founding of Maryland by the English came a few years later than the establishment of Dutch settlements on and near the coast between Maryland and New England, we return to that middle area to report developments that took place some years after Maryland had become a proprietary English colony.

Just as occupation counts for more than discovery, aggressive action by a strong military power counts for more than homestead rights which are not defended when challenged. In 1624 a renegade Dutchman, Willem Usselincx, had enlisted the aid of King Gustavus Adolphus of Sweden in an effort to obtain a foothold in America. Royal approval was promptly granted, but in war-burdened Sweden the financing and equipment of an overseas expedition proved difficult. Two companies were organized but folded up. Finally in 1638, commanded by the self-same Peter Minuit who had bought Manhattan Island for the Dutch but who was now working for Sweden, two small shiploads of Swedish adventurers reached the Delaware River and built Fort Christina on the site of present-day Wilmington. First, however, Minuit, perhaps seeking to surpass even the record for sharp trading he had established when he acquired Manhattan Island for the Dutch twelve years previously, bought from the Indians—different ones this time—most of what later became the State of Delaware together with a big slice of southeastern Pennsylvania, "appropriately rewarding them with articles of merchandise." Gradually Swedish outposts were built farther and farther upstream. Within five years Johan Printz, the third governor of what was by that time known as New Sweden, had built a fortified trading post on Tinicum Island in the Delaware River between the present sites of Chester and Philadelphia. Numerous small Swedish settlements sprang up on both sides of the

3. Many widely-traveled visitors have expressed the opinion that the Supreme Court building in Washington, D. C., is the nation's most impressive structure. It is east of the Capitol and near the Library of Congress, the dome of which is seen on the right.

74. The bridge across Chesapeake Bay at Annapolis.

75. Painted on the barn of an Amish farmer, a moral admonition
greets the wayfarer in southeastern Pennsylvania.

Sargent F. Collier

6. This great beacon on the site of Thomas Edison's workshop and "invention mill" is a landmark in eastern New Jersey.

77. These spheres store liquids under moderate pressure at the grea
     chemical works at Belle, West Virginia.

78. An oil refinery on an island in the Kanawha River near Charlestor
     West Virginia.

Gallowa

). Grinding paint at a pigments plant just west of Wilmington, Delaware.

80. The glee club of Johns Hopkins University, Baltimore, gathers ov
the steps of Gilman Hall for an evening of singing.

1. Looking east over the national Capitol and nearby public buildings.
The Supreme Court building and the Library of Congress have already
been identified. The Senate office building is at the left, that of the
House of Representatives at the right.

2. The modern replacement of the bridge at Wheeling, West Virginia,
which enabled the National Road to join the east with the middle west.

83. The Pittsburgh Triangle, where progress replaced decay. At th
point the Allegheny and Monongahela Rivers merge to form the Ohi

84. The middle portion of Atlantic City's miles-long water fro

Delaware, some of them well above Tinicum Island. It was the Swedes who introduced the log cabin into North America.

To these encroachments on what they considered their own territory, the resistance of the Dutch was fitful and ineffective. Leaders on both sides were soldiers of fortune. Explorers and professional colonizers sold their services to the highest bidder. Allegiance was a transferable commodity. Today's enemy might be tomorrow's ally. So for a while there prevailed a state, not of cold war but of intermittent and often half-hearted hostilities with many friendly interludes; in short, an unstable mutual toleration. No such half-peace, of course, could continue indefinitely; precarious international relations have a way of getting worse rather than better.

New Netherland had long been languishing, partly because of restrictions upon immigration which had been lifted even prior to the Swedish invasions, and partly because of weak and irresolute government. In 1646, however, Peter Stuyvesant, known to every schoolboy for his peg leg and his peppery disposition, took charge. The determined governor subdued the Swedish settlements, though it took him nine years to do it. But Swedes were not the only challengers of Dutch authority. Six years before Stuyvesant became governor, Englishmen from Connecticut had begun to cross over to Long Island, supposedly Dutch territory. The Mohegan Indians from the Hudson Valley, while Stuyvesant was engaged with the Swedes along the Delaware, almost wiped out New Amsterdam itself.

From year to year the inroads of Englishmen from New England upon New Netherland became more threatening. England greatly feared Holland as a commercial rival. So in 1664 England's "Merry Monarch," King Charles II, though England was at peace with Holland, took a step quite worthy of a twentieth-century dictator: Without warning or a declaration of war, he blithely sent a fleet to take over New Amsterdam and with it all New Netherland. Stuyvesant, repudiated by his peace-loving burghers (who didn't like the old curmudgeon anyhow), had no choice but to capitulate. New Amsterdam became New York, and the area between the South (Delaware) River and the North (Hudson) River became New Jersey. And so they remained, except for a brief Dutch comeback in 1673–1674 when a European war had curious repercussions in America.

New Jersey in the early years of English rule had a minimum of autonomy, for it was regarded as conquered territory. Gradually, however, as its English population increased, it acquired a political status similar to that of the other English colonies. Two years after its re-recovery from the Dutch, it was divided into West Jersey and East Jersey. More appropriate names would have been Southwest and Northeast Jersey, for the line of demarcation ran from a point on the coast a few miles north of present-day Atlantic City to the great bend of the Delaware River near the present city of Trenton. (This can still be traced in certain county boundaries.) Northeast of the line lies the two-thirds' portion of the state that is more or less closely associated with metropolitan New York; the other side faces the city of Philadelphia and the State of Delaware.

In the 1600's the entire eastern seaboard from the Potomac River to French Acadia had been a welter of conflicting claims and overlapping grants. If a profligate English king had borrowed heavily from a nobleman to support his mistresses and their joint progeny, what was easier than to discharge the debt by granting his creditor's son lands in America? Perhaps the boundaries between grants were ill-defined, but what of that? Let the proprietors worry! William Penn, to whom we now return, was the serious-minded son of a wealthy admiral who had advanced considerable sums to Charles II. Penn had become a Quaker and sought a refuge for members of his sect in America, which for nearly half a century had been sheltering English Catholics. So Penn bought what was to become Pennsylvania (with little Delaware thrown in for good measure) from the king for the price of a modest estate. Later he had the good sense to re-buy it piecemeal from the Indians at subnominal prices which, however, so far exceeded those paid by Minuit before him that he was applauded both by the Indians and by historians for his princely generosity.

As an American colonial proprietor, Penn was little more than an absentee landlord, for he visited his new realm only twice. The first visit, to set up the new colony, was in 1682–1684; the second, equally brief, came after fifteen stormy years devoted, in and out of English jails, to promoting the cause of religious and political liberalism.

Penn's short sojourns in the new colony made up in beneficent activity for what they lacked in duration. It required clairvoyance, when Philadelphia was a tiny ex-Swedish hamlet in a wooded wilderness, to lay out a city whose population would top the 2-million mark and whose chief traffic handicaps in an undreamt-of motor age would consist of its departures from Penn's original, grandiose layout. It took diplomacy to keep eastern Pennsylvania, scene of a constantly advancing frontier of European settlement, relatively free from Indian forays. Though Penn's problems were greatly simplified by the elimination some years before his time, first of Sweden and later of the Netherlands as neighboring colonial powers, throughout his lifetime and long afterwards Pennsylvania's boundary disputes boxed the compass. Yet the local and regional "wars" with which the musty records of the time are filled were for the most part minor conflicts.

Eventually Pennsylvania won most of the contested areas, doubling its north-south span as compared with Penn's original holding. The long-disputed southern boundary was fixed, in accordance with a compromise advantageous to Pennsylvania, by the line run by Mason and Dixon generations later in 1763–1767 and meticulously described (to the nearest 10 feet) as N. Lat. 39°43'26.3". In a gradual and not unfriendly separation, Delaware acquired an assembly of its own in 1704 only three years after Penn's second visit to America, and became an independent state in 1776 and the first state to ratify the national Constitution in 1787.

So it was that the middle colonies got started. New York, actually a northern state, is commonly associated with the middle states but is treated separately in this book. The fifth of what we call the central eastern states, West Virginia, as we have already observed, had no status as a political unit until the War Between the States. Immediately after the secession of the Confederacy, West Virginia, non-slave because of its mountain-and-frontier culture, seceded from the Confederacy. President Lincoln and his advisers were faced with a poser: Should they welcome into the Union a twice-seceded state to help them reject, by force of arms, the theory that a state could rightfully secede even once? Accepting with practical realism the less unwelcome horn of a tough political dilemma, Congress admitted West Virginia into the Union on the theory that, just as two negatives make a positive, that state wasn't no part of it and therefore belonged in and not out. And the Union never had cause to regret this decision.

The people of the American colonies in the mid-1700's were a hardy lot. Most of them, or their forefathers, had come from the British Isles.

Some of these were, as we have seen, adventurers and some were refugees from religious persecution. Others came to escape landless poverty or to surmount the economic barriers of a stratified society. Less numerous were the descendants of Swedish and Dutch immigrants who craved elbowroom and the farming and commercial opportunities of a new land.

Also, especially into eastern Pennsylvania, there had been an influx from Germany of members of Protestant sects that were severely persecuted in their native land. Known variously as Moravians, Mennonites, Amish, Brethren, and Dunkers or Dunkards—there is considerable confusion in nomenclature—these sects had and still have in common certain beliefs and mores, notably an austere rejection of everything suggestive of luxury or ostentation. It was this characteristic, presumably, that attracted them to a Quaker colony. These are simple folk, industrious and frugal. They are the backbone of one of America's most productive farming districts. Tourists visit Lancaster, Lebanon, and nearby towns to gawk at them, and are prone to grumble when these reserved and dignified people fail to appear in buggies and at markets as advertised by their would-be exhibitors.

In the pre-Revolutionary period, not a few Virginia Puritans found the Anglican slant of that colony uncongenial and crossed the Potomac into Maryland, whose Toleration Act of 1649 granted religious freedom to all avowed Christians and set the pace for Pennsylvania. Few French entered the middle colonies, for French Catholics emigrated to New France prior to its fall in 1763, and French Huguenots preferred the English colonies farther north or south to those of the central group. From other European countries than those we have mentioned, immigration in colonial days was negligible.

By natural increase, which was prolific, and by immigration, the central east was filling up. The Indians had never been numerous—at the most a few tens of thousands—in the area in which we are now interested. Europeans soon outnumbered them. In the year 1729, for example, 6207 settlers came to Pennsylvania, chiefly from northern Ireland; in 1750, 4317 Germans. In certain other years Scottish and Welsh settlers predominated. By 1750 in Pennsylvania alone there were a quarter of a million people. At the time of the first national census (1790) the population of the four central ex-colonies was almost exactly a million, to which should be added perhaps 100,000 in the northwestern portion of Virginia which later became West Virginia.

In the second half of the eighteenth century there was a decided trek to areas west of the mountains. Trouble with hostile Indians and with the French made frontier life precarious, but the lure of the unknown and word of the rich prairies and rolling lowlands of present-day Kentucky and Ohio proved irresistible. Thousands of settlers undertook the difficult journey through mountain passes over fantastically crude roads and risked their own and their families' scalps in the glamorous districts of Vandalia, Transylvania, and Louisiana whose boundaries were so vague as to baffle even the most imaginative map maker.

As a youthful surveyor, George Washington knew the mountain trails of this region well. He charted a route from western Maryland to the strategically located fork of the Ohio where Pittsburgh now stands. In the French and Indian War this site was bitterly contested. A British general, Edward Braddock, used Washington's trail as commander of an expedition to take Fort Duquesne from the French. Nearing that stronghold, Braddock disregarded the advice of Washington, who was familiar with Indian warfare and was serving as one of his officers, and led his men into ambush. Braddock was killed, and Washington was largely instrumental in saving what was left of Braddock's force.

A famous contemporary of Washington was Daniel Boone, a frontiersman who became a legendary figure throughout the vast region from the Appalachians to the Rockies. Counties, towns, and hotels are named after him from West Virginia to Missouri. It was Boone who in 1775 opened Wilderness Road leading from the Potomac in eastern Virginia through Cumberland Gap to Kentucky.

In selecting the *dramatis personae* for even the sketchiest summary of the late colonial and early national period, it would be unthinkable to omit Benjamin Franklin. For Franklin had everything: wisdom pleasantly salted with occasional folly; strong personal morality along with the faculty of sowing wild oats without reaping a bitter crop; anonymity which only enhanced his fame; immense popularity de-

spite the implacable hostility of a few active enemies; diplomacy in
his mature years replacing a perverse youthful belligerence; enormous
literary success with a minimum of sustained literary effort; the great
luck to be born in an age when one could achieve distinction as a
scientist without being a mathematician, as a statesman without first
being a lawyer or a general or a millionaire.

Franklin was the first American to base a career on democracy's
most characteristic activity, journalism, and it was his good fortune
to do so just at the right time. In Franklin's lifetime, Philadelphia increased twelvefold in size. When he arrived from Boston as a youthful
printer in 1723, British America was largely rural. No city north of
New Spain (where there were several cities of considerable size) had
as many as 10,000 people. At that time Boston led Philadelphia and
New York by narrow margins. By mid-century Philadelphia had forged
ahead of both its rivals. It kept its leadership until 1830, when New
York surpassed it.

In small but booming Philadelphia, whose somnolent quality was
as mythical then as now, the self-educated Franklin became the arche-
type of the modern go-getting civic leader. Grown wealthy—for those
days—by shrewdly tailoring his not-too-arduous writing and publishing
activities to the popular demand and capitalizing upon an early-
discovered aptitude for couching homely sentiments in still homelier
language, and already an expert promoter, he "retired" in his forties
to turn over the mossbacks and to needle the recalcitrant into public
enterprises that seemed always to click. In short, he was an arch-
Rotarian in a pre-Rotarian age.

Would it benefit Philadelphians to have an organization for the exchange of ideas? Franklin started one; it thrives today. Were books
hard to obtain? Franklin started the country's first circulating library.
Were fires too frequent and too costly? Franklin started a fire department and America's first fire-insurance company, besides inventing the
Franklin stove. Was it a nuisance to keep changing one's spectacles
for near and distant vision? Franklin invented bifocals. Was police
service inefficient? Franklin reformed it. Was there need for organized
care of the sick or injured? Franklin founded America's oldest hospital.
Was higher education in Pennsylvania lagging behind that of other
colonies? Franklin founded what became the University of Pennsylvania and was a co-founder of Franklin and Marshall College in Lan-

caster. Was the colonial postal service poor and running in the red? Franklin as postmaster general of the colonies improved it, reduced the rates, and made a profit for the several governments. Did the colonies need protection against the French? Franklin contributed money and supplies and became a colonel of militia. Did the colonies need a representative in London to interpret their views and seek mitigation of oppressive laws? Franklin for many years was that emissary. Was American independence inevitable? Franklin at seventy helped to draft the Declaration and signed it with firm but fine-lined calligraphy. Were the Articles of Confederation inadequate for the needs of the new country? Franklin at eighty-one as a member of the Constitutional convention urged compromises that broke deadlocks, and was one of the six signers of the Constitution who had likewise signed the Declaration of Independence.

During the late pre-national period the colonies west and south of New York were not only filling up but growing up. Life was becoming more complex. The balance of a simple agricultural economy shifted between subsistence and commercial farming as the market for tobacco waxed or waned. Slowly the beginnings of an industrial economy dotted the landscape. A multitude of small forges refined the low- or medium-grade iron ore which underlay highlands and lowlands alike. Small-scale manufacturing enterprises of every conceivable sort from the casting of pots and cannon to the blowing and engraving of fine glassware enriched many entrepreneurs and broke others who were less shrewd or less fortunate.

Shipbuilding, as in New England, grew apace. Steam was used by William Henry to propel river craft on the Conestoga—also famous for the wagon that became the prairie schooner—before the year 1765, as we are reminded by a plaque in Lancaster across the street from another tablet boosting the less authentic claim of Robert Fulton to priority (John Fitch, chronologically in the middle, being ignored by both plaqueteers). Coastwise and overseas commerce became highly profitable. The gold and silver coins of Spain, France, Holland, and even Arabia became *de facto* legal tender and continued in circulation into the early national period.

Restrictions imposed by the mother countries encouraged smuggling and even piracy. Lonely wave-washed sandspits and secluded bays from Hatteras to Block Island and even Cape Cod were rendezvous of bootleggers, tax-evaders, and hijackers operating under eighteenth-century names. So bold were they that New York's customs revenue declined while New York merchants grew fat on the sale of European and Asiatic merchandise landed in minor ports in New Jersey and slipped across the North River under cover of darkness. Pirate ships no longer flew the defiant skull-and-crossbones emblem; but, flagless, they took their toll of commerce on Delaware and Chesapeake Bays. Piracy, already a problem in Penn's time, a half-century later was still a circulation-building topic for young Franklin's journalistic balladry and a target for Franklin's maturer activities as a crusader for the suppression of lawlessness.

The birth pangs of the United States have been told in schoolbooks too many times to warrant retelling them here. The scene of the Revolutionary War, which as everybody knows began in New England, soon shifted to the middle colonies and eventually spread farther south. What is generally conceded to have been the decisive battle of the war was fought in northern New York, and the war ended in Virginia; but the long midwar travail, when soldiers were cold and hungry and discouraged, centered in Valley Forge. Pennsylvania was the heart of the new nation's struggle for existence, and it was a heart that almost broke under excessive strain.

In the first twenty-four years of our national existence the seat of government shifted from place to place like the party conventions of a later era. For a total of eighteen of those years, Philadelphia was the national capital; for five years—the notable quinquennium which included Washington's first inauguration—New York was the capital. During interruptions in Philadelphia's holding of this title, Congress, for periods ranging from a few days to nine months, met in Baltimore, Lancaster, York, Princeton, Annapolis, and Trenton, all of which therefore are correctly designated as former capitals of the United States. And since our present District of Columbia, which is coextensive with the city of Washington, consists wholly of land carved out of the State of Maryland, it is apparent that eight of the nine cities that have ever served as our national capital are in territory now or formerly within the east-central state group, and the ninth is just across a state line.

In the first decade of the nineteenth century there was considerable interstate and intercity rivalry. New York's regard for Philadelphia or

Boston's or Baltimore's regard for either may be likened to that of Los Angeles for San Francisco forty years ago or to Dallas' affection for Fort Worth today. Several eastern and southern cities wanted to be capital. Setting a precedent since followed by Australia and (in prospect) by Brazil, Congress solved a touchy problem neatly by awarding the honor to no city then in existence, and by accepting the offer of Maryland and Virginia to give up all title and sovereignty to a 10-mile by 10-mile tract straddling the Potomac. (In 1846 the part of the District lying southwest of the Potomac and including about twenty-nine percent of its total area was returned to the State of Virginia. Not only was that state unhappy over the failure of the Federal Government to develop the tract where almost a century later the vast Pentagon was built; in the mid-1800's the burgeoning city of Alexandria foresaw a greater future for itself if it could give up suburban status and return to near-autonomy.)

When the District of Columbia was set apart in 1791, the only towns within its limits—both small but growing and ambitious—were Georgetown north of the Potomac on the Fall Line and Alexandria on the right bank of the Potomac in the southeast corner. Both banks of the river were lined with plantations where flourished a polished and horsy manorial aristocracy based on rich soil, slave labor, and water transportation that made them largely independent of nearby towns. Wedged in between the larger land grants of a square mile or more and reaching out into the hinterland were irregular blocks and slivers of poorer, even marginal land where humbler farmers eked out a drab subsistence. North of the outlying farms the land resembled what the area between Washington and Baltimore would look like today if divested of its superhighways and if its original forests had not been replaced by second or third growth.

To rise just east of, and eventually to include, Georgetown a French engineer planned a city that in its streets and boulevards would rival Paris. Except for throughways built as afterthoughts at the cost of extensive demolition, Salt Lake City is perhaps the only American city that invites plat-with-plat comparison—and even Brigham Young neglected to provide for his city west of the Wasatch the broad and sweeping diagonal avenues so prophetically laid out for Washington by L'Enfant.

As a city, Washington had a hard time getting started. Other American cities had grown up in an orderly way where topographic and human factors combined to encourage their development. Let us, for a moment, replace the culture-hearth analogy with another that is equally homely: Chesapeake, Delaware, and New York Bays and the rivers to which they served as approaches were narrowing funnels into which Europe poured its people and its goods. Each had at least one major city. The lower Potomac, as a virtual arm of Chesapeake Bay, might have made commercial cities of Georgetown and Alexandria had those towns not been drawn into the Federal orbit. (Indeed this is what happened later to a cluster of cities at the mouth of Chesapeake Bay in Virginia.) But in the early 1800's the herculean task of building a city that would conform even approximately to L'Enfant's plan was so engrossing that competition with Baltimore was forgotten.

By the year 1800 greedy land speculators who came within an ace of smothering the infant capital had been paid off. Nuclei of the present White House and Capitol had been built, as had a Treasury and several other less important public buildings. All 126 of the Federal civilian employees had been moved, bag and baggage, from Philadelphia. A sprawling, muddy shack town was actually functioning as the nation's capital.

The new District of Columbia was soon to suffer a setback wholly unrelated to the difficulties that any artificial community has in establishing itself; and the impending calamity was to be the first of many indications that, for good and for ill, the history of the District of Columbia is the history of the United States of America in miniature.

"War Hawks" led by Henry Clay had long been shouting for war against Great Britain. The United States had grievances against Britain, to be sure, as well as against that country's enemies in the customary arena, Europe. But the War Hawks wanted Canada, to which this country could not, by any feat of casuistry, assert the slightest legitimate claim. So began the War of 1812. Derisively, those who thought it unnecessary or immoral named it "Mr. Madison's War" after the President in whose administration it was fought. Early in the war a United States force, in a kid-glove era when countries fought chivalrously (unless Indians were involved) and refrained from needless sabotage, had burned the government building in York, now Toronto, Canada. Late in the summer of 1814 a small British expeditionary force landed in the Chesapeake Bay region. Then followed a period of a few weeks that Americans would like to forget. A short third of a century after Saratoga and Yorktown, the "defenders" of the Chesapeake area abandoned it to invading Englishmen half as numerous as themselves, cringing before a raiding party which had ventured so far from its base of supplies that it could have been annihilated. Residents who didn't run were soundly beaten by inferior numbers. In retaliation for York, the British burned most of the government buildings in Washington, including the Capitol and the Executive Mansion. Years passed before the gutted interiors of these structures could be replaced. The wave of defeatism subsided with the valiant defense at Fort McHenry which gave us *The Star-Spangled Banner*, of which more anon.

Then came our era of greatest expansion. In 1814 Pennsylvania and Virginia west of the Appalachians were frontier country. Thirty-five years later the Gold Rush to California was on, to be followed shortly by gold-and-silver rushes, copper rushes, salmon rushes, timber rushes, wheat rushes, and cattle-and-sheep rushes into every territory and eventually every state of what we now, with continental perspective, call the west. Those are dealt with in other chapters of this book. But here, in the states of the central east and in the Federal District that is our capital, was developing the core of an industrial nation. New England specialized in manufacturing. The south and the middle west in those days were agrarian. The central east had a diversified economy. So did the far west, but that was another cosmos beyond the steppe land and the desert.

Just as Watt and Fulton and the Wright brothers and a hundred others got chief credit for innovations which they did not originate but which they improved or were the first to use successfully, so the central east figured prominently in the early development, if not in the actual invention, of devices and technological practices that revolutionized life in America and throughout the world.

Here, in Hoboken, was the test run of the first American locomotive, and here was built more than one of America's first railroads. Eventually three major lines surmounted the Appalachians and connected east with west. (Here also, within a century, the competition of airplanes and of busses running on publicly financed highways is bringing about the slow demise of railroad passenger traffic. One can no longer ride a train between Wheeling and Charleston, West Virginia, and passenger service has recently been discontinued on one line between New York and Washington.) On the rivers of these states plied the first American steamboats. In these states, during the epidemic of canal building that followed the opening of the Erie Canal in New York State, were dug a few canals like the one across the northern neck of the Delaware Peninsula that were a boon to commerce, and others that violated nature and became useless moats. And the central east pioneered in communication as in transportation. Here the telegraph was first tried out and the telephone first successfully demonstrated. And here, in our century, Westinghouse's Station KDKA in Pittsburgh pioneered in radio broadcasting.

Here the Western world rediscovered the values of coal, both anthracite and bituminous, and put to use the well-nigh inexhaustible deposits in the Appalachians. Here, for the first time in the western hemisphere, coal (via its derivative coke), iron ore, and limestone were brought together in vast quantities for the mass production of iron and of raw and fabricated steel. And in the very back yard of the world's greatest coal field petroleum first came into commercial use. For some decades it was consumed chiefly in the form of kerosene, which could be burned with the aid of wicks both for illumination and for heat. But petroleum really came into its own when it was found feasible to consume it explosively (rather than by slow combustion) in its higher-octane form known as gasoline, in internal-combustion engines for the propulsion of vehicles, boats, and aircraft. And here, as we have seen, began man's greatest salvage operation, the use of natural gas.

Petroleum and the internal-combustion engine brought about the automotive age. The contemporary era has been variously named— age of steel, machine age, air age, and now an atomic age that simultaneously promises unheard-of leisure and threatens us with extinction. Of all the changes that have been brought about by modern technology, undoubtedly the one that has had the greatest effect *thus far* on our way of life is the substitution of the automobile and bus, the truck, and the airplane for the buggy, the cart, and more recently the railroad coach. The central east had pioneered in the construction and improvement of roads for more efficient use of animal-drawn vehicles.

A hundred and fifty years ago the Lancaster Turnpike had been completed between Philadelphia and the city after which it was named. By the middle of the nineteenth century five east-west roads passed through Pittsburgh, and the long-contested bridge across the Ohio at Wheeling, where its stone abutments are to this day a prominent feature of the downtown district, had at last brought horse-and-mule through traffic from the Atlantic seaboard to the middle west via what later became U. S. 40. And today in Pennsylvania, New Jersey, and Maryland multi-lane turnpikes encourage fast travel with a minimum of halts all the way from the Atlantic to the western prairies. Chesapeake Bay is spanned at Annapolis by a mighty bridge, as is the Hudson to the northeast by half a dozen. Luxurious motels soothe the tired nerves of motorists who have driven six hundred miles between sleeps, replacing the wayside taverns that once refreshed the aching bodies of men who had coaxed and whipped draft animals into pulling loads a thirtieth of that distance.

Early in the national period of industrial development, in which these states played a leading part, came the long and tragic war known in the North as the Civil War and in the South as the War Between the States—the difference in names of course reflecting basic differences in political philosophy. In that war, as in the Revolutionary War and the War of 1812, the central east was deeply and intimately involved not only as a contributor of men and supplies but as a theater of actual fighting. Here took place the assault on Harpers Ferry, serving as a portent (to all who would see) that war had to come. The bloodiest battle of the entire war was that of Antietam in Maryland, and the most decisive, the Battle of Gettysburg in Pennsylvania.

After 1865 industrialization increased at an accelerated tempo; in fact during the war years the need for munitions and uniforms had stimulated industry. As in industrial areas the world over except the few, like the Ruhr, which are so jam-packed with factories, mines, smelters, foundries, and stockpiles that literally no room is left for crop fields, industrialization meant a parallel growth of mining, manufacturing heavy and light, and specialized agriculture such as dairying and truck farming. In the immediate vicinity of Pittsburgh heavy industries lined the river banks much of the way from Johnstown and

Altoona to Wheeling. "Smoky Pittsburgh" was a stereotype phrase un-til recent years when smoke-control measures, speeded up by the Donora smog deaths, made the air again transparent and inhalable. Johnstown, Pittsburgh, and Wheeling had their disastrous floods and sought to prevent repetitions. Pittsburgh replaced the sooty squalor of its old Triangle with glittering skyscrapers. Across the state in east-ern Pennsylvania Bethlehem was another smaller and comparatively sanctified Pittsburgh, and now Levittown joins Bristol in clamorous inroads on sedate Bucks County. Here, as on Sparrows Point near Bal-timore, iron ore from Venezuela is delivered without transshipment.

For half a century refineries had flourished midway between the light indoor activities of New York City and the chemical and phar-maceutical plants of east-central New Jersey. And let us not forget the landslide of industrial development that was jarred into motion by Thomas Edison, the Wizard of Menlo Park. *His* contributions were not local or regional or national, but world-wide.

All these industries depend on materials taken out of the earth, and in most cases the key materials are coal and iron. Back in the nine-teenth century it became cheaper to bring to the vicinity of the coal fields iron ore from mines south and (later) west of Lake Superior by a chiefly-water route, than to use the less concentrated ores that underlay the east. The coal fields of Pennsylvania remained its indus-trial foundation. The oil flow of Pennsylvania continues, but has in this century been vastly exceeded by that of the southwest, from which the product is piped to the vicinity of Philadelphia.

Meanwhile more and more factories were being built farther south. In Delaware since the early 1800's there has been a virtual industrial dynasty that has combined private enterprise with social conscience. Founded on materials for destruction whether of rock or of men, it has prospered. Some of its proliferations can be seen in what is per-haps America's most impressive industrial area. Witness the chemical works of South Charleston, West Virginia, at night, and you sense the mastery of mind over matter—and perhaps ask yourself, "Is matter about to triumph over mind in a final catastrophic rebellion of in-animate nature?"

Pennsylvania and West Virginia have had their industrial growing pains, for both coal mining and the iron-and-steel industry developed during that almost forgotten era when ownership had the bulge on labor. The Pittsburgh area has been the scene of some of the nation's most dismal steel strikes. And for decades, indeed into the 1930's, coal mining was in the popular mind not too incorrectly identified with intermittent work, pathetically low wages, long rows of blackened, unpainted "company houses," frowzy, despairing wives, and hungry, ragged children. Then came unionization and the towering figure of John L. Lewis, anathema still to coupon-clippers but venerated by the workers. Mrs. Miner has that washing machine we spoke of, and a painted house; and if the house doesn't have a toilet—most of them do, and radios and TV sets—the privy is painted. At least on the outside. Yes, the coal industry *was* sick. Oil was replacing coal on the railroads and in the factories and homes. But what can one do with coal if he can't sell it in the domestic market? Perhaps he can sell it abroad! And that, the miners say, is what J.L.L.'s union, under J.L.L.'s leadership, is doing—successfully and as a union. Miners are working 200 days a year at a wage many professional men would like to be assured of earning till they die. Sure, their lives are hazardous and many suffer from silicosis and die young; but they live while they mine, and their sons aspire to take their places, with that fierce occupational pride which is the earmark of a miner wherever there are minerals to be dug.

The central east's resort business is concentrated in a few spots. One of them suggests Old English type, cupolas, and community bathrooms. Another, White Sulphur Springs, frequented by politicos and affluent golfers, is for the relatively few. Atlantic City is the far-from-sacred Mecca of conventions, expanding southwestward (we hear) but in its middle and choicest reaches retaining the same rococo sky line, the same boardwalk, the same we'll-take-you-and-make-you-like-it flavor of forty years ago. With a few wartime suspensions and occasional concessions to other convention cities to keep up a genial pretense of competition, Atlantic City has been entertaining the big shots in education, labor, medicine and near-medicine, salesmanship, sport, and religion for half a century. They must like it, for they still go back for more. Once thought expensive, the proprietors of Atlantic City hotels and restaurants are pikers, hopelessly outclassed in their charges by keepers of less attractive hostelries from Anchorage to Acapulco.

In higher education and in the creative arts that flourish if they are not stifled by the anti-intellectualism of an age when material comforts are won too easily, our central east has not lagged.

Princeton University is the fourth oldest institution of higher learning in the United States. Franklin's Academy of Pennsylvania, as the University of Pennsylvania, became the nucleus of a group of distinguished colleges in eastern Pennsylvania. In 1867 the founding of the Johns Hopkins University at Baltimore helped to bridge the gap between the colleges of the central east and similar institutions in Virginia. Make a list of twenty-five or fifty American colleges and universities recognized as having the highest scholastic standards; write off any schools that are half research seminar and half panty-raid kindergarten, each remotely and disagreeably aware of the other —and you will find in the central east more than its share of the colleges devoted to education.

Forget for a moment the more academic arts and consider the beginnings of American music. More than a century after Bach and even in the days of Beethoven and well on into those of Brahms, America was musically a desert except for the central east where song-writers were making the most of music's simplest idiom. Here, the Marylander Francis Scott Key, exulting over the thwarting of the British at Fort McHenry after their humiliating successes in 1814, composed a national anthem for which audiences rise spontaneously. And here, in Pittsburgh, Stephen Foster charmed a continent with simple elegiac songs that became America's musical folklore. No wonder that Pennsylvania became a haunt of music lovers, with a Bach Festival in Bethlehem and two of the country's great symphony orchestras, one in Philadelphia and the other in Stephen Foster's home town.

In the realm of the printed word, Franklin, as we have already noted, pioneered with a forceful wisecracking journalism that attracted even more popular attention than did his candid, unaffected autobiography which became a classic. And let us not forget that Franklin had a part, though a minor one, in composing the Declaration of Independence, which is not only a political landmark but literature in its own right—whatever British critics may profess to think of its "rhetorical" quality.

After Franklin, the central east went into temporary literary eclipse while the sun shone farther to the northeast. In New York and Connecticut Cooper developed the American novel and Irving the American essay. In eastern New England, in the mid-nineteenth century there flourished a regional literature that was in many ways admirable and was hailed as national partly for that reason and partly because of lack of competition from other areas west of the Atlantic. Yet it was in the very middle of that age, when to most readers American letters meant New England letters, that President Lincoln composed his unforgettable Gettysburg address in a railroad coach on its jolting way through Maryland and delivered it on Pennsylvania soil that was to remain a national shrine.

Already in the mid-nineteenth century, Boston shared with New York and Philadelphia the publication of the lion's share of America's output of books; and even then, long before pulps or slicks catered to hotrodders, rapists, and wenches-in-rut, the chief centers of magazine publication were the cities just named.

Baltimore in the first half of the twentieth century was truly a meeting place of intellectuals, but call them that to their faces at your own risk! The Sunpapers attracted a galaxy of stars; in the mid-twenties Hendrik Van Loon's Baltimore apartment was a salon. In the late thirties and the forties Isaiah Bowman, geographer-president of Hopkins, kept open house for his friends, discussing weighty matters with them half the night and continuing their edification at a levee in his bedroom the following morning—if that was Sunday. In that same era a visitor to Baltimore might, if especially fortunate, find himself a guest at the Saturday Night Club, and if he kept discreetly in the background and didn't try to put on an act of his own he might be asked a second time or a third or a fourth. Perhaps he had come under the auspices of Heinie Buchholz, president and office boy of his one-man educational publishing house with its highly selective list of doctors' theses and its technical magazines. Once having achieved guest status, a visitor would be taken under Henry Mencken's wing. The musical prelude to the evening's sodality in the private room of a carefully chosen bistro was an amateur orchestral performance in a spacious and incredibly disorderly loft over—or was it back of?—a violin-repair shop. Within spitting distance of each player was a fiber cuspidor, target for so many tossed butts that in most cases it was the hidden core within a cone. Mencken the maestro whacked a decrepit upright piano while puffing at a stubby cigar, keeping time with emphatic nods and roaring at players who got too badly off-tone or off-beat. "Why don't you ever play so-and-so?" Mencken was asked one evening too late in the proceedings for the inquiry to be misunderstood as that unforgivable faux pas, a request. "What? These louts play *that*? That requires tone color. We just aren't good enough. This is a pitch-and-rhythm outfit, and if we don't stick to pitch-and-rhythm music we find ourselves insulting the composers."

Millions of active Americans in that bitter-sweet period of life so offensively referred to by whippersnapper statisticians and journalists as "aging" remember very well the schoolbooks and curriculum (then singular, not plural) of the year 1900. A study known as civil government began with the New England town meeting, handled city government rather briefly as a potato already getting warm, treated the county respectfully as a going concern, discussed the states as major political entities, and wound up with the national government presented as an alliance—recently, by force of arms, adjudged unbreak-able—of states sovereign both in theory and in fact. Sometimes the order, for obscure pedagogical reasons, was reversed; but the emphasis was always the same. The United States of America consisted of 45 states (the number in 1900) *and* a District of Columbia that accounted for somewhat less than one forty-thousandth of the total area. It was implicitly admitted that this tiny fraction of the country was more important than its size would indicate, for it contained a Capitol, a Washington Monument, a President in a White House, and at intervals a Congress. Somewhere in the fine print would be a patriotic tribute to the architectural merit of the Capitol and a statement of the impressive dimensions of the Washington Monument, easily remembered because of the odd recurrence of the digit 5. Reference might be made to Washington as a pleasant residential city of shade trees, which it still is today. But who, in 1900, could have foretold that within a little more than half a century, in a small mid-city area that you could stroll around in half a morning, housed in the world's greatest aggregation of public buildings, there would develop a slowly renewable but largely self-perpetuating leviathan of directive activity that would affect profoundly every city and hamlet, every isolated farm or mine or ski lodge or dude ranch or arctic outpost, in our three million square miles—three-and-a-half with Alaska?

The civilian Federal employees with headquarters in the capital city, 126 in the year 1800, have become a quarter of a million. While the population of the nation has increased 32 times, Federal workers in Washington have increased in number approximately 2000 times. In short, the capital's government personnel has grown 60 times as fast as the nation it both serves and administers.

Washington's growth was slow until World War I. It began a century before that war with the formidable task of cleaning up and rebuilding after the British raid of 1814. With a cozy concentration reminiscent of an Old World feudal manor but with mansions instead of cottages, a neighborhood directly or indirectly tributary to the Executive Mansion sprang up at a short but respectful distance from it. Here, to this day, is the Presidential guest house for visitors who don't quite rate White House hospitality. (That word "rate," by the way, looms large in Washington's thinking. Protocol, emphasizing man's inequality with man, has hamstrung the great majority of Presidents and has cramped the style even of the few who flouted it.) Toward the northwest there sprang up and expanded an embassy district, a community within a community, international, aristocratic, aloof. Off toward the northeast was—and is—the business district, small for a city of the size of Washington because of its preoccupation with government rather than commerce or industry. To the south and east lay the cruciform reservation for parks and Federal buildings. Beyond, in all directions except where the Potomac narrowed the city on the south, sprang up residential neighborhoods which, in their outward appearance, could have been in Philadelphia or Brooklyn or Boston. These were the homes of people of two races, set apart with a curious, friendly kind of spontaneous intrablock segregation—whites on the outside streets, Negroes along the inner alleys.

Slowly the L'Enfant plan materialized. The War Between the States had boosted the number of Federal employees within the District to 7000. In the decades that followed, buildings went up one by one along the Mall. World War I multiplied enormously the demands on and of government. Suddenly official Washington found its facilities inadequate. By the 1920's it became necessary for the Federal Government to buy the triangular tract between Pennsylvania Avenue and the Mall. Republican and Democratic administrations have vied with each other in the magnitude and magnificence of their building projects, which became a major vehicle of deficit spending and economic relief during the Great Depression of the 1930's. Once started, the building boom continued, until history repeated itself in World War II and not even makeshift "temporary buildings" could take care of the city's public needs. The need for private housing became so acute that palatial homes became lodginghouses and desk clerks in hotels became, figuratively, harem eunuchs fighting off intruders.

The story of Washington's expansion is the story of the evolution of government and concepts of government in the critical century and a half since its founding. During that time the world has gone far, in some respects far ahead and in others perhaps far astray. Radicals of yesterday become reactionaries of today. Vices of one administration, magnified in the next, become virtues. Spend-to-save and save-to-spend economic theories seesaw in public esteem, one up and the other down according to who is "in" and who is "out." Centralization of domestic government, desirable or undesirable according to one's point of view, proceeds relentlessly. World power politics becomes more and more baffling and forces Washington willy-nilly into the status of unofficial capital of half the world. The quiet, almost provincial city of a hundred years ago has become the seat of decisions that will determine the destinies of mankind. May they be wise!

New England

BY BERNARD DE VOTO*

"It is a small college," Daniel Webster is supposed to have said of Dartmouth, "but there are those of us who love it." The New England to which Dartmouth belongs is small, too, the smallest of our regions as well as the most continuously and diversely beautiful, and everybody has a lot of fixed ideas about it. Also about the people who live in it and who will be called here, with forthright originality, the Yankees.

The Yankees are a cosmopolitan breed, with an itching heel and a genius for adapting to far frontiers. That is why so many New Bostons, New Salems, Portlands, Newports, and Portsmouths are scattered over the other forty-odd states. So a friend of mine in San Francisco told me this: His daughter roomed at Smith College (Northampton, Massachusetts, providentially convenient to Amherst and Williams) with the daughter of a prominent member of the clan whom Mr. Cleveland Amory calls the Proper Bostonians. Last summer the roommate spent part of the vacation with my friend's daughter, and while in San Francisco had her nineteenth birthday. Her father telephoned his congratulations and affection. He had some difficulty hearing her pleased response and bade her speak up. She didn't speak up and he demanded, "What are you whispering for?" "But, Daddy," the girl said, "every-

* Revised and enlarged by Philip A. Knowlton.

body is asleep. It's only five o'clock out here." Then Boston: "Nonsense. I've been in my office for an hour."

Endlessly misconceived, misrepresented, and even caricatured as New England has been, the most striking thing about it is this: No American ever comes here for the first time. Wherever he grew up, whoever his forbears were, he seems to bring with him something that could be called an ancestral memory except that, most likely, his ancestors never saw New England, either.

Some elements of this feeling are easily accounted for. The history and literature which the visitor was taught in school were crowded with images and emblems of New England. Moreover, in this harried age there is an intense longing for our lost serenity, and nostalgia for what we may call Currier & Ives America has pretty well identified itself with the landscape of rural New England. That tranquillity of heart is associated in the visitor's expectation—by paintings, post cards, and calendars if by nothing else—with hillside fields marked off by stone walls, and village greens where a spire rises from a white meetinghouse and is seen through the branches of great elms.

Another element is more mysterious. For there is a faint, evanescent feeling of personal recognition. The visitor seems to have been here before. He lived here a long time ago; some part of his boyhood was spent here. He had forgotten about it but now, in momentary glimpses of things gone before he can identify them, he seems to be beginning to remember. In some profound and subtle way he has come home.

We have touched on two of the accepted symbols that mean New England to the general consciousness: the fields marked off by the stone walls that are so picturesque and signify so much labor through so many generations, and the elm-bordered village green with the meetinghouse topped by a spire that shows the influence of Christopher Wren—the Georgian or "Colonial" meetinghouse. But now we need several additional images and symbols of New England.

I take you first to a millpond anywhere in the region except the industrial centers. It provides fine swimming and fishing for boys but the masonry dam from which they dive, though built for eternity, is now functionless; the water that flows through its penstock turns no wheels. Next a reminder of the migration that Mr. Stewart Holbrook calls the Yankee Exodus—and this, too, could be anywhere in the region. Make it a marker in the village of Whitingham, Vermont, up a long valley, deep in the forest that has recaptured most of the fields once hacked from it. It looks like a gravestone till you get close enough to read the text. "Brigham Young," it magnificently says, "born on this spot, 1801. A man of much courage and superb equipment."

Finally to another church building, this one at Gloucester, Mass. Whereas the meetinghouse with the Wren spire is Congregational, this is a Catholic church, the Church of Our Lady of Good Voyage. Two things about it. The Yankees who make up its congregation are, most of them, of Portuguese ancestry. And Our Lady, whose image stands between the two towers, holds a fishing schooner on one forearm and has raised her other hand to still the stormy sea.

She looks out across Gloucester Harbor to the Atlantic and, because in New England the sense of the past is always with you and the sense of the sea seldom absent for long, we may begin with both. The Yankees, who invented a fair half of the machines and institutions and ideas that produced the contemporary United States, also invented about ninety-five percent of the American religions. Their sects have contended mightily without reaching agreement on what man's fate is. But there has never been any ambiguity about New England's fate: It is geographical. It begins here, at the coastline.

A long coast. Its western end is almost at the western end of Long Island Sound—Greenwich, Connecticut. It stretches to Eastport, Maine, and beyond it to where the St. Croix River comes out to meet the twenty-foot tides of Passamaquoddy Bay. It is multitudinously indented, an always changing succession of coves, inlets, bays, and estuaries. Most of them are short and narrow, but Narragansett Bay has room for the worlds' navies plus whatever multimillionaires' yachts may still survive; and Penobscot Bay, beautiful in all weathers and beloved by sailors of small boats, trends deeply into Maine. Creeks and rivers come down to many of these inlets. Most of the streams are short (though the Connecticut River bisects the region from north to south), but they were routes to the interior long before there were roads. They and the inlets they end in turned the Yankees to the sea.

So Mr. T. S. Eliot, who grew up in St. Louis and has spent his life in England but seems nevertheless to have lived some secret part of his boyhood in New England like the rest of us—Mr. Eliot hears the lost sea voices. Others heard these voices long before the Pilgrims got to Plymouth—Portuguese, Breton, Basque, and half a dozen other stocks who came to this coast for fish; and a gilded cod still watches over the proceedings of the General Court of Massachusetts. Fifty years after Plymouth, the Yankees were shipping lumber as far as Madagascar and long before that the King's men were ranging the forest to mark with a broad arrow the pines that would make masts for the royal navy. The Yankees have traded in timber, shingles, and the like ever since; if Paul Bunyan had a birthplace anywhere, it was in Maine. After the great days of lumber it was the coastwise trade; then it was the trade in slaves and molasses with Africa and the West Indies.

The whalers were in the Antarctic, the slavers off the Guinea Coast, and the merchant captains and supercargoes everywhere. Wherever there was a profit to be taken there was a Yankee shipmaster to lay his craft on her beam ends if need be, to get over the bar first and snatch it from the British. The names of Boston, Salem, Portsmouth, New London, and a dozen other towns were familiar in Asiatic ports and South Sea islands that had never heard of the United States. Yankee children worked into their counting-out rhymes such names as Surinam, Diamond Head, Pernambuco, Ilo-Ilo. The mansions that should be common beside the inland greens, but aren't, cluster at the ports. See them on Newburyport's High Street, on Portsmouth's Pleasant Street, on Salem's Essex Street, at Wiscasset, wherever the ships came home. They are gracious with carved interior cornices, mantelpieces, and dadoes by artisans who had learned their Adam and McIntire. They were full of treasure-trove from everywhere, chinaware, silk prints, ivory, lacquer work, jeweled statuettes of heathen gods.

Collateral heirs quarrel over that loot nowadays, or it has passed to the institutions which its collectors so handsomely endowed. The great age lasted to produce the clipper ship, which may well have been the most beautiful object American craftsmen have ever made, and then it ended. Bowsprits no longer thrust over the cobbled streets of the water fronts. You must look for the tall masts and intricate rigging in the museums—at Salem, New Bedford, Mystic, Newport. The shipyards build only small boats now except at Bath, Fore River, and Groton, where the Navy keeps the ways busy. But the big stone wharves still traffic in aromatic stuffs, coffee, spices, sandalwood; and New England, so early shaped by the sea, still looks out to sea.

Along the coast a man is a captain if he owns or sails a boat, any boat at all. At Chilmark, Chatham, Yarmouth, and many similar places you can be ferried about the harbor by weather-beaten, salty, indestructible sea dogs in their seventies, spouting their inherited lingo and recounting personal adventures with lovely brown wenches, cannibals, and mutineers—sea dogs doing their stuff for five dollars an hour, who have never been beyond the breakwater.

A rigid protocol is that of amateur captains and crews, from the myriad Snipes to the racing yachts whose balloon spinnakers, with the sunlight on them and clouds for background, make them almost as beautiful as the clippers. A landsman may not venture to say much about their rituals of precedence, procedure, idiom, and costume. Enough that the coast is the summer-sailor's paradise. A Sunday at Edgartown, Marblehead, or Boothbay Harbor is a maritime traffic jam. The Gloucestermen have not raced the Bluenoses for some years now, but there is nothing gentle about the annual Bermuda Race that sails from Newport. And from some headland such as Highland Light watch a freighter making out to sea, to the sea wine-dark with evening or slate gray with the anvil-topped clouds that mean a blow is coming up. It remains New England's portal on the infinite.

The blow coming up still brings the sea foaming over Norman's Woe, the Dry Salvages, and a hundred other reefs, shoals, and races. Every equinox and every winter adds to the heroic chronicle. Gloucester still needs the intercession of Our Lady of Good Voyage. It has an annual ceremony for those lost at sea, and on Memorial Day many another coastal town scatters flowers on the ebb tide. The Yankee names on the new gravestones are Portuguese, Scandinavian, Greek, or Italian for the most part, and they are those of fishermen. Fishing is the principal maritime commerce remaining to New England, with diesel-powered draggers and seiners, much different from the schooners of yesterday. No poetry celebrates the little hookers on their innumerable errands, and the lobstermen remain unsung.

At Bar Harbor and thereabout mountains rise sheer from the sea. Cape Cod is a long sandspit thrust eastward with nothing beyond it till you get to Spain. Cape Ann is a granite headland. The two big islands, Nantucket and Martha's Vineyard, are the maritime provinces of Massachusetts. Small islands cluster everywhere east of Long Island Sound. Some are fashionable—Mount Desert, North Haven; some famous for one or another reason, like Smuttynose and Deer Isle; most of them known outside the region only to summer sailors, vacationists, and artists. Sometimes the Federal Government sells a small one it no longer needs; the buyer gets at a bargain-counter price a lighthouse or a Coast Guard station that, like the inland dams, was built for the ages. Except those frequented by summer folk, the islands are as remote as Europe, or more remote. The islanders live mainly by fishing and lobstering, asking leave to go their way without regard to the mainland, unusually self-contained even for this region of individualists.

The rest of New England's geographical destiny is mountainous and glacial. The ice carved the cliffs, scoured the hills, rounded the valleys, and created the diversification of a landscape that changes continuously as you travel it. It put a curse on the Yankee farmer but bestowed two blessings, the innumerable lakes and falls in the creeks. It left a thin but rich soil on the hillsides where the forests of hardwoods and evergreens took root. The original stand, the Great Forest, was systematically despoiled, as has been the American habit everywhere, yet from the air New England remains hidden by trees. The loss of myriads of trees twice in a quarter-century when hurricanes have flattened a swath from Long Island Sound to the Canadian border is mercifully hidden within a few years by new scrub growth.

The lakes are at your choice and to your taste, from thimblefuls high in the Franconia and Presidential peaks, to Walden Pond, to the hundred-mile strip of Lake Champlain with the Adirondacks on one shore and the Green Mountains on the other. Champlain has been attracting painters and vacationists for well over a century. Indeed they all have—Moosehead and the other Maine lakes for which all the fishing tackle has been named (except such as is named for Maine rivers), Winnipesaukee and Memphremagog which are the most beautiful, unless you think Newfound or Squam or Caspian or the fiordlike Willoughby is. If you do, lovers of fifty others will denounce you.

The glaciers that bulldozed so much soil off the hillsides also filled the soil everywhere with stones. As true a symbol of New England as any I have named, though one little seen and less regarded by the tourist, is the stoneboat. Drawn by oxen, a horse, or a man's family, it was the sledge on which the stones that make those picturesque walls were dragged from the fields to make farming possible. The labor is not yet finished; it will never be, for every year when the snows melt more stones have risen to the surface.

No other agricultural labor in America has ever been so great as that represented by the hill farms. The Yankee pioneer cleared the hillsides because they did not have to be drained, were freer of frost than the lowlands, and for a brief time had the humus left by the forest he got rid of. This landscape, I repeat, is the landscape that means our lost serenity. It is the stage set of our fantasy. In the high mowing a whetstone clangs against the scythe blade long ago, a music as poignant and comforting as that of sleigh bells in the moonlight on the same hills about the lamplit village. Here are the spring into which the barefoot boy plunges his hot cheeks, the pasture he brings the cows from as evening comes on, the fire round which the swains and maidens chase each other at a sugarin'-off. Well, only a tough, tenacious, stiff-necked race could have cleared these hills or farmed them. But my point is not how the Yankee character was honed sharp right here but how it has remained constant through the tides of change and how the original stock has impressed it on the successive immigrations.

Years ago when William Allen White was working on his life of Calvin Coolidge, I drove with him to Vermont. Repeatedly he shook his head and asked, "Aren't there any fat men here?" And in the Coolidge barn, at Plymouth, looking at fragments of sadirons, old harness, and the usual clutter, he asked the question a Kansan must always ask, "Don't these people ever throw anything away?"

Yankees come in all sizes and configurations, but one marked type has always been common: lean and compact, thin-cheeked, bony, looking but little older at seventy than at thirty. As for throwing something away, not while a use for it can be conceived. Let dwellers in a more opulent geography waste their substance if the fools will; work has always been too hard here and solvency too hard to maintain.

They say that when Erskine Caldwell quitted Maine after an unsatisfactory venture there, he announced that he was going back to his own country, where there wasn't no difference nohow between ten cents and eleven cents. An exact awareness of that one-cent difference is at the very basis of the New England mind.

Hold this frugality to the light. One aspect of it has created ten thousand derisive anecdotes, and can indeed lead to meanness and miserliness that corrode the human spirit. And yet another aspect leads straight to the neatness, clarity, and precision that are true elegance.

This elegance is the swept and garnished New England countryside, the houses and town halls and meetinghouses whose white paint is spiritual dignity, the fanlights of the mansions, the scrubbed stoops (with a pumpkin on them at harvesttime) of the farmhouses themselves, sited not only so that they are sheltered from the prevailing wind but so that they take in the vista of the creek curving toward the fold in the hills.

It is almost inconceivable now that the hill farms were once a wheat country and a sheep country. That period could not possibly last; the upland soil washed into the creeks long ago. The Yankee Exodus that Mr. Holbrook writes about began even before the Middle West was opened up, and there was no stopping it once the Yankee farmer heard about cropland that was flat, had deep soil, and was free of stones. Concern about the abandoned New England farm became a fixture in American journalism. The forest began to take back the fields which that nightmare labor had cleared. Many miles of stone walls it was a weariness to build are deep in hardwoods now. Family burying grounds are thickets of weed trees. Lilacs, strayed garden perennials, and apple trees blossom among maples that have choked off what once were lanes.

The farmers who did not go west moved to the valleys and to whatever flatland New England has, mainly in Connecticut, Down East in Maine, and along the Connecticut River. Sometimes they moved their town halls and meetinghouses with them. Valley soil, truck gardening, and dairy farming saved the stricken agriculture. Commercial farming, with the increased efficiency of specialized one-crop agriculture but also with its greater risks, took the place of subsistence farming. Aroostook County has made the potato famous; Cape Cod has done the same for the cranberry. The Massachusetts cranberry rules supreme, but the Maine potato farmer has formidable competitors farther west. In summer the Connecticut Valley is wonderfully pleasing striations of green and white, the onion fields and the cheesecloth tents that shade the tobacco fields. But the truth is that not many of the original Yankees were talented farmers; their genius was of a different kind. So agriculture largely passed into the hands of those who had the talent: Poles, Italians, French-Canadians, Slavs, a few Russians and Greeks, and of course the Finns, who would work in a mill only long enough to raise the first payment on an abandoned farm. They knew how to make the glacial rubble yield the comforts that their predecessors could not get from it.

The hill farms ceased to be agriculture but remained landscape. New England has been a summer resort for more than a century and has steadily increased in popularity as a winter-sports center. Moreover, the exhausted fields and sagging houses, which up to the last war could often be bought for less than the timber in the wood lots was worth, attracted people who wanted respite from city noise and strain. "Summer folks" turned from renting to buying and so went on the tax rolls. Rich outlanders bought up such show places as the hill towns had, chiefly in southwestern Vermont and Connecticut's Litchfield Hills. Where nothing sufficiently imposing existed they built their own; because they invaded the Berkshires at the nadir of the national taste, a beautiful area is freckled with monstrosities almost as appalling as those at Newport. (Change has overtaken them, too; many are schools, hospitals, and religious retreats now.) But most of the summer folks who became taxpayers were professional people, especially academics.

A more important immigration that had been going on for a long time was accelerated by the depression, people whose workrooms or studies could be anywhere: writers, painters, musicians, handicraftsmen. A New Hampshire town is typical; it has an orchestra, founded by such an immigrant, that plays on antique instruments the music written for them. That some instruments are hard to come by does not bother its members, for they make what they cannot find. "Vermont's actual farming farmers amount to less than a fourth of its population," says a treatise just published. The explanation is not only the small industries; it is also the writers, clergymen, painters, etchers, illustrators, composers and dancers whom the state has attracted and the craftsmen who work in wood, metal, ceramics, glass, fabrics and plastics. In their small shops they practice an exquisite and fastidious workmanship, entirely true to the tradition of New England. What do you lack? Gunstocks, fiddles, cabinets, precision instruments of brass, ornamental ironwork, glass mosaics or stained-glass windows, carved semiprecious stones, models of the night sky or of molecules, laminated tables, chairs of inlay, miniatures, intaglio work? There are native or naturalized Vermonters to provide it.

Still another immigration has recently been making itself felt, even in northern New England. Manufacturing firms are establishing branch plants where highly skilled labor is abundant, and where there is quiet, and clean air and the rural outdoors. Thus a cycle of change has come all the way round to the beginning again.

Of the highlands, the most fateful were those farthest west, especially the Berkshires. For one fundamental feature of New England geography lies outside New England—the Hudson River. It is a water route for freight to New York harbor; and the Mohawk Valley which opens off it is a route, along which the Erie Canal was built, to the Great Lakes and the Mississippi. No canal could cross the granite spine of New England. New England lost the industrial lead that it had achieved over New York and Pennsylvania. It was forced back on the mechanical skills which have become its specialties and has flourished by means of them ever since.

For the Yankees who turned to the glacial waterfalls had found the genius of their breed. We may now return to those masonry dams that are the vestiges of another age. They are on all rivers and creeks and on some brooks so small that you can hardly believe the evidence. Beside them are brick walls it would take high explosives or a vagabond hurricane with its torrents of rain to demolish, though roofs and windows have been gone for two generations or more. The walls are those of little mills that were powered by the dams, the mills to which the Yankee genius brought precision, versatility, and unsurpassed craftsmanship. The Yankees were predestined smiths, mechanics, artificers, contrivers, innovators. The direct and orderly progression of machine processes was their intellectual idiom. Indeed it was their spiritual well-being, for what is the logic of machines if it is not the identical economy, exactness, propriety and neatness that I have already called elegance? At the village green, the exquisite steeple and the scrubbed stoop with a pumpkin on it; in the shipyards, the lines of the clippers; in the shop, a turret lathe or a drop forge growing ever more complex and automatic as Yankee logic works out its functions.

The mills were everywhere. The town where I have spent the pleasantest of my summers is far to the north; it has 500 inhabitants and a single woodworking mill. A century ago it had 1200 inhabitants and the two creeks powered a gristmill, a sawmill, a planing and turning mill, a fulling mill, a fanning mill, and one of those primordial "machine shops" that would do anything the surrounding market wanted done. What ended this happiest period of the industrial revolution was not only the spread of steam and, later on, of electric power that made industrial concentrations economical, but even more the development of the railroad network. Massachusetts and Connecticut, with their greater railroad mileage, developed the mill town as we now know it—and learned the vulnerability of a one-industry economy when later shifts came. But in upper New England the loss of the mills was a greater disaster than the passing of the hill farms. At about the same time large-scale lumbering began to peter out; the forest was as exhausted as the hilltop fields.

New England is a classic example, cited again and again by geographers of the modern school, of man's persistent refusal to let his destiny be governed exclusively by inanimate things—or by the lack of them. Years ago one heard a lot about geographic "controls": Where there were rich natural resources and a favorable climate, people would congregate and multiply. To that extent the older geographers were right; for in this crowded world hospitable land is seldom wasted. But there was a negative corollary to this truism to which New England gave the lie. Thin, rocky soils, rough terrain, and a scarcity of underground riches—with the noteworthy exception of granite, quarried here and there throughout New England except in the southwest, and Vermont's marble—did *not* keep New England from becoming well populated. For the entire United States, the population density is 57 persons to the square mile. For New England it is 147, or two-and-a-half times the national average. Southern New England (Massachusetts, Rhode Island, and Connecticut) has a population density of 550 persons to the square mile, which is nearly ten times our national average and exceeds that of India or China.

With pressures behind them such as immigrants from Europe into New England have experienced ever since the days of the Pilgrims; with invigorating temperatures and with a usual lapse of a good many years between serious droughts; with enough tillable soil to support a few generations of subsistence farmers; and with plenty of timber for a variety of uses—with these stimuli, the Yankees dug in. By natural increase and by continuing immigration, they became more numerous. Just across the state line in New York, being built up steadily during the nineteenth and twentieth centuries, was the greatest urban development in the western hemisphere. This eventually spilled over into southwestern Connecticut, already peopled with Yankee hatters and metalworkers.

New England was a land pleasant to live in. So the Yankees chose to stay. When coal-burning (and, later, oil-burning) engines and wholesale generation and long-distance transmission of electric current reduced their little water wheels to the status of quaint Americana useful chiefly for the delectation of tourists, the Yankees bought fuel or tapped the power lines, imported lightweight raw materials from all over the world, and kept on working. The value they added by manufacture more than offset their lack of cheap power and of locally produced raw materials.

So New England became increasingly industrialized. The loss of much of its textile industry to Southern mills close to the cotton fields and to a reservoir of less demanding labor was compensated for by quick conversion. When looms went out one door, work benches and lathes and spools onto which to wind coils of wire came in by another door. When a Yankee community collectively lost its job, it collectively found itself another. Certain staple and stable types of manufacturing, such as that of shoes and of shoemaking machinery, of course remained. The making of fine watches declined and came back. When the assembly stage of automobile manufacturing was scattered over the nation, New England got its share of the work. Garment manufacturing increased in volume in the Boston area. Printing held its own or expanded. Typewriters, guns, postal meters, kitchen and garden utensils, hand tools, brushes, clocks, insecticides, and miscellaneous hardware were turned out in increasing quantity and variety in New England's southwestern quadrant. When (and where) industry is in a perpetual state of flux, the need for co-operation becomes more than ordinarily evident. Many new England manufacturing and commercial enterprises share profits with their workers. Normally in this area, industrial relations are good.

So the towns hung on. I point again to the tenacity and ingenuity of the breed who built them, but something else is to be stressed more: The New England town, which is a political unit and may contain several villages, has always been a community. We speak of it as the society that first gave self-government to America; in the farmer on his feet in town meeting to hold the selectmen to account we see the primary mechanism of democracy. That is true enough, but the Ameri-

5. A Vermont ski lift. So great is the enthusiasm for skiing and other winter sports that winter resorts from Maine to California thrive in mountainous areas where the snowfall is sufficiently reliable and lasting to encourage investment in hotels, motels, lodges, and contrivances for making the inevitable ascents between descents briefer and easier.

86. A Harvard dormitory, in Cambridge, facing the Charles River. Harvard is the oldest Anglo-American university and has played important roles in education and in public affairs.

87. A dormitory at Smith College, Northampton, Massachusetts.

88.   A granite quarry at Barre, Vermont.

89.   Fishing boats in Gloucester harbor.

90.   A routine check of aircraft at the U. S. Naval Air Station, Quonset Point, Rhode Island.

Galloway

1. The Mount Washington Cog Railway. Cog railways have been used
Europe and in South America on steep mountainsides and escarpments,
ut only a few have been built. The one leading to the 6288-foot summit
f Mt. Washington has been used by three generations of vacationers
who prefer to do their mountain climbing the easy way.

92. The State House, Boston. Near the top of long-ago-truncated Beaco
Hill and overlooking the Boston Common, the original Bulfinch structur
has acquired granite wings. The dome is gilded.

93. East Corinth, Vermont, near a small tributary of the Connecticu
River, resembles scores of other peaceful villages in rural New Englan

94. Harkness Tower, Yale University, New Haven.

95. Moosehead Lake, Maine. Though only a few miles northwest of the geographical center of the state, this lake is farther north than Montreal.

96. Barnstable harbor, on the Bay side of Cape Cod.

cans were traveling toward that goal by other roads as well; the greater point here is that from the beginning the town was a society where people were members one of another. That explains its vitality and is the reason why anyone who writes about New England must keep coming back to the towns. On the successive New England frontiers civilization did not have to develop slowly, step by step. It was taken there fully developed in units already organized and of established community habits. Nor does the community stop at some Tenth Street boundary, with the fringe and farms excluded. It extends all the way to the next town line and incloses the proprietors of the farthest fields, trap lines, and summer camps in the common consciousness. It is remarkably independent of that next town, though practiced also in co-operating with it. And if the towns are independent of one another they are even more remarkably independent of the states. Independence is the other face of elegance.

As the towns hung on, so did a surprising number of woodworking mills. They had made everything for a wide market; now they made shoe pegs, heels, toothpicks, hoe handles, bowls, end tables, or toilet paper. Sometimes a town's solvency depended on a single mill that provided a small payroll and a market for the wood lots. You see them in the most thinly populated valleys; every few years they are rebuilt after a flood has swept them downstream. The forest began to return a larger yield; pulp mills came to utilize the wood that would not make lumber; the veneer and plywood business came into being. The mechanical specialties proliferated; as far up the Connecticut Valley as Springfield, Vermont, there are famous machine-tool plants, and your maple sugar may have been processed still farther north. Today the town is a complex equilibrium: truck farms, dairy farms, mills, summer residents and winter sports, the tourist trade, a preparatory school or a sanitarium. And now that the wheel has come full circle, the branch plants. The more the New England town has changed, the more it has remained the same thing.

We may note two types that, under pressure of change, lapsed from the town community. Some families clung in stubborn pride to the stripped uplands. Probably they have numbered fewer, all told, than the novels that have maligned them. And there were those who slipped rejoicingly into the encroaching forest. They went their own way and interfered with no one. The men hunted, trapped, gathered ferns, patrolled power lines, burned a little charcoal, hired out occasionally to a farmer or worked a spell for the lumber company. In the summer the girls went down to resort hotels to work as waitresses. The backwoods people lived better than has generally been believed, and they have seemed content in their secession. Good roads and the strengthening rural economy have reabsorbed most of them. Those that remain form at least one cultural service: South of the Maine woods they are the only Yankees who keep woodscraft alive.

Does this summary of rapid change imply that I am adding another lament to the long series of epitaphs on the New England economy and elegies for the extinct Yankees? No, though that form of poetic fantasy makes good reading. New England is decadent, we have been hearing for well over a century now. There are no Yankees left. As for their region, the next stanza has always said, it is headed toward bankruptcy, is becoming the Nation's No. 1 Economic Problem, and perhaps the best thing for everyone would be to set it aside as a national park.

Recall the Iowa farmer on tour who stopped his Cadillac to watch a New Hampshire farmer mowing with a scythe, the steep edge of a hayfield? The Iowan asked him scornfully what he did with his profits from this rocky barrens. He put 'em in Iowa farm mortgages, the Yankee said, and the remark, which issues from the difference between ten cents and eleven cents, expresses a bedrock principle of regional economics. What the century-old elegy on New England's "decadence" disregards is the disproportionate concentration of wealth and the density of manufacture in New England. The wealth must have been amassed somehow and from something; it capitalizes an enormous amount of national and international as well as regional business. The tears currently being shed over the shift southward of the (locally owned) New England textile industry have blinded mourners to the spread across New England of the electronics industry.

As for the long emigration of Yankees and their replacement by immigrants from a score of nations, the mourners leave two things out of account. They ignore the Yankees who did not join the Exodus but stayed home and bred mightily. And they ignore the vigor of the stock, folkways, and social institutions. That vigor has molded the immigrants in the original image, making of the latecomers Yankees indistinguishable from the firstcomers, who were themselves a very mixed stock. If a selectman is named Sullivan or Santucci or Scipola nowadays, he not only feels, thinks, and especially talks like Eli Perkins but looks like Eli's twin. . . . The immigrants came here with the hope of getting ahead in the world, and they found the educational system which the old stock had worked out to be a great help in achieving that ambition.

The general public, however, likes the cliché of Yankee decadence too much ever to give it up. Some part of it may be ascribed to one of the seasons. Spring here is short and is likely to be disagreeable, with the first hot spell close on the heels of the last untimely snowfall. The winter has been unconscionably libeled. Away from the seacoast it is stimulating and even beautiful, because the temperature, with infrequent exceptions, keeps consistently below the freezing, thawing, and refreezing level that makes the Fahrenheit thirties so unpopular throughout the middle latitudes of both hemispheres. The minus thirties and forties are sometimes recorded, and anyone who has experienced them in his youth has nostalgic memories of them as long as he lives. Summer is surcharged with opulence and fecundity, a violence of growth that makes the universal forest a jungle. It is a passionate season, attuned to the Puritan's passionate heart. But fall is an almost intolerable beauty, an ecstasy of color, a splendor too great for the frail senses of mankind. So a metaphor is inevitably imposed: the year is dying, this autumn loveliness must prefigure the region's death. Surely you can see that New England is autumnal and therefore dying.

Stereotypes about the Yankees are also much too beloved to be given up. Most of them go back to the Yankees of the Exodus. By the hundred thousand they went out to Oregon and Nebraska and Minnesota and Arizona, and to all wildernesses and way stations in between. They sowed the land with colleges and loan companies, with transcontinental railroads and inconceivably woozy utopian experiments, with revolutionary political ideas and Lydia E. Pinkham's Vegetable Compound. They furiously peddled the Yankee notions, both kinds: tinware and whittled bowls and brass clocks and, so the comic weeklies proclaimed, wooden nutmegs; the abolition of slavery and the prohibition of strong drink (which they had conspicuously omitted to institute in New England), humane treatment of the insane, tax-supported schools, and a passionate regard for civil rights in the state that executed Sacco and Vanzetti.

The stereotypes are as various as the actuality. The Yankee as bumpkin with a hat all bound 'round with a woolen string, chewing a straw and talking 'bout the caows—the earliest figure of farce in our literature and still a fixture on television. The Yankee as Sam Slick, just too dum'd smairt for other bumpkins and for you city fellers, peddling lightning rods for cows and swamproot bitters and stock in the Portland city hall. The Yankee as busybody, reformer, agitator.

And down this corridor are so many images of the Yankee as Puritan that I can only shrug and check the bet. I tell you severely that the Puritan had little to do with Maine, less with Vermont, and nothing at all with Rhode Island—or half of New England—and that he was a divided soul. With all his ascetic creed, he was a beset artist, a lover of fine glass and fine silverware, of bright colors, of the art of rhetoric; he created our most beautiful architectural styles. Often his temptations were mighty and his joys gargantuan.

Boxing the compass, the stereotypes assert too much. As one who is without New England blood, breeding, or inheritance but has spent his mature life here, I demur. The Yankees are supposed to be a taciturn and laconic breed, speaking little and in unstressed, epigrammatic irony, hiding their private thoughts and private lives behind a cool impersonality of speech. They are the most indefatigable talkers on earth, of a more than Sicilian volubility. It takes an outlander years to learn how to break in even momentarily on their logorrhea. The stranger who comes among them never gets accustomed to the reckless and unbuttoned outpouring of their most intimate secrets. A repressed people? Orgiastic is the better word; I would be happy to take you to a dog track or to any town or country fair. Graceless and bad-mannered? Well, yes, sometimes—especially behind the steering wheel of an automobile. Prone to eccentricity? Yes, thank God, both the old stock and the immigrant or galvanized Yankees. . . . It means that in the Yankee commonwealth the right for a man to be himself is exercised and respected.

Which brings us back, as always, to the New England countryside and the New England town. And to the question with which I began, why so many Americans from other regions, on coming here for the first time, feel at home.

By whatever distant rivers the Yankees sat down, they wept when they remembered Zion, and they still do. In the last desert between the last blue rocks, Mr. Eliot rejoices in the lost lilac and the lost sea voices, the bent goldenrod and the whirling plover. (Killdeer, he would have said if he were more recently from Zion.) On the far side of the continent Stewart Holbrook remembers great-aunt Sharon picking up a great pink-and-white conch shell to sound over the Vermont hillside the note which was a "warning that a Yankee God had brought noontime again." New England is those voices, that music, those wings, those hills and waters. It is an enduring perfume, a landscape not so much lost as found all over again and verified.

It is the street of a town. It is quiet, almost as quiet as the woods, the hill crest, and the pond that can be reached in ten minutes from the center. The town has no vision of becoming a city. None of its inhabitants expects to become a millionaire. The basis of its vigor and its magnetism is quite simple and it is also quite real. One is freer here than elsewhere to be oneself. There are space, leisure, and freedom for personality to develop. One may follow his calling and raise his family in decent self-respect with less pressure to conform to the prepossessions or timidity of others, with more immunity from the dictation of fashion or belief or group passion or group orthodoxy.

This is one part of the feeling I am trying to account for. The rest will be revealed by another immigration to New England. In my time at Harvard, the most beloved teacher was Dean Le Baron Russell Briggs. Shortly after he died, a friend of mine, trying to phrase our feeling about him, said, "To thousands of alumni he stood for the invisible Harvard." This other immigration is to the invisible New England. For the first instance, the Boston doctor.

Those who have intractable or little-understood ailments, or who need the most expert surgery, or who can't afford to pay for the needed treatment, come to Boston by the thousand every year. Now there has always been an honorable medical tradition among the Bostonians, and in some families medical talent seems to be hereditary. But the Boston doctor comes not only from New England but from everywhere else—London, Johannesburg, Vienna, Prairie du Chien, Podunk. He does not come to make a fortune. Having come here, he cannot be drawn away. He will refuse chairs and appointments that pay three times as much in money and power.

Other cities have medical schools, foundations, hospitals and research laboratories quite as distinguished as those in Boston. There is no reason why medical men should come to Boston in such numbers. No reason except one: that, like the townsman along the village green, they will live more fully here because they will be at home. They hold citizenship in the invisible republic.

Yankee Institutions were founded on the difference between ten cents and eleven cents. They grew out of the Yankee logic, the Yankee scorn for slovenliness, the Yankee passion for order and precision. They are magnificent. Take me, a man who practices his profession by means of libraries. Within reach of a fifteen-minute drive from my door there are two of the largest general libraries in the world, nearly a dozen specialized libraries that are unsurpassed in their fields, a good many lesser ones. There is no vocation dependent on collections, archives, museums, repositories, laboratories, or experiment stations for which the Yankee republic does not provide similar abundance.

Think of the colleges. And take for granted and so pass over the famous universities, the "name" colleges. To understand more fully, consider the little-known ones plentifully scattered over six states: the experimental colleges that spring up and flourish, the junior colleges and technical institutes and normal schools. A YMCA night school becomes Northeastern University. Brandeis in Waltham was born of dream and exile after the close of World War II. Institutes on back roads or over garages are founded for farmers' or workingmen's children, for bright boys in the mills, for immigrants and displaced persons. Once founded, they grow.

Think of the schools and again pass over those that are known in all parts of the country. Get on to two other groups, the upstate academies with the microscopic endowments that teach the young of eight towns and some from Iran and Luxembourg, and the small specialized schools that teach everything, posture or lip reading or electronics or foreign exchange or oratory or design to the ambitious, the elderly, the handicapped, and even the dimwitted. Now to complete the map of the republic, bring in the museums, laboratories, herbariums, arboretums, conservatories, experimental farms and forests and fisheries and print shops, and the membrane that connects them with one another.

People have kept coming to study at the Institutes, to work or teach at them, to pursue inquiries or investigations or researches, or simply to live where they are near at hand. In regard to their staffs and satellites, the word "Yankee" has come to have the same meaning that the generations have given it in the cities and towns and on the farms. Some are Yankees in that they came to New England and stayed. They came as the maker and player of obsolete musical instruments came to Littleton, the craftsmen in glass or walnut to Burlington, the medical researcher to the Back Bay.

For a long time only a trickle, this immigration has been in full flood for two generations. It has been partly a conscription, for the Institutions can call almost anyone they may want. But they attract more than they summon. Between the two wars brilliant and courageous people kept coming here in loathing of the Italian, German, and Russian tyrannies. During and since the second war the *émigrés* have been joined by exiles and refugees. A heterogeneous, miscellaneous, astonishing society. They were sent for, they were drawn here, they came in curiosity or in hope or in a restless, sad conviction that There Must Be Some Place. They found a place; it had been prepared for them a long time ago. They found they were at home. They are Yankees.

Let it not be thought that this Some Place is chiefly rural New England. No less truly, no less characteristically, it is urban, even metropolitan, New England. Just as in the United States of America Ivanovich is as American a name as Smith, in urban New England Mulcahy and Bozyczko are as Yankee names as Nickerson and Parker. And where is this polyglot, melting-pot big-city New England? Take a night plane from New York or Newark to Boston to find out.

Most of the way to New Haven you are over the Sound. Below you on the left, just beyond the blackness of the unseen water, is a vast network of lights—white for side roads, yellow-green for superhighways, red for night spots. Beginning far behind you in central New Jersey, these lights form an almost unbroken crisscross pattern as far as Westport. This is where Metropolitan New York overflows an adjacent corner of New England. (We'll disregard, as invisible from the air and irrelevant anyhow, the fact that an architectural undertow from the east has made Bedford Village, New York, down there just behind us, as Yankee as Bedford, Massachusetts, or Bedford, New Hampshire.) Then, for a few miles and a fifth as many minutes, the darkness from the north, like a long, black tongue, extends all the way to the shore beneath us. This is the southwestern extension of rural New

England, heavily infiltrated with celebrities who want privacy without loss of accessibility. Then come the lights of Bridgeport, another short stretch of darkness, and the bright circle of the New Haven area tapering off in the north into an endless succession of illuminated cobwebs. Except in the immediate foreground, these are the cities in the valley of the Connecticut River. On a clear night you can discern the lights of Springfield and Holyoke beyond those of Hartford. After all, what's a hundred miles after dark when you are a mile and a half up in the air?

At about New Haven we leave the Sound behind us and our north-eastward course takes us catty-corner across the State of Connecticut. Urban communities here are relatively small and scattered, with few patches of light to break the darkness. Then, perhaps fifteen minutes beyond New Haven, we see away off to the right the Rhode Island light-grid, chiefly Pawtucket and Providence. At about the same time, ahead and to the left, we see the light-island that is Worcester, and straight before us looms the glow of Metropolitan Boston. The plane's nose dips landward, and as we lose altitude we skim over the multitudinous lights of the easternmost major urban development of the North American continent. Almost continuously, the area within Route 128, the "circumferential highway" that makes it easier to drive from the North Shore to the South Shore than from any suburban point to Faneuil Hall in downtown Boston, is built up and consequently illuminated. New England may not be richly endowed with physical resources, but its Hub, seen from the air at night, reminds one of the twinkling vastness of Los Angeles where millions of people thrive in an area that has only a third of Boston's rainfall. Surely the fringes of this great land of ours demonstrate man's unwillingness, once he gains a foothold, to be frustrated by the limitations of his environment!

Greater Boston is one of this country's prime examples of what some scholars, with academic fondness for Latin derivatives, like to call a *conurbation*. "Supercity" would seem to be a simpler term, but no suitable Anglo-Saxon equivalent comes to mind. Geographers tell us that most conurbations suffer from lack of co-ordinated management: A community has the choice between remaining a hick town with inadequate services and a low tax rate, and absorption into the metropolis with better facilities and higher taxes. In Boston's Metropolitan District most of the smaller cities and towns have retained their political individuality, though once-separate cities such as Dorchester and Roxbury have long been parts of Boston itself. Within the entire area—roughly, within the magic circle of Route 128—there is an agency responsible to the Commonwealth (State) of Massachusetts. This unit of administration, known as the Metropolitan District Commission, provides efficient, integrated services that would otherwise be difficult or impossible. Here we see the principle of federation working at the local or semilocal level; each community, including the City of Boston itself, gives up a part of its autonomy but gains results that it could scarcely accomplish alone: adequate water supply, the most basic need of any group of people anywhere; sewage disposal, for which co-operative planning is especially important; parks and bathing beaches; highways and bridges; intercity public transportation; even co-ordinated police protection. Everybody gets services. Everybody pays high taxes; especially property owners in Boston and Cambridge, for in these cities the holdings, tax-free for operational though not for investment purposes, of churches and schools represent a formidable proportion of all wealth, and continued reliance upon the real-estate tax as the major source of public revenue puts the squeeze on householders and business enterprises.

Boston's facilities for land, water, and air transportation abundantly justify its Hub sobriquet but are not sufficiently superior to those of other large American cities to give it any great comparative advantage. Into the Hub converge many spokes. Excellent highways connect Boston with points west and north, average highways with points south and southeast. Some of the spokes are water routes to other cities of our eastern seaboard and overseas routes to the wide world. (Gone these many years, however, and lamented by lovers of leisurely travel, are the four lines of night boats that carried passengers between New York and New London, Fall River, New Bedford, and Boston itself via the Cape Cod Canal.) Airlines to Europe, to Canada, to Florida and the Caribbean, and to our own midwest and west offer nonstop flights to so great a variety of destinations as to assure Logan Airport a place in any list of the world's greatest centers of commercial aviation. But New England's railroads, in this air-and-motor age, are vestigial—important because of their needed carrying capacity but certainly far more ramified than they would be had the era of railroad building followed rather than preceded the establishment of competing means of transportation. As for the electric "interurbans" that once honeycombed all southern New England, they are so totally of the past that few remember them.

The growth of any type of land or water transportation depends in large part not on population figures but on the volume and weight of goods to be carried; that in turn depends largely on a surplus of local resources for export and on the need for importing, chiefly for use in manufacturing, large quantities of bulky or heavy products. Boston, combining its own catch with that of Gloucester and other fishing ports, is this country's largest fish-shipping center; for New England waters abound in fish and there are ten million Yankees and many millions of other Americans to eat them. But with ocean-freight traffic averaging about 50,000 tons a day, Boston, though ranking above Seattle and both Portlands, is hopelessly outclassed not only by New York and Philadelphia but also by numerous ocean and Great Lakes ports more favorably situated for handling heavy raw or partly processed materials, notably iron ore, coal, petroleum, and wheat, that are most economically carried by water.

Uniqueness, like virginity, is an absolute, not a comparative, quality; it exists, or it doesn't exist. But if there *were* steps or stages of uniqueness, we should be tempted to claim a special degree of atypicality for Boston. Among its suburbs, to be sure, are some that are Down East to the core, others that could be anywhere. Each type embraces some that are not very desirable and others where the realestaters tell you that you can "live graciously"—whatever that may mean in a neighborhood where motorists, not all of them kids, replace mufflers with megaphones and drive by horn, and a parking meter that doesn't say Violation is a curiosity. But Boston proper, including both Proper and Improper Boston, is *sui generis*.

We will not emphasize Boston's many historic shrines, for other cities, too, have their relics. Bostonians themselves are likely to neglect, and may even disparage, these reminders of the past, as did the police officer who, dropping in at a bar for a quick one, defended the proposal to dig up the Common in order to build a parking garage of widely debated value. Explained the cop, "If you ask *me*, we've got a damn sight too much historical —— in this town." And we won't stress the crooked streets near the water front; New York can almost match them. Nor will we make a great point of the fewness of Boston's skyscrapers; for with Boston's growing rivalry with Hartford and New York as an insurance center, and with insurance companies' well-known penchant for multistoried headquarters, skyscrapers in Boston are becoming more numerous. In fact, Boston's individuality lies not so much in major features that cannot be duplicated elsewhere, as in the impression jointly created by a host of little quirks and whorls that serve to fingerprint it.

Boston's unofficial civic center is its Common and the Public Garden which, separated only by the heavy traffic of a busy one-way street, are virtually a continuous park in the heart of the city. As big-city parks go, these are rather small. The venerable Common, however, accounts for 40-odd acres of the less than 1000 acres of peninsular downtown Boston, whereas the parvenu Garden, like Chicago's much larger Grant Park, is made land. The Common is unkempt throughout the balmy lounging and courting season when the populace, despite posted warnings, covers it with tattered newspapers, popcorn bags, peanut shells, and occasionally bottles faster than the attendants can pick them up. Yet there are compensations. Often in the summertime the fragrance of the linden trees is as overwhelming as a burst of DDT. If you get a whiff from one of the park incinerators, perhaps a sudden wind shift will immerse you in the scent of kelp and infinite expanses of salt water. Meanwhile over in the tidier Garden, flatboats adorned with huge wooden swans and propelled by human foot power noiselessly carry children and their elders over the knee-deep water of an artificial pond. Beside this pond every June in recent years, tents and a knockdown auditorium have sprung up to house a two-week Fine Arts Festival. Prizes have been awarded for paintings and other objets d'art, and Boston has upheld its reputation for egg-headism by invariably refusing to give top rating to anything "representational."—By November the paper-throwers and bottle-droppers have taken to their lairs. Just before Election Day the Common and the Public Garden get their faces lifted. America's most amazing collection of crèches and Christmas figurines and life-size simulacra of donkeys and shepherds and sheep comes out of the mothballs and is installed in these parks to remain until after New Year's. Snow, when there *is* snow, lasts longer and stays whiter here than on the trodden thoroughfares.

If these changes seem violent and these contrasts perhaps a bit contrived, one can only plead that in Boston variety is the very essence of living. Oddities are expected; lack of them subjects an individual to suspicion and a neighborhood to wholesale exodus in search of livelier surroundings.

On the steep, staggered side streets and dead-end lanes of Beacon Hill, with its mellow but unpredictable architecture, classic mansions are flanked by drab lodginghouses. Neighborhoods that are slipping and neighborhoods that have slipped interpenetrate. Only Louisburg Square enjoys a status of aristocracy so impregnable that ultimate decay is unthinkable. In sharp contrast to Beacon Hill is the quadrangular monotony of Back Bay, low and flat and straight on former marshland reclaimed from the backwash of the Charles River a century ago. Here the bay-windowed façade of each brick house is just one of an endless series of matching merlons in a street-long crenelation. To confuse one's own abode with its replica next door or in the next block would be so easy that the house numbers on the transoms are often of gigantic size.

Boston is replete with surprises. Some segments of the subway are a sure-enough underground railroad; others are grim catacombs noisily traversed by surface cars. Restaurants deservedly touted by Duncan Hines and Lucius Beebe and other experts in belly-lettres hide away in obscure alleys. In the heart of the overstuffed-parlor-suite district a servicer of razors, scissors, and sickles will sell you hair oil by the gallon or will sharpen horse clippers. A couple of streets over and around the corner, you can have your old hat not only cleaned and stretched but completely remade in any stipulated size. Across from the Park Street Church is a school for wigmakers. The telephone company's classified directory is a delight to read.

But the variety of goods and services at your disposal is insignificant when compared with the mental cyclopedia of intimate information about your wants and tastes and those of hundreds of your fellow Bostonians that is acquired as a matter of routine by each of the many persons who minister to you. Magazine write-ups of a local chain of high-grade food-and-drink stores commend it highly, and rightly so, for its personalized service to customers. But that is just Boston! Everywhere you go, your wants are anticipated. Without being asked, your waiter orders up your favorite dish and maybe your extra-extra-dry this or that as soon as he sees you coming through the door. The second time you sat in your barber's chair, he knew exactly how you wanted your hair trimmed. The blind news vendor at the head of the subway stairs gropes for the right paper as soon as he hears your morning greeting. Your tobacconist has your favorite cigars ready for you by the time you reach the counter. Probably your priest, if you have one as most Bostonians do, remembers your favorite pattern of sinning and expedites your confession.

Many theories have been advanced to account for the even tenor of life in this old American city whose economic structure long ago outgrew its supporting hinterland. May not this extraordinary rapport between and among a multitude of diverse human beings be a part of the answer? Like the slowly undermined brick walls of old Back Bay houses, the Bostonians support each other.

East
North Central

BY WALTER HAVIGHURST

The East North Central is not a name but a designation, and so it has no echoes. But say the Old Northwest and the echoes start—Indian war cries and the crash of falling timber, the boatman's horn and the bells of Conestoga wagons. It calls up other names—Fort Recovery and Fort Dearborn, Chillicothe, Tippecanoe, Shawneetown, Kaskaskia, Michilimackinac—names that smolder on the map like old campfires. The Old Northwest means a country of distance and danger, the first public domain of a new nation, a territory five times as big as England. It means the Ordinance of 1787 which extended the Union westward, creating five states in the huge wild land between the Ohio River and the Great Lakes.

Or say the Midwest, and see another set of pictures. Farmlands extending for six hundred miles, long straight roads leading in to the county seat with its wooded courthouse square, the rolling sheep pastures of Ohio, the endless cornfields of Illinois, the trampled stockyards of Chicago, long trains of coal, cattle, wheat rolling by, tractors and gang plows striping the level land. The Midwest means miles of government grain bins glinting in the sun, elevators above the railroad siding, cattle milling in the loading pens. It also means the smoke of steel mills, mile-long motor factories, the towers of cities rising from the river landings and the long lake shores.

In fifty years the brooding Northwest became the busy Midwest, the states of Ohio, Indiana, Illinois, Michigan, Wisconsin. And in a century the five states became the central region, the heartland of the nation.

America has a short and eventful past. The first land office in the Northwest Territory still stands—a weathered one-room building beside the Ohio at Marietta, the original settlement beyond the mountains. The Indians were curious about the white man's camp. They understood the cabins and the cornfields and the log fort on high ground in the clearing. But they were puzzled by the low building with two sloping decks and a plank table strewn with record books and rolls of paper. No family lived there, no clothes or implements hung on the wall, no smell of cooking came from the blackened fireplace. Men stooped under the doorway, pondered the papers on the boards, counted out money and signed their names. It was a small room where the white man made big medicine. The first land office, with its plots and transfers of their hunting country, was beyond the tribesmen's comprehension.

Now every scene is two scenes, as the land was and as it is: the wild free earth of the Indians, *Wesheasiski* in the musical Shawnee tongue, and the tamed, possessed, toiling, striving, hugely productive Midwest of America. In 1778 when George Rogers Clark led his ragged regiment against the British and the Indians north of the Ohio, it was all wilderness. From Fort Pitt, the jumping-off place, the wild land rolled westward. It was a silent, somber country with all its memories yet to come. An Indian trail came down to the empty river, where big white packet boats would line the Cincinnati levee. Beaver were gnawing trees on the Cuyahoga where Cleveland would spread above Lake Erie. Wolves roamed the prairie where Abe Lincoln, with law books in his saddlebag, would ride the circuit court. Blackbirds swayed on the reeds in the Chicago River. Beard grass was blowing where John Deere would hammer the first steel plowshare out of an old buzz saw and Joseph Glidden would twist a steel barb around a strand of fence wire. Indian signs on a tree trunk were the only writing in a country where Spencer would teach penmanship, McGuffey would compile his readers and Ray his arithmetic. Black night hung over Milan Creek where a boy named Thomas Edison would watch the whale-oil lights of wheat schooners, and passenger pigeons streamed over the Miami valley where the Wright brothers would experiment with flight.

West from Pittsburgh for four hundred miles stretched the Black Forest, threaded by the rivers, Muskingum, Hockhocking, Scioto, Miami, Wabash, and worn occasionally by the track of the great game animals. It was a deciduous forest, green and murmuring in summer, a riot of colors in the fall. Its great trees were oak, ash, maple, walnut, sycamore, chestnut, and beech, with a flowering undergrowth of redbud, dogwood, pawpaw, hawthorn, and wild plum. Shadowed trails led from one river to another, to moss-lined springs, to salt licks trampled by deer and buffalo. They led at last to open places where sunlight was blinding after the forest dark. The "plains" of the Ohio country were Indian town sites, smoke seeping up from cooking fires, women hacking at the cornfields, dogs sniffing at scraps of deer hide on the ground. Towards the upper Wabash the plains grew larger and more frequent, though seven-eighths of future Indiana was dark with forest.

Beyond the Wabash the Grand Prairie began its long sweep westward. Here the gloom of the forest ended in space, light, distance. Every traveler halted at sight of the prairie, as though he stood on an ocean shore. George Flower of Hertfordshire, England, described it in 1817: "A few steps more and a beautiful prairie suddenly opened to our view . . . lying in profound repose under the warm light of an afternoon's summer sun. . . . From beneath the broken shade of the wood, with our arms raised above our brows, we gazed long and steadily, drinking in the beauties of the scene which had so long been the object of our search." This was the scene from just beyond the Little Wabash, on the edge of the great Illinois grasslands. Fertility shouted from the wind-rippled bluestem and rank bull grass, the tangle of pea vines in the hollows. On the swells profuse cornflowers mingled with waving stems of blazing star and bluebells. The prairie lay many-colored under its bending sky.

For two hundred miles the grassland, broken by thickets of bottom timber along the Kaskaskia, the Illinois, the Spoon River, and the Sangamon, rolled on to the Mississippi. In this country timber was rare, infrequent groves rising like islands from the sea of grass. Some of Illinois' early place names designated the exceptional woods—Downers Grove, Troy Grove, Little Grove—as in Ohio the exceptional "plains" were distinguished.

Northward, toward the long loop of Lake Michigan, the forest began again. The "oak openings" of Wisconsin and Michigan were meadows framed with timber. And halfway up Lake Michigan came the deep, unbroken woods. At Saginaw Bay on Lake Huron, at Green Bay on Lake Michigan, at LaCrosse where the Black River joins the Mississippi, the North begins. A dense, dark, difficult country, it had few trails and no clearings; the Indians pitched their camps on the lake shores. Rivers were the route of exploration and early trade. Over them moved the land's first traffic, bales of peltry and barrels of trade goods, to the swish of canoe paddles and the *voyageurs'* songs. The rivers rose out of black cedar swamps, they flowed through a twilight of pine and hemlock toward the Great Lakes and the widening Mississippi.

The East North Central is generally level land, with no mountains or near-mountains except on the rugged shores of Lake Superior. The huge region is like an inverted plate without a discernible height of land, though it drains in two directions. Some of its rainfall plunges over Niagara and finds its way to the cold Gulf of the St. Lawrence; more of it joins the Mississippi and flows into the Gulf of Mexico. Only farther west is there any drainage into Hudson Bay. At no place did explorers find a range of hills to mark the watershed. There was merely a dwindling of one stream, a few miles of portage path, and then water running in a new direction. The "carries" of the Indians and fur traders are now the sites of cities—Akron in Ohio, Fort Wayne in Indiana, Joliet in Illinois, Portage in Wisconsin. In the 1830's canals were cut through the inland counties, linking the Great Lakes to the great rivers, and a generation later railroads webbed the level land. The region's topography gave it unity from the start.

Thomas Jefferson never saw the Old Northwest, except in the strong light of his imagination, yet he pictured future commonwealths that would grow up in the wild territory. In 1784 he drew a map of the interior, filling in its emptiness with such names as Chersonesus,

Assenisipia, Metropotomia, and Polypotamia, the states that would be formed by independent, enterprising settlers from the original seaboard colonies. A year later James Monroe made a journey to the Northwest. Indian wars shortened his tour, but he came back with a positive impression of the interior country. "A great part of the territory," he reported, "is miserably poor, especially that near Lakes Michigan and Erie, and that upon the Mississippi and the Illinois consists of extensive plains which have not had, from appearances, and will not have a single bush on them, for ages." He doubted that the region could ever attract enough people to form a government. Both Jefferson and Monroe lived to see Ohio, Indiana, and Illinois take their places in the Union.

In his most sanguine moments Thomas Jefferson could not have foreseen the Midwest of today. It begins with miles of smoking industries on the upper Ohio, steel, coke, chemicals, where the old Indian forts stood on the edge of wilderness. Past the old dreaming towns of Gallipolis, Madison, and Shawneetown flows the Ohio, and past the busy cities of Portsmouth, Cincinnati, Evansville. The southern counties of the river states keep some of their forest and some of their leisurely folkways. They were the first districts to be settled by immigrants who came west on the broad Ohio. The old state capitals of Ohio, Indiana, and Illinois were in the south—Chillicothe, Corydon, Kaskaskia. As settlement spread northward the capitals were moved midway up the states. The northern counties lagged; not till the Erie Canal was opened in 1825 did traffic on the lakes rival the commerce that for thirty years had moved on the Ohio River. Cleveland, Toledo, Detroit, Milwaukee, Chicago were still villages when Cincinnati and St. Louis were the commercial centers of the frontier. Statehood moved quickly west, to Ohio in 1803, Indiana in 1816, Illinois in 1818. It was longer in moving northward—to Michigan in 1837 and Wisconsin in 1848. After the Civil War a rush of population came to the Great Lakes, and the cities along the forty-second parallel spread for miles over their lake and river shores. The great Illinois grassland became the corn belt and the oak openings of Michigan and Wisconsin a land of dairy farms.

The East North Central is the most tamed and occupied of American regions. But a part of it remains primitive. North of the forty-fourth parallel stretched the great pine, spruce, and hemlock forest.

In a generation of wasteful and epic labor it was all logged off. Now there are miles of stump land and whole huge counties of second-growth forest with an occasional sawmill snarling through pine and poplar logs. Where the big timber booms once choked the rivers there are summer colonies, and long ships laden with iron ore trail their smoke over the lakes. Across the six-mile Straits of Mackinac the second-growth forest is a dense domain of deer, bear, beaver, with towns dotting the iron ranges and wilderness around them. Now the last spans have been fitted into the Mackinac Straits Bridge, and the upper peninsula of Michigan is linked to the populous land below. Still it remains a big, rough, lonesome country where one can drive through the woods for fifty miles without passing a human settlement.

The people of the north country are different from the Midwesterners of the Ohio valley. They are miners, lumbermen, fishermen, lake men, living far from the influence of cities, speaking with the sing-song inflections of Scandinavia or the clipped accents of Cornwall, relishing the hardy life and traditions of their remote country. A hundred years ago mail to Sault Ste. Marie or Marquette was addressed to "L.S. (Lake Superior), Michigan," as though the northern peninsula were a separate country; and people bound for Lansing or Detroit spoke of going to the United States. The north country is still a land apart. At its edge, on a border that seems final and ultimate, stretch the lonely beaches and dark headlands of Lake Superior.

It was a man from the Midwest who said, "Everybody talks about the weather, but no one does anything about it." Mark Twain remembered the somnolent summers and bleak winters of a Mississippi River town. All over the Midwest the climate is a sequence of extremes. Without barriers the weather sweeps and swoops over the land. Chicago is the Windy City. The Great Lakes have storms as violent as any ocean; forty big lake ships were lost in the great November storm of 1913. Generally the region has a short and wavering spring, followed by a long, hot, heavy summer. The early Scandinavian settlers were dazed by the fierce heat of midsummer when horses were lathered and a man idle in the shade was drenched with sweat. For fifty years Ohio valley people had the "shakes," a malarial fever that alternately chilled and steamed them; they accepted it as a part of frontier life and frontier climate. The hot humid summer wilts everything but hogs and corn; it is a season of burning sun briefly broken by crashing storms of wind and rain. Yet the precipitation is dependable, averaging thirty to forty inches a year and assuring the crops that fill the storage bins with more than a prodigal people can consume.

Winter is the other extreme, raw, sunless, chill in the Ohio valley with alternate frost and thaw from December to April. It is a bleak season so slow to pass that people invented ground-hog day in their wish for an early spring. In the north the climate is described as "eleven months winter and one month poor sledding." Summer is brief there with a scant ninety-day growing season and clear, cool air that attracts vacationers from the steaming cities below. Winter in northern Wisconsin and Michigan is long and dependable, deep snow, weeks of zero temperature, clear skies and a cold dry invigorating air. Ski slopes now mark the old iron-mining towns and winter sports draw thousands of visitors.

Over the entire Midwest autumn is the gracious season. September brings cool, clear days and starry nights. Quickly the colors warm and brighten, slowly they fade. It is a time of beauty and serenity, with a haze on the horizon and a yearning sky. Cornfields grow crisp and sere, like the ranks of a tattered army, the pastures turn brown, at sunrise frost lies silver on the tawny grass. In the towns the streets are carpeted with color and the evening air is spiced with burning leaves. A new ardor comes to the cities as the days grow shorter and lights come on in the early dusk. The American fervor for football, so marked in the Midwest, is as much a zest for the season as for the sport. Thanksgiving brings it to a reluctant end. No one ever wished for a short autumn.

For much of the year the climate is an adversary—the blizzards of midwinter, sudden windstorms whipping the land like anger, menacing thunderheads in the hot summer sky. This mid-American weather has stirred and prodded its people, made them restless and resistant. "Take it easy," is a folk phrase rarely followed in this strenuous region. Midwestern people can thank their willful climate for that.

For twenty thousand years, after the last glacier crept back from the Ohio valley, the land was wild and silent. Two hundred years ago it was still a timeless country, the home of a dozen wandering tribes, some thirty thousand people, where now it is the home of thirty million. The Indians lived in it like deer and foxes, without changing the country. The only sign of their possession was an infrequent village beside a river, a path through a thicket or the charred ground of an old hunting camp.

But time came, like the quick northern spring, with a pent-up urgency. It brought incredible changes in the span of a lifetime. Rangy long-striding Gurdon Hubbard, whom the Indians called "Swift Walker," crossed the wild prairie when there was no dwelling for a hundred miles. He brought a string of pack ponies to the upper Wabash and herded the first drove of hogs into the huddled village of Chicago. When he died Chicago had spread for twenty miles over the lake front, and long trains brought cattle, hogs, and sheep to the huge packing plants. By that time the prairie was webbed with railroads, the lake skies were stained with smoke, and the city at the mouth of the Onion River was getting ready to hold a World's Fair.

Indian wars held back settlement north of the Ohio in the years after the Revolution. But in 1794 Mad Anthony Wayne, the "Big Wind" of the Indians, swept through western Ohio and humbled the tribes at Fallen Timbers. The next summer 1100 chiefs and warriors filed in to Fort Greene Ville to feast on the army's beef, pork, brown sugar, and coffee, and to sign the treaty which opened the doors of the Ohio valley. Nearly twenty million acres were outlined in the treaty terms, for which the tribes received $20,000 in trade goods. It came to one tenth of a cent an acre. At about the same rate, during the next forty years, the rest of the Old Northwest was acquired by successive treaties with the tribes, until the entire region was cleared of Indian title.

Meanwhile the great land rush was on. Surveyors hacked lines through the country; they notched their witness trees and marked the boundaries of sections and townships. Revolutionary veterans arrived with land warrants in their pockets. Migrant families rocked over Zane's Trace toward the "land of the first quality . . . valuable and unsettled lands" described in the *Emigrant's Guide*. All through the East the "Ohio fever" ran like a contagion. Connecticut children played a game called "Going to Ohio," and Yankee farm boys sang,

> Says I, my boys, we'll leave this place
> For the pleasant O-hi-o.

Farmers, blacksmiths, millers, speculators thronged the new land of-fices in the Ohio valley. Said the shrewd traveler Harriet Martineau: "The possession of land is the aim of all action, generally speaking, and the cure for all social ills, among men in the United States. If a man is disappointed in politics or love, he goes and buys land. If he disgraces himself, he betakes himself to a lot in the West."

There were three ancient ways to the West, trails long traveled by migrating animals and by Indian hunting bands. In the early 1800's these wild trails became the paths of history. The Wilderness Trail brought people from Virginia and the Carolinas. The Cumberland Trail brought settlers from the central seaboard. The Genesee Trail, later the route of the Erie Canal, brought men and families from New York and New England. People from all the older states made the Ohio valley the first all-American frontier, where settlers from the North, South, and Middle colonies formed a new society. Someone said that if an Ohio town had a Congregational church and a college it was of New England origin; if it had a Presbyterian church and a distillery it was settled by Virginians. The Western Reserve, along the shore of Lake Erie, was "New Connecticut"; each of its towns gathers around a white-spired church in the village green. In towns along the National Road, halfway between Lake Erie and the Ohio, rows of brick houses front the street, each with a stone stoop above the side-walk in the Maryland manner. Ohio's old river towns still contain a few Virginia mansions with fanlights over columned doorways and deep side porches.

The Wilderness Road was a roundabout way over the mountains, down the great valley of Virginia to Cumberland Gap at the border of Kentucky and Tennessee. Here the emigrants sang:

> Cumberland Gap is a noted place,
> Three kinds of water to wash your face.

The waters flowed east, west, and north, and the best kind led toward the Ohio. Daniel Boone had come this way, marking the trace to the bluegrass country. He was followed by hunters, land-lookers, pioneer farmers and their families. By 1800 they had grown to a great proces-sion—pack horses laden with flour, salt, gunpowder; freight wagons creaking under bags of seed corn, rye, malt, and bundles of blankets and booting; farm wagons bristling with hoes, scythes, axes, plow-handles, cradles, and spinning wheels. Hill farmers in Virginia and the Carolinas working steep fields and brushy pastures, heard of land a-plenty, upland and bottom, timber and grassland, north of the Ohio. Some of them stopped for a generation in Kentucky, like Abe Lincoln's people, and then pushed on again. In the government land offices, spaced across the valley from Pittsburgh and Marietta to Shawneetown and Kaskaskia, they could buy land for two dollars an acre. The Harrison Land Act, allowing the purchase of 160 acres for eighty dollars cash with four years to pay the remainder, opened the public domain to the common man. In these years "a land-office business" came into the American language.

West from Baltimore ran the Cumberland Road, wholly unrelated to Cumberland Gap. It led through Cumberland on the Potomac and then struck across the green Allegheny ridges, forking out to Pittsburgh and Wheeling on the Ohio River. Another route, Forbes Road, linked Philadelphia to Pittsburgh. These roads were worn by a motley procession of wheeled vehicles: wagons, carts, carryalls, traps, flies, buggies, even wheelbarrows. At Pittsburgh or Wheeling travelers reached the end of the road but only a halfway point on their journey. They sold their horses and loaded their goods onto flatboats. At the riverbank one stream of commerce ended and another began. The shining Ohio carried them on to the western country. In the summer of 1791 John Pope started west from Pittsburgh in a keelboat, with a brick fireplace in its littered cabin, named the *Smokehouse*. Taking turns at the heavy steering oar were six men—a Virginian, a Kentuckian, a Welshman, an Irishman, a German, and a man born at sea. In 1802 the French naturalist Michaux traveled down the Ohio. He had but one eye, the other having been shot out by a rifle bullet in his youth, but he saw the myriad species of nature and the many strains of men. At every landing he heard the repeated greeting, "What part of the world do you come from?" It was a varied population that traveled the western waters.

The Ohio is a river without a source or a mouth. It begins as the stem of a Y under the hills of Pittsburgh, where the clear waters of the Allegheny meet the muddy Monongahela and the joined streams flow west toward the Mississippi. After 981 miles between curving hills and sloping meadows it ends at the tip of Illinois, still a thousand miles from the sea. It is the only great river of the mid-continent that flows west—in line with the American destiny. So the Ohio was more than a river, it was a moving, gleaming highway ready to carry the future to a new country. The settlers journeyed by arks, scows, broadhorns, flatboats, keelboats, bringing their horses and cattle, plows and wagons, axes and log chains, pigs and chickens, bundled nursery shoots and bags of seed corn. Some came on rafts as big as a barnyard, with a haycock at one end and a tent at the other. A bright green parakeet or a bronze wild turkey might settle down on that floating island to feed with the poultry.

The year 1811 was a time of wonders in the West, with earthquakes in February, hailstorms in summer, a September eclipse that darkened the sun, and a fiery-tailed comet in the autumn sky. In this *annus mirabilis* the greatest wonder was described by Zadok Cramer, editor of the *Navigator:* "There is now on foot a new mode of navigating our western waters, particularly the Ohio and Mississippi Rivers. This is with boats propelled by the power of steam." At Pittsburgh all that summer there was a clamor on the river front. Men shouted, ropes creaked, hammers clattered as the steamboat *New Orleans,* 138 feet long, capacity 350 tons, grew at the landing. At the end of October the lines were cast off and the big paddle wheels churned the water. Like a marvel the first steamboat passed down the Ohio and the Mississippi. Sixty steamboats were on the river by 1820, and the landing at Pittsburgh was thronged with emigrants awaiting passage to the West. Said Henry Rowe Schoolcraft, who was soon to explore the headwaters of the Mississippi River: "The Children of Israel could scarcely have presented a more motley array of men and women, with their 'kneading troughs' on their backs and their 'little ones,' than were here assembled on their way to the land of promise. To judge by the tone of general conversation they meant, in their generation, to plough the Mississippi valley from its head to its foot. There was not an idea short of it. What a world of golden dreams was there." By 1837 three thousand steamboats kept the frontier commerce moving. In the upper cabins tourists mixed with Southern planters, Yankee merchants, land speculators, army officers. Below, amid bags and bales of cargo, were the hopeful immigrants and settlers, crowding the rails in fine weather, crouching against the boiler walls when the river fog blew in. The pound of the paddle wheels was the new pulse of the valley, and sometimes they heard a voice from the past. Over the water came the long, sad call of a boatman's horn, and then the plaintive song:

> Hard upon the beech oar!
> She moves too slow
> All the way to Shawneetown,
> A long time ago.

The northern route, west from Albany through the Mohawk valley, was the way to New Connecticut, first traveled in 1796 by burly Moses Cleaveland and his task force of fifty woodsmen and surveyors. In 1818 the Genesee Road became the route of the Erie Canal, and three thousand Irish workmen began clearing the forest and shoveling out the Big Ditch. It was opened in 1825, a procession of packet boats passing from Buffalo to New York Harbor, with cannon booming, bands playing, church bells ringing in every town along the way. Off Sandy Hook a cask of fresh Lake Erie water was ceremoniously poured into the salt sea; so the inland waters were wedded to the ocean. Then began the business of the canal, barges leaving at every hour of day and night, carrying plows, axes, anvils, and emigrants to the West, bringing back pork, wheat, wool, apples, cheese, and whisky from the frontier.

On the wharves of Buffalo a dozen tongues and dialects clamored while people streamed into the immigrant ships for Cleveland, Toledo, Detroit, Milwaukee, Chicago. The line of steamers running up the lakes was known in the market towns and embarkation ports of Europe. People who knew no other words of English called the immigrant boats by name and bought their passage to Milwaukee or Chicago. Charles Fenno Hoffman, a one-legged traveler writing frontier news stories for the *New York American*, described the arrival of the steamer *New York* on a wild and gusty night in Cleveland. Above the rumble of wheels and the slap of water rose the cries of stevedores, the shouts of the ship's officers, and the clamor of immigrants "screaming at each other in half as many languages as were spoken at Babel." That night, limping behind the captain on a tour of the ship by lantern light, the newspaperman saw Swiss, German, Scotch, Scandinavian, and English immigrants stretched out among their baggage and their household goods. A painted German wagon was loaded with ploughs, shovels, saddles and sideboards, chairs, clocks, and carpets. Its sides were hung with kettles, bake pans, frying pans, iron candlesticks, old shoes, and broken tobacco pipes. Under it, with a crooked pipe in his mouth, lay a man in a blue cotton blouse and a woolen cap. "That man," wrote the correspondent, "had probably not the slightest idea of the kind of country he was coming to. He looks, indeed, as if he came from another planet. But visit him on his thriving farm ten years hence and you will find him happily at home among his neighbors."

The twentieth century has brought another commerce to the lakes. Three hundred big freighters carry iron ore from Lake Superior to the blast furnaces of the lower lakes and wheat from the great plains to the mills and elevators of the East. The immigrant ships of a century ago made the new trade possible. They brought the German and Swedish wheat farmers, the Norwegian and Finnish lumberjacks, the Cornish, Irish, Italian, and Croatian miners who opened up the iron hills. Most of them could not speak the New World's language, but they understood what it offered them—freedom, equality, opportunity, participation.

Migration to the Midwest moved with a tidal power and rhythm, advancing, subsiding, pushing forward again. The first big move swept in after the Harrison Land Act of 1800, which opened the public domain to the small farmer. The War of 1812 slowed the march, but briefly. Its end was the signal for the Great Migration, which filled five expanding years. The panic of 1819 stemmed the movement for a decade, but a greater surge came in the 1830's when new roads and canals carried new multitudes to the public lands. Sales in the National Land Office swelled from two million acres in 1831 to four million in 1833, to twelve million in 1835, to twenty million in 1836. The figure dropped to five million with the panic of 1837. But even in that dark year a traveler in frontier Springfield, not yet made the Illinois capital, reported: "Our far west is improving rapidly, astonishingly . . . like the marks of enchantment. . . . The state of Illinois has probably the finest body of fertile land of any state in the Union. Population will continue to advance, admirable farms and town lots may be purchased with a certainty of realizing large profits. The country here is beautiful—equal in native attractions . . . to the scenes I visited and admired in Italy. The vale of Arno is not more beautiful than the valley of the Sangamon, with its lovely groves, murmuring brooks, and flowery meads." In this panic summer of 1837 Daniel Webster, snorting with his annual hay fever, visited the frontier. Excited by the sweeping Illinois landscape, he bought a thousand acres in Sangamon County and plotted a townsite named Salisbury for his birthplace in New Hampshire.

Ohio was only the first "fabled region." As the migration broke across the near frontier, farther lands glowed with promise; the Ohio fever was followed by the Illinois fever and the Michigan fever. By 1840 Ohio with a million and a half population was the third state in the Union; Indiana had nearly seven hundred thousand, Illinois almost half a million. In Ohio one-tenth of the public land was still for sale, in Indiana one-fifth, in Illinois one-half. To these tracts of wild country came thousands of wagons with family goods jammed between the sideboards. Meanwhile the tide was reaching into the northern states. In the spring of 1851 Ralph Waldo Emerson made a lecture tour of the western country. He took a steamboat down the Ohio, slept in buffalo robes on the deck of canal barges, drove in stages and buckboards across the roads of Illinois to the steep little town of Galena on the Mississippi River near the border of Wisconsin. There in his tavern room he wrote to Thomas Carlyle in London, describing the upper Mississippi country. "On all the shores interminable silent forest. If you land there is prairie behind prairie, forest behind forest, sites of nations, no nations." But nations were coming. On a summer night while his letter was still on the way to England two steamers collided in fog on Lake Erie. Quickly the big *Atlantic* filled with water, and in the gray dawn the *Ogdensburg* saved 250 immigrant passengers who finished their journey to take up land in Wisconsin and Illinois. Every day in the navigation season Germans, Irish, Scandinavians, Hollanders, Scots streamed off the immigrant boats at the western lake ports. In the winter of 1853 fourteen river boats lay icebound at the junction of the Ohio and the Mississippi, while two thousand German and Irish settlers fumed at the delay that kept them from pre-emption lands along the upper Mississippi. That summer nine thousand immigrants changed trains in Chicago in a single day.

After the Civil War fresh waves of settlement surged into Illinois, Michigan, and Wisconsin. With prairie to plow, forests to fell, minerals to mine, the states sent immigration agents abroad to recruit new citizens. Germans poured into Chicago and Milwaukee and the lake towns all the way to Green Bay. A Dutch population grew in the towns of Holland, Vreeland, and Vriesland on the Michigan shore.

The Polish came in large numbers in the 1870's; one group hired by a lumber company halfway up Lake Huron cut the timber, bought the stump land with their wages, and developed some of the finest farms in Michigan. A great wave of German and Scandinavian settlement came to the northern states in the 1880's. The largest of all Polish migrations arrived between 1910 and 1920, thousands settling in the industrial centers of Michigan and Wisconsin, others going north to the lumber and mining towns. In the years of the first World War came the first migration of Negroes to the Midwest cities. Recruiting agents toured the southern states, bringing trainloads of Negro workmen and their families to the industrial centers along the Great Lakes. It was the beginning of a population movement which has steadily continued.

Behind the people on the roads and rivers, the lakes and the canals, were the social and economic pressures that have always sent people into new regions. Native population in the older states was growing, and a Yankee farmer could not leave each of his ten, twelve, or fifteen children a farm. Hard seasons in New England, like the year 1816, with frost in every month—the year of "eighteen hundred and froze to death"—sent thousands to the frontier. When Yankee farmers had a scant crop and southern farmers watched the price of cotton falling, a new light shone in the west. And Americans were restless and hopeful by nature; life on the edge of a new continent had given them an instinctive belief in the new chance. "To move," said a squatter, "all I hafen to do is put out the fire an' call the dog." Wrote Englishman William Faux, seeing how lightly a man could load his wagon and leave his past: "The American has always something better in his eye; he lives and dies on hopes, a mere gypsy in this particular."

For European immigrants there was the pressure of poverty and oppression behind them and the lure of opportunity ahead. In the late 1840's the potato famine in Ireland and the unsuccessful revolution in Germany sent millions to America. At the port of Bremen German emigrants were asked what they expected to find in America. "*Kein König dort,*" they answered—"No king there." They might also have said "Acres," for they had read in "America letters" that one day's labor would buy an acre of farmland. To hungry Ireland came reports of high wages and cheap land, of peaches and apples rotting on the ground and grain ungleaned in the fields. By 1850 Irish immigrants were sending a million dollars a year to families in the Old Country, where all the young men dreamed of coming to America.

And along with opportunity was the lure of equality and independence. From Wisconsin a Norwegian wrote home: "Here I take off my cap to no one—not even the minister—not even the President." A Swedish settler wrote: "Here a man can come to something by his own efforts." In Scotland after a visit to the Indiana frontier John Melish wrote of the western farmer: "None dare encroach upon him; he can sit under his own vine, and under his own fig tree, and none to make him afraid." Wrote a Welsh settler in Ohio to his brother in Glamorgan: "We have done very well in this country. Have a fine farm which would sell for about 6000 dollars, and every other thing in proportion. . . . Thank God no orthodoxy, no tithes, no high church, no king but good and wholesome laws."

The Midwest has had the great gift of diversity—deep forest and wide prairie, vast lakes and mile-wide rivers; coal, oil, and gas; sand, clay, and limestone; copper, iron, and the deep rich soil. But the greater gift has been the diversity of its people. Early Michigan settlements were said to be made up of Yankee, Hoosier, Yorker, Yahoo, Buckskin, Buckeye, Chegoe, Sucker. These were varieties of native-born Americans. And more diversity was coming, with the thirty nationalities that crowded the immigrant trains and ships. Each strain brought its own vitality, its distinct temperament and its special gifts. The mingling of the blood streams gave the Midwest a strong, bright life force, capable of many pursuits, resourceful in various ways, and sharing a common future. In Europe more than a century ago a young seaman, Herman Melville, saw the emigrant ships crowded with many peoples bound for the midlands of America. He wrote: "You cannot spill a drop of American blood without spilling the blood of the whole world."

In describing his travels through the Midwestern frontier, Charles Dickens referred to towns and villages. Then he corrected himself: "I ought to say city; every place is a city here." In the frontier period every crossroad had expectations and the poorest settlement dreamed of becoming a commercial center. Prospect Street is a familiar designation in Midwestern towns. In Illinois the name Stone's Landing was changed to Napoleon, as more appropriate to its outlook, and Goose Run became the Columbus River. Spunky Point was renamed Warsaw.

Commerce City, Illinois, consisted of two shanties on the Mississippi, while Eastern speculators circulated engraved plots of a burgeoning metropolis. The Mormans bought Commerce City in 1839, changed its name to Nauvoo, and raised one of their elaborate temples on the riverbank. When they went on to Utah a few years later, Nauvoo was a ghost town beside the lordly river.

Some of the frontier's best-advertised cities existed on paper only. Speculators in the Maumee valley, where Toledo was not incorporated until 1837, printed maps showing Manhattan at the mouth of the river, Lucas City, Oregon, Orleans, and Austerlitz above. City lots were sold by Eastern agents, but when the owners arrived there was only a straggle of huts along the river. At the site of Austerlitz they found an empty swamp. In 1852 a group of colonists arrived at Galena on the upper Mississippi, asking for steamboat passage to Rollingstone City—a place no riverman had seen or heard of. The Easterners had maps of the town, showing wharves, business streets, a hotel, a lecture hall, a public library. Finally a steamboatman recalled a site that seemed to fit the location of the plotted city. The place, just vacated by the Sioux, was empty except for a squatter's shack.

The most ambitious non-existent town, the "future metropolis of the Mississippi," was Nininger City, the dream of expansive young Ignatius Donnelly. Seeing the swelling river trade, the huge rafts of upper Mississippi pine, and barges laden with lead, wheat, cheese, pork, lard, potatoes, and whisky, Donnelly chose a site near the head of navigation, twenty miles below St. Paul. With the financial backing of a Philadelphia man named Nininger, he laid out his city. "Western towns have heretofore grown by chance," he said; his city was completely planned, with thirty streets running parallel to the river and fifteen avenues named for Donnelly and his friends. In 1856 the *Emigrant Aid Journal,* Ignatius Donnelly, editor, appeared in English and German editions. It was published in Philadelphia but dated Nininger City, and it was entirely concerned with the bright prospects of that new metropolis. A running head across the front page expressed both Donnelly's taste and his temperament: "Dost thou know how to play the fiddle?" "No," answered Themistocles, "but I understand the art of raising a little village into a great city." A year later, after the panic of 1857, Nininger City was a weedy riverbank, and Ignatius

Donnelly began working on a cipher to prove that Bacon wrote Shakespeare.

The actual cities of the Midwest began by chance more than by plan and without unusual expectations. Illinois had been a state for twenty years before Chicago, with 4117 people, was incorporated as a city; at that time nearby Michigan City was more vigorously pushing lots for sale, as were Vienna in Illinois and Liverpool in Indiana. In the summer of 1796 when General Moses Cleaveland paced off a ten-acre common above the Lake Erie shore and told his surveyors to plot town lots around it, he dared to hope that the town of Cleveland would grow as large as his native village of Old Wyndham, Connecticut. South Bend, at the old carrying place on the southernmost bend of the St. Joseph River, was a mere trading post until 1830. To attract settlement the town's founders offered free land and a cash bonus to sober tradesmen. Still South Bend remained a village until the 1850's when the Studebaker brothers began making their rugged high-wheeled farm wagons.

In retrospect it appears that the art of raising a little village into a great city lies in choosing a location on a waterway and peopling it with one or more uncommonly enterprising men.

Cincinnati was originally named, by a wandering frontier schoolmaster, Losantiville. By means of L for Licking, *os* mouth, *anti* opposite, this fanciful name designated the town opposite the mouth of the Licking River. The Licking flows north from bluegrass Kentucky, and Cincinnati was also at the mouth of the rich Miami valley, on a historic Indian trail from the north. It quickly became a bustling town, farmers creaking in with corn, potatoes, and apples, drovers herding hogs through the muddy streets, a fleet of flatboats at the landing and families trudging up Broadway past the blockhouses of Fort Washington. In the Miami valley, after Wayne's defeat of the tribes, the towns of Hamilton, Middletown, and Dayton were planted, and over the valley roads came hogs that made Cincinnati "Porkopolis." In 1817 a talkative Cincinnati barber told a newcomer: "Now, sir, in dull times when money is scarce these hogs are not weighed, they are not counted, they are *measured*, sir, not individually but aggregately; measured by the lot and sold by the acre. So much for a lot of five acres and so much for a lot of ten acres. The western people, sir, love

7. Chicago's skyline, especially at night, is as exciting as that of any city that is built on level land. Note the streaks of light (from headlights) resulting from the prolonged exposure.

98. Frank Lloyd Wright designed both this unusual industrial buildin
in Racine, Wisconsin — home office of a major producer of wax prod
ucts — and the office furniture.

99. A Wisconsin cheese maker checking wheels of blue cheese in th
curing room to determine the amount of "age."

00.   Nuclear and atomic research at the University of Wisconsin, Madi-
n. Working here are visiting scientists of the Midwestern Universities
esearch Association. These are days of co-operation rather than competition in efforts to extend man's knowledge of the physical universe.

101. Reading meters on the control board of a giant boiler at a ste[am]
plant in South Chicago.

102. Filling, stoppering, capping, and packaging bottles of antibioti[cs]
at a pharmaceutical plant in Indianapolis.

103. Rims, engineered to eliminate tire wobble, being rolled off an
assembly line at Akron, Ohio.

104. The completion of the giant bridge across the Straits of Mackina ended the comparative isolation of Michigan's Upper Peninsula.

105. A huge automobile factory on the outskirts of Detroit.

406. The water front of downtown Cincinnati. Note how the rise and fall of the water level in the Ohio River affects land use along the riverbank.

407. A concrete wall built by the U. S. Army, Corps of Engineers, between Portsmouth and New Boston, Ohio, for protection against flooding.

108. Downtown Cleveland is dominated by the lofty Terminal Tower, visible to airplane passengers far out over Lake Erie.

109. Coal mining in southern Illinois. A huge conveyor belt makes it possible to bring out 1300 tons per hour.

to do business upon a great scale, and this selling hogs by the acre suits their mind."

In 1827 the Miami and Erie Canal began bringing beef and bacon, salt and saddle-trees, tallow, timber and tobacco, and the big white steamboats at the landing carried Cincinnati cargoes all the way to New Orleans. So the Queen City grew, spreading up from the river basin to its ring of hills. Besides its packing plants it had big breweries and tanneries, brass and iron foundries; it did a large business in steamboat bells and supplied church bells to all the interior country. Until the Civil War it was the largest city west of Philadelphia. Cincinnati was a center of culture as well as commerce, a city of churches and colleges, a publishing center, a place known for its concert halls and fine hotels. Thousands of Germans came in the mid-century, settling in "Over the Rhine" across the canal. They manufactured stoves and musical instruments, they ran jewelry stores and breweries, on the banks of the Ohio they tended gardens and vineyards. They published German papers and formed a colonizing committee to attract their countrymen from Saxony and Hannover. At the same time Cincinnati had a Southern flavor, with Kentucky just across the river and strong commercial ties to the South. When railroads webbed the Midwest the river and canal trade dwindled, and the Queen City was overshadowed by the new cities to the north. But it kept its cosmopolitan flavor, its love of music, art, and learning, and the river still washed its levee. Now the big white packet boats are gone, but diesel towboats push long strings of barges loaded with coal, sand, sulfur, oil, and steel for Cincinnati's soap and machine-tool factories.

When Moses Cleaveland died, back home in Connecticut, in 1806, there were not yet forty people in the town he had planted ten years earlier on Lake Erie's shore. Cleveland was a remote village with a huddle of houses around a wharf under the steep Cuyahoga bank, and a few more dwellings on high ground around the public square where at nine o'clock each evening an iron wagon tire was rung with a hammer to mark the end of day. On the far side of the Cuyahoga, near the lake, a few Irish families squatted in the rushes, trapping muskrats and catching fish. In 1816 young Alfred Kelley, mayor of the village, watched muddy teams toil over a wretched road bringing pork, wheat, and flour to the Cuyahoga mouth where it was loaded into schooners for Buffalo. Ten years later in the State Assembly at

Columbus, Kelley became the "father of the Ohio canal system"; he had not forgot the wagons lurching beside the smooth waters of the Cuyahoga.

When the first segment of the canal was opened in 1827, ten thousand barrels of flour, whisky, pork, butter, and cheese passed through Cleveland and the town was booming. By 1840 Cleveland had six thousand people and its harbor was filled with canal boats, lumber scows, and grain schooners. Steamers lay smoking at the wharves and the masts of sailing vessels rose above docks laden with wool, lard, lime, fish, and grindstones. Above, on the high ground where Moses Cleaveland had measured the town common, rose the white dome of the new courthouse, four church spires, and two hotels. On the roofs of the hotels were sentry boxes where lookouts watched for the approach of steamers. At every arrival runners raced down to the docks to meet prospective guests. With lake and canal traffic Cleveland was a crossroads of water-borne trade.

In 1852 six barrels of iron ore were shipped from Lake Superior to Cleveland—after being hauled around the falls at Sault Ste. Marie and re-loaded into a second vessel. This was the first cargo in a trade that was to make Cleveland a great city and America an industrial nation. In 1855, after two years of construction, the St. Mary's Falls Canal was open, linking Lake Superior to the lower lakes. That season 1447 tons of iron ore passed through the Soo locks. In half a century it became the largest single commerce in the world. Though it affected a score of other cities, the growing lakes commerce became centered in Cleveland. The enterprise of its iron merchants and a location close to the coal fields of Pennsylvania made Cleveland the capital of the Great Lakes trade. For miles the twisting Cuyahoga was lined with docks, elevators, coal and lumber yards, oil tanks, foundries and blast furnaces; and Euclid Avenue, once a game and Indian trail, was spaced with the mansions of the industrialists. Now high-level bridges span the smoky Cuyahoga basin, carrying a ceaseless traffic to handsome suburbs on the lake shore.

Toledo, at the mouth of the Maumee River, began its existence with misfortunes. An epidemic of cholera in the 1830's, aggravated by the miasmic air of the swampy Maumee valley, was followed by drought which burned up the crops and reduced the Maumee to a trickle. Between these calamities came the "Toledo War," a dispute

unique in the history of the United States. For a year armed militia-
men of Ohio and Michigan patrolled the straggling town, each state
claiming protection of its own property. The "war" resulted from a
geographical error, in which map makers had drawn the southern end
of Lake Michigan ten miles too far north. Michigan's southern boundary was designated as a line drawn due east from the tip of Lake
Michigan to the shore of Lake Erie. The error gave Michigan claim
to a strip of land ten miles wide across northwestern Ohio, a strip containing the town of Toledo and its harbor. Soon after Michigan's
21-year-old governor, Stevens T. Mason, sent militia onto the disputed
ground, Governor Lucas of Ohio arrived with a thousand troops. There
were fist fights and some stray shooting in the muddy streets while
Federal agents from Washington urged a truce until Congress could
take up the question. By good fortune casualties were limited to two
work horses and some hogs, but tension hung over Toledo for months.
Finally Congress upheld Ohio's claim to the Toledo strip, and in return ceded to Michigan a big wild territory beyond the Straits of
Mackinac. Michigan accepted the Upper Peninsula under protest, not
knowing of its prodigious veins of copper and its ranges of iron ore.

Toledo soon became the terminus of canals reaching southward to
the Ohio and Wabash rivers and a great shipping port. When gas was
discovered in the Maumee valley the first glass factories were established at Toledo. They grew into a big industry, supplying glass to the
automobile makers of the Midwest. Now the Maumee is lined with
oil refineries, coke ovens, blast furnaces, stone crushers, and coal docks.
With long coal trains arriving day and night and deep-loaded freighters whistling under the bridges, Toledo is the greatest coal-shipping
port in the world.

Detroit, which in the twentieth century has put America on wheels,
was named for navigation; it is "the strait" between Lake Erie and
Lake Huron, and its first commerce was canoe caravans bringing the
peltry of the North to the French fur traders. In 1800 it was a straggling
settlement six miles long and one street wide. Its little farms with their
"ribbon fields" of grain and pasture lined the river from Belle Isle—
then called *Isle au Couchon*, Hog Island—to the marshy mouth of
the River Rouge. Whitewashed French cottages looked across the
river to a Wyandot village where old men scarred with smallpox sat
on mangy bearskins and women tended the cooking pots. At evening

the shore twinkled with their supper fires. Around Detroit lay tribal lands of the Wyandots, Miamis, and Ottawas. From Lake Huron the Chippewas brought canoe loads of peltry, down the interior rivers paddled the Wea and Piankeshaws, across the prairie came Kickapoo and Potawatomi. From the start Detroit has been a place of mingled tongues.

Thirty years later with the Erie Canal pouring commerce into the western waters, Detroit was a bustling gateway to new settlements in Michigan and northern Indiana. Tall ships fretted the river front and up the streets swarmed merchants, speculators, army men, horse and cattle traders, westward-moving Yankees and the polyglot tide of immigrants. In the month of May, 1833, ninety steamboats arrived at Detroit, each one bringing hundreds of eager settlers to the West. During the 1840's hundreds of thousands came ashore at Detroit, loaded their goods into carts and wagons, and pushed on to the public lands.

On a summer day in Indiana in 1894 Elwood Haynes cranked up his horseless carriage and drove for three miles down the dusty Pumpkin Vine Pike. From that event came the phenomenal industrial growth of Detroit in the twentieth century. Now the long freighters steam through the river, under the Ambassador Bridge and past the new glass-and-steel buildings of the Civic Center. At Ecorse and Wyandotte the once-green shores are mounded with black coal, white limestone, green sulfur, red iron ore. The River Rouge, once a hunting area for waterfowl, is heavy with blast furnaces and the huge spread of the motor factories. Now it takes trains, trucks, and ships to carry the endless products of Detroit's assembly lines. But the lakes are still a route of transport. Long freighters with solid ranks of automobiles across their decks steam out of the historic river for the markets of the Midwest.

The last Indian trouble east of the Mississippi was the pathetic Black Hawk's War in 1832. When it was over, the beaten warriors fled across the Mississippi and southern Wisconsin was open to settlement. Two years later three men bought land on Lake Michigan at the mouth of the Milwaukee River—Solomon Juneau a French fur trader, Byron Kilbourn a New Englander, and George Walker from Virginia. Milwaukee's growth began in 1835 with ships from Buffalo bringing immigrants and settlers, merchants and speculators. In the summer of 1836 sixty buildings went up in seven months, ferries plied the river, and Byron Kilbourn published the town's first newspaper. At mid-century thriving Milwaukee received an influx of German "forty-eighters"— liberal, learned, cultivated people who promptly enriched the life of the city. In 1856 a Great Lakes schooner loaded Milwaukee wheat for the long voyage to Liverpool, the first cargo in an epic trade. After the Civil War Milwaukee industrialists exploited some of the richest lumber and iron lands of the north country. Since then grain and lumber, meat packing and metalworking, breweries, tanneries, shoe factories, and machine shops have made Milwaukee famous.

One of the terms of General Wayne's Indian treaty at Fort Greene Ville in 1795 was the cession of six square miles at the mouth of the Chicago River. It was not a likely place for a city. There was no harbor—a sand bar blocked the mouth of the shallow river—and the low Lake Michigan shore was covered with reeds and swamp grass. It was merely a portage, a place for carrying canoes through fields of wild onion which the Indians called *che-ca-gau.*

For years Fort Dearborn, built in 1803 at the river mouth, was the loneliest post in the West. When the Potowatomis burned it and massacred the garrison in the summer of 1812, there was no life there at all. But it was a strategic point where the Chicago River wound lakeward from the Des Plaines and the Illinois. In 1816 Fort Dearborn was rebuilt and a few huts sprang up on the riverbank. Two years later Illinois became a state. That summer 18-year-old Gurdon Hubbard, a trader for the American Fur Company, walked to Chicago from Mackinac. At the end of the journey he found the fort by the river, across from it the cabins of John Kinzie and a couple of other families, and the endless prairie beyond. It remained a lost place until 1830 when surveyors began running lines for the Illinois and Michigan Canal. The town of Chicago was incorporated in 1833; then the prairie silence gave way to a clatter of building and a clamor of men. In 1837 it became a city, with 4117 excited people. A merchant in an unpainted store on Lake Street stated that Chicago would become the greatest commercial city in the world. Four years later the editor of the first city directory wrote soberly that he could see no limit to the city's growth.

Chicago owed nothing to nature except its location where the wide prairies met the broad far-reaching lake. The ground on which the city rested was soft, low, barely above the river level. At first the streets were paved with heavy planks, but they sank under the city's traffic. Cobblestones were no better. Finally in the late 1850's the city streets were raised twelve feet above their natural level, and in a few strenuous seasons thousands of buildings were jacked up and given new foundations. By brute strength Chicago lifted itself out of the mud.

With sand bars dredged and the channel deepened the Chicago River was thronged with lumber schooners, grain schooners, passenger vessels. In 1839 when wheat fields were spreading over the prairies two grain merchants built the first Chicago elevator and the brig *Osceola* loaded the first cargo of grain for Buffalo. Railroads fanned into Chicago from six directions in the 1850's, linking the young city with the East and also with the Mississippi River; already the Illinois and Michigan canal was obsolete and Chicago was on its way to being the greatest railroad center in the world. Long trains of cattle cars brought western cattle to Chicago's growing stockyards. Down the lakes came endless cargoes of lumber, lumber to build the barns and houses of the prairie farms and to build the prairie cities. In 1870 Chicago was a wooden city with thirteen miles of wooden docks along the river and its branches, twenty-four wooden bridges, seventeen wooden elevators, miles of wooden warehouses, hundreds of livery stables, and long cliffs of lumber on the landings. Some men wondered what a fire would do.

All around Lake Michigan the summer of 1871 was hot and dry. Chicago had a bare third of average rainfall. All through the prairie country wells and cisterns ran dry and mud cracked open on the river banks. The pine woods of the north were parched. In the first week of October smoke dulled the skies of Lake Michigan; the forests were burning at a dozen places. When the wind came the town of Manistee was rimmed with fire, the men of Menominee dug a fire-block and fought for their lives, seven hundred people were trapped in the burning town of Peshtigo. Then came word of another disaster at the foot of Lake Michigan. Chicago was burning.

The wooden city burned furiously. At half-past nine in the evening fire broke out in Patrick O'Leary's barn on DeKoven Street. By midnight the whole loop within the river was a tempest of wind and flame, and fire was leaping the river. At daybreak came thunder but no rain; on the north side firemen were dynamiting blocks of houses in the path of the flames. A hundred thousand people fled to the lake shore and the open prairie. After twenty-seven awesome hours the heart of Chicago was a smoking ruin.

When dazed officials could survey the wreckage they reported a third of the city destroyed and 70,000 homeless. Relief contributions poured in and rebuilding began. Tents and barracks went up on the lake shore, architects began planning a new city, thousands of men hauled rubble to a huge dumping ground in front of Michigan Avenue. So began the magnificent lake-front parks that adorn the Chicago of today.

Fire had not lessened Chicago's advantage on the east-west line of the nation's commerce, and this was a phenomenal time in America's growth. In a few years the marks of fire were erased; in a decade Chicago had half a million people, nearly double the population of the city that burned. The new city was more robust and confident than before. In 1892, on the 400th anniversary of the discovery of America, it prepared a World's Fair that drew visitors from every country on earth. Then it was a city of a million, two-thirds of them foreign-born. Now, with four million, it is a city of soaring beauty and sullen ugliness, of violence and of aspiration. It has given the world the reaping machine, the Pullman car, and the steel skyscraper. Into its vast railroad yards come products from every corner of the nation and to its docks come the raw materials of heavy industry. Soon the St. Lawrence Seaway will open the Great Lakes to foreign commerce and the prairie city will become one of the great seaports of the world.

Politically the Old Northwest was an outlying region, though geographically it was mid-continental. History soon made it central, as it will remain. Now America's center of population is in south-central Illinois and the Midwest is the heartland of the nation.

It was not a hard-won land. Most of its people came to it without hardship or hindrance and they quickly found freedom, opportunity, independence. So the region has no lost causes, no shadows, and few cherished memories. Its critics find it monotonous, prosaic, and undistinguished, perhaps because the land lies open and its people have prospered. Happy countries, say the French, have no history, and the East North Central is an astonishing success story. Still the Midwest has had meaning for its people. All his life Mark Twain was haunted by a drowsy town beside the Mississippi, and Abraham Lincoln never forgot the long morning light on the prairie with the future coming up like sunrise.

The Plains States

BY JACK SCHAEFER

Turn the map as you wish, balance out the great continental land mass as you will—always the geographic center is here, somewhere here, in the vast expanse of rolling sea-like land, more than 500,000 square miles of it, that is the north central section of the United States.

All of it, except the relatively narrow valley of the Red River of the North which drains into Canada and the relatively small pointed piece of Minnesota which adjoins Lake Superior, is on the western slope of the mighty Mississippi basin. All of its major rivers, the Arkansas, the Republican, the Platte, the Missouri, again except the Red, finger eastward and southeastward across it from far sources in the Rocky Mountains to join the Mississippi and sweep to the Gulf.

Seven states. In two tiers, side by side. Three states in the one tier, Missouri and Iowa and Minnesota, eastern in appearance on the map; that is, suggestive of those eastward to the Atlantic, odd-shaped, outlined chiefly by geographic factors. Four states in the second tier, Kansas and Nebraska and the twin Dakotas, definitely western in the drawing, like those westward to the Pacific, straight-shaped, symmetrical, outlined primarily by arbitrary lines drawn on surveyors' charts. And that is as it should be.

This is the transition area, where east becomes west in New World terms, where the land itself changes and the conditions it imposes change with it.

The Laurentide glacier in its time crept down out of the northeast over some of this area, roughly the eastern tier of states, and melted back leaving its rich deposits of soil drift. Huge lakes marked the surface later, drying and bequeathing their own rich alluvial deposits. Off to the west when the Rockies had reared upward in crinkling of the earth's crust, streams fed by endless snows coming in from the Pacific, rushing down the steeps and slowing out on the comparative levels, had begun the long building eastward of a blanket of debris, stone and sand and silt, out over the wide-ranging sheets of marine rock that underlie the whole region and slope slowly but steadily down towards the Mississippi. In the long sweep of geologic time this covering blanket thickened and spread ever eastward to meet and merge into the glacial and alluvial deposits—and east and west met and merged then as they meet and merge today in the heart of this rolling sea-like expanse that is the heartland of the continent.

Sea-like. . . . The term is not derived from water-action beginnings. It is not condemned by the fact that in the present age, through much of this area, a lack of water is the single most important problem. When settlement broke past the Mississippi and faced out over the open treeless spaces, people sought for comparisons with the land, the environment behind them—and not alone behind them east of the Mississippi but beyond in the Europe from which they had originally come. They sought in vain. They were confronting a newer world in the New World. Inevitably they thought of the sea, the lonely land-markless expanses of the world's oceans. The same phrases recur in the old records. An ocean of land. A sea of grass. . . .

That is the dominant characteristic, the vastness of wide open stretches of land rolling wave-like into seemingly limitless horizons.

It is not all open, leveled in the long view. It is broken along the eastern edge bordering the Mississippi by the erosive action of the tributary rivers and streams and occasional flood waters, again along the western fringes where flash-flood violence of few far-spaced but torrential downpours beating upon semidesert have created the bad-lands formations. Those are rippings downward below the general level. There are mountains too. In southwest Missouri the old Ozarks look towards the flats of Kansas. In western South Dakota the Black Hills, which are not hills but rugged mountains, the world's oldest, rise sharp against the horizon rolling into Wyoming. Up in North Dakota, straddling the Canadian line, the Turtle Mountains, which are not mountains but sturdy hills, hump strong against the northern sky. Yet all these, sizable each as old-time kingdoms elsewhere in the world, are little more than islands almost lost in the vastness, the ocean of land.

It was not all treeless, even discounting the patches of timber in those mountains, when settlement broke into it. It is not all treeless today despite despoiling by men to whom the concept of conservation meant nothing. This is the transition area and the transition is not abrupt. East merges into west in successive stages, successive zones, three of them, determined by rainfall. The lines are blurred today under the impact of modern technology. They were distinct when the westering migrations first crossed them.

The eastern timber region which once covered most of the United States east of the Mississippi with a close carpet of forests extended on beyond the great river to form the first zone. Unbroken forest covered most of Missouri, much of Minnesota. There was a gap, treeless except in patches and along watercourses, roughly what is now Iowa. Perhaps Indian tribes here through countless generations, setting fire to grasses and brush as part of their periodic collective hunts, cleared this break and kept forest seedlings from taking hold again. That is one of the questions still puzzling prehistorians. The important fact is that this first zone, first strip west of the Mississippi, forested or close to forests, well-watered, dotted with lakes in the Minnesota portion, was essentially an extension of the eastern portion of the country, an environment already known, familiar, still friendly in terms of the basic ingredients of early settlement: land, water, timber.

Beyond the forests, the prairies.

Vast in unexperienced immensity they rolled westward, an ocean of land, a sea of grass, a wide, wide zone traversing the entire region out of what would be Texas and Oklahoma to the south into the overwhelming wilderness that would be Canada to the north. Strange. Different. Raw and violent with blazing shadeless sun in summer and fierce storms in winter that would demand a new name and get it, blizzards, and endless wrenching winds and the nameless panic of space and distances that would twist many a man into a mindless creature wandering directionless to a lingering death. . . . And yet, not too strange, not too different. Treeless, timberless, yes, except in ironic teasing small lowland bits along the few watercourses soon exhausted. But still friendly in the more vital ingredients: land, water. Land enough, most of it rich and fertile beneath the matted sod, to absorb millions of the land-hungry. Rainfall enough, though not to nourish forests, on the average over an appreciable period, good years outbalancing bad, to make of that land one of the world's great agricultural empires.

And beyond the prairies, the plains.

Vaster, huger in massive humping shoulders of limitless horizons, they too rolled westward, again traversing the entire region south to north. Rawer. More violent. No longer friendly at all in terms understandable to settlers out of the east. Indifferent instead, if not actively hostile. Semiarid; beyond the line, roughly the 98th meridian, of 20-inch annual rainfall, minimum for soil-crop farming without irrigation. Scantiness of rainfall, accentuated by periods of complete drought, was abetted by rapid runoff of what rain did fall and by rapid evaporation under beating sun and constant dry winds.

No timber. Insufficient water. There remained only land.

Not even mineral resources in any significant quantity. Some lead and zinc in the Ozarks and by the Des Moines River in Iowa. Some gold in the Black Hills. Some coal and natural gas in eastern Kansas and Iowa. Some oil far underground in the far northwest corner of North Dakota shading into Montana. Small patches only in the vastness. Land was and remains the major resource, the one constant through the three zones. It was no accident, no mere quirk of history, that here in the heartland of the continent land-hunger would be unleashed on a scale never before known.

Three zones. Eastern, transitional, western. Forest, prairie, plain. Trees, deciduous hardwoods and white pine; tall grasses, sodded; short grasses, bunched. And always and forever an ocean of land.

The Mound Builders were the first people. At least the first to leave tangible evidence of their presence.

They belonged to the dim prehistoric people or peoples who once spread through much of the Mississippi basin and the Gulf coastal plains and left their burial mounds and earthwork enclosures and strange snake-and-animal-shaped artificial hills for later folk to find. They were artists in pottery and copperwork. One of their customs has endured and spread now around the world, the smoking of tobacco in pipes. Their range was primarily east of the Mississippi itself, but they did penetrate into this section, pushing up the Missouri as far as southeast Dakota. Perhaps they were of the stock that would produce the Central American civilizations, spreading early through the Mississippi basin and dominating the lesser roving tribes there. Perhaps their penetration up the Missouri was part of their last stand in far out-of-way places as their time in the basin waned and the roving tribes overran them. Those too are questions still puzzling prehistorians.

The known tribes of today were next. At least the next that can be cited with some assurance. Even that is difficult because from the beginnings of colonization after Columbus there were dislocations, tribe pushing against tribe in chain reaction westward, and that process was long under way before there were serious efforts at assembling accurate data. What is reasonably clear, however, is that at the time of the discovery of the New World by European explorers, this section was a reasonably well-defined area.

It was Siouan territory, inhabited and held by peoples of the great Siouan tribal family. Their names are written indelibly across our modern section maps; five of the seven states, cities and towns and rivers. It is enough simply to cite major groups: Missouri, Iowa, Kansa, Omaha, Osage, Oto, Ponca, Yankton, Mandan, the Dakotas (Eastern, Santee, Teton). They held the west bank of the Mississippi and westward almost all of the section, a huge island of Siouan territory virtually surrounded by the Algonkin tribes along the east bank of the Mississippi and northward through Canada above them and, with some of the Caddoan tribes, on down the western edges beyond them.

They held it then, firmly. They would stop the brief spreading dominance of the aggressive Iroquois and allies there at the Mississippi. Still holding, they would block the original tribes of the original Northwest Territory along the Great Lakes from retreating westward before the white frontier and thus compel them to make a last ruinous stand in Ohio and Indiana. They would not, could not, hold when the white frontier reached them. But, driven westward in their turn, they would make, those that remained of them, primarily the Dakotas, the final and the strongest stand of their race out on the far northern plains.

Names they would leave, blanketing the land. And a tradition.

To the popular mind American Indians are Sioux Indians, the Dakotas, the Indians of the buffalo nickel. Thanks to movies and the convention of popular artists, they are imbedded in the national, to some extent the continental, consciousness as the prototypes of their race. Their costume, in deference to popular expectation, has become the ceremonial dress of the remnants of almost all tribes from coast to coast except those of the deep southwest whose own tradition is strong. They have entered the national, even the world, folklore, symbols of a conquered race and a vanished way of life.

But they left no impress on the land itself. They lived with it, in balance with it, a natural part of it, making little or no attempt to conquer it in the white man's manner, subdue it, exploit it, wrest wealth from it for an acquisitive, strongly materialistic civilization. When, in the old phrase, Indian title to any portion of it would be "extinguished," whether by treaty or trickery or military action, the land itself would be there, waiting exploitation by the whites, unchanged, almost untouched by the centuries of Indian occupation.

A date to remember is 1541. In that year Coronado, searching out of the southwest for Quivira and its fabled cities of gold, reached a corner of what is now Kansas. In the annals of recorded history, he and the few soldiers with him were the first white men to set foot in the section.

The fact of a strange different land, unexperienced in kind even by the Spanish whose own land in Europe came closest to it, emerges at once, seen now in long hindsight. Coronado turned back because his corn supply was low and he was afraid his horses and men would starve. Unaware, he was traveling through a sea of buffalo grass, finest year-round forage of the entire continent, through herds of buffalo, finest single complete food ever known. . . . And in contemporary accounts of his and other explorers' wanderings the misnaming of the animals of the strange different land was fixed for all later time: buffalo that were not buffalo but bison; prairie dogs that were not dogs but squirrels; rabbits that were not rabbits but hares; antelope that were not antelope but a distinct new species, pronghorn.

No Spanish occupation followed. Gold and silver and manageable natives to convert and to exploit were the New World attractions for the Spanish. There were no precious metals here. The natives were not manageable, did not live in settled towns like the Pueblos of the southwest, were all too many roving raiders and independent warriors themselves. In time some Spanish and the emerging mestizos, the future Mexicans, would do some trading into the area. Inadvertently they would give it the horse and, later, the longhorn. But there was no Spanish colonization.

Something more than a century later the French, working south from Canada and north from the Gulf lowlands, claimed the area, held it—if loose juggling of a huge section of largely unknown land on inaccurate maps in far-off Europe can be called holding it. In simple fact, of course, it was still held by the Siouan tribes, who still lived as they had always lived, only those out on the prairies and plains becoming horsemen now, and tolerating and trading with the few French coming among them.

To the French themselves this was part of the immense tract, almost the entire Mississippi basin east and west, which they claimed under the name of Louisiana. They held it in the loose holding of the time just about another century. But they too made little impress upon it.

What they did do was the first true exploring. By 1700 men like Radisson and Marquette and Joliet and Hennepin had traversed most of what is now Iowa and Minnesota. By 1750 Dutigné had raised the French flag in Kansas, others had followed the Platte through Nebraska, and the Vérendryes, father and sons, had swung through the Dakotas. Fur traders were establishing a few temporary posts. Jesuit missionaries were erecting a few crosses. But all actual French settlements, and these only small compact villages, were on the east side of the Mississippi.

All but one. On the west bank of what is now Missouri was the little village of Ste. Genevieve. From here trips were made westward to salt licks near the Ozarks and on to the lead deposits in the mountains. Ste. Genevieve remained—and remains—the one enduring legacy of the period of French holding, the first town in the entire section.

Off to the northeast the French and Indian War, American phase of the Seven Years' War in Europe, flared through the forests and on the Plains of Abraham by Quebec and in the aftermath those inaccurate maps in far-off Europe were juggled again. By the Treaty of Paris, 1763, France ceded all of Louisiana east of the Mississippi to England, all west to Spain. The area was beginning to be defined on the white men's maps too: the western portion of Louisiana, at last, more than two centuries after Coronado, a Spanish holding.

That made little practical difference, however, little more than a change in royal governors. Spain's time as a world power was passing. The first Spanish governor did not even arrive for the formal transfer until three years after the treaty. Through the forty years of Spanish title only a few Spanish even entered the area. For the most part French officials already there simply carried on. The first new settlers were French too, moving out of the now-English region east of the Mississippi into what would be Missouri. Life drifted on in the area as a whole with little change except an increase in periodic lead mining in the Ozarks and in the fur trade edging up the Missouri River. Even the American Revolution barely touched it, caused only one real flurry of excitement when Virginians under George Rogers Clark advanced to the east bank of the Mississippi to forestall a British advance down the river from Canada which, however grandiose in paper plan in London, dwindled away into nothingness.

There were only three developments of this period of abiding significance. One was the founding of St. Louis as an administrative post up the Mississippi and a further defining of the area as Upper Louisiana, regarded now as a separate province with a lieutenant-governor for it stationed at the new post. The second, by permission of the Spanish authorities, was the pressured removal by the new United States of the once mighty Delawares and some Shawnees, already driven from their lands along the east coast into the Ohio region, on westward across the Mississippi to loosely defined areas in what would be Kansas and Missouri, a foreshadowing of the general policy to be followed as white settlement pushed forward. The third was an even more drastic portent, the start of truly American expansion beyond the big river.

The infant American Congress touched this off with the Northwest Ordinance of 1787. That profoundly pregnant act established not only the principle that American territory beyond the original states would in time be translated into new states but also the method of surveying land in neat mile-square units that would turn vast portions of the growing nation into big symmetrical checkerboards. It also, by prohibiting slavery in the Northwest Territory of the time, deflected pioneer movement from the slave states directly westward instead of northwestward, even caused slaveowners already in the territory to leave. Some of them crossed the Mississippi, most of them into what would be Missouri. And a few years later the Spanish authorities, troubled by British pressures from Canada, particularly in the fur trade, began actively to encourage immigration from the States on the now-seen-to-be-quaint assumption that the hostility of Americans to England would become loyalty to Spain. Land was offered at no expense beyond small fees. Even those payments could be deferred. Religious freedom was promised.

Out of Kentucky and Tennessee into Missouri they came, sons of those who had followed Boone over the Alleghenies, lank backwoodsmen and their families who had licked one wilderness already, the vanguard of American continental empire. They would be Americans wherever they went. But their independence erupted in no trouble. There was no need for it.

Another date to remember is 1803, here the most important of all, to the nation as a whole second in importance only to 1776.

The year of the Louisiana Purchase.

At one stroke the land area of the United States doubled. At one stroke all of this section and more, west and south, became American, direct European influence canceled. The new nation, itself only a string of colonies not long ago, now had a colonial empire of its own, separated from it not by a wide ocean but only by a great river in itself a tremendous asset for trade and travel. And this colonial empire, with the later additions, would be, in a sense, the tail that would wag the dog.

It would intensify, make definite, a process already begun, the turning of the attention and energies of the new nation westward, away from the Atlantic and the long look towards Europe, westward across the great land mass to the far Pacific—a turning, an attitude, that

would become the isolationism of later years and bring the bitter political debates of this present era of world-wide wars.

It would break the balance between North and South and make
the Civil War inevitable—break the balance distinctly in favor of the
North and thus determine that the ideas and ideals of the North would
become dominant.

With its wide stretches of land for the taking it would help push
the new nation, despite temporary panics and depressions, towards unprecedented prosperity, a prosperity based for nearly a century until
the rise of large-scale industrialism upon the steady increase in the
value of land.

And this huge public domain, held by the nation as a whole rather
than by individual states though it would become states, would be a
profound nationalizing force—an area accustomed to look to Washington, not state capitals, for guidance and aid and the solution of
problems. Under its influence the strong federalism of the first eastern states would fade at last into the new nationalism of Theodore
Roosevelt and the new freedom of Woodrow Wilson and the New
Deal of Franklin Roosevelt.

An ocean of land. . . . To be juggled and rejuggled on American
maps now, carved and recarved into territories and finally aligned in
states.

The tempo too changed now with the transfer of title. The whole
process, from still largely unexplored expanse to complete statehood
throughout, would take less than a century, just about eighty-five years.

And the land itself too would be changed, the face of it, the use
of it. The Indians lived with it; the Spanish barely touched it; the
French roamed over it and accepted it and its inhabitants, lived with
them, intermarried with them, were content to take out furs and establish a few tight little villages. Coming now were the Americans
and the increasing tide of immigrants, primarily from north Europe,
who would become Americans—a different breed, hardy, aggressive,
land-hungry, who would sweep the native inhabitants aside and spread
out themselves in ever larger graspings of land units, eager to seize
and exploit every asset of the new land.

How can it be described here, the part played by this section in
the great historic movement that leaped in less than a century west-

ward to the Pacific, farther and over a much greater expanse than had been covered in the previous three centuries? Only in deceptively simplified generalities.

Explorations first, American explorations. Almost immediately the Lewis and Clark expedition struck north and west, up the Missouri and through the northern plains to the true northwest beyond. Then Zebulon M. Pike led his men across what is now Kansas to Pike's Peak and the sources of the Arkansas in the Rockies. A few years later Stephen H. Long led his, following the Platte through what is now Nebraska.

Those were the most important, all within the first years. The reports, particularly those of Pike and Long, in part at least popular reading at the time, made the new nation aware of its colonial empire—and fostered a myth that would plague it. They described the prairies and plains in terms, using the precise word, that created the concept of the Great American Desert. For decades all maps marked much of the section, all textbooks described it as such. There was some truth in the concept in that the land was different, a new kind of land that would not yield to pioneering as known in the east. But it was overdone. It was inaccurate when applied to the prairies, only partially accurate when applied to the plains. The true deserts were further west, in the big bowls between the Rockies and the Sierras.

And the desert concept, the firmly held belief that most of the land west of the Mississippi on to the Rockies was actually desert, uninhabitable in civilized manner, fit only for uncivilized barbarians, had a direct and blighting influence on the nation's Indian policy. Why bother even to face the problem of how to fit the native peoples (those not simply exterminated) into the growing nation, make them a part of the emerging national pattern, when there was all that land, fit only for them, into which they could be driven or deported? And that, in general, passed for Indian policy until there was no more west into which they could be driven or deported and they had been herded onto reservations.

Meanwhile, during those first American years, the first wave of migration beyond the Mississippi was moving into what would be Missouri. This was the portion already fairly well known, already invaded by the vanguard. It was also the portion closest to the southern states whose people, under the impetus of the plantation and slavery system and expanding cotton empire, were pushing westward more rapidly in this period than those of the northern states. The movement slowed with the War of 1812; then, right after the war, swept forward. Within a few years the whole pattern that would be repeated in the other portions was laid down: a forward sweep, collision with the Indians, their removal westward by treaty and trickery and some military action, intense and rising speculation in land, wildcat banking and inflation, temporary collapse of optimism and paper values, then a resurge of hope and forward movement.

By 1820 Missouri Territory, population doubled and trebled in about five years, was clamoring for statehood. The balance between North and South, maintained until now east of the Mississippi, was threatened by developments west.

An attempt to match Missouri with Maine failed. The question of what might happen elsewhere in the vast colonial empire was becoming too strong to be answered with a simple matching of admissions. Out of the great debate came the Missouri Compromise. Missouri would be admitted as a slave state, but slavery would be "forever prohibited" in all the remaining portion of the Louisiana Purchase north of 36°30′, approximately the southern border of what is now Kansas.

In 1821 Missouri was admitted and the United States as a union of states crossed the Mississippi.

On up through the bulk of the vast expanse the land waited, inhabited by its Siouan tribes and the tag ends of others being pushed across the river, crisscrossed increasingly by the trappers following the beaver along the few far watercourses. Some settlers were crossing the Mississippi above Missouri, again the hardy vanguard, but staying close to it and only in small numbers.

The opening of the Erie Canal in 1825 stirred new currents of trade and travel. There was a good route now from New England and the Middle Atlantic states into the Great Lakes region and the land beyond. Another wave of western movement followed, filling in the Indiana and Illinois and Wisconsin area—and spilling on across the Mississippi. The flow was chiefly from the northern states now, emphasis on New England, augmented by strong immigration from Germany. What would be Iowa was the main target west of the Mississippi in this period. Again the forward sweep, the removal of

Indians in the way, the rising speculation in land. By 1838 Iowa was detached as a separate territory and soon after was a state.

Movement into the section slowed in the '40's. Most of Missouri was now settled and the eastern portion of Iowa. There was an edging of settlement up through what would be Minnesota. Much of the first zone, that similar to the eastern states, was now occupied, claimed by the white frontier. What lay ahead was the prairie zone and, beyond, the plain, both marked on all maps and still regarded as the Great American Desert.

The western movement slowed—then leaped across and beyond.

The drive to keep Oregon from the British began the leaping. In the early '40's the Oregon Trail became a well-worn route, out of Independence and Fort Leavenworth on the lower Missouri, up across the prairies to strike the Platte and follow it across what would be Nebraska, on through the Rockies to the true northwest. By '46 Oregon was American territory, clinched by treaty, and the movement slackened—and as the decade approached a close a new call came: Gold in California!

By the thousands the gold seekers and the fiddle-footed and the adventurous streamed across the prairies and plains, deepening the ruts of the Oregon Trail and leaving it in the Rockies to angle towards the Sacramento-San Francisco area, deepening too those of the Santa Fe Trail that swung down through the southwest out of what would be Kansas for a southern route to the golden fleece.

In the one long leaping and the one decade the frontier advanced more than a thousand miles—crossing and spurning the new land, the new kind of land—to a region, timbered and well-watered, like that already known and experienced back in the east.

But this remained: Those crossing had seen the new kind of land, not on maps under the desert label but as it was, and in time many of them would backtrack to it. And out across the expanse in a scattered sprinkling along the main routes were a few Army forts established to protect the travelers from Indian raids and a few trail or road ranches where those travelers could stop to rest and trade for fresh draft animals and regroup before moving on.

And out of the necessity to cross the prairies and plains, to get across, had come the symbol of western pioneering that in its turn would enter the national folklore: the covered wagon, the long train of covered wagons wheeling ever westward into a limitless horizon.

The '50's, for this section, belonged to Minnesota and Kansas.

They opened with the Minnesota Road Act pushed through a reluctant Congress by representatives of the adjacent area, providing for the construction of four roads and survey of a fifth in the territory recently separated and organized under the Minnesota name. Similar aid had been tried experimentally a few years before in Wisconsin. But this act with formal annunciation of policy can be regarded as the beginning of direct action through the national government, other than exploratory or military, to aid settlement and commerce across the Mississippi, a policy that would be followed in other territories and in encouraging transcontinental railroads.

Again the forward sweep of settlement, completing now the claiming of the first, the timbered zone, edging out some into the next, the prairie, and the collision with the Indians, ended this time by the Treaty of Traverse de Sioux which moved them into the western part of the territory. Again rising speculation in land, the influx of settlers primarily out of the northern states, augmented again by German immigration and, as the tide of general immigration was swelling, by many peoples now from the Scandinavian countries.

The panic of '57, the collapse of the nation-wide inflation that had been boomed for nearly a decade by the flow of gold from California, pricked now when the New York banks suspended specie payments, slowed the movement almost to a halt. That winter, too, was the worst of many years, the land itself showing its prairie strength, discouraging further advance. No matter. Minnesota had been claimed. It was admitted as a state the following year.

Meanwhile, southward in what would be Kansas, another movement was taking place, not as important in terms of actual settlement, much more important in another sense, as a preview of the Civil War.

The new Compromise of 1850, hammered out over the admission of California as a free state, had revived the issue of slavery in the western territories despite the "forever" prohibition of the Missouri Compromise. The weight of these western territories was swinging the balance inevitably in favor of the North. Acquisition of southwest territory with the Mexican War and annexation of Texas had made no real difference. These were definitely southern, yes; but nature had provided an effective block to expansion of the plantation system and the cotton empire. Simple insurmountable facts: lack of rainfall and rising altitude with too-short growing season. The South, as an economic and political sectional entity, was hemmed in, steadily losing power and influence in the growing nation. There in eastern Kansas it would make its last struggle short of actual secession.

Out of Illinois, itself a "western" territory not long ago, where northern and southern settlers had mingled and sectional rivalries meant little under frontier conditions and the democratic spirit was strong, emerged Stephen A. Douglas with his slogan of "popular sovereignty." The Kansas-Nebraska Bill was enacted in mid-1854 creating two territories, Kansas and Nebraska, opening them to settlement with the provision that each, when later admitted as a state, should decide for itself by popular vote whether to be free or slave. A noble experiment, a well-meant attempt to preserve the Union by democratic means. And also against the temper of the times, an open invitation to trouble. The implication was plain. There would be no more compromises.

Nebraska was too far north for any immediate southern hopes. Eastern Kansas became the battleground.

Disorder and actual strife over control of the territorial government flared within a matter of months as the opposing vanguards of settlers met. Emigrant societies were organized in the northern states to encourage and help finance free-soil and abolitionist colonies. Crates of "Beecher's Bibles"—Sharps rifles—were sent to those colonies. Missourians in armed bands stormed across the border to swing the scattered locality elections for territorial delegates. Each faction organized a territorial government and clamored for recognition by Congress. The rising town of Lawrence, stronghold of the abolitionists, was besieged and partially destroyed by the southern faction. John Brown and sons, fanatic free-soilers, staged their infamous Potawatomie massacres. Raids and bloodshed became common and the first impromptu battles of the coming war were fought on the Kansas prairies.

The outcome, of course, was never in doubt. Kansas was prairie-plain. Slavery and a system based upon it could not flourish there. The North, already much more populous, could furnish more settlers. Several years of turmoil and the troubles in Kansas subsided with a free-state government in control. But the distant thunder of the advancing storm that would shake the nation had sounded; the preview complete to inevitable outcome had been provided.

The movement into Kansas slackened, as had that into Minnesota, with the panic of '57 and under the impact of the prairie itself. Settlement had not pushed far west, was confined to the eastern border. Discovery of gold in the Rockies, in what is now Colorado, shifted attention again on beyond, on across. New implements, new ways of pioneering, would be needed before the real claiming sweeps out onto the prairies and the plains.

The Civil War intervened. That has scant place here, pertains primarily to the states east of the Mississippi. There was border warfare in the border area of the section, Missouri and Kansas, a particularly nasty kind of warfare as such semiofficial, semiguerilla groups as Lane's brigade (Union) and Quantrell's raiders (Confederate) burned and pillaged and outraged more like outlaw brigands than military forces under orders. Yet that was merely peripheral activity insignificant against the great struggle eastward.

There are several points, however, to note. One is that this section, what there was of it settled, was a strong asset to the North, supplying men and regiments out of all proportion to population. Another is that the section held as a section; the influence of the land, the westward-looking land shaping its people to their own independent individualism and strong nationalism, held throughout. Even Missouri, southern in general character, settled by southerners, admitted as a slave state, numbering thousands of slaves on its census rolls, active southern leader in the struggle for Kansas—even Missouri, when the final test came, swung to the Union. In the special state election held on the specific secession issue, the Union ticket won with a decisive majority.

Up to the war the first tier of states had been organized and admitted. Kansas too, of the second tier, had become a state, admitted in early 1861—though that was as much a political maneuver (another free-soil state at a critical time) as a recognition of settlement. The first zone, the timbered and well-watered, had been claimed and an edging made out on the prairies, chiefly along the watercourses and the cross-section trails.

During the war movement into the section continued, not on any major scale but consistent, most of it confined to the filling in of still-open patches in the first zone. Travel on across to the other frontier, California and the Oregon country, continued too, even picking up momentum again with the discovery of gold in what is now Montana. The desert myth was dying—just as the time was approaching when renewed respect for the residue of truth in it might have tempered the suffering and misfortune of many an over-optimistic immigrant family.

In the decades following the war the greatest land settlement surges in all history were unleashed.

Conditions and the time were right.

The eastern portion of the nation was now, in terms of the still largely agricultural economy, closely settled. In many areas were actual population surpluses that would have to spill on westward. In the northern states the war, taking thousands of men from their homes, had created a new restlessness, a widening of horizons. In the southern states were thousands more, the defeated, the dispossessed, unable or unwilling to re-establish themselves in the bitter reconstruction era, who looked westward for new opportunity. Out on the prairies would begin the first real binding of the nation's wounds as streams of northern and southern settlement would meet and merge and under common circumstances and shared hardships forget the sectional animosities of the past. Immigration too into the United States was now rising to its peak. Land, freehold land, the dream of millions in Europe, not under an age-encrusted aristocratic system but under a democratic laissez-faire government, was a reality across the Atlantic. Westward that land waited.

The pattern of the Minnesota Road Act was being followed, pushed on an enlarged scale. Roads and road surveys were starting across Nebraska and Dakota Territories. Railroads now gridironed the east, up to the Mississippi, beginning to push past, one line already to St. Joseph on the Missouri. The national government, accustomed by the war to huge expenditures, taught by it the value of sectional rail links, was encouraging rail building towards the Pacific with enormous bond and land grants. The Union Pacific and Kansas Pacific were creeping out over the southern prairies. The Northern Pacific was surveying its new right of way across Dakota. In the east railroads had followed population. Here in the great open spaces they would lead and settlement would follow and boom construction towns would rise and keep pace westward with them.

The basic land laws covering the public domain had been changed. Long since the original notions of the early Federalists that the public domain should be opened in segments, a single territory-to-be-a-state at a time, and that the sale of public lands should be a primary source of revenue, had been abandoned. Popular pressures had demanded ever more indiscriminate opening of territory and ever cheaper prices for the land itself. Now the Homestead Law, passed during the war, had gone the whole way. It threw open virtually the entire western domain and with no price tag at all, no cost for a plot of land beyond a negligible filing fee, subject only to the requirements that a homesteader live a certain part of each year on his claim for five years and that he make certain minimum improvements.

And it reversed a trend that would have been definitely crippling. From the beginning American land laws had whittled down the size of land units available to settlers, from the 640 of the first laws to the 40 of the period just before the war. That had been sensible, logical, in the forested east. There a pioneer family, with the tools of the time, could not well clear and cultivate more than 40 acres—and, since the land had a price tag, usually did not want more. There a pioneer family, in most areas, could manage to extract a living from 40 acres of the moist loamed soil. Ahead now was the new kind of land. Forty acres, with or without a price tag, would be a joke, a grim joke, for anyone trying to eke out a living from them in that vast sun-baked wind-swept expanse. The Homestead Law raised the figure to 160.

That too was inadequate except in the richest stretches of bottom land along the watercourses or when applied to possible townsites. It would be utterly and tragically ridiculous out where the prairies faded into the plains. It would encourage fraud and evasion, make these almost necessities in the scramble for land in large enough chunks to be practically useful. It would encourage too the scramble for land, not to be used, simply to be held long enough for title to be established then sold. But it did give the true settlers more of a fighting chance against the new environment.

With singular appropriateness the first homestead taken was in Nebraska, just beyond the Missouri, where the prairies rolled on westward. The law was to go into effect January 1st, 1863. Just after midnight on New Year's Eve the land office at Nebraska City was opened to permit David Freeman (even the name was appropriate), a Union soldier on brief furlough, to file the first claim before leaving to rejoin his regiment.

Explorer . . . fur trader . . . miner . . . cattleman . . . farmer. That was the historic procession and sequence marking every western frontier across the continent. These prairies and plains had known explorers, Spanish and French and American. Fur traders had penetrated through them, trapping out the beaver, turning to the traffic in buffalo hides. Miners had crossed them to the gold fields beyond. Now came the cattlemen and the farmers.

They came together, at the same time. There was land enough for a while for them both, then out of the conflict of interests, of land uses, emerged the general division, the cattlemen on the plains, the farmers on the prairies.

They came better equipped than those who had preceded them. The breech-loading rifle had been developed during the war. The metallic cartridge, easy to carry, simple to load, was coming into use. The revolver, the six-shooter, the famous Colt equalizer, was at last being produced in quantity. Ideal weapon for the horseman, it had already tipped the scale against the plains Indians down in Texas and would blaze its way, not only against Indians, across the prairies and plains. The steel plow was becoming common, able to rip through the tough prairie sod that had blunted and balked the old wood and iron shares of the firstcomers. Methods of dugout and sod-house construction, the only immediate answer to lack of timber, had been developed. And those firstcomers had learned from the Indians the use of buffalo and cow chips and twisted hay for fuel. There would be surprisingly efficient hay-burning stoves invented during the next years.

Down in Texas during the war, with men to ride roundup almost as scarce as markets, semiwild longhorns, descendants of the original Spanish cattle, had multiplied into the millions. There were markets again now—in the populous north and east. Fortunes dangled for the men who got them to those markets.

Trail drives northward started in '66. Within a few years they were a wide, multitudinous movement. The first were aimed at the advancing railheads for cattle shipments eastward. One by one the once-famous cow towns, Abilene and Wichita and Ogallala and Newton and Dodge City and others, bloomed and blazed in brief wild wickedness with cavorting cowboys and gamblers and prostitutes and gun-toting marshals and then were tamed and dwindled into normal railside towns. Meanwhile more and more of the trail herds stayed in the section, spreading out over it and into the territories beyond, seeding the great range industry whose swift sweeping heyday was one of the wonders of the period.

A sea of grass . . . western grass, those tough scrawny varieties, poor-looking to eyes accustomed to lush eastern pastures yet amazingly nutritious for stock and, better yet, winter-curing on the stem, good forage in winter as in summer. There were only two real obstacles in the way: the Indians and the myriad buffalo, the one dependent upon the other.

Since the Kansas-Nebraska Bill and the start of settlement out on the prairies there had been increasing Indian trouble. The last strongholds of the native peoples were being invaded. During the war the Sioux in western Minnesota had risen and been driven on into Dakota. All through what would be the second tier of states there was now scattered raiding and fighting, always with the same ultimate result. The Indians might win battles as they did in the Red Cloud War of '67–'68 and again in the campaigns of the '70's which included the Custer "massacre." Always when the fighting waned they had been pushed on westward or confined to reservations.

The countless movies and western stories of these later days have not yet even begun to exhaust, let alone to handle adequately, the epic material of the western Indian wars. In an historic sense, however, those wars fade before the even more drastic war against the buffalo. When the buffalo were gone, the plains Indians and the remnants of the tribes pushed out on the plains were literally starved into submission. They were defeated, in the ultimate sense, by the destruction of the economic base of their way of life.

Inroads had been made on the tremendous herds before and during the war. Hunting to feed road and rail construction crews now became a business in itself, soon dwarfed by hunting for the hides alone. The heavy Sharps breech-loader was the perfect weapon. Railheads were now available for shipping. Hides by the hundreds of thousands, then by the millions, went eastward. By 1875 the southern herds, separated now from the northern by the westering railroads, were virtually cleaned out of the section, existing only in scattered remainders down through the Indian Territory and the southwest. By the early '80's the northern herds too were gone, the last survivors being pursued into the final fastnesses of Wyoming and Montana. The stench of rotting carcasses would linger a while and bone-collecting for eastern fertilizer plants would help homestead families eke out a living for a few years. But the buffalo were gone.

Hard on the heels of the hunters came the cattlemen. This was the era of the open range, when land titles meant little and range rights meant much and he who could first claim a water hole or stream controlled the grassland of the watershed. Within little more than a decade the herds had swept over the prairies and plains and cattle grazed even in the broken badlands of Dakota. This was the true era too of the cowboy, before he became romanticized and conventionalized into the over-costumed caricature of later years. Usually young, ignorant, narrow-minded—and at the same time hardy, resourceful, intensely loyal to his outfit, faithful to far lonely trust, gallant in his own way, courageous in simple acceptance of daily often hourly danger and life-risk as part of the underpaid job—he took the semiwild longhorn through hell and high water and drought and Indian raid two thousand miles and more out of Texas to the farthest shores of the sea of grass.

Ranching was suddenly popular, even fashionable. Money poured into it from the east, from Europe. Wealthy easterners and titled Europeans went west to inspect their investments on the hoof, a few to try the "strenuous" life, young Theodore Roosevelt with them. The winter of '80–'81 gave warning. It was not heeded. The boom raced on; overstocking of the range continued. The winter of '86–'87 clamped down early; blizzard followed blizzard, packing the fine snow hard over the vital grasses. Late spring, long delayed, saw herd losses of from 50 to 90 percent across the great expanse. The boom was broken. The cattle business on the prairies and plains settled to the long pull into a more prosaic, more practical operation.

It had never been as important as it has loomed, still looms, in folklore and popular imagination. At its peak it could not number nearly as many cattle as there were on the myriad farms east of the Mississippi. What it had was flavor, sweep, scope, the handling of cattle not in small barnyard lots but in big herds on wide open range. Its symbol, the cowboy, would soon become literally just a hired man on horseback, later a hired man in a jeep. But briefly, superbly, he had had his day.

The homesteader, the sodbuster, was having his day too. He was more important in numbers and impact, but he did not stand out as distinctly. He was part of a mixed motley movement that was making all previous frontiers of settlement seem almost neat, orderly developments.

In the release of the Civil War's ending, "western fever" swept the nation. By the thousands, by the tens of thousands, land seekers streamed westward. Land unending! Land without forests to be cleared away! Land without a price tag! Land to live on and farm. Land to acquire and sell. Land for townsite speculation in pyramiding of prices. And not only land. Because of it, because of the skyrocketing of population in the territories, wonderful opportunities, economic and political, for the shrewd and the farsighted and the unscrupulous too.

Even old-hand settlers already established in the first zone were caught in the fever, carried on westward again. And the backwash from the west coast and the mountain mining camps added impetus, presenting the paradox of people moving eastward to take up western land.

Wildcat banking and all manner of speculative schemes were rampant. Town building became a mania. Rival town companies and the railroads, themselves establishing towns on their railside grants, sent agents and advertising everywhere. Competition for county seats erupted into election frauds and kidnapings of records and pitched brawls. Towns boomed—and died. Here and there some boomed—and endured.

Town building became a mania—and a swindling device. Prepare a fine-looking town map, sketch in streets not yet graded and never to be graded, buildings not yet built and never to be built—and go back east a bit and sell town lots to suckers. Why not? Almost everyone seemed to be either heading west or looking for a chance to invest in the western boom.

Through the turmoil and confusion and speculation, the true land seekers, the land-hungry, were moving, fanning out over the prairies, first along the old trails and stage lines and new rail lines, then filling in between, staking their claims and hurrying to the land offices, adding to the national lexicon the popular phrase: "land-office business." The population of Kansas doubled, tripled. Almost overnight Nebraska was a state. Early comers there told of seeing 500 to 1000 wagons a day rolling past. Farther north in Dakota, not yet on the same scale, they were rolling into the "Jim" River and the Red River valleys.

Westward, out on the prairies, encouraged by several years of fair rainfall and relatively mild winters. Then smack into a series of disasters. Easter week of '73 and a blizzard started, caught the homesteaders unprepared, killed off their livestock, killed some of them too, blocked travel. Before the year was much older the panic of '73, caused primarily by collapse of overblown confidence and speculation in the western railroads, was chilling the western fever in the rest of the country too. Then, in '74, the grasshoppers came.

That is still known as the grasshopper year.

It started well, with a favorable spring, a crop-promising early summer. And late in July the swarms came, darkening the skies, piling up inches deep over the ground, stopping trains with oily heaps over the tracks, devouring almost all crops, everything green. Not everything. They seemed to be a scourge directed deliberately at the settlers, an agency of the land striking at those who had broken its ages-old sod. They devoured the crops the settlers had brought with them, even eating turnips right out of the ground, stripping the planted fruit trees —and left untouched the native grasses.

The westward movement slowed, stopped, even dropped back. Many a homesteader faced eastward again in defeat. Many another hung on just long enough to wangle a mortgage, supposedly for improvements, from some still-optimistic eastern company with an agent in the field—and departed, figuring that was the best he could ever extract from the land. Many a town dwindled, died.

The western fever was broken, finished as an overall excitement. But not the land-hunger, the itch, the ache of tens of thousands back through the eastern states and of the immigrants streaming across the Atlantic for a piece of land, a new start in life. Perhaps gold in the Black Hills of Dakota started the resurge of optimism. No. That was only a ripple in the new advance. Land-hunger still dominated in a still largely agricultural era. And westward great stretches of the ocean of land still waited. The western movement swept forward again.

And again better equipped than before.

The homesteader with his 160 acres would still be the basic unit. But the land laws were beginning to recognize the need for larger units. They were still not adequate, would never be adequate, because framed by easterners unable or politically unwilling to grasp the true conditions. Major John Wesley Powell made his now-famous then-ignored report, outlining the types of land available, urging claims up to 2560 acres out on the plains where grazing was the sole practical use. It was promptly shelved. But some concessions were made. Under special provisions (timber culture, irrigation, ridiculous notions for a region where trees would not survive, water for irrigation was scant and beyond the reach of individuals) more land could be acquired— and ways of winking those provisions aside were soon learned.

Farm machinery adapted to big units was becoming available. The gang plow, the steam plow, the harvester, the thresher, developed in the midwest, were ready now for the attack on the wide open spaces.

Fencing, vital problem in a treeless land, had been licked. Several decades of experiment with hedges and smooth-wire devices had culminated in a rush of patents. Out of these had come barbed wire, and this was rolling west by the ton, by the carload. It would be the major weapon of the homesteaders against the cattlemen. They had welcomed the passing herds at first. These left a good supply of drying chips for fuel and calves born along the way, too small and weak to be taken along, were usually left for the homesteaders to claim. Now, with settlement filling in whole areas, the conflict between crop-farming and open-range grazing was becoming acute. Barbed wire would help decide it and arguments over fencing-in vs. fencing-out laws and bitter fence-cutting feuds would develop before the final decision.

Wind, a constant of the land, was being turned to advantage. In conjunction with well-drilling, which was replacing well-digging, the new small-solid-bladed self-adjusting windmill could bring up subsur-

110. An infrared photograph of a couple strolling in the Ozarks of Missouri.

111. Missouri River commerce. This towboat, with a 1600-ton cargo of steel, averaged 6½ miles per hour upstream between Kansas City and Omaha.

112. Downtown St. Louis.

113. Downtown Kansas City.

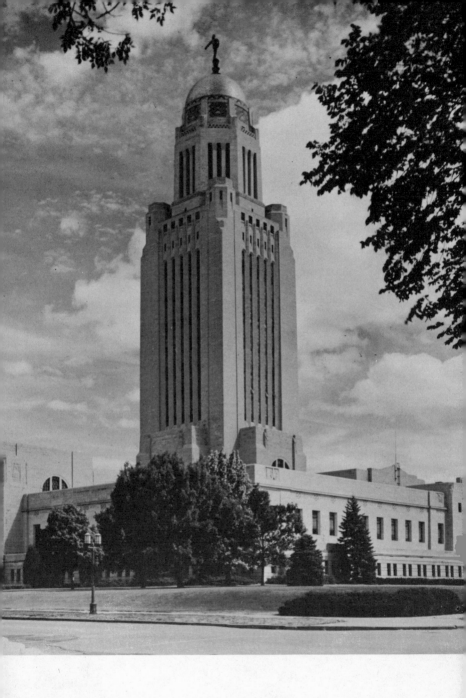

114. The state Capitol of Nebraska, at Lincoln. This is one of the few state capitols that either omit or subordinate the dome as an architectural element.

115. Evidence — if that were needed — that there is oil in North Dakota.

116. In the Badlands of southwestern South Dakota.

7. At Lake of the Woods, where Minnesota, Ontario, and Manitoba
meet, the international boundary swings northward about 30 miles beyond
the 49th parallel.

118. One of the processes involved in the corn-hog economy of Iow

119. Another familiar sight in rural Iowa.

120. Here, the corn is converted into hogs.

21. Strip farming in Minnesota. Like contour plowing, such an arrangement of crops avoids runoff of water and retards erosion.

122.   Harvesting wheat in Kansas, the heart of the winter-wheat belt.

123.   On a cattle ranch in South Dakota.

face water. Not many settlers could afford ready-made windmills at once—but homemade contrivances patterned on them would suffice for a while.

The movement accelerated in the late '70's and by the '80's was at full tide, the biggest, the solidest land rush in the records of the westering frontiers. The territorial and new-state governments were pouring forth literature and all types of publicity, denouncing each other's possibilities, boosting their own. The railroads now had agents scattered even through Europe, offering special rates for migrations of whole colonies at a time. The population of Kansas doubled again, that of Nebraska tripled. That of Dakota, still one territory (division and twin statehood came in '89), soared. There were weeks when an average of 9000 immigrants a day passed through Chicago, 8000 of them ticketed to Dakota. The famous bonanza farms bloomed through the Red River valley and on westward. Individuals, partnerships, syndicates gathered land by whatever means, some by purchase in big chunks from the rail grants, and with the new machinery sowed wheat in 1000-acre fields. Abraham Lincoln's prophetic reference, in his second annual message to Congress, to the territories of the Mississippi basin as the "Egypt of the West" was becoming a definitive fact. Within a few years the center of American wheat production swung west across the Mississippi, followed fast by that of corn.

Westward, ever westward, out across the second zone, the prairies, with the homesteader, the little man with his little piece of land and his high hopes, leading the way, driving his stakes, struggling with his sod house or tar-paper shack, ripping with his steel plow through the ancient sod, bringing with him the courage and persistence and willingness to work that had conquered two-thirds of the entire continental sweep, that was completing the conquest of two-thirds of this section, this ocean of land.

He was led westward by several seemingly good seasons. Westward, out onto the plains themselves—to collide at last with the true west, the land that would not be tamed, that would not be domesticated to farm land and populous towns, the land that would only be lived with, co-operated with, accepted on its own stern terms.

Courage . . . persistence . . . willingness to work . . . even the new equipment—these were not enough. In the further western territories, in the Rockies and the bowls beyond, the attempt had not, would not ever be made to spread out and subdue the land. Population would remain in separated clusters in the valleys and a few favored locations and the mining areas. Here, on the plains, the battle was fought, the settlers against the land. The wave of settlement thrust forward and expended itself and fell back and renewed itself and fell back again. The American pioneer was defeated at last. Not defeated. Matched. Forced to adapt himself and his ways after the tempering of the transition zone to the environment of this third zone as before, across two thousand miles and on the west coast, he had adapted the environment to himself and his ways.

Even today signs of the defeat, the matching, remain. Humped earth of old dugouts, tangles of old wire, marks of old furrows and ruts of old roadways are scattered across the rolling sea-like miles where home-steaders tried and failed and the land endured them for a few years and in the callous indifference of its own strength drove them back. Old weathered boards, once freighted long miles, lie among the bunched native grasses and sagebrush where false-fronted hopeful towns once sought to defy the limitless horizons. Those who tried and retried to use this land in the eastern manner failed and were driven back. Those who could adapt to it remained, but they were few against the immensity of the spaces.

So few that large tracts, despite the areas set aside for Indian reser-vations, were still public domain, unclaimed, and the land laws were amended and amended again on into the early years of the new cen-tury, offering larger units, up again to 640 acres, a mile square at a time. More people came through the years, a thin sprinkling out over the spaces, no longer settlers in the old manner, westerners adapting to the land. And still long stretches remained, and remain, public domain.

The cattlemen learned that barbed wire was an asset—barbed wire coupled with the windmill bringing up water, not much perhaps but enough for them, where wanted. With it they transformed the big-range country into the big-pasture country, in the process taking back to grazing much territory once plowed in vain by the home-steaders. With fenced pastures, though these might be huge in extent, breeding could be controlled and they turned to improvement of stock, the squat, bulky Hereford and the shorthorn and some Angus replac-ing the rangy, bony longhorn. The great partnership between cattle raising in the western portion of the section and cattle finishing in the big feed lots of the grain-growing eastern portion took shape. There in the eastern portion a steadily increasing proportion of the great grain crops went to market on the hoof, in the form of western cattle finished on milled feeds and local hogs fattened on the tall field corn.

In the transition edging where rainfall was uncertain, sometimes adequate, more often not, the farmer became the farmer-rancher, achieving stability by diversifying his land uses. The windmill was his salvation. It had scant potentialities for irrigation. But its small steady supply of water sufficed for family use, for a family garden, and for some stock. He could make out, get by, in the drought years— and once in a while, in a good year, temporarily replenish his pocket-book with a cash crop. Contrast with the east was evident. There a small pasture was an adjunct to cultivated fields. Here a cultivated field was an adjunct to pasture land.

The development of dry farming, particularly strong in Nebraska, helped him too. New methods of cultivation, conserving what moisture fell during several seasons between plantings or early in one good season, made more frequent crops possible. Crop farming pushed again a bit farther west—and stopped again against the plains.

Generalities . . . generalities. . . . Never take them as gospel. They make markings and movements seem sharp and distinct, neatly out-lined, and miss the endless overlappings and shadings and mergings. They skim off the thin layer of summing fact and miss the reality beneath. These were people moving westward out of the burgeoning east, out of far old Europe, into the new land. Not statistics, not im-personal moving forces, not abstract entities in mass, but people. In-dividuals in an individualistic society taking the American dream of independent competency for the common man and the white Ameri-cans' arrogant belief in manifest destiny westward with them.

The frontier pattern had repeated itself west of the Mississippi, sharper, more distinct, on a larger scale, just as the physical aspects of the advance were larger, life moving faster and with more momen-tum, expanding into more space towards more remote horizons. These people had put their impress upon the land, made it theirs. They had converted the first zone into an extension of the eastern states, checkerboarded into fertile farms, spotted with growing towns, the best-located becoming true cities, each firmly based on the past and in the present: St. Louis, once gateway to the west and great river town becoming a great railroad city; Kansas City, sprawling trade center where the old Santa Fe and the Oregon Trails had started; Davenport, strategically located at the most practicable bridge-crossing along the upper Mississippi; Des Moines, dedicated to the making and distribution of farm equipment; Minneapolis-St. Paul, milling capital of the wheat country. They had turned the second zone into an agricultural empire, again checkerboarded on the basic survey pattern but in larger units, known now and not in jest as the breadbasket of the western world. They had penetrated the third zone and achieved there a truce, a balance with it. Land, the ocean of land, was the major resource. They were using it. And that too was not enough.

The nation was changing. Agriculture was losing predominant importance. Industry and finance were taking over. These controlled the railroads, the shipping facilities, the crop markets and the money markets. The people of this section, like many in the midwestern states east of them and most in the territories-becoming-states west of them, were caught in the squeeze between high freight and interest rates and low prices for their products—all beyond their control, manipulated in the industrial and financial centers of the eastern states. And the physical frontier had faded, the land had been overrun; no new opportunity, new impetus for hope, now lay just over the western horizon.

But the land, this ocean of land, had in its turn made its impress upon them. Advancing into it, adapting to it, they had become, more sharply than their pioneer antecedents eastward, innovators, radicals in the true sense of the word, accustomed to change, to devising new ways, new techniques. Unfettered by federalism, they had become accustomed to direct national action to meet problems. It was logical, inevitable, that this section should become a breeding ground for grass-roots reform movements, develop co-operatives, demand national regulation of railroads and antitrust legislation, send to Washington senators and representatives called progressives at home, regarded as sons of the wild jackass in the conservative east. The Grange movement, the Greenback party, the Populist party, these were strong in their times all through the section. It was no accident of birth that

a William Jennings Bryan, asserting that mankind must not be cruci-
fied upon a cross of gold, should come out of Nebraska. It was logical
too that the people of this now-depressed agricultural section should
eventually join, in a merging of basic interests, with the depressed
workers of the industrial areas eastward in support of the sweeping
farm and labor reforms of recent decades. And it is at least symbolic
that the swing to national action on wide social and economic fronts
should have become definite, taken firm shape, under Theodore
Roosevelt, chronicler of some aspects of the western movement and
first President to have had direct personal experience beyond the Mississippi, out on the ocean of land.

That was the strength of the people, the tough, resilient practicality
of pragmatic folk adapting to a new environment, refusing to accept
an inferior economic position as an immutable fact beyond manipulation. The point has often been made that the United States, in its
growing stages, was not so much a nation as a huge commercial enterprise devoted to the grabbing and exploitation of vast territories. That
was particularly true of this section, where pioneering was telescoped
in time, the swift transition in area after area from open "wild" land
to settled "civilized" exploitation compassed in less than a single
generation. The conquest of the land and the struggle against the last
unconquerable portion, the drive to establish a practical primarily
middle-class society as rapidly as possible where only a few years
before Indians had roamed, monopolized attention and energies.
There was scant time for art and literature, what were usually referred
to as the refinements of culture. In the inescapable pioneer pattern
these were regarded as fringe adornments, relatively unimportant
against the problems of material progress, simply accepted from elsewhere at second hand. Innovators, radicals, progressives in politics
and economics, the people of the great growing inland empire looked
eastward for cultural leadership just as, for so long and so subser-
viently, those of the eastern states looked even further eastward to
Europe.

They had strong respect for education in the tradition of the westering New Englanders scattered among them; established schools
everywhere almost as quickly as stores and banks and saloons; soon
spotted the region with small colleges and burgeoning state universities on the model of those in the region just east, Wisconsin and

Illinois and Michigan and Indiana. The pressures of practicality dominated again. There was increasing emphasis upon ever more democracy in education, upon meeting the needs of all the population, upon vocational training and applied science, particularly in engineering and agriculture. Education too was a practical matter, more a preparation for earning a living than a disciplining of the mind in the liberal humanities.

Here, if anywhere, one might say, in the heartland of the continent, far from both coasts and foreign influences, where the American dream had its widest open-handed application, truly American voices would rise in the arts, speaking for a native culture. They were few, most of them feeble, no match in their field for the vigorous shoutings of the politicians and businessmen in theirs. Practicality reigned; the lonely talented usually departed for the east where cultural standards, still based primarily on Europe, were set.

A Mark Twain came out of Missouri sounding the healthy barbaric yawp of the back country and the west, the voice of the new democracy that would do its own thinking, see with its own eyes, put value only on the vital and the genuine—and went east and settled in Connecticut and ended his career writing about Christian Science and a Connecticut Yankee in old-time England and the medieval Joan of Arc. A Hamlin Garland came out of the midwest, calling for a new Americanism in literature, writing with earnest honesty about the land and its people—and was seduced to Boston and became almost petulantly critical of that land and its people because they were not rushing ardently ahead to establish outposts of pure Bostonian culture.

And meanwhile an Ed Howe and, a little later, a William Allen White, novelists and newspapermen in Kansas, were the real spokesmen for the section, accepted as such, successful as such, able men, down-to-earth sharp-witted men—and basically staunch exponents of practical material-progress common sense.

The pioneer cycle always repeats. The first generations, overcoming or adapting to the wilderness, push the crudities of beginnings as rapidly as possible into the background, tend to ignore them, be ashamed of them, try to forget them. In the urge to acquire comfort and "culture," they look to the older regions, miss most of the significance of what they themselves are and have done and what is about them. They are busy doing—and thinking in terms of that doing. It is their children or grandchildren who, later, when comfort has been achieved and the imperatives of doing have lessened and there is more time for leisure, begin to look back at the beginnings and their results and grope towards native self-expression. Just so here. In the first decades of this century new voices were rising. Out of Nebraska came Willa Cather, writing of youth in pioneer times seen now through the golden haze of remembrance, and John G. Neihardt with his long swinging songs of splendid wayfarings and old Hugh Glass and the grizzly and the Indian wars. Out of Iowa, Ruth Suckow, writing of the farms and their people with realism and understanding, and Herbert Quick with his solid readable novels of the early days and a Vandemark's pioneer folly. Out of Minnesota, lean red-topped Sinclair Lewis slashing at the babbitry of a hundred monotonous stifling main streets. Out of Dakota, O. E. Rolvaag with his superb, strangely moving stories of Norwegian immigrants who wrestled there with the giants in the earth.

There were others and there continue to be others; names plucked almost at random out of recent reading memory: Paul Corey, Paul Engle, John Selby, Mari Sandoz, Hartzell Spence, Wallace Stegner, Phil Stong. Some stay staunchly at home in the region; others, in the fluidity of the times, wander the whole country; but the touch of their own beginnings remains.

The universities too are strong in the stirrings. Still firm and practical in vocational training, they have broadened their curricula, widened their horizons, drawn scholars and creative artists to their faculties. Their presses publish steadily, outside the stream of strictly commercial works, with emphasis on the history and development of the region itself. The very practicality of their beginnings is perhaps an asset. They are freer of the usual strictly academic blight, less tinged by arty, avant-garde, cultish, little-quarterly folderol, than so many others eastward toward the Atlantic.

And, paradoxically, yet not so, this is the region which has given the strongest leadership in a truly American art. Three names stand out: John Steuart Curry of Kansas, who early saw the environment of the region, the life and the land about him, not as something to escape from, to be shunned, but as his inalienable birthright as an artist, and has caught it on canvas with a combination of haunting realism and poetic personal understanding; Grant Wood of Iowa, who tried to escape in a sense of cultural inferiority and again and again made pilgrimage to Europe—and always returned and at last, in rebellion back with his own beginnings, broke through to his own dynamic, personally stylized interpretations; and Thomas H. Benton of Missouri, who too turned away and sought inspiration in the art circles of Paris—and came back, in rebellion too, and has painted, in all its strength and vulgarity and richness and restless changing and aspiration, his America in his own way.

The section lines are gone now, marked only on maps. The first zone merges, indistinguishable in essentials, domesticated in the same manner, into the area bordering it on the east. The third zone merges imperceptibly, with no discernible change, into the area bordering it on the west. Only in the middle zone does it remain distinct, something in itself, where the east meets the west in the heartland of the continent. Even here the picture blurs, the standardizing uniformity of modern America overlays ever more the national similarities. This is no longer a section but an integral part of the United States, absorbed into the nation. What happens elsewhere, happens here.

And yet . . . nowhere else across the whole sweep of the continent is land itself still so predominantly the basic resource. Cities rise, towns multiply, the few mineral resources are tapped, industry creeps out over it—and still the land rules, the land and the people using it. Not many are rooted in it in the old-time European sense of the peasant and his plot of land. They are modern Americans in tune with the fluidity and flexibility of the times. By the thousands every year the old folks, having used their pieces of it, extracted a competency from it, sell out or turn over to the young folks—and depart for the softer climate and easier living of, say, Florida or southern California. But they have lived here, on the ocean of land, have used it and been used by it, and its impress is forever upon them.

To fly out over it now, westward as the migrations moved, is to see the past stamped indelibly into the present.

Westward, across the Mississippi, out over the first zone, where the only real cities of the whole section sprawl, becoming huge, ungainly, sending out their streamers of billboarded neon-lighted motel-spotted business districts through the housing-development suburbs, where growing towns, each a copy of the others, dot the wide areas and all between is an almost unbroken checkerboard of neat farms, wood lots marking many, barns and silos overshadowing the neat frame houses that long since replaced the original cabins.

Westward, out over the prairies, and the cities are left behind, there are only towns, almost all on rail lines striking due west, a few approaching the city stage but not yet sprawling, far-spaced, marked by their water towers and grain elevators and big feed lots surrounding them, and almost all between is still a checkerboard of neat farms but on a larger scale, big field after big field stretching away interminably with the farmhouses, few and far, almost hidden among them.

Westward, out over the plains, and the towns too seem to have been left behind, small and sparse in their distant dotting over the immensity, little more than crossroad settlements with an occasional moteled tourist mecca. The checkerboard effect is gone, though it might be discerned in part by faint tracing of barbed-wire lines. Patches of cultivation show where some farmer-ranchers are making a stand, aided nowadays by farm-program subsidies, then these too are gone and the remote scattered ranch houses and corrals are merely natural features of the land itself, lost in it, and the sea of grass, over-grazed always but stubbornly clinging, indifferent to the long-ranging fence lines and the occasional cowboy in a jeep riding them, rolls on as it did when Coronado saw it towards the dim distant haze of the Rockies.

Here is where the long migrations ended, where settlement out of the east met the backwash from the west coast and the mountains and was matched by the land and made its truce. Here electric lines and paved highways and the standardizing of modern technology make their way gradually, only gradually. In time, no doubt, the conquest, armed ever more efficiently, will cover this too. Oil derricks rise in the Williston basin of North Dakota. Huge dams are being built to harness the Missouri and its main tributaries and provide power for industry and reservoired water for irrigation. The tourist blight will spread and deepen, industrialization will increase and become big business, intensified farming will crawl out over the plains.

Not yet. Not quite. Always, somewhere out by the far shores of the ocean of land, there will be places where Stephen Vincent Benét's words will stand:

But, where the ragged acres still resist,
And nothing but the stoneboat gets a crop,
Where the black butte stands up like a clenched fist
Against the evening, and the signboards stop,
Something remains, obscure to understand,
But living, and a genius of the land.

The Rocky
Mountain West

BY WALLACE STEGNER

When I was a boy on the steppe-like Saskatchewan plains I used to
watch, full of fantasies and longings, the crests of the Bearpaws that
floated on the heat-waves along the southern horizon far down in
Montana; and I can remember well when, at the age of eleven, I
finally got to the mountains for the first time. The Bearpaws and the
Little Belts, outlying ranges, would in themselves have been wonder
enough after the withered plains. The forests, lakes, glaciers, and
geysers of Yellowstone left me bug-eyed and awed. But what I most
remember is a camp we made by Upper Mesa Falls, on Henry's Fork
of the Snake.

I knew neither geography nor history. I didn't know that this mar-
velous torrent rose on the west side of Targhee Pass and flowed barely
a hundred miles, through two Idaho counties, before joining the
Snake near Rexburg; or that in 1810, only four years after Lewis and
Clark came back across Lolo Pass with the first authentic information
about the Northwest, Andrew Henry built on Henry's Fork near modern St. Anthony the first American post west of the continental divide.

The divide itself meant nothing to me. My imagination was not stretched by the wonder of the parted waters—the Yellowstone and Gallatin and other rivers rising only a few miles eastward to flow out toward the Missouri, the Mississippi, and the Gulf, while this bright pounding stream was starting through its thousand miles of canyons to the Columbia and the Pacific.

All I knew was that it was pure delight to be where the land lifted in peaks and plunged in canyons, to sniff air that was thin, spray-cooled, full of the smells of pine and fir, to be so close-seeming to the improbable indigo sky. I gave my heart to the mountains the minute I stood beside this river with its spray in my face and watched it thunder into foam, smooth to green glass over sunken rocks, shatter to foam again. I was fascinated by how it sped by and yet was always there. Its roar shook both the earth and me.

When the sun dropped over the rim, the shadows chilled sharply; evening lingered until foam on water was ghostly and luminous in the near-dark. Alders caught in the current sawed like things alive, and the noise was louder. It was rare and comforting to waken late and hear the undiminished shouting of the water in the night. At sunup it was still there, powerful and incessant, with the sun tangled in its spray and the grass blue with wetness and the air, scented with campfire smoke, as heady as ether.

By such a river it is impossible to believe that one will ever be tired or old. Every sense applauds it. Taste it, feel its chill on the teeth: It is purity absolute. Watch its racing current, its steady renewal of force: It is transient and eternal. Listen again to its sounds, get far enough away so that the noise of falling tons of water does not stun the ears, and hear how much is going on underneath: a whole symphony of smaller sounds, hiss and splash and gurgle, the small talk of side channels, the whisper of blown and scattered spray gathering itself and beginning to flow again, secret and irresistible, among the wet rocks.

In the day or two we spent on Henry's Fork I think I got from the mountains one of their most precious gifts, wonder; and I learned something about their most precious resource, water. Both are indispensable to any discussion of the Rocky Mountains. Wonder, delight, freedom, adventure, excitement, are as much a part of the mountains as peaks and forests. Realism is for tamer landscapes; the mountains are inescapably romantic. And water, while an exhilarating element of the mountain scene, is in the West of more than aesthetic interest. By Upper Mesa Falls I had the wit to be awed by what was most vital. The water of the Rockies is the very source and fountain of the West's life. Without it the dry plains that front the mountains and the deserts that back them would be all but uninhabitable.

Let us limit the area under discussion. What we speak of is the Rocky Mountain states, but not the entire Rocky Mountains, whose multiple ranges extend all the way from Alaska down through Mexico, and which may, with no great distortion of topographical fact, be made continuous with the ranges of Central and South America. We do not even include all of the American Rockies, for our region stops in the middle of the Sangre de Cristo range in southern Colorado, at the foot of San Luis Valley. Below that is the Southwest, which ethnography and history, if not topography, have made another country.

Six states—Montana, Wyoming, Colorado, Utah, Idaho, and Nevada—comprise the Rocky Mountain West as distinguished from the Southwest, California, and the Pacific Northwest. Even these six are by no means all mountains. The whole eastern side of Montana, Wyoming, and Colorado is high plains, the gently-sloping "long hill" which the swinging rivers have built and down which they run. Montana, named for its mountains, is three-fifths high plains; in Wyoming and Colorado the mountain chain is wider and the plains correspondingly narrower. But plains or mountains, these states are all within the "West," they lie beyond the invisible boundary which marks the true West's beginning. The boundary is the isohyetal line of twenty inches. Beyond it unassisted agriculture is dubious or foolhardy, and beyond it one knows the characteristic western feel—a dryness in the nostrils, a cracking of the lips, a transparent crystalline quality of the light, a new palette of gray and sage-green and sulfur-yellow and buff and toned white and rust red, a new flora and a new fauna, a new ecology. The boundary is as unmistakable as if a wall had been built between East and West, roughly along the 98th meridian. If political boundary lines were logical, that is where our western states would begin, about a third of the way across Kansas, Nebraska, and the Dakotas.

But the Rocky Mountain West, if topography dictated boundaries, would begin at the mountains. Walling the high plains along the West, tilting the earth violently upward, they reach down out of the north-west corner of Montana, from where Chief Mountain is overthrust onto the short-grass prairie before Glacier National Park. Widening as they go, they run south-southwest, a chain of linked and inter-locking ranges with several isolated outliers—the Sweetgrass Hills, the Highwoods, the Bearpaws, the Little Rockies, the Little Belts, the Big Snowies, and farther south the Big Horns and the Black Hills—until they reach a kind of corner at the Laramie Range, west of Cheyenne, Wyoming. There the whole system, which has now reached its widest spread, turns due south. The ranges that leap up in waves back of Boulder, Denver, and Colorado Springs are the highest in the whole American Rockies, with fifty-four peaks over 14,000 feet. Front Range, Park Range, Sawatch, Sangre de Cristo, San Miguel, La Plata —they fill western Colorado nearly to the Utah border, where the plateaus begin; and southward they reach into New Mexico to link the Rockies with the Southwest.

The eastern tier of Rocky Mountain states is thus made of plains on the east, mountains on the west. The western tier, not quite so sym-metrically, is made of mountains and plateaus on the east and deserts on the west. Nevada, in fact, almost a region in itself, is nearly all desert, and its mountains, though they sometimes lift out of the Great Basin to lofty altitudes, are transitional between the Rockies and the Sierra Nevada rather than an integral part of the Rockies chain. Throughout the region, altitude has both good and bad effects: The mountains not only catch rain, but they throw a rain shadow. As the Montana, Wyoming, and Colorado plains lie in the rain shadow of the Rockies, the deserts of southwestern Idaho, western Utah, and Nevada lie in the rain shadow of the Cascade-Sierra-Coast Range up-lifts. And these deserts, says the historian Walter Webb, are the truest West, its dead and arid heart. The rest of the West is a semihabitable fringe subject to cyclic disasters and dust bowls, and to a chronic and incurable shortage of water.

Professor Webb's thesis, whose central points were first phrased by Major John Wesley Powell in his extraordinary *Report on the Lands of the Arid Region* in 1878, needs periodic and stentorian restating in a region where optimism consistently outruns resources. But I should like it stated in a slightly different way. Instead of a country with a dead heart and semiarid fringes, I conceive the Rocky Mountain West to be composed of two long belts, one of dry steppe-like plains and one of true desert, with the multiple fountain of the Rockies between them. The fountain, even if every reclamation damsite should be developed, cannot water a fraction of the land that lies under it, but it is a fountain nevertheless. A simple comparison of annual rainfall figures, such as that between the 35-inch precipitation of the Yellowstone plateau and the 6-inch precipitation of the Big Hole Basin, tells only part of the story. The difference is actually much more than the apparent six-to-one, for the snowpack in the higher, cooler altitudes melts more slowly, the forest cover retards the runoff, the evaporation rate is much lower. Both the surface streams and the underground water table for hundreds of miles out on the plains may benefit from the fact that water is not only made in the mountains, but stored there. Without the highlands, the lowlands would be at the worst utter desert, which parts of them are anyway, and at best a thinly populated grazing country always on the dusty edge of trouble. And despite the help of the mountains, great sections of the plains periodically suffer terrible drouths and dust storms, loss of topsoil, ruin of farms and ranches. The 1950's repeated the 1930's, which in turn repeated the late 1880's and early 1890's.

Apart from its abiding unity of aridity, the Rocky Mountain West is a region of bewildering variety. Its life zones go all the way from arctic to subtropical, from reindeer moss to cactus, from mountain goat to horned toad. Its range of temperatures is as wide as its range of precipitation; it runs through twelve degrees of latitude and two miles or more of altitude. It is bald alkali flats, creosote-bush deserts, short-grass plains, irrigated alluvial valleys, subarctic fir forests, bare stone. It is, by common consent and the advertising of local booster clubs, the biggest, the best, the widest, the highest, the most invigorating, the friendliest. And of this gigantic sandwich with its two dry slabs and its moist center it is possible to cite the statistics of the Promised Land.

Within its area of roughly 400,000,000 acres—about one-fifth of the United States—lived in 1950 only 3,644,224 people. They were densest in Colorado, at 12.8 per square mile, thinnest in Nevada at 1.5 (the population density over the whole nation that year was 50.7). More than that, this skimpy population was concentrated in certain areas of plentiful water, and rather surprisingly, showed in the statistics as more urban than rural. Over half of Colorado's people were packed into the ten counties along the east face of the Rockies, the rest scattered thinly through fifty-three counties; more than two-thirds of Utah's population made a narrow dense band of settlement in the six counties along the foot of the Wasatch, the other third occupied oasis spots through Utah's remaining twenty-three counties. And what was true in a marked way for Utah and Colorado was true to a somewhat lesser extent for the whole region. As Professor Webb has remarked, the West is an oasis civilization.

Room, then—great open spaces, as advertised. Also, those great open spaces contained the mineral heart of the country, the source of much of our gold, silver, lead, zinc, copper, molybdenum, antimony, coal, iron, petroleum, uranium. The single mine of the Utah Copper at Bingham produces, year in, year out, roughly thirty percent of the country's copper, ten percent of the world's. Now that the Mesabi Range in Michigan approaches exhaustion, Iron County in Utah becomes one of our major sources of iron ore; the steel industry based upon Utah ore and limestone and on Utah, Wyoming, and Colorado coal is the indispensable first step in the West's industrial maturity. It has been estimated that the upper Colorado River basin contains a sixth of the world's known coal reserves. Since the railroads dieselized, and towns converted to natural gas, all but the coking coals lie nearly untouched, and coal mining is in a deadly slump; but at least the coal is there, in case anyone wants it. When the accessible petroleum, including that in the extensive fields in Montana, Wyoming, Colorado, and Utah, is used up the oil shales of eastern Utah and western Colorado, already in experimental production in Parachute Canyon, may be literally the world's major resource of oil. And though there are no public figures, it is a foolproof guess that most of the uranium mined in the United States comes from the San Juan country where Utah, Colorado, New Mexico, and Arizona meet. Recently, on a road across the top of the Navajo Reservation near the Four Corners, where a few years ago you were lucky to meet so much as a lizard, I was stalled by an oil exploration rig that broke an axle fording Chinle Wash after a cloudburst. Behind me, in the hour I waited, stacked up fifteen or twenty cars and parts of three other exploration outfits. And who pulled the broken-down one out and let us get on? A truck loaded with twenty tons of uranium ore. At Farmington, Ship Rock, Grand Junction, Moab, the wondering traveler will see repeated, with the addition of a mechanization then undreamed-of, a frenzy of boom not matched in this country since the gold rush.

The statistics say that the Rocky Mountain region is extravagantly endowed with sources of energy, including solar energy. And more: Down its entire length from Alberta to New Mexico, nearly a thousand miles by airline and much more as the ridgepole bends, the mountains form the nation's roof, and on them are generated the three great western river systems, the Missouri, the Columbia, and the Colorado, not to mention the Southwest's great river, the Rio Grande. Along all those rivers, and along all their tributaries, most of the most feasible power, reclamation, and flood-control damsites are already developed; for the others, two great government agencies and an assortment of private power companies now contend. But never mind, for the moment, who develops and harnesses the rivers, whether Corps of Engineers or Bureau of Reclamation, Idaho Power, Montana Power, or Utah Power and Light. Whoever puts them to work, they are formidable fountains of energy. Just one installation, Grand Coulee, made an industrial revolution in the Pacific Northwest; and Hollywood's Sunset Strip glares with the light of water falling through the penstocks of Hoover Dam on the Colorado. The Upper Colorado River Basin Project, already authorized and elements of it begun at Flaming Gorge and Glen Canyon, will provide the power for the exploitation of rich mineral and oil deposits, especially in the Uinta Basin of Utah and Colorado, and may well turn into an industrial complex "beyond the Urals" a region that until now has been submarginal farm land, desert grazing land, or total wasteland.

Power. Also, at least hopefully, the power of attraction, though historically the mountain region has never had this except sporadically. Even yet most people go, not to it, but through it. Much as it means to the six mountain states, the tourist business of all six is still minor—their total take of $715,000,000 in 1955 was less than that of California alone, and far less than that of New York or Florida. They are too far from the great centers of population—one is inclined to add Thank God—to be overrun with visitors. But within the region lie some of the continent's most impressive natural spectacles, including Glacier, Yellowstone, Rocky Mountain, Grand Teton, Mesa Verde, Zion, and Bryce Canyon National Parks and twenty national monuments, besides hundreds of square miles of mountain, forest, plateau, and canyon that anywhere else would be called superlative. Within them also are many of the country's finest ski resorts—Sun Valley, Jackson Hole, Alta, Brighton, Aspen, Steamboat Springs. Some indication of the discrepancy between resources and use may be gained from the fact that so famous a ski area as Alta, held by many to have the finest snow and the best slopes on the continent, has accommodation for no more than 250 people as of 1957, and its sister resort, Brighton, a few miles of lovely high-altitude ski-touring over the divide, has only one real ski lodge, the Alpine Rose. Though even at the present rate of visitation, so unsatisfactory to local improvement committees, the annual visitors to the mountain states outnumber the native population by at least five to one, the fact remains that in the tourist business, as in the field of industrial energy, what so far exists is an enormous potential.

When you have run through the extravagant statistics and assayed the promise of the future, add this: That all the West's resources, even water power, even scenery, are more vulnerable than the resources of other regions, and that the social and economic structure of much of the West is tentative, uncertain, and shifting. The reasons are partly short-haul freight rates and partly distance from sizable industrial markets; but a more compelling reason is that the basic resources of water and soil, which can be mismanaged in other regions without drastic consequences, cannot be mismanaged in the West without consequences both immediate and catastrophic—consequences, moreover, that may spread far beyond the boundaries of the mountain states proper. The overgrazing or clear-cutting of a watershed on the Milk or the Yampa can carry consequences clear to St. Louis or Yuma. And the history of the Rocky Mountain West, when we hold at arm's length the excitement, the adventure, the romance, and the legendry, is a history of resources often mismanaged and of conditions often misunderstood or disregarded. Here, as elsewhere, settlement went principally by trial and error—only here the trials were sometimes terrible for those who suffered them, and the errors were sometimes disastrous to the land.

Specifically, the history of the Rocky Mountain West until very recently has been a history of the importation of inherited humid-land habits (and carelessnesses) into a dry land that will not tolerate them;

and of the indulgence of an unprecedented personal freedom, an atomic individualism, in a country which experience says can only be successfully tamed and lived in by a high degree of co-operation. The inherited wet-land habits have given us an endangered and partly-damaged domain; the exacerbated personal freedom of the frontier has left us with a myth, a folklore, a set of beliefs and automatic acceptances, that are often comically at odds with the facts of life. Because that myth and that folklore have been embedded in a literary—or sub-literary—tradition, and through the movies and television and radio have the widest and most incessant distribution, this West is a place where life may very often be seen to copy art. Nobody so devours Westerns as the bona fide cowhand; nobody so religiously attends horse opera; nobody is so helplessly modeled by a fictitious image of himself. And what directly affects the working cowhand affects, in its subtler and less stereotyped forms, a lot of people in professional or service or industrial occupations, in cities like Denver and Great Falls and Salt Lake City and Boise. The West, and the Westerner, are partly what in fact and history they are and have been; and they are partly what the romantic imagination has made them.

Bernard De Voto once described the West as a plundered province. Certainly, until the industrial boom that began with World War II, its products generally went to provide dividends for corporations chartered in Missouri or Maine or New Jersey, and to enrich investors living in Boston and Upper Montclair. And certainly, for at least seventy-five years from the opening of this frontier, it was not so much settled as raided. Until the 1880's it saw few true settlers except the Mormons, and some of the few it did see should have been talked out of coming, for their heroic efforts to make homesteads in the arid belt succeeded mainly in making dust bowls. Mainly what the West saw was explorers, through travelers bound for Oregon or California, and a series of hit-and-run plunderers, picturesque, robust, romantic, and destructive.

Newest of our regions, raw, brash, still nascent, still discovering its endowment and still learning how to live within its natural conditions, the Rocky Mountain West cannot fairly be charged with its cultural limitations, as one literary easterner did in describing the vacant, stunned, deprived or undeveloped "Montana Face." I suspect that the Montana Face is an illusion as romantic, in its way, as the archetypal figure of the Westerner that the Westerner himself is likely to accept. And it would be remarkable indeed if the cultural stirrings that agitate the campuses and the clubs of the West were not often naive, almost always derivative, and frequently fumbling. It is as permissible for a region to be young as for an individual to pass through the stages of childhood. The Rocky Mountain region has a total recorded history of hardly more than a century and a half, and a settled—or exploited —history of not much more than a century—some parts of it much less than that.

Before the beginning of the nineteenth century white men had seen the Rocky Mountains twice. In 1743 Pierre and Chevalier de la Vérendrye, exploring far down into the plains from the Saskatchewan country, described "high" and "well-wooded" mountains that might have been the Big Horns, the Black Hills, or even the Laramie Range. In 1776 Fathers Escalante and Dominguez crossed from Taos to the Utah Valley, turned southwest along the eastern wall of the Great Basin, recrossed the Colorado at the Crossing of the Fathers near the present Glen Canyon damsite, and found their way back across the Painted Desert to New Mexico. They left both Escalante's journal and Miera's map, and both added immeasurably to knowledge. But the history of the Rocky Mountain states for Anglo-Americans begins with the official explorers from the United States, with Lewis and Clark in 1804–06, with Zebulon Pike in 1810, with Major Stephen Long in 1820. Especially with Lewis and Clark, the first, the most intelligent and resolute, incomparably the most successful. Pike, whose impetuosity got him into difficulties first with the country and then with the Spaniards, has left his name on the great landmark peak above Colorado Springs. Long, as over-cautious as Pike was headstrong, retreated without major discoveries but also left his name on a peak, this one above Estes Park. Lewis and Clark left their names on no such peaks, but they opened the West.

From St. Louis up the Missouri through the plains that would some day be Nebraska, the Dakotas, Montana; past the Great Falls and through the "Gates of the Rocky Mountains," up the dwindling forks, they went by water until the water would no longer float them. Then they stalked Sacajawea's suspicious Snake relatives until they caught some and made friends, and with a few horses and information about a difficult way over the mountains, they struggled up over Lolo Pass and stood, the first Americans to do so, on the western slope of the continental divide. Next spring, having passed a dreary winter in the rain at the mouth of the Columbia, they came back over the Bitterroots, split forces so that Clark could explore the Yellowstone while Lewis went up the Marias, and were reunited below the mouth of the Yellowstone, from where—Lewis with an accidental gunshot wound in his thigh—they floated the long river homeward to St. Louis and triumph.

Their word on the unknown reaches of Louisiana and "the Oregon" was added to by Pike and Long, as well as by Frémont, who surveyed the Oregon Trail in 1842 and other parts of the West in 1844–46. It was given detail by the Pacific Railroad Surveys of the 1850's, and topographical knowledge was brought close to its final form by Major Powell's brilliant exploration down the Green and Colorado Rivers in 1869. The last act of all in the record of official exploration belonged to Powell's brother-in-law, Almon Thompson, who in 1871 added to the map of southern Utah the last-discovered river—the Escalante, whose mouth Powell had missed. But long before the 1870's, when explorers had become surveyors and the King, Hayden, Powell, and Wheeler Surveys were triangulating the West, another breed had lived its short hot life and disappeared: the first of the raiders, the first of the picturesque and destructive ones, the first shapes of myth—the mountain men.

Returning out of the wilderness on Clark's heels in 1806, Lewis had met, below the mouth of the Yellowstone, two trappers named Dickson and Hancock, the first to follow upriver the path the explorers had opened. One of the expedition's men, John Colter, turned out to be still unsated with wilderness after two years of hardship, starvation, wounds, scurvy, and venereal Chinook squaws. He asked leave to turn back with the trappers, and having been a faithful man, was granted it. He helped build in 1807, at the mouth of the Big Horn, the fort that was the first building in Montana and probably the first in the Rocky Mountain states. That same year he returned from a trip up the Yellowstone with tales of boiling springs, fountains of steam, quaking and smoking earth, mountains of glass. Sixty-five years later a body of enthusiasts assisted by members of the Hayden Survey and armed with photographs by William Henry Jackson and water colors by Thomas Moran would succeed in having Congress set aside

Colter's Hell as Yellowstone National Park. Both the discovery and the reservation are significant; they bracket a substantial part of the West's history, from uninhibited exploitation of the public domain to federal ownership, conservation, and management of the more crucial parts of it in the interest of all the people and of the future. A hundred and fifty years after Colter made the first white moccasin tracks in the Yellowstone country, an annual invasion of a million and a quarter tourists would be threatening to trample it to death, and would have done so long since except for the protection of a federal bureau, the National Park Service.

After 1808 the Northwest Company had posts in western Montana, in 1810 Andrew Henry built his post on Henry's Fork, in 1829 the American Fur Company erected Fort Union at the mouth of the Yellowstone, and this was for a time the ultimate outpost of the raiders in a hostile country. But the trade was already shifting westward, away from the river that was so unreliable and dangerous a highway, with so many belligerent tribes in a constant boil along its banks. Soon the raiders would operate without bases; and in their wanderings they would locate a road. Wilson Henry Hunt led his fifty Astorians down the Snake and the Columbia in 1811, following roughly the route of Lewis and Clark. Next year, Robert Stuart brought a small party back, swerving southward in search of an easier way; crossing the mountains far to the south and east, he may have made the first crossing of South Pass. The effective discovery of that route, the one with consequences, was made by a party of General Ashley's trappers under Thomas Fitzpatrick and Jedediah Smith in 1824. Intent upon new beaver country, they prepared the way for a new phase of the frontier.

Over the same featureless plateau, Jason Lee and the Spaldings and Marcus and Narcissa Whitman would go missionarying to Oregon. Whitman would drag a wagon over it all the way to Fort Hall in 1836; in 1840, mountain men and other missionaries would print the mark of wheels all the way to Whitman's mission at Waiilatpu. While fixed posts such as Fort Laramie and Fort Hall began to take over from the annual rendezvous of the fur brigades, and while Nathaniel Wyeth disputed the Snake River country with Peter Skene Ogden and John Work of the Hudson's Bay Company, the fur trade guttered out. Marcus Whitman would enforce the new order on the imagination of the nation, first making his epic journey from the west coast to preach the gospel of Oregon into eastern ears, and on his return in 1842 taking a wagon train all the way through, to show that it could be done. These things would take time, almost two decades after the effective discovery of an easy wagon pass, but the discovery made them inevitable. There lay the open track to—or through—the West; the route of the Donner-Reed party doomed to their grisly ordeal in the snow-blocked Sierra in 1846, the way of the Mormon pioneer company, moving out of the infested bottoms at Winter Quarters, on the Missouri, in 1847; the road of the Gold Rush; the road that the Handcart Companies would walk to their snowdrift graves along the Sweetwater in 1856.

Stand on South Pass now, and you will find it as still and peaceful as if no clamor of empire had ever surged through it. Antelope will drift close to see what you are up to; no smokes stain the dark blue sky; the riotous rendezvous of the fur brigades, held in this vicinity for a dozen years after 1825, have left neither mark nor echo, not even a tepee ring. The wheels that between 1836 and 1869 rocked and creaked and squealed up the Sweetwater and down past the westward-falling trickle of Pacific Creek have left ruts that are still visible in places among the sage and bunchgrass if you look hard, but modern travel does not go this way. Both Highway 30 and the railroad cross the divide at Creston. All that crosses South Pass now is Wyoming 28, a secondary road.

And here is a lesson, not only in history, but in the fallibility of prophecy based on false premises. In 1860 William Gilpin, first territorial governor of Colorado and a loud voice for Manifest Destiny, foresaw that South Pass would become a gateway more thronging than Gibraltar, and that the population of the Rocky Mountain region would be numbered in hundreds of millions.

Ask the antelope, coming back after a long period of near-extinction, where those hundreds of millions are. Ask the people from the Bureau of Land Management, the Soil Conservation Service, the Bureau of Reclamation, and the Forest Service, who have the job of restoring the overgrazed ranges and impounding the little available water and protecting the watersheds, how they would like to entertain that many guests. Look back eastward a little, back where the Sweetwater flows down into the North Platte, and see in the Seminole, Kortes, and Pathfinder Dam, one of the salient reasons why this part of what Gilpin called the great Cordilleran Region is habitable at all. The dams represent sanity, acceptance, planning—the act of acquired wisdom, the acknowledgement of inexorable aridity. Gilpin made one principal error: He forgot that people live on water as much as on land.

Nobody stopped here to accommodate Gilpin's prophecies. Except for the Mormons who after 1847 were building an agricultural society in the irrigable valleys of Utah and southern Idaho and the western edge of Nevada, nobody stopped anywhere in the Rocky Mountain country—especially after John Marshall stooped to examine the glitter in the bottom of Sutter's millrace at Coloma, California, in January 1848. For a round decade everybody went straight on through, cussing every dusty mile that lay between him and the Pacific coast. From John Colter on, men with the itch of the wild in them had found the Rockies a place of savage freedom; but they apparently offered nothing to the homemaker, and their minerals were not yet discovered. Oregon wagons and Forty-niners were part of the history but not the life of the Rocky Mountains. The Mormons were another matter. They were not headed anywhere else; their destination was a desert valley between the Wasatch and Great Salt Lake. On the very first afternoon they made their peace with at least one of the West's inflexible conditions. They diverted water from City Creek to soften the ground for a potato field, and began Anglo-American irrigation on this continent— began, that is, the adjustment that north-European peoples were compelled to make before they could learn to live in the West.

The ferocious partisans of the fur companies had cleaned out the beaver by 1840, and turned to guiding wagon trains, scouting for the United States Cavalry, or hunting buffalo for the hides. Nearly twenty years before they had the buffalo wiped out and the cavalry had suppressed the last desperate Indian uprisings, a new wave of raiders swept in upon the Rockies from both east and west. 1858 saw gold strikes on Clear Creek, near modern Denver, and on Cripple Creek back of Pike's Peak, and on Gold Creek in Montana. The next year the fabulous Comstock Lode sucked half the miners in California over the mountains into Nevada, and intercepted most of the emigrants from the east. Idaho joined the excitement with the strike on Orofino Creek in 1861, and in 1862 with strikes in the Boise Basin and at Bannack in the Beaverhead country. In 1863 the discovery of the richest of all placers brought into existence a Montana Virginia City to match the Nevada city of the same name on the Comstock. By that time General Connor's soldiers, posted in Salt Lake City to keep an eye on the Mormons, had been turned loose to find gold in Bingham Canyon and in the Wasatch, and a Gentile society of raiders, which gradually transformed itself into a more permanent cluster of camps to exploit lode mines, was developing in competition with the Mormon society of irrigation farmers.

Insofar as the non-Mormon West was settled at all by 1869, when Union Pacific and Central Pacific bumped cowcatchers at Promontory and opened a new age of accessibility for the mountains, it was settled by miners, and miners are notoriously prone to vanish from their mushroom towns as quickly as they gather. Quartz mines can last a long time, and new discoveries and new mining and smelting methods have kept alive such towns as Bingham, Butte, Anaconda, Park City, Ely. For that matter Salt Lake City, the heart of Mormon agrarianism, is the largest nonferrous smelting center in the world. But if the West depended entirely on minerals to support a civilization, it could look forward to an extinction as complete as that of the Land of Midian, where King Solomon's mines have heard only dry whisper of blowing sand for millennia. Mineral resources are not renewable, and placers especially are resources of a year or two or ten, hardly more; the early placer camps went out like blown matches. In such of them as now show any standing buildings, the doors swing in the wind and snow blows in the broken windows of saloons and stores, the nails are tufted with the hair of animals, the gutted gulches spill their gravel into the valleys on the spring freshets or in summer cloudbursts, and the mountainsides whose pines went to prop shafts or flumes show now the deep scorings of erosion gulleys. Some lode camps, like Virginia City, Nevada, or Leadville, Colorado, survive as fractions or remnants; some, like Virginia City, Montana, Aspen, Colorado, and Alta, Utah, have been rejuvenated as resort or ski towns. But many of these too are ghosts. Tourists and antiquarians often profess to find them charming, and it is true that some of them, buried among the mountains, occupy spectacular sites. But charming they hardly are with the single exception of Aspen. They are the leavings of the second careless rush of hit-and-run exploiters, a breed generally as thoughtless of the future or of consequences as the mountain men slaughtering their way through a wilderness of fur and meat that seemed inexhaustible and then was suddenly gone. The towns which *did* expect a future, looking upon their mineral wealth as inexhaustible, and which erected opera houses and ice palaces and hotels and cultivated the high-toned arts (the two Virginia Cities, Leadville, Central City), have a rather wistful lease on life as quaint tourist attractions or as sites of summer opera festivals. They survive, that is, on transfusions.

Montana, Colorado, most of Idaho, and Nevada all drew their first inhabitants to the mineralized mountains, not to their agricultural land. Utah and its southern Idaho outposts maintained their pastoral and co-operative societies based on irrigation even through the mining rushes, and made money selling services, farm produce, mules, and Valley Tan whiskey to the infidel. Wyoming, with vast ranges of grasslands, became above all a cattle country. The raid here, as on the plains of Colorado and Montana, was on the grass. Many of the cattle corporations, like the fur companies and the mining companies, were absentee-owned, some in England and Scotland. The men who set out to get rich from the western grasslands shared the psychology—and the ignorance of consequences—of the men who had cleaned out the beaver streams and were busy cleaning out the precious metals. Who among the mountain men would have paused to consider, or would have cared, that beaver were a water resource, and that beaver engineering was of great importance in the maintenance of stream flow and the prevention of floods? Who among the miners worried about what happened to the watersheds where they logged their timbers or the stream beds where their monitors or dredges tore up the gravel? Who among the cattlemen knew, or cared, that in a dry land grass, like minerals, might be non-renewable; that some of the best grasses were annuals that reproduced only from seed, and that overgrazing both prevented reseeding and encouraged erosion? The cattleman like his predecessors lived a large, free life; he is even more deeply embedded in our folklore than mountain man or miner; in terms of the enduring capacity of the West to sustain a civilization, he did more harm than either.

Late as they came to it, settlers were in the West before much of it was surveyed, before there were laws adequate to its conditions. The public domain lay wide open to anyone with the energy to take it. Also there were, for those who chose to use them, short cuts to an empire. By having your cowhands homestead a quarter-section apiece and commute it to you for a small consideration, you could assemble the core of a noble range. By homesteading, buying, or merely appropriating the land along the watercourses or around sources of water, you could dominate many square miles of dry grazing land. By using the public domain as if it were really your own, you could perhaps convince yourself that you had exclusive rights to it, and by intimidation or the method known as dry-gulching you might discourage rivals or sheepmen or nesters, saying in justification that they were trespassers or rustlers. The history of the West is full of murderous quarrels over property that neither of the contestants owned, and over rights that no law had approved. Transformed, these quarrels are often the stuff of horse opera. Read, for instance, the history of the Johnson County War in Wyoming, when cattlemen rode northward from Cheyenne with a list of "rustlers" and "trespassers" they intended to rub out. They rubbed out two before the law belatedly began to assert that the rustlers and trespassers had as much right where they were as the cattlemen who tried to gun them off. That is an ugly story. But put in the terms Owen Wister gave it in *The Virginian,* it takes on all the beguiling qualities of myth. The culture hero, torn between friendship and duty to "law," does not seem like a lyncher and a vigilante. By such transformations it is even possible to make a sort of hero of Tom Horn, the cattlemen's hired assassin, or of Billy the Kid, a psychopathic killer.

The mythic West is the West that everyone knows. Every American child grows up in it. The dream of total emancipation from inhibition, law, convention, and restraint is a potent dream. The West, wide open, fostered it as few environments have. And if the emancipated and uninhibited were also lawless, if they were scoundrels as so many western characters turn out to be on close examination, let us make them rebels against the system, friends of the poor, according to a formula well known to the creators of Robin Hood and Jesse James. If law officers turn out, on close look, to be bandits with badges on, and if the posses who made themselves judge, jury, legislature, and executioner look sometimes like dupes, sometimes like a bloody-minded rabble, put into their mouths such excuses as the Virginian uses, and further palliate their vigilantism by making them courteous to women and tender to little children and to old men; give them a stern faith in honesty, property, the sanctity of contract. Commit them

fully to the mores of the middle-class community and give them all
the lineaments of the Lone Ranger, let them be lawless in defense of
law, unconventional in the service of convention, and the peculiarity
of their ethics, like the dubiousness of their exploitation of natural resources, blurs and disappears in a blaze of picturesqueness.

The mythic western hero, the apostle of a most rugged individualism, is a curious hangover, and may sometimes be caught sanctifying
some odd practices and policies. He has codified and perpetuated an
honor as high-colored as the feudal code of the old South—which, by
way of the Virginian and a lot of ex-Confederates among the Texas
cattle drivers, was probably its source. He suggests that the resolution
of every quarrel is ultimately violence: The walkdown is a fixture of
all highbrow horse opera, as the stagecoach chase is of the lowbrow
variety. He represents a Cockaigne, a Poictesme, a Never-Never
West, but he is propped with the most scrupulous and niggling realism. Try to write a Western with your gun lore crooked, or with holes
in your lingo! He is sometimes—and this is the principal danger in
what would otherwise only be wistful or amusing—invoked to justify
new outbreaks of rugged individualism, irresponsibility, intemperance,
and the economics of the raid. The real people of the West are generally not cowboys and never myths; they live in places like Denver
and Salt Lake, Dillon and Boise, American Fork and American Falls,
and they confront the real problems of real life in a real region and
have gone a long way toward understanding the conditions of western
life and accepting the agencies that have been slowly evoked to meet
them. But those who live by the myth, or pretend to, have never yet
admitted that they live in a land of little rain and big consequences.
Whether they are resisting the gift of Grand Teton National Monument from the Rockefellers to the people of the United States, or
maneuvering for the transfer of grazing, timber, oil, or mineral lands
from national parks and forests to state and ultimately to private
ownership for the quick profit of a few, they represent the survival of
a gospel that left to its own devices would ultimately reduce the West
to a desert as barren as Lebanon. One would be more inclined to in-
dulge the fiction of western largeness and western freedom if it did
not consistently obfuscate the facts that Westerners who can learn
have been painfully learning for a century.

Say of the mountain West that it is extravagantly endowed, but that it has one critical deficiency, water, and that therefore its soil, its watersheds, its timber, and its grass are all vulnerable. There have been man-made deserts before in the world's history; some, like the valley of Oaxaca, in Mexico, are being made while we watch. The West could be one of those, and it is not comforting to know that its range is at least fifty percent deteriorated under our handling, and that its rivers run muddy where they used to run clear. The very jokes that strike us as most western are likely to have an edge of grimness: "Throw a gopher in the air, and if he starts to burrow, it ain't a clear day"; "The best place to locate a farm in western Colorado is in eastern Kansas."

Say of the West too that it has been plundered and has plundered itself, or collaborated with its plunderers, but that little by little whole communities and districts have learned how to manage their environment and have made superb living-places out of their oases. Say that the West is everyone's romantic home, for we have all spent a part of our childhood there. And say that in its territory, as in its legendry, much of the West is public domain.

Next to aridity, this is the most important fact about the Rocky Mountain states. Of their 400,000,000 acres, more than half is federal land. Of the state of Nevada, you and I own eighty-seven percent. Drive from Glacier Park to the Spanish Peaks, and from the Sierra Nevada to the high plains, and you are never out of sight of lands reserved and managed by public agencies in the public interest. Why? Not because Westerners are more socialist than other Americans; they are, on the contrary, inclined to conservatism politically. And not because a conspiracy within the government is using the West as a pawn in a game to overthrow the American way of life. Some of these lands have been reserved to keep them from ruinous private exploitation, some to protect the regions in which they lie, some simply because despite all its efforts the government was never able to get anyone to homestead or buy them.

Some of the management is a good deal less effective than it ought to be. The Bureau of Land Management's 116 million acres of range and wasteland are overgrazed, partly because of heavy pressure from permit holders against reduction, partly because the bureau has never been given a budget big enough to do anything: In 1956 the Forest Service was handling 6 million acres of rescue work as "land utilization projects" because the Bureau of Land Management had no staff to put on them. And if history means anything, any future bureau which did get an adequate budget and start seriously to work to bring the range back would find itself bucking the embattled graziers and leaseholders and stockmen's associations.

Who else runs the public West? Well, in our six states the Bureau of Reclamation has 5½ million acres reserved for dam and canal sites, there are 4½ million strictly set aside for "use without impairment" as national parks and monuments, there are 3½ million acres in game and bird refuges and feeding stations run by the Fish and Wild Life Service. The Bureau of Indian Affairs, apart from the Indian Reservations proper, which are not federal but tribal land, has 188,000 acres. The withdrawals for the use of the armed services are large—islands in Great Salt Lake and patches of the salt desert for bombing ranges, A- and H-bomb testing areas near Las Vegas, desert proving grounds, airfields, training centers, the Air Force Academy near Denver. But it is the 75 million acres of national forests in these six states which are the most critical acres in the whole West. They are important for their resources—their reserves of timber, their annual crop of water, their summer grazing, their priceless and mushrooming value as places of outdoor recreation for millions of people—but even more for what they prevent. The Forest Service lands lie almost entirely in the high country and on the watersheds where the West's life is made and stored, where floods can begin, where erosion can be most disastrous. Any forester these days is likely to admit that watershed control, and after that recreation, are both more important in the national forests than the growing, selective marketing, or conservation of trees for timber. The Forest Service is a key bureau because, operating on a policy of multiple use and sustained yield, it harvests some of its resources, especially lumber, water, and grass, each year, and is always under pressure to let go of more. If watershed control, or recreation, or the maintenance of wildlife habitat, or any of the other interests involved, are in conflict with the interest of holders of grazing permits or the bidders for timber-cutting contracts, the service has the unpleasing job of deciding among the conflicting claims. It takes a steady pounding, year in and year out; and year in and year out it is the principal force which keeps the short-term profit-takers, the raiders who see no farther than mountain man or miner, from doing the region in.

The fact is, neither the Forest Service nor most of the other federal agencies are likely to go out of business in the West, because too many Westerners have found out how important is the work they do. It is not merely a question of federal payrolls in local communities, though those are an item. Who, for example, can measure the dollar value of the A-bomb testing area to Las Vegas, or the dollar value of Rocky Mountain National Park to Colorado? The annual payroll for Denver's more-than-two-hundred federal bureau offices was over $20,000,-000 as far back as ten years ago. Not many Westerners are inclined to question federal participation in the local life when it means a power or reclamation or flood-control dam in the area: Listen to the logs rolling among western senators on that issue! Few Westerners will deplore the spending of public funds to rescue the trumpeter swan from the edge of extinction, or to cure ducks sick with botulism in the Bear River marshes, or to winter-feed the elk in Jackson Hole. The collaboration between state fish and game departments, which hatch and plant and manage the fish and game birds, and the Forest Service, which manages the habitat, is close and cordial, and the degree to which Westerners actually make use of the national forests for "harvesting" the fish and game is clear from one figure from Utah. On the opening day of the 1957 deer season, one Utahn out of every six was out with a rifle, and along with them were tens of thousands of out-of-state hunters, mainly from California.

No Westerner in his right mind would dream for a moment of trying to get along without the constant aid and support of the federal agencies. It is easy to see why. Stand, as I did once, on the high grade of the Union Pacific between Salt Lake and Ogden, and watch a cloudburst roll a fifteen-foot wall of mud and rocks and water down the canyons onto the farm land, and come back later to see houses full to the second story with mud and gravel, and gravel and boulders ten feet deep over the fields. Reflect that floods like that arise from one cause alone—the stripping of the mountain slopes of timber in the 1880's. And then visit the regional forest office in Ogden and learn what they are doing in watershed research and (in small, local pilot projects) in watershed restoration, and you will know why this and other agencies have friends when the sniping begins. Watch the parachutes of smoke-jumpers balloon out against a sky ominous with the smoke of forest fires, and the lesson acquires excitement, even heroics.

For research that preserves a national forest helps state forests or private forests, saved watershed reflects good all around it, a fire halted in your woods and mine is money in the pocket of everyone anywhere near there. To give the public lands to the states, as the raiders periodically propose—they say "restore," but the word is a smoke screen, for the public lands have never belonged to the states—could have only one of two effects. The states would go bankrupt trying to keep them up, or they would let them deteriorate. Most people in the West know when they are well off.

It is a pity, in a way, that so many Americans know the West only from the roadside. The original Oregon-Mormon-California trail through it has proliferated into many through routes—U. S. 2, 12, 14, 20, 30, 40, 50, with their north-south links U. S. 85, 87, 91 and scores of good secondary roads. But present and past are alike in this, that the majority of travelers see the West on the fly, customarily on their way somewhere else, and that in consequence roadside accommodations and services are a primary function of western towns. They are considerably less open to criticism than the stage stops on the Overland against which Mark Twain complained so bitterly in *Roughing It* ("At the Green River Station we had breakfast—hot biscuits, fresh antelope steaks, and coffee—the only decent meal we tasted between the United States and Great Salt Lake City . . ."). You do not rough it now, and you may choose among many caravanserais, so many that a lot of western towns appear to exist only as adjuncts of the road. A town on a through highway, such a town as Ely or Elko, Nevada, or Rock Springs, Wyoming, crouches like a spider on the trip-thread of asphalt, and everything in it vibrates to the passing thunder of wheels. Being oases, western towns are inevitably way stations as well.

The West invented the motel, and the motel here has come a long way from the homemade cabin with "running water" and "flush toilet" that used to be advertised along western roads. It has graduated from the back-yard home-labor class and become big business. Nowadays it is likely to be the equal of a first-rate, often a luxury, hotel; it may be one of a chain; the best ones are likely to belong to an association bent upon improving the tourist's comfort, and if you follow one of the guides (the AAA publishes a good one) you can sleep every night

124. The Lower Falls of the Yellowstone River in Yellowstone National
Park. This national park, famous for its wildlife and its scenic wonders,
occupies the northwestern corner of Wyoming and extends for short
distances into Montana and Idaho.

25.   A Montana sheepherder, with his faithful assistant, watches his flock.

126. St. Mary Lake in Glacier National Park, Montana. With the adjacent Waterton Lakes National Park of Canada, this area has been given the name Waterton Lakes-Glacier International Peace Park.

127. Hoover Dam, Nevada. From this picture, which shows details at the top of the dam, the reader would not suspect that it is our highest — 726 feet.

128. Salt Lake City. At the right is the Mormon Temple; in the left center, the turtle-shaped roof of the Tabernacle; in the center background, the Utah state Capitol.

129. Bingham Canyon, Utah. A terraced mountain of copper ore is being removed by strip-mining methods, and the end is not yet in sight.

Galloway

130. The Teton Range of Wyoming seen from across Jackson Lake.

131. Skiing in Colorado. Colorado, like Idaho, northern California, and New England, has all the facilities.

132. These Idaho homesteaders are digging potatoes grown in soil that
was covered with sagebrush until late in 1947.

133. Cattle ranching in southwestern Montana.

134. Dude ranching in Montana. A couple of weeks may or may not make plausible buckaroos out of the new arrivals at the right, but they will "work" off extra pounds and enjoy themselves.

in a tastefully decorated room, on a posturpedic mattress, insulated from traffic noise, and in the morning after your shower you can open the curtains quite often on a superb view through your picture window. If you do not follow a guide, you can get stung, but not nearly so badly as in some other regions, because here competition does what competition is classically reputed to do. When a motel fails, it is much more likely to fail in taste rather than in comfort, and it is for their breaches of taste, rather than for any failure of essential service, that one has to deplore the roadside institutions that have learned to cluster around the motels on incoming and outgoing roads: the hamburger stands, diners, drive-ins, restaurants, bars, taverns, service stations; the drug stores featuring postcards of cows stepping on their dragging udders, over the caption, "You think *you* got troubles!"; the curio shops featuring strange wooden and leather items and Ute beadwork made in Hong Kong. No matter how well designed and carefully planned these roadside businesses may be individually, they are collectively an eyesore. With their advertising, they make the outskirts of nearly every western town feverishly ugly. Here again, the West is not so different from the rest of the country; the trouble is only that in a dry country, without masking grass, shrubs, trees, the ugliness shows more.

Sooner or later the West will learn that scenery, the natural beauty which is the region's noblest endowment, can be ruined as surely by billboards, neon, and the ferocious glare of competing colors, as range can be ruined by overgrazing or a watershed by indiscriminate timber cutting. Somebody should read to the western roadside the story of the man who killed the goose that laid the golden eggs. Anyone can sample the goose, before and after killing: Drive through a typical motel strip, say that of Colorado Springs, and on through the desecrated entrance to Ute Pass, and then on into the unbillboarded wilderness—unbillboarded because certain federal bureaus, here the Forest Service, have had the will and the power to prohibit the posting of outdoor advertising and the smearing of paint on cliffs, even the paint that says "Jesus Saves."

Maybe He does save; maybe He will some day save the West from its habit of exploiting and destroying by human heedlessness resources that are not automatically renewable. Add outdoor advertisers, big and little, to the list that contains mountain men, miners, and cattlemen. Add scenery to the things that haste and folly can destroy.

It is too bad, one insists, that America knows the West from the roadside, for the roadside is the hoked-up West, the dude West, the tourist West, the West with its eye on the traveling dollar. Remembering earlier and more innocent years when I knew this country all the way from the Canadian border to Monument Valley, I have taken to traveling whenever possible by the back roads, and giving up the comforts along with the billboards. That is one way of getting behind the West's roadside face. Another is to live in some part of it a while, sample it as a human dwelling place, as the formative stage of a unique civilization, as a place to go *to*, not through.

Try, since this is an oasis civilization, some of the oasis cities. Try Denver, Salt Lake City, Reno, which, spaced like the stars in the belt of Orion, span the Rocky Mountain West at its broadest part. Highway 40 will lead you through all of them, across 1100 miles of mountain, plateau, and desert, and will lead you also through all three of the West's zones. Denver is a plains city, Salt Lake a mountain city, Reno a desert city. Each is the metropolis of its subregion, each one of the earliest settlements in its cultural area. They all depend for their life upon the water of the mountains that overhang them—Denver upon the Rockies, Salt Lake upon the Wasatch which forms the eastern rim of the Great Basin, Reno upon the Sierra which forms its western rim. They are all recognizably western, they know the same high, dry air, the same purity of light, the same quality of youth and cleanliness. But they are very different, nevertheless.

Denver, being a plains town, is spread wide; in spite of the mountains behind it, and in spite of its altitude of one mile, it impresses a visitor (and for all I know a native) as the Midwest at its farthest west remove. It has more in common with Wichita than with Salt Lake City or the Pacific coast. It is a family town, a home-owning town, a business town, a regional-office town, a town proud of its schools, its parks, its civic center, its community spirit. In the *Denver Post* and the *Rocky Mountain Herald* it has two newspapers each unique in its way and with more-than-metropolitan influence. It is a good place to grow up, though it has its own local segregations and snobberies, and East High may hold itself above South or Manual Training High, and Indians, Mexicans, and more recently Negroes have had to resist survivals of frontier prejudice. But a good town, and one its children are proud of, and one that illustrates something about the whole West and about the whole habit of man as a homemaker and a builder of civilizations. Lacking adequate rainfall, Denver has made its water supply from the mountains, even tapping the watersheds of the western slope by tunnel. Lacking natural greenery, it has produced it by pooled effort, and the qualities of Denver as a park city are in direct proportion to the community co-operation it has taken to create them. The great agricultural civilizations, we are reminded, were born in deserts: Egypt, Mesopotamia, the Indus Valley. And the most settled and civilized Indians in the territory of the continental United States were desert agriculturists—the Pueblo, Hopi, and Zuñi of the Southwest. There is much to be said for a civilization that has to be planned for and continuously worked for. No one need be afraid of Denver's future; she will remain the "Queen City of the Plains and Peaks"— though my private reservation is that her influence is shed east, north, and south much more than it is shed west. Before you get very deep in the mountains, you begin to feel the influence of the next metropolis.

Salt Lake City is less than half Denver's size, but it is even more surely a provincial capital. A mountain town, it does not spread like Denver: It is cupped, cradled, in the broad valley between the Wasatch and the Oquirrh Range. As Denver lies at the beginning of the Rockies, Salt Lake lies at their end; it is exactly at the breaking line between mountains and desert. It too is a business town, a milling and smelting center, a center of deferred shopping (watch the stores and shops during the spring and fall conferences of the Mormon Church, when out-of-towners combine the godly with the necessary). Like Denver, it lies a little to one side of the main transportation routes—the Union Pacific hits Cheyenne and Ogden rather than Denver and Salt Lake, and the airlines characteristically fly right over nonstop to Chicago or New York. Nevertheless, the Utah (and Mormon) symbol of the beehive is very apt. This is an industrious and thriving city, intensely domestic, intensely self-sufficient. Hidden behind its mountains, it feels the winds of politics and international hysteria less than most places; it has, uniquely, the qualities one might ask of a "home" town. Since it was my own home town for fifteen years or more, I speak from prejudice, but I know of no evidence to confute the local boast that this is "the most beautifully situated city in America," and I know few cities which display more community spirit in keeping themselves attractive. At least as much as Denver, this is a city of parks, of broad grassed parkways, of clean streets, of monuments. The monuments are a little hard to account for, in spite of Mormon devotion to the Church's history and an almost Shintoist reverence for ancestors. I suspect that partly they derive from the heavy proportion of Danes among the early converts, and from the Danes' inherited tradition of sculpture. In any case the city has the beginnings of a monumental quality: Its pioneer Mormon company of 1847 is commemorated in Mahonri Young's "This Is the Place" monument at the mouth of Emigration Canyon. The Mormon Battalion of the Mexican War has its memorial in the Capitol grounds, Brigham Young's solid frock-coated figure dominates the intersection at the corner of the Temple Block, the Temple Block itself has its grateful sculptural acknowledgement to the sea gulls who descended to end a locust plague in 1848.

Somehow the monuments are symptomatic: These were people who intended from the beginning to stay, and they brought their gods with them. As the holy city of the Church of Jesus Christ of Latter-Day Saints, Salt Lake City has its religious shrines and its religious tourist attractions, but even for a "Gentile," or non-Mormon, it is a good town to grow up in. And Mormon or Gentile, these, much more than the mythical men in high heels and big hats, are the people of the West. They do little dry-gulching or racing after runaway stage coaches, but they do a lot of sprinkling of their fragrant lawns in the evenings when the canyon breeze begins to feel its way down from the mountains toward the more-slowly-cooling lake; they dig night crawlers with flashlights after dark; they do a lot of fishing and hunting; they haunt the canyons which open in their very back yards—the Wasatch National Forest in 1956 entertained, of all kinds of visitors from casual travelers to campers and hunters, nearly 13,000,000 people (if we count repeaters), most of them locals. These are mountain people and they use their mountains.

From Salt Lake City it is nearly 600 miles by road to Reno—600 miles of desert, salt flats, arid ranges half buried in their own alluvium. There are some minor oases on the way, such as Elko under the Ruby Mountains, but Reno is the true oasis because it has the Sierra behind it. It lies on the Truckee Meadows, the Truckee River flows through its heart and provides a suitable wishing well for divorcees to throw their wedding rings into. It has long been known as a divorce capital and a gambling mecca, and it is both. But it is also, like Denver and Salt Lake City, a university town—the University of Nevada is situated there. And back of or behind or interwoven with the divorce mills and the resorts and the clubs is a surprisingly stable and sober community. I lived in it once for a good part of a year (for non-divorce purposes), and found it astonishingly like Salt Lake. It even smelled the same, and on some of its streets in June the whole sky snowed down cottonwood fluff from big rattly-leaved trees in just the same way, and the climate was variable and stimulating and the nights had the same softness, the moon the same silvery paleness, the horizon the same abrupt thrusting into the sky. Even if you don't want to gamble or shed a wife, Reno is a good town.

I cannot, personally, say the same for Las Vegas, once a sleepy way station on Highway 89 and now the focus for A- and H-bomb testing, for a lot of shenanigans by refugees from Hollywood, and for an extravagant night-club life. It is all very hectic and glossy, but I have not liked it since I went a few years ago into a bar I had used to frequent —a real oasis in prohibition times—and found it a place of chrome and blue glass, with a bartender who was above conversation and a clientele that was beneath notice. While I was there a prospector with a dog came in, put a nickel in the juke box, and started the dog to dancing. The bartender ran him out. We went out too. They can have Las Vegas.

They cannot have a lot of other western towns. They can't have Great Falls, where I used to wade in the Missouri and catch carp with my hands, where I used to sell ice-cream cones in Black Eagle Park and take Boy Scout hikes up the river to Third and Fourth Island. They can't have Boise, where I know the best Basque restaurant that ever made a delirium out of lamb. They can't have the green, irrigated Mormon potato towns along the Snake River. They can't have Jackson, Wyoming, in spite of the fact that the gamblers and the Hollywood refugees have come in there, too. They can't have Missoula or Provo or any of the small, provincial college towns, for whenever I visit them I am brought to the conclusion that the word provincial is a very dangerous word: It means, generally, "different—different from what I am used to," or it means "inadequate by the standards that I have chosen to set." I do not care whether or not Missoula may be provincial by the standards of New York or Cambridge. By standards appropriate to this fledgling civilization, it is something new and potentially fine and exciting. It has health and hope and ambition and a future.

The Rocky Mountain West is good at any season, and it has all four, sharply defined. Try Denver or Salt Lake in May, when the chestnut trees are tossing up cones of blossom, and the scent of lilacs and snowballs perfumes the whole air and mockingbirds go wild on moonlit nights. Try the Aspen or Alta or Brighton or Jackson Hole snow, any time from Thanksgiving to April. Try the summers, with their sharp distinction between sun and shade, their hot days and shirt-sleeve nights. Or try autumn, after all the tourists have gone home for the summer, and the winter ones have not yet arrived, when for a brief while the mountain people have their mountains to themselves. The color of autumn in the mountains is gold, and it is gold the "Aspencades" go out to see. But gold is a limited word. On a single aspen, if you stop to examine it carefully—examine it, say, from the chair lift at Aspen, as you cruise up over the glowing mountainside toward the Sundeck—you can see thirty shades of gold, all the way from the purest palest jonquil to a red-gold that is nearly vermilion. Every leaf of every white-boled tree is in motion; the very air is gold; the mountainsides opposite, and the mountains beyond those, lift into view wider and wider tilted planes of color. You could bottle the air and sell it for vintage prices. At Aspen, where taste has restrained garish advertising and where the natural setting was superb to begin with and where the old mining camp had a certain Victorian charm that later buildings have not departed from too markedly, there is more the feeling of a Swiss village, more a feeling of community within the mountains, than in most Rocky Mountain towns. Another of the same, not known to skiers because skiing has not been developed there yet, but known to Salt Lake City families who for four generations have used it as a local, quiet resort, is the Heber Valley, sixty miles southeast of Salt Lake in the Wasatch. Lie there in your bed in the Homestead Inn at Midway, under the magnificent terraced east face of Mt. Timpanogos, and in the high pure morning before sunup listen to the tuned Swiss bells of Mormon cows going down the village street.

There are a hundred things to do and know in the West that the roadside-tourist does not do or know. If you want to fish and camp and climb, and swim in lakes so cold they electrocute you at the touch, try the Permanent Wilderness of the Grand-daddy Lakes Basin, in the Uinta Mountains of eastern Utah. Try the rivers, though this is not notably a country of rivers. Try boat trips on the Yampa or the Green, or down Glen Canyon of the Colorado as far as it is still possible to float. Or try any mountain creek in an inner tube—that is the way kids from Provo or Ashton or Jackson would do it. Try getting out in back country and breaking down; stick yourself in sand or mud and learn the unfailing hearty helpfulness of the people who will rescue you. Heedless of their resources they may be, but never of a fellow creature in a jam. I have been stuck by cloudbursts in the Arizona Strip, below Zion National Park; and in both sand and cloudbursts in the Navajo Reservation; and by car trouble in the Capitol Reef and in Clear Creek Canyon in central Utah, and by washouts on Togwotee Pass in Wyoming, and by other cloudbursts out in the barren sagebrush stretches of the Wyoming Plateau; and I have slept in root cellars with mud dripping through on me, and in a shack where the bach homesteader had a water bucket full of rattlesnake tails—his hobby and consolation—and under cottonwood trees and beside irrigation ditches—(in Idaho pronounced "airigation" ditches) and I never failed to end by loving the catastrophes that marooned me among so much human kindness.

There is no Montana Face—there is no Western face. The people of the West come from everywhere, practically, and it takes more generations than they have yet had in this home to stabilize a breed, as the Yankee was stabilized. It takes more generations than they have yet had for the making of a native culture. The West is still nascent, still forming, and that is where much of its excitement comes from. It has a shine on it, it isn't tired: Even the sometimes-dubious activities of the boosters reflect an energy that doesn't know what it means to be licked or to give up. The face of the West changes; a decade is much. Generally speaking, the country lives up to its water supply. As long as there is only so much water, for so much farm land, so many towns, so much industry, Mormon boys from the Salt Lake and Utah Valleys, boys from Montana cow towns and mining camps, boys from Sheridan and Ucross and Twin Falls, will be heading toward the West Coast or toward the Midwest or the East: The Rocky Mountain states export manpower as a general rule, though all of them grow in population—Nevada most because it has no state income tax, Utah and Colorado next because they have richer mineral and industrial possibilities. They will continue to grow until they again crowd the limits of their water; if they want to grow indefinitely they will have to make the sort of effort for water that Los Angeles makes, and bring it in, perhaps, by an 800-mile pipeline from condensing plants on the Pacific Ocean. The fountain itself, the Rocky Mountains in their many folds and ranges, can produce even with maximum efficiency a crop of only so many acre-feet per year.

There will always, that is, be some open spaces. Not all the irrigation works of the next two hundred years are likely to affect the climate enough to take that dry clarity out of the air or change the gray and tawny country to a green one. There will still be the smell of sagebrush after a shower, the bitter tang of aspen in the mountains; the smoke of juniper or piñon fires: western smells. Thanks to the collaboration between private and public, local and federal, that western conditions have begotten, there will always be some roadless wilderness, quite a lot of accessible national forests, the indispensable scenic core of the national parks and monuments, a managed harvest of fish and game, a touch of the old wonder at mountain water, mountain peaks, mountain sky. Angry as one sometimes gets at what heedless men do to a noble human habitat, one cannot be pessimistic about the West. This is where optimism was born. And when the West learns more surely that co-operation, not rugged individualism, is the quality that most characterizes and most preserves it, I will seize the harp and join the boosters, for this will be one of the world's great lands.

The Pacific
Northwest

BY STEWART HOLBROOK

Possibly because the United States is still a young country, Americans have come to romanticize their pioneers and like to describe this or that region as the Last Frontier. Oregon and Washington have some claim to the distinction. As parts of what originally was known as the Oregon Country they comprise the last corner of the United States to be settled.

New England had a permanent settlement in 1620. By then what is now our Southwest corner was an established colony of Spain. The Southeast corner dates its settlement from before the American Revolution. Although the Northwest corner had a trading post as early as 1811, the classic American settler, who was the farmer-pioneer, did not arrive until the 1840's.

It was a late beginning in a disputed territory. Great Britain claimed it as a part of Canada. Americans chose to believe that the purchase of Louisiana from France gave it to them. It remained in doubt for more than four decades, or until 1846, when the Oregon Question was settled not by gunfire but by treaty, and two years later Oregon Territory was organized. It comprised the present states of Oregon, Washington, and Idaho, together with parts of Montana and Wyoming. It has the distinction of being the only region added to the Union of the States by three different means none of them military— discovery, exploration, and occupation.

Taken together Oregon and Washington today extend roughly 500 miles north and south and 350 miles east and west. In this Northwest corner is almost everything from stark desolation to lush green jungles of almost tropical growth. Two of its counties each contain more than half a million people. Some of the other counties can scarcely muster crowd enough for a decent Fourth of July picnic.

This is the proper place to mention, for the sake of clarity, that any account of the exploration and development of the entire region will be easier to follow if two major geographic features are kept in mind. One is the Cascade Range which runs from British Columbia all the way to and into northern California and divides both Oregon and Washington into two astonishingly different climatic zones. The other is the Columbia River, a stream that antedated the emergence of the mountain masses on both sides of it and cut its way through the mountains as they slowly rose.

Only half a century after Columbus first saw the New World, Spaniards who had already claimed South and Central America and raided the treasure houses of Mexico and Peru were sailing up the west coast looking for new golden stores. Apparently they got as far as the southern coast of Oregon before storms drove them back to sea. A little later came an English ship, the *Golden Hind*, Captain Francis Drake, to sight the Oregon coast. His vessel already packed with treasure pirated from the Spaniards, he was looking for that celebrated mirage known to history as the Northwest Passage, a strait alleged to connect the Atlantic and Pacific Oceans. Finding no sign of it, he was obliged to return home by sailing west across the Pacific, around Africa, and so to London.

No profession of the time enjoyed more or wilder rumors than that devoted to exploration and piracy, and a false report was soon current throughout Europe that Drake had really found the Northwest Passage. Spaniards hastened to return and cruise the northwest coast of America to seek it. Russians, the advance guard led by Vitus Bering,

a Dane, and later settlers led by Alexander Baranov set forth to establish trading posts in present Alaska and even attempted to found a
colony in northern California. It was they who first learned that the
Chinese would pay immense prices for the fur of the sea otter, with
which the northwest coast of North America was swarming. The news
got around. Both the English and the Spanish sought to trade for
sea otter and, of course, to look for the Northwest Passage, or the
River of the West as some called it.

Meanwhile, the British colonies in present United States revolted
and declared their independence. Ships flying the Stars and Stripes
began to trade in foreign parts. Among these was the brig *Columbia*,
of Boston, Captain Robert Gray, a curious man who, while cruising
the west coast for furs, sent his ship plunging full sail over a foaming
white bar that had caught his attention, and history began on the
River of the West. It was the cloudy morning of May 11, 1792.

Captain Gray appears to have been the laconic type of Yankee.
Three lines in his log serve to bring his ship over the terrible bar, and
so into a stream he judged to be a good ten miles wide near its mouth.
Some six lines are devoted to sounding and bearings, one line to
pumping out the casks and filling them from the stream. Then "So
ends," he wrote. He might better have written it "So begins," for the
story of the great river begins with Gray. It was his discovery that also
gave the United States a fairly stout claim to the area it drained.

A few days later Captain Gray bethought himself to declare this to
be the Columbia's River, then went to trading with the natives, large
numbers of whom came in canoes to the vessel, some with salmon,
some with elk meat, and all with furs. Among them he got 160 prime
sea-otter skins, for which he was happy enough to trade sheets of shining copper and bolts of bright cloth. The otter skins fetched up to
$100 each in China.

Probably more pleased with his successful trading than with his discovery and naming of a river, Captain Gray sailed promptly out of
the stream and virtually out of history too. It is known that he returned safely to Boston and that he died, either there or elsewhere,
obscurely in 1807, or even earlier. If it seems odd that this man who
first took the American Flag around the world and on his next voyage
discovered the Columbia River should have passed almost unobserved,
it is particularly satisfying that the name of his ship endured and that

she obliterated the apocryphal Northwest Passage, along with the River of the West.

It was only a few years since a Yankee adventurer named Jonathan Carver had gone so far as to state in a book that the River of the West is really the River Oregon and it rises "in about the center of this great continent" and "falls into the Pacific ocean." This was in keeping with the native legend. The name of the river, a tributary of the Mississippi, had undergone notable mutations since it first appeared on a map prepared by the French explorer Lahontan. It was then the Ouriconsint, obviously a heroic effort to put the sound of the native word Wisconsin—the name of an entirely different river 2000 miles farther east—into something a Frenchman could pronounce. The French alphabet contained no W. Jonathan Carver was not particularly careful of facts, but he was a lively, free-wheeling writer and in his *Travels* produced a fascinating narrative read widely by British and Americans, among the latter being the young Yankee poet William Cullen Bryant, who was so moved by Carver's prose about the wondrous stream that his own lines on the river, brief as they are, were of such majesty as to immortalize the name Oregon. The river, true enough, became the Columbia, but *Oregon* was sonorous, inimitable, far too good to remain without an object. Hence the Oregon Country.

When Gray entered the Columbia, nobody of course knew who "owned" the region it drained or even its limits. Gray's bold action was the first of a series of explorations by which the United States established its "right" of domain. Before other Americans could capitalize on this discovery, however, there came the British in Captain George Vancouver's three-vessel fleet. Captain Gray had met the Vancouver party both before and after he entered the Columbia. On the latter occasion he told them of his discovery and gave them a copy of his chart of the river's entrance. Then he sailed away to sell his sea-otter skins in China.

Gray had no more than disappeared into the Pacific when Lieutenant William R. Broughton, commanding one of Vancouver's vessels, entered the Columbia. He proceeded upstream far enough to sight a "remarkable mountain clothed with snow" which he named for Samuel Hood, a noted man of the Royal Navy. Captain Vancouver himself was meanwhile exploring what he named Puget Sound. He also named other geographic features including Hood Canal and Mount Rainier.

It seems more than possible that the interest in exploring the West Coast by both British and Americans was less with the idea of future dominions than because of the immediate cash value of the trade in sea-otter skins. In any case, the importance of a foothold on the Pacific Coast appears to have been appreciated by few American statesmen of the period. But because one of these was Thomas Jefferson, this was not left wholly to chance. Even before the Louisiana Purchase of 1803, Jefferson had started planning an expedition overland to take advantage of Gray's discovery.

In 1804 a party headed by Captain William Clark and Lieutenant Meriwether Lewis was moving up the Missouri River. It was mid-October a year later when the explorers laid eyes on the stream which had been flowing in and out of men's imagination for so many years. If they felt any emotion on seeing for the first time this River of the West, they did not confide it to their remarkable *Journals*. They were worried at the loss of some of their remaining stock of trade goods due to capsizing of a dugout.

From here, near present Pasco, to the river's mouth the party were to live in the midst of the ages-old salmon economy. Everywhere were the big fish floating in the river, lying rotting in heaps along the shores, untold more of them split and drying on miles of scaffolds. On they went, and were cheered by a sign that told them they could not be far from their goal—two scarlet blankets and a blue one, trade goods from coastwise ships. On November 7 they camped where they could see, between the receding banks of the river, the bright expanse of the Pacific, and Clark noted the event. "Ocian in view," he wrote. "O! the joy!" They were looking fair on the Great South Sea. The waves were coming in from China.

During a bleak, damp winter the two captains busied themselves with their *Journals*. These were conscientious men determined to carry out in the smallest detail the instructions of their good friend, Mr. Jefferson, who wanted to know everything possible concerning the great void beyond the Mississippi. Their botanical and zoölogical notes, anthropological observations, and sketches of geographic features turned out to be astonishingly accurate considering the general knowledge of the period. They even noted that the left arm of one of the native women was tattooed in memoir of "J. Bowman." It was late in March when the party began the homeward journey, and on September 23, 1806 they arrived at St. Louis.

For a century and a half historians have been assessing and reassessing the importance of Lewis and Clark. Some writers have tended to credit the expedition alone for acquisition of the Oregon Country, which was *not* a part of the Louisiana Purchase and was at best of doubtful sovereignty. But, granting that the expedition was of "paramount importance" in regard to Oregon, Bernard De Voto believed the greatest contribution of this first exploration by land was that it gave the entire West to the American people as "something the mind could deal with." Before, this void had been a region of rumor, guess, and fantasy. But when Lewis and Clark had peopled the unknown with specific tribes of Indians, mapped its mountains and rivers, and described its varying climates, they had dissipated forever the ancient myth* of a Northwest Passage. Thus, after Lewis and Clark, the mind could "focus on reality."

Simultaneously, the minds of both British and Americans began at once to focus on reality. In the same year when Lewis and Clark came down the Columbia, men of the Northwest Company of Montreal, fur traders, came over the Canadian Rockies and set about exploring and naming rivers and establishing trading posts. And by 1811 one of these men, David Thompson, who had already found the source of the Columbia, shoved off to follow that stream to its mouth.

It was an epic voyage, during which Thompson and his paddlers wore out three canoes. They made one purposeful pause while Thompson posted a notice by which he claimed the region for Great Britain, adding that the Northwest Company of Canada planned to "erect a Factory at this Place for the Commerce of the Country around." This was clear enough. But when the doughty Briton arrived at what is now Astoria he was dismayed to find a stockaded compound over which flew the American Flag. It was a spearhead of John Jacob Astor's plan to make his American Fur Company into a trading monopoly of the North American Continent.

---

* The Northwest Passage as conceived a century or two ago *was*, of course, mythical. An actual passage north of the Canadian mainland, first traversed by Amundsen in 1905, is too far north and too ice-clogged to be of much value for navigation.

Disguising both his surprise and his disappointment, Thompson gave Astor's men to understand they would waste their time should they attempt to erect posts east of the Cascade Mountains. Why, said he, his own outfit had found the interior to be barren of furs. Then, after civil entertainment, he took off upriver—followed by a party of Astorians just to make sure Thompson did not secure all the good interior locations.

John Jacob Astor's plan was as magnificently bold as it was feasible, and fully as dangerous: He would plant at the mouth of the Columbia a central establishment, with subordinate posts throughout the interior. The furs would thus be gathered at the point nearest to their sources, and nearest also to the richest market which, as said, was China. Having disposed of the furs, Astor's vessels were to reload with spices for the United States and return to New York.

It might have worked out that way, too, had the War of 1812 not interfered. In the face of reports that British men-of-war were in the Pacific, Fort Astoria was sold to the Northwest Company of Canada, and HMS *Racoon* entered the Columbia to take possession. As new Fort George, the post opened for business under what appears to have been a cynical, hard-boiled crew who ruled the poor natives with rum and bullets. When the war ended, the Treaty of Ghent declared that all territory, places, and possessions taken by either party from the other during the conflict should be restored. Fort George was returned to the United States. Astor decided not to resume operations, and the Northwest Company of Canada was permitted to continue in business. A convention of joint occupancy was entered into between the two nations.

In 1821 the Northwest Company was taken over by its ancient competitor, the Hudson's Bay Company, an outfit whose policy indicated a dogmatic belief in the permanence of the British empire. For a century and a half it had seen trading concerns come and go. It was patient with the wisdom of the ages. It was also as relentless as time, and its Governor and Gentlemen Adventurers were no men to desert the empire in time of need. So, presently to Fort Astoria came George Simpson, soon to be knighted, and with him Dr. John McLoughlin, whom Simpson had recently made chief factor, to consider matters in this, their new western department. At a spot on the Columbia opposite present Portland, they established what was to be the Bay's headquarters in the Oregon Country, with McLoughlin in charge, and christened it Fort Vancouver.

Born in Quebec and educated in Scotland, Dr. John McLoughlin stood six feet four inches, a hulking figure topped by prematurely white hair, who had long since displayed ability to trade with Indians and was moreover a man of strict honor and integrity. At Fort Vancouver he was soon the most important person in the vast region between the Pacific and the Rocky Mountains, not only as an able trader but as a sort of benign baron. Though of simple tastes himself, he carried on the old feudal customs of the Bay Company, setting a table graced with fine china, silver, and linen, with a kilted Highlander to pipe officers and guests into the dining hall. In the entire establishment usually lived some seven hundred persons, the most populous village in half a continent.

The location of this imposing post had been chosen with care. It was near the head of navigation for deep-sea vessels. It was the natural starting point for parties going up the Willamette River or overland to Puget Sound. Governor Simpson believed that nothing could keep American settlers from entering the Oregon Country and instructed Factor McLoughlin to steer them so far as possible to lands south of the river. If the Yankees could be thus herded and somehow kept there, then when the joint occupancy was over, the Columbia might well turn out to be the boundary between the United States and British Canada. Half the Oregon Country was better than none.

Simpson had been right. On came the Yankees, many of them inspired by the urging of Hall Jackson Kelley, a strange and consecrated New Englander who, though he had never been nearer Oregon than Lake Champlain, considered himself God's own messenger in respect to settlement of the Oregon Country. Fur traders, fish packers, missionaries, and families seeking land, on they came. One and all they called to see Dr. McLoughlin, who was kind, courteous, yet persuasive in urging them to settle south of the Columbia in the Willamette Valley.

One of the American missionaries, the Rev. Jason Lee, opened a school for Indians, then turned his talents to politics. Making the rounds of the scattered settlers, about half of whom were retired veterans of the Bay Company's trap lines, he got signatures to a petition asking Congress to provide a territorial government for Oregon. This he sent to Washington. When nothing came of it, Lee took off on foot overland to the Atlantic Coast and in person presented a second petition to Congress, then went about recruiting settlers. In May of 1840 he returned by ship to the Columbia, with him a party of fifty-one new settlers whom Lee's eloquence had shaken from their native homes. This party went into Oregon history, with capitals, as The Great Enforcement. Most of them took lands in the Willamette Valley. When a little later a settler died intestate, the settlers held a meeting "with probate powers." They elected justices of the peace and four constables, and named a committee to frame a constitution and draft a legal code. This was the first of several get-togethers out of which came a provisional government that was to last from 1846, when the Oregon Question was settled, until Oregon Territory was formed in 1848.

Dr. McLoughlin must have known, with the arrival of Lee's Great Enforcement, that the end of joint occupancy could not be far off. Try as he would, he could not contain the Americans south of the Columbia. A trickle of them were not to be denied. They moved north to settle on the Cowlitz River and Puget Sound in present Washington. Then, in 1843 and again in 1845, came great migrations which together brought some four thousand American settlers, to rut the Oregon Trail so deeply it could be seen a century afterward and to make of the Covered Wagon a symbol fit to join the *Mayflower* in the legendry of America. The ship of the great plains, the prairie schooner, was on its way into song and folklore.

Until the very last of the Covered Wagon people had crossed the vast expanses east of the mountains, they remembered the biggest sun and the biggest moon in the biggest skies they had ever seen. It was the hottest sun, the coldest moon. Mirages danced ahead of their wagons, or flickered in their wake; and the youngsters cried with joy, then wept bitterly as a handsome blue lake suddenly appeared, shimmering cold and inviting for a few moments, then sank out of sight into the horizon. It came to seem that their goal and the horizon were moving in unison; they were not getting anywhere. The wind never ceased. It blew straight out of hell, then from the antipodes. It piled up dark murk that split in thunderous crashes, and out of it came salvos of cast-iron hailstones to stun the imagination and to fell oxen in their yokes.

The sun was worse than the wind. Here in the great void there was no getting away from the sun. You could not hide from it. Worse was its confusing brightness. A gopher was seen plainly to be a coyote, a clump of sagebrush became a mounted Indian; a wrecked and abandoned wagon grew and grew until it loomed like a monstrous barn, then fused with nothingness. But on went the covered wagons, and out of the wagons, when desperate men saw that Time was passing them, that they must mend their pace lest they be caught in a mountain winter—out of the great wagons went a massive bureau of carved oak, or a chest, a chair or two, or even an organ. Winter must not find families on the trail; out went the furniture. . . . Parkman the historian saw the furniture strewn along the trail that led to Oregon. He recognized, as did lesser men, that these things were not the mere trumpery of households, but were the last physical evidence of family importance or at least of family continuity. They were not discarded lightly. Next to food and powder, they were the last things to be left along the way. A family that jettisoned them was a family in desperate straits.

These were among the things talked or thought about in later years, when the pioneers gathered for reunions and remembered their youth in the circle of campfires blinking like small red eyes in the endless dark.

The Great Migration of Forty-three astonished and dismayed the Hudson's Bay Company, and also the British government. From England came men-of-war to anchor in the Columbia. The United States also sent a warship. The tension increased, and James K. Polk was elected President on a campaign slogan of "Fifty-four forty or fight." The grasping Americans were demanding all of the Pacific Northwest to the Russian territory of Alaska, or northward to 54 degrees and 40 minutes, North Latitude. Mr. Polk went in. Congress passed a bill serving notice upon Great Britain of the end of the so-called joint occupancy. The British government rejected the proposal. For a time it looked like war. Great Britain, however, proposed as a compromise to relinquish its claim to all land (except the southern part of Vancouver Island) south of the 49th parallel, provided the United States would give up its claim to land north of that line. This offer, clearly advantageous to the United States, was accepted and war was averted. By this time the Hudson's Bay Company was moving out of Oregon, to set up new headquarters in British Columbia.

The Oregon Country had not yet been admitted as a territory of the United States, but an event of violence hastened legislation to make it so. This was the Whitman Massacre in the Walla Walla region of present Washington, when Marcus Whitman and his wife Narcissa, Presbyterian missionaries, together with twelve of their people, were murdered by Cayuse Indians. The provisional government of Oregon, whose treasury contained exactly $43.72, acted swiftly and well, raising and arming 500 men to run down the guilty braves, five of whom were later hanged at Oregon City.

Provisional Governor George Abernethy also dispatched a messenger overland to Washington. He was the huge, buckskinned Mountain Man, Joe Meek, whose sensational appearance with the tragic news stirred the nation. The Oregon Bill which had been languishing so long in Congress was promptly passed and signed by President Polk, who appointed General Joseph Lane territorial governor. Five years later those settlers who had taken lands north of the Columbia petitioned for separation from Oregon under style of Territory of Columbia. This was done in 1853, though the new subdivision was designated Washington Territory. Idaho Territory was later created from Oregon and Washington Territories; and from Idaho, in good time, came Montana and Wyoming. Oregon gained statehood in 1859, Washington in 1889, respectively the 33rd and 42nd states admitted to the Union.

Neither Oregon nor Washington was to suffer overmuch from Indian uprisings; and neither gained notably from a few minor if typical local gold rushes. Once the trappers had passed, and with them the economy of furs, the classic symbol of the Pacific Northwest began to take shape in the form of the man with an ax. You will find him today in the murals of our barrooms and statehouses, and even on one capitol dome.

The sounds that have influenced us in the Northwest are the crash of timber and the savage music of the whining headsaws on the sandspits of Puget Sound, on the banks of the Columbia, and elsewhere in the two states. The aroma that stirs us most is that of fresh sawdust wild on the wind. Roughly sixty cents of every dollar in the region derives from forest products. Thirty years ago the figure was slightly larger. New industries, including aluminum, have cut into the Northwest dollar, yet the woods are still the incomparable source of livelihood. Their influence is felt everywhere, and in a recent year their varied products were valued at two billion dollars.

There are two distinctive forests in the region. West of the Cascades is the forest dominated by the massive Douglas fir, with which is mixed hemlock, and where, in the coastal strip called the Rain Forest, stands the gigantic Sitka spruce. East of the Cascades are the immense timber stands of pine bordering the grasslands and deserts. Logging here was not of major importance until the arrival of the several transcontinental railroads.

Rain is the great tree maker, and rain up to the extreme measure of 130 inches a year falls in the coastal region of the two states. At the summit of the Cascades, however, the moisture lessens markedly, and presently all but disappears. It is here that the Douglas fir forest begins to diminish and the pine takes over. This is the dividing line between two vastly different climates. It often divides the political thought of both states. Perhaps nowhere else in the United States is the transition from one climate to another so sharp and sudden as in the Cascade Mountain passes, including the Columbia River highway. Less than half an hour takes you from one to the other. The change can be felt and seen.

The geographic and economic isolation of the region continued to hamper population growth until the first of the transcontinental railroads arrived in the early eighties. In 1880 there were but 175,000 people in Oregon, a mere 75,000 in Washington. During the next decade Oregon's population doubled, that of Washington increased almost four times. The pattern of settlement remained as it had been fixed since the 1850's, concentrated in the Willamette Valley and along Puget Sound. Comparatively few chose the region east of the Cascades where cattle and wheat empires were taking form and the vast pine forests were just beginning to attract the attention of lumbermen.

The early migration of eastern lumbermen to the Northwest had been by sea around the Horn. Now came timber cruisers by railroad from the lake states attracted by the new lands made available by grants to the transcontinentals. Sawmills soon marked the lines between Spokane and Portland, Tacoma and Seattle; and only a bit later from Bellingham on the north to Coos Bay and Klamath Falls near the California border.

Once the railroads came, the entire region was a magnet for an army of town promoters whose favorite gospel was that a railroad plus a good big sawmill was the certain way to Metropolis. The struggle for supremacy of this or that town was a characteristic of settlement all over the American West, and it was never more bitterly fought than in Oregon and Washington. New Tacoma boomed with sawmills and a railroad, while the older Seattle languished without rails until the determined settlers started laying rails of their own and eventually attracted the Great Northern. Portland flourished on its sawmills and on the shipping of wheat facilitated by its rail connections with both California and Chicago. Spokane grew because of rails plus a mining boom in the nearby Coeur d'Alenes of Idaho.

Meanwhile there were also the cities where gaslights flickered and went out, or perhaps never emerged from the hopeful conditions described by the town boomers' favorite adjective "projected." These were often cities of paper, illusions on a map, bolstered with pen-and-ink sketches by artists of riotous imaginations. Ocosta, Boston Harbor, mighty Frankfort-on-the-Columbia; Garrison City, Umatilla Landing, North Dalles; Grays Harbor City, Empire, Lower Cascades—one and all, and many more, arose and disappeared like the mirages they were, leaving little more residue than the handsome town plats and deeds to lots which may still be found in attics of homes all the way from Bangor, Maine, to the West Coast itself.

In contrast to the standard type of city boomer, talking shrill and fast of projected railroads, gaslights, and streetcars, the Puget Sound region attracted an extraordinary number of settlers who were seeking not the conventional metropolis, but the ideal community symbolized in the anagram of "nowhere" which Samuel Butler, an Englishman, used as title for his celebrated philosophical novel. *Erewhon* had no slums. It had no poor. It had a great deal of milk and no little honey. All hands lived on the sunny side of the street. Later and still more influential came a book called *Looking Backward*, by Edward Bellamy, an American, who also seemed to think the future of man lay in co-operative effort.

Because the Northwest corner was a new region and not yet wholly corrupted by materialism, it seemed—in the eighties and nineties to thousands of Americans—that this was the place to establish the perfect Erewhon. So they came, the idealists, to found their Edens, under various names, mostly on the bays of Puget Sound and adjacent waters. There was the Puget Sound Colony, or Model Commonwealth, near present Port Angeles; the Glennis Socialists near Tacoma; the Co-operative Commonwealth of Equality, near Edison; the Co-operative Brotherhood of Burley; the Freeland Association on Whidby Island; and the Mutual Home Colony Association of Home, on Joe's Bay.

One and all they published organs like the *Model Commonwealth*, *Industrial Freedom*, the *Co-Operator*, *The Islander*, and the red-eyed *Discontent: Mother of Progress*. Early and late the new Edens attracted national and international figures generally described as "dangerous radicals," people like Emma Goldman, Elbert Hubbard, Harry Kemp, Big Bill Haywood, and William Z. Foster. The single tax, birth control, socialism, anarchism, and finally communism, such were the labels "outsiders" attached to these experiments in living, which bloomed a while, then faded, yet achieved a reputation for nonconformity that has survived. It seems odd that scarcely a writer on the political and economic atmosphere of western Washington has paid any heed to the possible influence of these unorthodox colonies. There is almost nothing about them in the standard local histories.

Until the 17th of July, 1897, Alaska had meant little to the Pacific Northwest. It was merely a remote place humorously referred to as Seward's Icebox. But early on this particular morning there docked at Seattle from Alaska the SS *Portland,* her decks and cabins filled with bearded men and in her hold what the press described as "a ton of solid gold." It hardly mattered that the solid gold turned out to be gold dust (the total weight was authentic), or that the diggings were not in Alaska but in the part of Canada called Yukon Territory. The news electrified a United States which for three years had been suffering deflation and economic distress, while as for Seattle, according to one commentator, "the hard times vanished in a single day."

The fortuitous circumstance that the miners and their gold arrived

in Seattle took that city's name across the United States and around
the world; and hordes of men, rich and poor, clerk and farmer, set
out for the Puget Sound city as the gateway or jumping-off place for
the new Eldorado of the North. Warehouses were turned into hotels.
So were tents. Shipyards mushroomed into being all around Puget
Sound. By late fall Seattle and nearby towns were filled with the thousands waiting to take part in what went into history as the Gold Rush
of Ninety-Eight.

Although there was a backwash of dreary prospectors during 1899,
the mining boom did not bust. New discoveries were made, both in
Canadian and American territory, and all of western Washington
prospered famously from the impetus of gold until the national depression of 1907. The census of 1910 showed what had happened:
Washington had passed the million population mark, to lead Oregon
by a margin that has never materially diminished. It had also taken
first place nationally in the production of lumber, which it was to hold
until 1938 when Oregon supplanted it.

The great salmon industry of Alaska continues to be directed largely
by packing concerns on Puget Sound and the Columbia River, whence
crews go north and return annually from the canneries.

East of the Cascades the "wheat counties" of Washington and the
"cattle counties" of Oregon gained population slowly. Around the turn
of the century the latter region was the scene of sporadic violence, a
part of the classic cattle-and-sheep wars of the short-grass frontier.
Irrigation efforts, begun in pioneer days, rose and fell as the experiments of settlers failed, or were taken over by companies able to risk
capital in the enterprises. Both the Northern Pacific and the Great
Northern railroad companies came to the rescue at critical periods
in eastern Washington, which resulted in large areas successfully
planted to fruits and berries and vegetables. State and Federal agencies later lent a hand.

Hydroelectric power, first developed in this region at Oregon City
Falls by a progenitor of the Portland General Electric Company and
on the Puyallup River by what later became the Puget Sound Light
& Power Company, kept pace with population and industrial needs
until national and even international events conspired to harness

the incomparable source of hydroelectric energy in North America—
the majestic stream which in its distant solitude had so appealed to the
imagination of the youthful poet Bryant, dreaming in New England of
"the continuous woods where rolls the Oregon, and hears no sound,
save his own dashings."

Men had long been looking at the Columbia with the urgent eyes
of ambitious engineers. It is a mere 1210 miles long which, in the
world of rivers, is only medium mileage. But its source, on the roof
of the continent deep in British Columbia, is 2650 feet above sea
level. In the matter of fall, which is to say power, the Columbia ranks
high. When it has been dammed to capacity, the river will develop
50,000,000 horsepower. The first dam to harness the Columbia was
built in 1929–1931 by Puget Sound Light & Power at Rock Island
in the so-called wasteland of eastern Washington. It touched off
what can properly be called the dam-building era in Oregon and
Washington.

By the time the Rock Island project was producing power, the
Corps of Engineers of the United States Army was well under way
with an overall survey of American rivers. Two years later work was
started on a dam named for Captain Benjamin Eulalie de Bonneville,
French-born graduate of West Point and a prominent if controversial
figure of the Old Oregon Country. Bonneville Dam was built just below the Falls of the Cascades, described graphically by Lewis and
Clark as "The Great Chute." Transmission of power from the Bonneville turbines started in 1938. By then a tremendous controversy
was under way as to where the next Columbia dam should be built.
It was settled in 1933 when the Federal government selected a site
at Grand Coulee, one of scores of abandoned river channels in eastern
Washington.

The Coulee is a thousand feet deep in places and some fifty miles
long. A pioneer explorer, Alexander Ross, stood in awe to see it
and wrote that "Grand Coulee was the wonder of the Oregon Country." For another century other men looked at the Grand Coulee, to
contemplate turning the Columbia into it by construction of a gigantic dam that would not only develop immense horsepower, but
would hold back in a reservoir water that could be used for irrigation
purposes to reclaim some two million acres of desert land in Grant
and adjoining counties of Washington. Then, in 1933, when bread

lines were the longest that the United States had known in this century, thousands of men went to work on what the press liked to call "the biggest thing on earth." When it was finished, the lake behind the dam was to extend 151 miles back to the boundary of Canada.

Grand Coulee dam is big, certainly, but it has to contend with too much vacant space to *look* big. Set in the midst of appalling distances, it appears like a play dam of children, lost in the terrifying wastes that are now threaded with transmission lines. And when, in 1952, the first irrigating water was released from the reservoir, the main canal alone was said to be capable of holding "the flow of the Niagara River" and to be "longer than the Potomac." Grant and other counties were on the way to reclamation.

Next came the project at Umatilla Rapids where the river has turned west to form the Oregon-Washington boundary. Named for Charles McNary, long-time senator from Oregon, this dam wiped out the rapids, added many kilowatts to the Northwest Power Pool directed by Bonneville Power Administration, and in time will pump water to hundreds of thousands of acres now arid. Other dams on the main Columbia followed McNary—one (not far below Grand Coulee) named for the noted Chief Joseph of the Nez Percé tribe; another, The Dalles, named for the nearby Oregon city. At least two dams are being planned (1957) for the main river in Canada, while others have been built or are a-building on tributaries in the United States. The Dam Era of the Columbia is thus far from finished.

The influence of the Northwest Power Pool, which comprises electric energy from both public and private sources, is felt in all parts of the two states and often beyond their borders. When transmission of power is interrupted for any length of time, men may be laid off at the aluminum plants at Spokane, Tacoma, and Vancouver; and in the great sawmills, plywood mills, and pulp and paper plants of Port Angeles, Everett, Camas, and Longview, Washington, and Lebanon, Springfield, Medford, and Coos Bay, Oregon. It may well affect the operations of smelting and concentrating mills in the mining regions of Idaho. The shearing of sheep may be hampered on the far ranges. The canning of salmon at Astoria may be halted. What the regional press periodically calls a critical shortage of power can make a headline.

One reason often cited for power shortage is the vast and still mysterious plant of the Hanford Engineer Works, a title of utmost euphemism. Hanford is nothing less than an atomic plant where some of the essences of the Hiroshima bomb were made. What Hanford's power load amounts to in watts is not known to the public. How many watts are required to produce one pound of plutonium 239, which is the product of Hanford, is a closely guarded secret. Hanford started coming into being in 1942. At the peak of war activity in 1944, no less than 51,000 workers lived in Hanford alone, while thousands more came to work daily from tents and trailers within a radius of sixty miles.

One hardly knows how to go about describing Hanford. From a distance it seems suddenly to rise out of the desert along the mid-Columbia like an enormous mirage of almost templelike buildings, glinting silver and white in the sun, with illusive things like detached columns and isolated globes, the whole mass changing shape as one watches, confused and certain of nothing at all save that one is looking at an hallucination. After dark it is transformed into a carnival nightmare of white and yellow and green and red lights, astonishingly brilliant in this never-never land that is still enveloped with the enduring silence blanketing it when Lewis and Clark were here. One leaves Hanford reflecting that the two brave captains would comprehend no more of what went on there than the tourists of mid-twentieth century.

If, as has been said, it pleases the people of Oregon and Washington to think of their Northwest corner as the Last Frontier, it is a harmless brag characteristic of the American West. Time has made of pioneers a romantic company sitting high in the Valhalla of national memory. It is more accurate to say of Oregon and Washington that they are in a new frontier period, that of the industrial frontier; and to say, too, that a large majority of older residents dislike it. It has done havoc to their formerly easygoing way of life.

The industrial frontier arrived rather suddenly when the needs and emergencies of World War II created new and tremendous military installations and manufacturing plants accompanied by vast dispersions of population. Almost exactly a century after the covered wagon trains of the so-called Great Migration of Forty-Three, several hundred thousand Americans came to train or work through the war period, and many of them remained. Many more returned after service abroad.

What had been the pioneer airplane plant of Boeing expanded again and again. So did shipyards. The Northwest Power Pool was hard put to furnish heat to keep the new aluminum pot lines heated; to turn the saws for what since early times had been the leading industry of the region; and to operate its newest industry, if that is the term to apply to the Hanford Engineer Works.

The end of the war did not bring a backwash. Instead, there began at once a movement of small industry from the east and midwest and south; of families seeking agricultural lands, including those reclaimed from the desert by the new irrigating facilities.

In the decade after 1940 approximately one million population was added to the two states. It was a rare chamber of commerce indeed which could not note its community's "enormous gains," while speaking softly if at all of industrial slum districts. Like it or not, Oregon and Washington were no longer a Last Frontier but in the midst of an industrial civilization and the problems that go with it.

History has moved swiftly here in the Northwest. Scarcely a century separates the end of the fur trade and the Hanford Engineer Works. One after the other the stagecoach, the stern-wheeler, and the steam locomotive have gone over the hill, or over the falls, or to take their place in a museum. The bewhiskered and footloose logger, yelling at his bull team lurching down the skid road or kicking in the windows of brothels and saloons, has become a smooth-faced young man with a family and his major vice is cigarettes. He operates power machines. The Indian fighter is now with Custer. The Indian himself buys his salmon in cans, and if he wants firewater he is at liberty to buy it in a state liquor store. If his fathers lived on a timbered reservation, he may well buy Cadillacs.

Looking back no more than a century, one may ponder on the cultures that were brought here by the varied waves, some of them mere ripples, of immigration. The fur companies were officered by Scots and manned in large part by Canadian French. Many of the latter retired to farms in the Willamette Valley. They were Catholics, and missionary priests soon came to minister to them.

The first immigrants who came purposely to take up land were native Americans of English stock, and in their vanguard were Methodist missionaries who founded the first college. The first hospitals were Catholic institutions. The "father of public education" in the old Oregon Country was the Rev. George H. Atkinson, a Congregationalist from Massachusetts. The first territorial governor was Joseph Lane from North Carolina.

In the covered wagon trains of the forties were many men who came simply because they had suddenly been taken with the newest fever of their kind, the Oregon Fever. Either they or their fathers had been through migrating fevers before. The urge had taken them from the Atlantic coast states to the Ohio country, next to Illinois, then to the Missouri. It was a habit. In the process they had become virtually a professional class of pioneers, and they took to the Oregon Trail with little more thought of danger or hardships than if they were heading for a Fourth of July picnic or a camp meeting.

New Englanders were more likely to come by ship. Among these were many founders of Oregon towns, promoters of stagecoach, steamboat, and railroad lines; and always of schools and libraries. Immigrants born in Europe did not arrive in any number until the transcontinentals came. By then Washington was a territory about to be admitted as a state. Germans seemed to favor Oregon. A majority of Scandinavians chose Puget Sound and Grays Harbor. Finns concentrated on Astoria. As elsewhere in the West, Chinese had been imported to build railroads, after which they followed the mining camps, then settled in colonies in Seattle and Portland. Japanese were scarce in the Northwest until well after the turn of the century. So were South Europeans.

For decades lumbering, agriculture, and fishing have been the major occupations; and for decades little or no thought was given to the expendable nature of the forests, the soil, and the fish. Year after year the Columbia was over-fished with nets, with traps, with "Chinese lines" of multiple hooks running to hundreds each, and great salmon wheels, thirty feet in diameter, turned by the current day and night, which scooped all fish seeking to move upstream in certain channels and dumped them into a hopper. Wheels were eventually banned by both states. So were the Chinese lines, and the taking of salmon was regulated by laws.

Farmers here as elsewhere were destined to try, and to be defeated by, the one-crop idea—usually grain—before they accepted the new religion of diversification; and many more discovered what is sometimes the fatal illusion of dry farming. Yet neither state quite became a dust-bowl problem. Several of the biggest irrigating projects in the country helped to save them.

The loggers arrived in the Northwest still cherishing the idea they had held for nigh three hundred years: There was always timber, plenty of timber, just over the next hump. They had already cut a swath of it from eastern Maine through the lake states, and some had moved south to do as much for the timbered states bordering the Gulf of Mexico. The rest loaded their gear and themselves into the steam cars for Oregon and Washington.

Loggers never looked backward, eastward. Had they done so, the more reflective among them might have seen what was happening— that as fast as they abandoned their old works a horde of farmers, traders, and city promoters moved in to grub stumps, plat towns, and make highways of the grass-grown logging roads. It was the loggers' ancient enemy, Civilization, following hard in their wake, and they wanted none of it.

Yet here on the west coast, loggers and lumbermen were in their last stronghold, their backs to the sea. There was no hump to go over from here. Civilization had at last caught up with them; and it was going to tame them, too. Time out of mind their war cry had been to let daylight into the swamp, then to move on West. And now there was nothing west of the continent's west shore.

Conservation of timber, or forestry, is too complicated a story to go into here. A beginning was the setting aside of forest-reserve lands by the Federal government. Much of the timber of Oregon and Washington was long ago locked up in the National Forests, where it is harvested by private concerns operating under strict regulation. As for the rest, the loggers went to work on it with a terrifyingly efficient machine-age technology. "Timber barons" became "devastators," fit to be damned with other menacing figures. A younger generation of loggers and lumbermen still bears some of the blame directed at their fathers and grandfathers, but it grows less by the year, and rightly.

Nobody denies that the old timber barons were greedy, though probably no more so than other men. They were also charged with waste. Both haste and waste dogged the industry for decades in large part because the tax system placed a penalty on standing or uncut timber; and standing timber was accounted so great a risk it could not be insured. Thus the thing to do was to cut it as quickly as possible. This resulted in the classic curse of "cut-out-and-get-out" which had followed the loggers from Bangor to Seattle. When the tax system was revised and the tax collected when the timber was cut, lumbermen were encouraged to retain their cutover lands, to care for the new growth, even to reforest where areas had suffered fire. Tree farms were the result.

For more than a decade the larger lumber companies in the two states have had their own private nurseries from which selected tree stock is removed for planting on logged-*over* but not logged-*off* lands. Smaller outfits get their seedlings from the great co-operative nursery at Nisqually, Washington. The industry is operated today on the theory that timber is a crop, to be harvested in cycles. It is no longer merely a lumber industry, but due to the new techniques of utilization, it is known properly as the forest-products industry, which includes not only pulp, paper, and plywood, but many more items such as alcohol, plastics, material for rayon, and soil conditioners.

The logging camp as an isolated community has virtually disappeared. So has the traditional logger. The new logger is a mechanic or a technician, and he lives at home with his family in a town, city, or community, from which a highway leads to where the logging camp would be if there were any logging camp.

The forest is still the incomparable source of livelihood in Oregon, which leads all other states in the manufacture of forest products; and in Washington, which is in third place. (California is second.)

At mid-century, Seattle is the first city in the Northwest. It rises from the shore of Puget Sound and rambles up and over high hills. Its citizens like to call it the Gateway to Alaska, sometimes the Gateway to God's Country. Its setting is spectacular. In front is the blue sparkle of the Sound. At the city's back is Lake Washington. West across the Sound rise the jagged, glittering peaks of the Olympics. To the city's north, east, and south loom the Cascades. Commanding all, when there is no haze, is the tremendous mass of Rainier—The Mountain—alone, aloof, majestic.

Seattle's character is simple and clear. It is the perennial boom town—gay and grim by turns, but always loud and lively, brassy and friendly, a backslapping place given to roaring, boasting Vision. There is perhaps no more hospitable city in the United States. In its Pioneer Square stands what is locally described as "the tallest totem pole in the world"; and along the water front runs a major thoroughfare named Alaska Way. Both the totem pole and the street are evidence of Seattle's pride in its commercial and emotional ties with the forty-ninth state. The city's position in relation to the short great-circle route to the Orient also gives it an advantage in shipping over other west-coast ports.

The Northwest's second city, Portland, is a deep-sea port more than a hundred miles from the ocean. Less spectacular than Seattle, its setting is dramatic enough, what with two great rivers flowing past or through the town and three major snow-capped peaks rising from the somberly beautiful Cascade Range. The older part of the city spreads west from the Willamette, then mounts to the handsome semicircle of modest hills called The Heights. The city's east side is flanked by both the Willamette and the Columbia.

In character and atmosphere Portland is in contrast to Seattle. One of the oldest towns in the West, it was settled in some part by aggressive if conservative New Englanders whose heritage is to be seen in the hundreds of acres of elm-shaded village green bisecting the downtown section, a sort of Boston Common called the Park Blocks, inviolate these past ninety years. The pioneer Yankees also bequeathed attitudes and institutions, including a really great library, a college, and an art museum which have had no little to do with the oft-quoted remark that Portland is the "Athens of the West." One of its two newspapers, *The Oregonian*, observed its centennial in 1950. Portland is one of the world's large exporters of grain and of forest products. It has long had close shipping ties with Hawaii and with Japan.

The Northwest's third city, Spokane, rightly enough calls itself the Capital of the Inland Empire, a region embracing the rich Coeur d'Alenes and other mining districts, vast forests of white and ponderosa pines, wheatlands, and cattle ranges. Its rise was meteoric when the Northern Pacific came through, and was followed by the Great Northern and the Milwaukee railroads; the Spokane International and a branch of what is now the Union Pacific. This network of rails has given it a commanding position as a marketing and distribution center for the entire northern intermountain country. Concentrated around the handsome falls of the Spokane River, the city has spread eastward over the level valley floor and southward over the rocky rim of low pine-covered hills.

During the past two decades, the Northwest with new highways and airways has kept abreast of America's phenomenal growth in travel. Its mountains, rivers, and coast have much to offer the tourist or the vacationer. A vast complex of Federal and state forests and parks preserves the wilderness of Mounts Rainier and Hood, and of many other scenic spots in the Cascades, as do the superb national parks named for the Olympic Range and unique Crater Lake. These and other areas of native wilderness have, since the end of World War II, been building up the new industry, tourism, which many profess to believe will one day seriously contend with forest products in importance.

135. Mount Rainier, Washington, seen from a lake high up on its southern slope. Visible in clear weather from as far away as Portland, this great
mountain dominates landscapes throughout western Washington.

136. An advanced-model jet transport plane being assembled at Renton, Washington, a few miles southeast of Seattle. From such a view, one realizes that talk of "flying" tractors to distant places is not nonsensical.

137. Grand Coulee Dam, dwarfed by the magnificent proportions of its environment.

38. Where the Columbia River, older than the mountains, cut through
     them as they were uplifted.

39. "Yarding" logs in the Cascade Mountains prior to loading them
     and hauling them to sawmills.

140. Portland, Oregon, looking east toward Mount Hood.

141. Cool weather and inviting scenes make picnicking one of the favorite activities for visitors to the Oregon coast.

142. Railroad loading station for sugar beets in Washington's Columbia Basin.

143.   Helicopter bringing men and equipment to fight a forest fire near Mount Shasta, California.

144.   The San Francisco Bay Bridge. In the background at the right is the main part of San Francisco which was swept by fire in 1906 and rose from ashes to become a greater city.

Galloway

145.   Large-scale harvesting of lettuce in California.

146.   Death Valley, California. Appropriately named before the days of modern highways and air conditioning, Death Valley is now a "must" for tourists.

Galloway

147.   Looking eastward over the business district of Los Angeles.

California

BY SCOTT O'DELL

The story of California, for all its diversity of sea and mountains, deserts and mesas and sunny lowlands, its dozens of cities and hundreds of towns from the Mexican border to Oregon, is really the story of its two principal cities, San Francisco and Los Angeles. The story began like most stories of America some four hundred and fifty years ago in Spain.

It is said by Cervantes, the man who should know, that Don Quixote was a great and greedy reader. Happy with the bogus knighthood conferred upon him by a mischievous innkeeper, tilting through the grim countryside of La Mancha with a farm laborer on assback for a squire, he was equally happy book in hand beside a tavern fire.

The books he liked best, it seems, were those that dealt with fantasy. Of these his favorite by far was *The Exploits of Esplandian* by Montalvo, written in 1510. It is easy to see why:

"Know ye that at the right hand of the Indies," wrote Ordoñez de Montalvo, "there is an island named California, very close to that part of the Terrestrial Paradise, which was inhabited by black women. . . . In this island, named California, there are many griffins. In no other part of the world may they be found. And there ruled over that island of California a queen of majestic proportions, more beautiful than all others . . . their arms were of gold and so was the harness of the wild beasts they tamed to ride, for in the island was no metal but gold."

Amazons, griffins, and gold! The vision stirred Don Quixote from boot to pasteboard helmet and resolutely he rode forth to break new lances against the churning mills.

But there were others less dreamy who read Montalvo too and instead of tilting against imaginary foes, their blood afire, crossed the seas, remembering the island where love reigned and booty abounded. One of them was the conqueror of Mexico and Montezuma, Hernán Cortés.

A curious youth, this son of a curious nobleman. Martín Cortés, like the knight of La Mancha, spent most of his leisure reading books of romance. He was practical about only one thing: his son. Though puny, a frequenter of taverns, more interested in twanging a guitar than in studies, Hernán would someday be a soldier. Martín had a large and knotty whip which he frequently used to further that end.

At 19, bored with the beatings, the scorched landscape of Estremadura, his head spinning with countless fantasies (Amazons, griffins, and gold—love, adventure, and booty—if they existed in a book they must surely have reality somewhere, possibly beyond the seas), Hernán Cortés took ship for Santo Domingo.

In 1521, 17 years later, a soldier now and a tough one, Cortés stood in fabulous Tenochtitlán, heart of the Aztec Empire. He had seen beautiful women, had taken one as a mistress; his sword and his cunning had conquered Montezuma. Amazons and adventure in full measure, but where, he asked himself and his lieutenants, were the storied hoards of gold?

One of his men, the brutal de Guzmán, was sent northwest into the land of the Tarascans, but de Guzmán, though he had the Tarascan king dragged behind a horse and finally tortured to death by fire, found nothing but golden trinkets. The hoard lay elsewhere.

To bring it in Cortés dispatched expeditions by foot and ship, as far off as the Colorado River. All returned empty-handed. Still convinced of its existence, Cortés himself sailed up the Pacific Coast. He went ashore upon what he took to be an island, which, remembering Montalvo, was named California, though nowhere were there Amazons or griffins or gold. Only sun-burned mesas, barren hills, and thorn forests stretching to a fiery horizon.

The treasure lay far beyond the tip of Lower California where Cortés stood, 1500 miles to the northwest, in fact, locked in the granite jaws of the Sierra Nevada. It would take another man, a carpenter who had never heard of Montalvo, or Cortés for that matter, and more than three centuries to unlock it.

The man was James W. Marshall, and the year was 1848.

Marshall had just completed a sawmill on the American River, some 90 miles east of San Francisco. On this morning of January 24, having shut off the water from the river, he was inspecting the tailrace when his eye caught the glitter of something that lay lodged in a crevice, submerged under six inches of water. He picked up the substance and found that it was heavy, of a peculiar odor, unlike anything he had seen in the stream before. For a few minutes he stood with it in his hand. It was too heavy for mica. Could it be sulphuret of copper? Recalling that this mineral is brittle, he put the specimen on a flat stone and struck it with another. The substance neither cracked nor flaked off, merely bent under the blow.

Marshall was sure that he had found gold, but during the next few days he collected other specimens from the tailrace and on the morning of the fifth day, with three pieces of the yellow metal tied in a handkerchief, started off on horseback for Sutter's Fort, 50 miles away. He arrived there in a blustery rain, wild-eyed and almost inarticulate with excitement, sought out John Sutter, his partner in the sawmill venture, and asked if they could talk in secrecy.

Sutter took Marshall into his bedroom and locked the door behind them. He watched in uneasy silence while Marshall dumped the yellow pellets on the table. But then, without a word, he quickly reached for a volume of his encyclopedia, found the information he sought, tested the pellets with *aqua fortis*, and balanced them against an equal amount of silver. He glanced up from the scales and stared at Marshall.

"It's gold," Sutter cried. "At least 23-carat gold!"

Three and a half months later, on May 12, though John Sutter and James Marshall did everything possible in the meantime to prevent it, America learned their secret. Riding his horse pell-mell into San Francisco with nuggets in his pocket, waving his hat and lifting his voice to the hills, adventurer Sam Brannan shouted:

"Gold! Gold! Gold from the American River!"

The treasure chest that Hernán Cortés and countless other conquistadores had frantically sought was now unlocked. Sailors in the harbor deserted their ships, schools closed, newspapers suspended publication, doctors left their patients sitting in the anteroom. Outside the city farmers let their crops wither in the fields. At Sutter's Fort the tanners packed up and headed for the diggings, leaving 2000 hides to rot. The workers in Sutter's newly completed flour mill followed close on their heels.

Brannan's stentorian shouts did not die out at the Sierras. They reached across the Rockies, through the Middle West to the Atlantic seaboard. Young men took down their geography books and studied the maps.

Where was this country, not yet a state, wrested from Mexico just two years before? They saw a misshapen parallelogram, standing on its end, canted from southeast to northwest. A coastline over 800 miles long with a vast indentation two-thirds of the way along this serpentine shore marked Bay of San Francisco. Into the bay, joining there like the arms of a gigantic parenthesis, flowed two rivers, one from the south, the San Joaquin, and one from the north, the Sacramento—both fed along their courses by icy streams from the Sierra Nevada, a chain of snow-covered mountains that formed the central third of California's eastern boundary.

What these young men did not find in their geography books, and what they would fail to find elsewhere, for it had not yet been written down, was the lineaments of the dream that had inevitably led to this moment in history.

When Cortés left the thorn forests of Lower California and sailed back to Mexico and hence to Spain to repair his unraveling fortunes, the search for gold went on at a fresh pace under the questing gaze of Antonio de Mendoza, the first Viceroy of New Spain. Mendoza sent Francisco Coronado—he was 28 at the time—into the southwest at the head of an army with banners to seek out the fabled Seven Cities of Cibola whose dwellings, it was said, were fashioned of emeralds, turquoise, and gold. He dispatched Hernando Alarcón into the upper and unknown waters of the Sea of Cortés (Gulf of California) to look for them by sea and river.

Impressed with the command to bring back "the secret of the gulf," at all costs to effect a juncture with Coronado's army then traveling overland and in need of the supplies he was carrying, Alarcón by sheer will power forced his three small ships through the tidal maze formed by the meeting of the gulf and the Colorado River.

Before him, while his caravels were buffeted about like so many chips, loomed a gigantic bore (the second largest in the world), formed by the collision of the racing waters of the Colorado and the tidal waters of the sea. He might have waited there, in good conscience, for Coronado; but ambitious, fearless, and vain, dressed in his finest clothes, with his personal orchestra of three pieces at hand to refresh lagging spirits, Alarcón lowered two boats and headed upriver. He charmed the recalcitrant Indians whom he soon met by posing as the Son of the Sun, and enlisting their aid, cordelled his longboats to a spot near the Gila River. Here in the fall of 1540, not having met Coronado, he erected a cross and left the inscription: "Alarcón reached this place; there are letters under the tree." The first white man to stand on the soil of present-day California.

Viceroy Mendoza dreamed of other things besides gold. One of them was a passage said to join the Atlantic and Pacific Oceans—called the Strait of Anian by the Spaniards and the Northwest Passage by the English. To find this elusive strait, which might serve as a new route to the Kingdom of Cathay, he commanded Juan Rodríguez Cabrillo to sail north along the coast of California as far as reason and discretion would permit.

A skilled navigator, the Little Goat—as his name translates—followed the viceroy's orders and brought his two open-decked caravels to the vicinity of the Bay of Monterey. Confronted by a heavy storm and suffering from an injury to his arm, he turned back to the Channel Islands, near Santa Barbara, where he died from his injury. His command was taken over by Bartolomé Ferrer, who once again set out to the north and sailed as far as the southern coast of Oregon before turning back.

Ferrer missed the great Bay of San Francisco both coming and going—from the deck of a ship standing off at a safe distance from the coast, the Golden Gate (especially in foggy weather) looks more like a headland than a harbor entrance. Sir Francis Drake likewise missed it in 1579, as did Gali, Unamuno, and finally Vizcaíno in 1602.

In that year the search for the Strait of Anian ceased. Spain at the moment was concerned with establishing a refuge for her treasure ships—galleons plying between Manila and Acapulco—which were regularly at the mercy of English freebooters. She owned such harbors as San Diego, which Cabrillo had founded, and Monterey, explored by Vizcaíno. But the current viceroy of New Spain was the Marques de Montesclaros, a pompous sybarite who thought that a refuge should be established near Japan. Moreover, he was bemused by the myth that in this vicinity were two islands—the Isle of Silver and the Isle of Gold.

The mythical islands were sought but not found and Montesclaros' folly, unique in the annals of Spanish exploration, introduced a policy of inaction that lasted for more than a century and a half. It was 167 years, to be exact, after the successful voyage of Vizcaíno before another expedition was sent into California!

This *entrada*, organized by José de Gálvez, had a single purpose. Peter the Great had long nursed the idea of opening an eastward passage between the Pacific and Atlantic Oceans; at his death, in the pursuance of the scheme, Russia began to explore the coast of Alaska, build ships on Kodiak Island, and encourage her fur traders to scour the Aleutians.

Alarmed at Russian encroachment on the territory of New Spain, Charles III dispatched a plan by special messenger to his viceroy in Mexico City which was immediately put into effect. Franciscan priests were sent into California to found a chain of missions from San Diego to Monterey. Accompanying them were soldiers who were to establish presidios at each mission. Thus soldier and priest, working together, would bar the path to Russian aggression. At least their presence would be visible evidence of Spain's claim upon California—something that had been missing since Alarcón had first seen it centuries before.

The missionaries were led by Junípero Serra, the soldiers by Gaspar de Portolá, the newly appointed governor of California. Leaving Loreto, capital of both the Californias, the expedition safely traversed the 600 miles to San Diego. There Serra founded the first mission of the chain and Portolá, gathering a force of 64 men, pressed on to his destination.

At the latitude set down for the Bay of Monterey he found not the magnificent harbor described so sanguinely by Vizcaíno but a small *ensenada,* open to wind and wave. A Catalan soldier of courage and tenacity—both qualities were endemic among early Spanish explorers —he decided that Monterey must lie farther to the north.

But at Half Moon Bay, ill and exhausted, Portolá was forced to halt. He was certain that Vizcaíno was a liar and that Monterey had somehow been passed; nevertheless he sent out two small scouting parties. One topped a ridge and looked down upon the lower reaches of San Francisco Bay; the other, trending north, came upon the southern promontory of the Golden Gate. They reported their find to Portolá, but somehow unimpressed, positive that he had not found Monterey and conscious of failure, he retraced his steps to San Diego. There he unburdened himself to Father Serra, who had also had his own troubles.

"Don't fret," said the priest. "You have merely been to Rome without seeing the Pope."

"I've been to hell," said the soldier, "and have shaken hands with the Devil."

A presidio and mission were established at San Francisco in 1776, the same year Captain Anza arrived overland from Mexico with 240 colonists and founded nearby the pueblo of Yerba Buena. On the day in 1848 when Sam Brannan rode through the town shouting "Gold from the American River!" it was no longer a Mexican pueblo. The name had been changed to San Francisco the year before to coincide with the end of the Mexican War in California.

Brannan's shouts not only sent the able-bodied citizens of San Francisco scurrying for the mines but also the population of every town and village from San Diego to the Oregon border. Three weeks later, by the first of June, 2000 men were in the Sierras; one month later the number had doubled. Working a full day, anyone could pan $15 of gold dust; many struck it rich. A miner named Hudson in six weeks dug $20,000 worth near Coloma. Young Mr. Davenport found 167 ounces in two days. A Frenchman discovered $5000 while removing a tree stump.

Summer passed idyllically, with plenty of gold and elbow-room for everyone. The Gold Rush was a local, California affair. But in December the director of the Philadelphia mint received a shipment valued at $26,000. Simultaneously a government messenger carried $3000 worth of gold in a tea caddy to President Polk, which the President publicly displayed and referred to in his message to Congress:

"The accounts of the abundance of gold are of such an extraordinary character, as would scarcely command belief were they not corroborated by the authentic reports of officers in the public service."

Brannan's shout had been heard across America; Polk's message made it official and took in the world. Before the end of 1848, the forty-niners were California bound.

They came by wagon and by horseback. Some 16,000 sailed around the Horn, a six months' voyage considerably longer than halfway around the world. Others—the more energetic—sailed to Chagres, threaded the Panamanian jungles by foot or muleback, and completed the six weeks' journey by ship. They arrived singly and in companies, with or without guidebooks, these young men from China, Peru, Mexico, and Europe; from the neat little towns of New England and the farm lands of Ohio.

Most of those who came by ship were city men, described by Bancroft as "editors, ministers, traders, the briefless lawyer, starving student, the quack, the idler, the harlot, the gambler, the henpecked husband, the disgraced . . ." Among them were also many honest men and devoted women. Those who made the 2000 mile journey westward from the marshaling points in Missouri were largely farmers and mechanics—experienced frontiersmen.

By the end of 1849 the population of California had skyrocketed to 100,000 exclusive of native Indians. Of this number the vast majority were somewhere between Sutter's Fort and the various mines, at such places as Red Dog, Poker Flat, Rough and Ready, or Hell's Delight. They were in possession of what remained of the $10,000,000 pried from the earth that year. With the arrival of the bulk of those who had left home in '49, the value of the pannings jumped to $41,000,000—to double that amount in 1851.

The diggings were fabulously productive and yet, so dense was the horde that worked them, the earnings of the average gold miner totaled less than $600 a year. The men who struck it rich were generally those who stayed in the booming town of San Francisco and went into business. Ships moved in and out of the bay in an endless phalanx; cargoes often failed to reach the merchants they were consigned to, so great was the demand, and were bid for on the wharves. Flour brought as much as $400 a barrel, cabbages $2 apiece; pills sold for $20 a pill; eggs were $1 each; doctors charged $32 a visit; tents rented for $20 a week, a two-story house for $1000 a month; *nymphes du paye*, arrived from Paris, asked $16 merely to sit on a bar stool and converse for an evening, $250 for more demanding favors.

But while San Francisco's entrepreneurs grew rich from the mines, their counterparts in the other towns along the Royal Highway—Monterey, San Luis Obispo, Santa Barbara, San Buenaventura, and San Diego—flirted with ruin. Only at Los Angeles, then the third largest town in California with a population of some 1500, did they fare better. All the foot-loose males of course were in the diggings, but the pueblo happened to sit directly at the gate of the southern route into California. Gold seekers traveling the Old Spanish Trail, experienced miners from the silver reefs of Mexico's Guanajuato and Sonora, stopped here to replenish their supplies. Some of the more daring merchants bought cattle from the great surrounding ranches, where fresh beef was practically worthless, drove them north to the gold fields, and sold them at a profit.

The Los Angeles merchant, however, did not get rich. The pueblo he served was still, despite the argonauts who came and went, a dusty collection of flat-roofed adobes, grouped around the traditional Spanish plaza. The roofs were mostly fashioned of reeds laid down in tar, which under an enduring sun melted and ran down the earth-and-straw walls. The streets were wide and straight—Governor Felipe de Neve, when he founded the town in 1781 with 22 colonists recruited from the old silver city of Alamos in Sonora, had laid them out that way.

They were for the most part somnolent. Guitars twanged in the dusk, it is true, señoritas promenaded in the square, and bibulous shouts rose from a few cavelike cantinas. But there was nothing approaching the life or gaiety of the boom town to the north where gaming tables never closed down, where champagne was quaffed from ladies' slippers, and cosmopolites gladly paid $65 a seat to watch Lola Montez, ex-mistress of a Bavarian king, perform her famous "Spider Dance."

Its somnolence, in addition to the drain put upon it by San Francisco, lay partly in the fact that it was caught, dead-center, between two eras—the Spanish-Mexican period which had ended with the Mexican War and the American period which had just begun.

The Mexican War in California, instigated on a national scale by a land-hungry administration operating under the excuse and compulsion of Manifest Destiny, was, in a large measure, opéra bouffe. Hostilities began in the north with name calling, graduated to bloodless sorties when politically ambitious John C. Frémont rode onto the scene, and ended in the north with the raising of the Bear Flag over the country domicile of a Spaniard who, surprised to learn that war had been declared, invited his besiegers into the parlor to have a drink of brandy.

South of the Tehachapi Mountains—the traditional boundary between the two parts of California—the war had a different aspect. The Southern *Californios*, whose ties to Mexico were still strong, resented the easy capitulation of their northern neighbors as well as the high-handed tactics of the army which arrived to take over Los Angeles. They drove the Americans from the pueblo and defeated the forces sent by sea to reënforce them.

They were later subdued, but rallied again at San Pasqual, and with a small band of horsemen—probably the best in the world at the time —waylaid the Army of the West commanded by General Kearney. Using homemade lances, the *Californios* surprised Kearney at dawn and cut his little army to pieces in a matter of minutes, killing 18 of his men and wounding as many more. The war in California ended two months later, in January of 1847, with a show of friendship on both sides. The friendship was not too sincere in either case.

Besides the lifeblood it was losing to the Sierra gold fields, and the resentments of the transition period following the war, Los Angeles had yet another cause for somnolence: The pueblo was the heart of California's pastoral economy, and this economy was threatened by ruin. The threat had its origin some 75 years in the past.

When Portolá left San Diego to seek out the Bay of Monterey, Father Serra set to work in earnest. Short, thin, lame, and no longer young, with deep-set eyes beneath a high Spanish forehead, Serra combined saintliness with the obstinacy of a medieval fanatic. There were thousands of pagan souls to save; he proposed to save them, whatever reluctance they might show, however difficult the military proved to be, in the few years that God had left to him.

He first moved Mission San Diego de Alcalá to a more favorable site nearby, and then set out to establish a chain along the Royal Highway, roughly marked out by Portolá. Building of ashlar, mud, and timber—on models taken from San Pol in Spain—he erected in three years the Missions San Carlos Borroméo at Monterey; San Antonio de Padua, about 70 miles south of Monterey; San Gabriel Arcangel, just east of Los Angeles; and, closing the gap between Los Angeles and Monterey, Mission San Luis Obispo de Tolosa. He was infinitely patient with the Indians, impatient with the military, and when the latter began to chafe at his demands, he went over their heads and hobbled his way to Mexico City to see their superiors, returning to California only when his demands had been met.

At his death, Serra's work was taken over by Father Lasuén and others, so that all the gaps in the chain were filled. The original plan was complete and 21 missions extended for some 600 miles along the Royal Highway, approximately a day's journey apart.

Their lands were large—often exceeding 100,000 acres. With the guidance of the priests, Indians set out orchards and vineyards, raised stock, built dams and ditches for irrigation and mills for the grinding of wheat and corn, and engaged in many other activities ranging from beekeeping to the making of rowels and musical instruments. Women were taught to spin and weave. The missions at their peak had under cultivation about 200,000 acres and owned 320,000 sheep, 245,000 cattle, and 65,000 horses.

This wealth was bound to excite cupidity. The King of Spain had decreed that the missions should not hold the land forever, that their role should be simply one of colonization; it was likewise not intended that they should be despoiled. But as soon as Mexico won its independence from Spain, the Mexican governors of California and their friends got busy. With the Secularization Act of 1833, which decreed that mission property henceforth belonged to the State, they began to nibble away at it. At the start of this confiscation there were less than a hundred private ranchos in California; at the finish, with the end of the Mexican War in 1847, they totaled ten times that number. Thus, in a short period of 15 years, all mission land passed from the Church (and the Indians who first held title to it) to new owners. The missions themselves became a shambles, many were abandoned. The commodious church and once ample granaries of Mission San

Juan Capistrano sold for $710, those at San Luis Obispo de Tolosa for $500.

The Indians fared worse. Serra had beguiled them out of the hills with bright trinkets and gifts of love; they came to the missions reluctantly, and, for the most part, reluctantly stayed, abjuring work, preferring a diet of grubs, insects, and seeds to more staple food, and when fortune favored, a hunk of dead whale washed ashore on some handy beach.

They were children—backward children at that—of a Mongoloid race untouched by the past 5000 years. And they were treated as children, punished for their misdeeds, rounded up if they fled. It would have taken six generations of Franciscan priests, if not more, to make them independent members of a new era; unfortunately, there was only one. With the result that as the missions broke up the Indians returned to their ancestral lands to find themselves unsuited for either the old life or the new, their homes preëmpted by a race whose ways they could not understand.

Those who had acquired these lands through old or recent grants —Spaniards, Mexicans, and Americans married to *Californio* women —found to their consternation, as California changed hands, that the United States was a devious landlord.

In 1850 California became the thirty-first State; one year later the United States created a land commission of three men whose powers abrogated the Treaty of Guadalupe Hidalgo and its protection of prior titles whether granted by the King of Spain or by Mexico. In short, if any owner failed to submit his title to the commission's scrutiny within two years, or if it were submitted and deemed faulty for whatever technical reason—and there were dozens of reasons lying about—the title became forfeit. And this, though he and his forebears had lived on the land for 50 years.

It was true that some method of clarification of titles and boundaries was needed. For example, Rancho San José, typical of many, was laid out by two chain bearers who started from a willow tree marked by a cross of twigs, one of the bearers riding at full gallop trailing a rope about 250 feet long with stakes fastened at each end. As he reached the end of the rope his partner set a stake, and the gallop continued until the two bearers had satisfied themselves that the 15,-000 acre grant had been defined. This particular romp enclosed the boundaries of the present cities and towns of Pomona, Claremont, La Verne, Spadra, and Glendora in the Pomona Valley.

The boundaries during the Spanish-Mexican period were therefore approximate. If the grantee received a thousand extra acres, who cared? No one, until the Americans came along. They cared a lot, about this and other things. One of those concerned was the senior Senator from California, the equivocal John C. Frémont, who filed a claim on Rancho de las Mariposas and had it approved by the land commission—the first such approval made by that body. Senator Frémont, incidentally, had instigated the Land Act.

The result of this new American law was confusion in the quiet pueblo of Los Angeles and among her surrounding ranches. Accumulative and deadly, its full effects would not be felt for another ten years.

San Francisco, meanwhile, far from pastoral, unconcerned with who owned ranches as long as they produced food for its well-heeled citizens, had a problem of her own.

In the three years since the discovery of gold, law and order in the city had broken down. Businessmen were too busy getting rich to do jury duty or to vote; judges were in cahoots with venal lawyers, of whom there were hundreds; hoodlums who would have been hung if they had lingered in any of the mining camps found happy asylum among the scourings of four continents, pouring by the thousands into the port. The elite of this criminal element were at first the Sydney Ducks, former members of the Australian penal colony, but their leadership was soon challenged and taken over by a gang of bully boys from New York who called themselves the "Hounds," later, since it was more euphonious, the "Regulators."

Ducks and Regulators, dividing the city into loose precincts, robbed, murdered, threatened, and blackmailed, much as it is done today. Their favorite trick was to set part of the city afire, and while the lawful element was dealing with the conflagration, to rifle those sections that had been left unguarded. The Regulators would have gone on indefinitely regulating and starting fires had they not overstepped themselves and elected to run the Chilenos (a general term for all South Americans) out of town.

Razing the verminous Chilean settlement, looting its saloons, they swaggered about the city for 24 hours until disgusted citizens, finally aware that they had a menace on their hands, got tired of the display. Sam Brannan, who the year before had announced the discovery of gold on the American River, climbed on a barrel in a public place and harangued a large crowd into action. Two hundred and thirty volunteers started off to round up the Regulators, most of whom by now had skipped; those who were caught were sentenced to the penitentiary. There being no penitentiary, they were freed and told to follow their departed friends.

San Francisco settled back to normal business, well-satisfied with itself, and hundreds of ruffians plied a quieter trade. Two years later a couple of thugs entered the store of C. J. Jensen, a popular merchant, beat him unconscious, and robbed the safe of $2000. The thieves were captured, but the populace, certain that the culprits would go free as was the custom, marched 5000 strong into Portsmouth Square to hear Mr. Brannan shout: "We are the mayor, the hangman, and the laws. The law and the courts never yet hung a man in California."

Out of this meeting grew a Vigilance Committee which described itself as "A group of responsible citizens, bound together by a permanent organization, with the declared purpose of protecting lives and property in emergencies where lawful means prove ineffective." The Committee hung four ruffians in all, brought 90 to trial, and more importantly, caused hundreds of others to seek sunnier climes.

One of the sunniest, if quiet, was Los Angeles, now in 1851 still a pueblo though officially an incorporated city and the county seat. The mayor and council, following the lead of the North (the habit of trailing along after San Francisco in civic matters is one that Los Angeles has found difficult to break), met the inrush of murderers, thugs, horse thieves, and highwaymen with a Vigilance Committee of their own. But outdoing San Francisco and establishing the precedent of extravagance in affairs once undertaken, southern Committees, formal and otherwise, hung 37, not counting the "legal" hangings which numbered 40!

Their work was greatly augmented by Sheriff James F. Burns, whose specialty was chasing mounted highwaymen. One he pursued for 200 miles into the cactus wastes of Baja California, returning to claim his reward with the grisly proof of their meeting—the deceased's unique, six-toed foot.

Other highwaymen—lawyers and moneylenders who flocked in with the Land Act—were unfortunately outside the sheriff's jurisdiction. In the five years of its existence, the land commission passed on more than 800 cases involving some 12,000,000 acres; 520 titles were verified, 275 were rejected. In each instance, faced with proving his title, the California ranchero was compelled to seek legal advice. Advice was expensive (one case dragged through the courts for 35 years; the average was 17 years), and while the rancher was often wealthy, he was wealthy in land and cattle, poor in cash. Lawyers frequently eased the situation by taking a mortgage on his property; if not, moneylenders were happy to make a loan at usurious rates, ranging from 5 to 10 percent a month, compounded monthly.

The Land Act was necessary, but it ruined dozens of ranchers: combined with the drought it put an end to cattle raising in Southern California.

The drought began in 1862 and by '64 held the Southland in a searing grip. Alfilaria and burr clover dried to powder. Streams fell to a trickle, springs failed. Thousands of cattle died on the range—more than 70 percent of the total herd—and their carcasses piled up in mountainous hedgerows, filling the countryside with a nauseous stench and the sky with wheeling phalanxes of carrion birds. Wild horses were rounded up to save what pasture remained and driven over the vaulting cliffs at San Pedro and other promontories from there to San Diego.

The Land Act and the drought and the ruinous prices that followed the drought (steers sold for 25 cents) also ended the way of life established by the Spanish Don. Gone in a few short months was the era of princely estates, horned herds on a thousand hills, a pastoral existence based on the slow turning of the seasons. Dignified, relishing danger, a man of his word, loving display and hating physical labor, open-handed, prodigal and prolific, the philosophy of the California ranchers is best summed up by Don Ignacio Palomares who, asked why he did not join the Americans in the gold fields, replied: "What do I want of gold? All these fertile leagues of land are mine. Every smoke you see rising is from the home of one of my children or one of my friends to whom I have given land. Every year I lead my *carretas* and take my hides and tallow to the ocean and the Yankee ships. Every year I trade them for all those things I and my family need—silks, shawls, fans, combs, and such folderols for the women; Chinese sweetmeats for the children, salt, sugar, coffee, tobacco— enough of everything for another year. What would I do with more?"

Scarcely aware that the old era in Southern California had passed and a new era had begun, San Francisco rode high on a new wave of wealth—a gold and silver tide pouring down from the Nevada side of the Sierras, from the deep shafts of the Comstock Lode. And more remarkable still, a group of men, known as the Big Four, were busily engaged with a scheme that would soon dwarf the combined riches of the Comstock and California fields.

The biggest of the Big Four was Collis P. Huntington. Known to his friends as a "cheery old man" who was "scrupulously dishonest," and to his enemies as a bandit "ruthless as a crocodile," Huntington arrived in the first months of the Gold Rush, worked a half day in the diggings, and then, like most of the smart forty-niners, became a merchant. By 1860 he was wealthy, launched with his three partners —Mark Hopkins, Leland Stanford, and Charles Crocker—on a project to build a railroad from San Francisco to Ogden, Utah.

The project was delayed by the Civil War, whose opening shot in California was fired by United States Senator David C. Broderick on September 13, 1859.

Broderick was a Democrat, immensely popular, the leader of the wing of the California party set against the extension of slavery. The most vocal of his opponents in the pro-slavery wing was David S. Terry, Chief Justice of California's Supreme Court. Judge Terry ridiculed his rival in a convention speech; Senator Broderick read the remarks while at breakfast in the International Hotel, smiled grimly, and said, "Had the Vigilance Committee disposed of him as they did of others, they would have done a righteous act." He alluded to Terry's arrest by the Vigilantes three years before on a knifing charge.

Broderick's remark was overheard by one of Terry's friends, the incident led to an exchange of letters between the principals, the letters to an arrangement for a duel. The men met at sunrise on the 12th of September, only to be placed under arrest by the chief of police. Efforts were made that day to halt the proceedings, but both men were determined to have it out. They met again the next morning on the sand dunes of Laguna de la Merced, about 12 miles from the city, with seconds and 80 spectators.

Broderick received a hair-triggered pistol, unfamiliar to him, and as the command "Fire! One—" was given, it discharged before he could bring it to the level. A second later Terry fired, his ball striking Broderick in the chest. Three days later Broderick was dead and 30,000 San Franciscans gathered in the plaza to mourn him.

His death left California with two Senators, both secessionists, and of the two congressmen one openly proposed the establishment of an independent Pacific Republic if the Union were dissolved. The Knights of the Golden Circle, secretly formed to promote these views, were opposed by Union clubs. With the firing on Fort Sumter skirmishing broke out, and Union troops were hastily marched in from Oregon and Fort Mojave to quiet the city.

The Civil War in Southern California tended, characteristically, to more extravagance of speech and action. The *Los Angeles Star*, a four-page weekly, had called Lincoln's First Inaugural Address a "grand failure." The *San Bernardino Patriot* now took up the Union cause and reported that the Knights of the Golden Circle daily grew stronger.

"Secret meetings continue to be held all over . . . and secession and disunion are boldly avowed in our streets. Shooting continues to be the order of the day, and drunken desperadoes and Southern cut-throats damn the Stars and Stripes . . ."

Southern efforts were centered upon a conspiracy called The Great Hastings Scheme. Hundreds of men, secretly recruited and hanging around in the San Bernardino Mountains under the pretext of mining, were to be used to overthrow Federal control of Arizona and New Mexico. Landsford W. Hastings, its originator, hurried to Richmond to present the plan to Jefferson Davis. He would first issue a pamphlet, he told Davis, describing the mining resources of Arizona and New Mexico, distribute it through California's secret societies, and organize several mining companies which in turn would hire miners. These soldiers would join those already in the San Bernardino Mountains, set out for the mining properties in northern Mexico, rendezvous on the Colorado River, and then suddenly march upon Fort Yuma. The plan was bold and might have affected future events, but since it was now late in the war, the Southern leaders decided that it would be impossible to raise the amount of money required and safely transport it to the West. Their decision ended all thoughts of formal resistance in California.

With the close of the Civil War, Collis P. Huntington resumed work on the Central Pacific Railroad. In a moment of blinding inspiration he saw that since the government offered a subsidy of $16,-000 a mile for track built in flat country and $32,000 a mile in the foothills, millions could be made by interpreting flat country as hilly. It was a simple matter to change topography on the maps by a few scratches of the pen, and he conscientiously did so with the connivance of his partners.

The city jumped high in the air and clicked its heels when the Central Pacific's tracks joined those of the Union Pacific at Promontory, Utah, early in May of 1869. Sedate citizens danced in the streets, toting a giant transparency lettered "San Francisco annexes the United States," beside tipsy denizens of the Barbary Coast's Deadman's Alley, Murder Point, Moketown, and Bull Run, and the companions of Iodoform Kate, ineffable Queen of Maiden Lane. San Francisco at last was the Pacific terminus of a transcontinental railroad!

Wealth poured into the city, pyramiding the silver treasure from the Comstock Lode. William Chapman Ralston began to build the Palace, a hotel that would out-dazzle any in America, and to equip it set up his own furniture factory. Overnight San Francisco consolidated its position as the banker for the West—a position which it has never relinquished.

In this moment of general euphoria, Huntington found it easy to eliminate his competitors. He acquired two branch roads, forced another out of business, absorbed two proposed short lines and a river navigation company, and persuaded a complacent city council into granting him control of half of San Francisco harbor.

The dusty little pueblo of Los Angeles meanwhile sat by enviously eyeing the new riches of the northern city, particularly the transcontinental railroad. True enough, it had a railroad of its own, the Los Angeles and San Pedro, with a locomotive brought around the Horn in pieces. The trouble was that Phineas Banning's line didn't go anywhere—just 20 miles in one direction and 20 miles back. There was also Butterfield's Overland Mail, now a year old, which halted twice weekly on its 2800 mile trip between St. Louis and San Francisco. But a stagecoach that carried only four passengers was not a transcontinental railroad.

Fortune smiled.

Clawing its way through the Tehachapi Mountains, boring 18 tunnels along a corkscrew gradient in a major feat of construction, the Southern Pacific arrived at Los Angeles on September 5, 1876. The pueblo tried to match San Francisco's spree of seven years before. Cannons boomed and oratory flowed; the streets blazed with day-long bonfires.

The slow awakening, as the Southern Pacific strangled existing competition, raised freight rates, and fought the Santa Fe's entrance into California, was painful. The railroad hired Eastern lecturers and publicists to advertise Southern California. Local boosters sent out crates of literature. Few responded. By 1880 the population had fallen from its peak of 16,000 to 11,000, and some foresaw the day when Los Angeles would be a collection of huts beside the river, like the old Indian village of Yang-na upon which the pueblo had been built. They failed to discern a small white cloud on the horizon, far to the east. The cloud was dust, and the dust was made by the construction crews of the Santa Fe Railroad, snaking down through the Cajon Pass to the discomfort of its rival, the Southern Pacific.

Once established in Southern California, the Santa Fe took on its competitor in a reverse, jacks-wild poker game that thrilled the nation. It cut passenger rates from Kansas City to Los Angeles from $100 to $95. To $80 when the Southern Pacific countered the move, and then successively to $50, $25, and to $8. The Southern Pacific cut the ante to $6, and, misinformed that this figure had been met and lowered, to $4, then, in a rousing flourish, to $1.

Thousands of Americans owned a dollar and wanted to spend it (the Southern Pacific alone sold over 100,000 tickets) on a trip to Southern California. Trains in four and five sections, loaded to the roofs, steamed into Los Angeles daily. Hotels slept six or nine to a room, three to a bed, often handled guests in shifts, one shift sleeping while the other roamed. The overflow found shelter in tents, countless makeshift houses, in a wide circle around the town.

The prices of lots doubled and tripled; property sold and resold as many as four times a day. Prospective buyers lined up in block-long queues for daylight excursions to outlying subdivisions where the food was free though not the land. Moonlight excursions—and some of the property looked better by moonlight—with bands playing soft Spanish music appealed to the romantic.

Along the 45 miles of the Santa Fe main line between Los Angeles and San Bernardino two dozen towns sprang up before the end of 1887. But by the following summer, to everyone's dismay, the boom had burst, a third of those who had journeyed west had returned home, and those who stayed found values depreciated by a half.

The pueblo, however, had become a city of 80,000 in a single year. Built on a dollar fare and speculation, it would grow (to a population of 2½ million, reach confidently toward 3) on a factor not then generally considered. The factor was climate.

An early observer, with a taste for rainbow prose and large visions, alluded to it while conducting an auction at Santa Monica. "At one o'clock," he told his listeners, "we will sell at public outcry to the highest bidder the Pacific Ocean, draped with a western sky of scarlet and gold. . . . The purchaser of this job lot of climate and scenery will be presented with a deed of land 50 by 150 feet. The title to the ocean and the sunset, the hills and the clouds, the breath of life-giving ozone, and the song of birds, is guaranteed by beneficent God. . . ."

Exaggeration, but not much. Climate and its accompanying causes and backdrop are what he had to sell, and what the millions who have come after him have bought, lived with, and thrived upon.

The determining feature of California climate is the Pacific Ocean. Out of it in summer come the prevailing westerlies, fog-laden and fairly constant. In winter it breeds cyclonic storms that bring heavy rain in the north, diminishing as they move south. At northern Eureka, for example, the annual rainfall is 46 inches, at San Francisco 22½, at Los Angeles 15, at San Diego, on the Mexican border, a scant 10 inches.

The ocean's influence is countered and changed throughout California by the immensely varied elevations. Thus in the mountain village of Julian, only 50 miles from San Diego, the annual rainfall is 38 inches and snows of four feet are not unusual. At the foot of the southern Sierra Nevada—a continuous rampart over 400 miles long, with 50 peaks above 13,000 feet—where snow lies into midsummer and reaches depths of 20 feet in winter, sprawls the great cauldron of Death Valley. There rain is scarcely measurable and temperatures nudge 134°.

The Pacific is especially felt along the coast and in the adjacent valleys. During the summer, these areas are visited almost nightly by what are called velo clouds, which sometimes sweep in as low fog. Usually they're a high fog, obscuring the sky until late morning, and serving both to moderate the summer heat and to retard evaporation. The influence of these unique clouds stretches as far north as San Francisco, but it is decisive in Southern California where it extends farther inland.

Another unique feature of the State is the San Andreas Rift, a zone of faults which starts on the northern coast, runs through the San Francisco Peninsula, through the great Central Valley, twists east of the San Gabriel and San Bernardino Mountains near Los Angeles, and loses itself in the Gulf of California. A break in the earth's surface, its action is roughly comparable to that of hands held palms down and side by side, then moved backwards and forwards.

A violent movement of the earth's fractured crust (which has occurred only five times since 1812), results in a major earthquake similar to the one that struck San Francisco in 1906. Starting at daylight and lasting 48 seconds, the temblor shook buildings loose from their foundations, lit fires that raced in all directions, and in two days left the heart of the city a heap of smoking debris.

The righteous saw in the city's disaster divine punishment for her sins. But Charles Field—a cousin of Eugene—learning that a friend's liquor warehouse had survived intact, penned a dissenting quatrain:

> If, as they say, God spanked the town
> For being over-frisky,
> Why did He burn His Churches down
> And spare Hotaling's whiskey?

A San Francisco reporter, Will Irwin, writing at a newspaper desk in New York from hourly dispatches, summed up the city's feelings: "The old San Francisco is dead. The gayest, lightest-hearted, most pleasure loving city of the Western continent . . . is a horde of refugees living among ruins. It may rebuild; it probably will; but those who have known that peculiar city by the Golden Gate, have caught its flavor of the Arabian nights, feel that it can never be the same. It is as though a pretty, frivolous woman had passed through a great tragedy. She survives, but she is sobered and different. If it rises out of the ashes it must be a modern city, much like other cities and without its old atmosphere."

San Francisco did rise out of the ashes, a modern city, but not at all like other cities as Will Irwin predicted. She did lose some of her old atmosphere, though this would have been lost anyway without earthquake and fire, in the process of growing up. What is important, she did not lose her spirit. She stands today confident and alive on her hilly tongue of land between the sea and a magnificent bay—really a series of harbors—much the same as she did in the past.

San Francisco in the old days was a doorway from Asia. It was through the Golden Gate that some 30,000 Chinese came to California in the first few years of the Gold Rush; Huntington later used thousands of them to build his railroads. Today the city is a doorway to Asia, sending its planes winging westward; trading heavily with Japan and the Philippines; shipping rice, funneled in from the great fat valleys of the Sacramento and the San Joaquin to Pakistan, Hong Kong, and Singapore. Ahead of rice, among the exports, are cotton and machinery from the two valleys. (For American consumption, excellent wines come down from the gravelly hills of Napa and Sonoma.)

Commerce is inevitably crippled by the embargo on Chinese trade in effect since 1950. Businessmen, internationally minded, favor the lifting of the embargo and are working politically by opening branch banks and starting businesses in Asia against the time when trade can move freely. When it does, San Francisco will be ready.

Meanwhile the city, invigorated by weather that can change three or four times in a single day, and usually does, lives in the present, proud of her past and her arts, with the leisure and wealth to enjoy them. Proud too of the University of California across the bay at Berkeley which specializes in Asian studies and with its various branches throughout the State is the world's largest.

Above all, San Francisco is proud of her heritage of hospitality; it is among my fondest memories. I remember one occasion especially when as a new author with a new book I had gone north to launch it in a hopeful bookstore. The sale was not brisk, indeed, disappointing; but suddenly there appeared a small man in a rumpled suit who introduced himself as Albert Bender and bought 45 copies to distribute among institutions and his friends.

Moreover he invited me, a stranger an hour before, to his apartment, beautifully furnished with Chinese antiques, to meet two of the loveliest women I had ever seen or have seen since, and fed me pressed duck besides, and Pol Roget in a Chinese crystal goblet. Philanthropist Albert Bender is now dead, but others have taken his place. Where else in California can their like be found? Where, as a matter of inquiry, in America?

Los Angeles is hospitable, too, in a quite different way. The most extensive city in the world with an area of some 421 square miles, she has greeted and dazzled the multitudinous sun-seekers of America.

The eighty-seveners—those who were attracted by the one-dollar fare—came mostly from the Middle West. Thus Pasadena was founded co-operatively by Indianans; Quakers from Illinois and Iowa started the town of Whittier; similar groups grafted themselves upon the Mormon population of San Bernardino, itself largely recruited 30 years earlier from the Middle West.

Unlike the forty-niners, who sought adventure and gold, who brought with them the ways of the world and gave San Francisco its worldly flavor, these later settlers brought the taste and look of the old home place beside the Wabash, the Missouri, and the Ohio. When they found the California climate salubrious (San Francisco rightly complained that "the average mind conceives of California as a small tract of country situated in and about Los Angeles"), far more congenial than the Middle West's icy winters, unstable springs, and hot summers, they imparted their enthusiasm by letter.

Relatives and neighbors responded, so that throughout the early 1900's and into the '20's immigration was predominantly from the same source. Other sections of the country, other parts of the world, participated after this date. (Los Angeles and vicinity now has the biggest Mexican population in any city outside of Mexico City itself, and thriving Japanese and Filipino colonies grew in size and influence though they could not match San Francisco's Little Italy, Little Manila, or Chinatown.)

But even to this day the average Angeleno's loyalties are divided. His equivocations, for example, may be dramatically observed at any Rose Bowl game, where football teams from the Pacific Coast meet those from the Middle West's Big Ten. The man in front of you and in the row behind, although a Californian in good standing—which means he has been in residence at least 10 years—to your discomfort is wildly rooting for Old Illinois, and successfully as a rule, against the University of California at Los Angeles.

The Queen (her official name is El Pueblo de Nuestra Señora la Reina de los Angeles de Porciúncola, or The Town of Our Lady the Queen of the Angels of Porciúncola), stands on a plain, but her flower-decked skirts sweep from the mountains to the sea. The plain is cut by two rivers, the San Gabriel and the Los Angeles, both of which can be torrential in winter and dusty in summer.

Los Angeles climate has been called Mediterranean and is generally thought of as subtropical. Neither term applies: The country is semi-arid and would support little in the way of vegetation if it were not for water brought in from the Sierra Nevada and the Colorado River, hundreds of miles distant.

In the days of the Dons the pueblo dipped water from the river, but as the population grew (until 1930 it either doubled, tripled, or quadrupled every decade except one) new sources had to be developed. In 1903 the shortage became acute and the city turned to rainmaker Charles Hatfield for relief. Hatfield, who used a system of tanks and acids, produced some rain or at least rain fell, but the next year the problem worsened and Mulholland, the city engineer, went afield on a desperate hunt.

He found water 250 miles away in Owens Valley, Sierra snow water which he brought to the thirsting city by a remarkable engineering feat though the massive conduits were repeatedly dynamited by citizens of the valley not satisfied with the water contracts. This source was adequate until 1923 (population was now reaching toward its second million at the rate of 100,000 new residents a year).

Mulholland began to eye the Colorado River. By the time Boulder Dam was finished, so were the plans to bring Colorado water into Los Angeles, supplying several counties on the way—one of them the county of San Bernardino, the largest in the United States, is considerably larger than Massachusetts, Connecticut, and Rhode Island combined.

These twin sources of water replenished the reservoirs and helped to make Los Angeles County first nationally in agricultural production, first in the raising of eggs. It also helped the orange growers of this and other counties such as Orange, Riverside, and San Bernardino to contest first place in orange production with Florida, a contest which has now been lost. Fifteen years ago orange groves were the dominating feature of Southern California's landscape. Two trees brought from Brazil and planted at Riverside in 1872 grew into hundreds of thousands, waves of blue-green running through the sunny valleys, into the canyons of the San Gabriel, San Bernardino, and Temescal Mountains. In the last six years more than half of this acreage has been bulldozed out to make room for subdivisions.

But the Owens Valley and the Colorado River have not solved the water problem. As subdivisions expand toward the Mexican border, Southern California still needs water. A current project plans to tap the Feather River northeast of San Francisco at a cost of $1,800,000,000.

Another source seems to offer better possibilities. The Pacific Ocean lies offshore, and though Southern California has done nothing toward experimentation, scientists believe that sea water can be desalted and delivered at an economic price. By the time the Feather River Project is completed—in an estimated 12 years—giving the southern half of the state, with 55 percent of the population, only 6½ percent of the available water, it is very likely that a system of desalting will have been invented. Probably by a New Englander (the Maxim Silencer Company of Connecticut leads in the field with a plan to desalt at a cost of 20 cents per 1000 gallons, against a present cost of 6.8 for Colorado water and the probable price of 14 cents for the Feather River Project).

Until ample sources are found, Los Angeles with a predicted population of 5 million by 1970, and Southern California with 15 million, will continue to be dogged by this problem.

Los Angeles has other worries. One is her dependence upon a shifting aircraft industry which employs more than a quarter of a million of her manpower. This worry is balanced by the fact that the area leads the nation in oil refining (early Spanish grants that sold for 25 cents an acre were later found to be floating on lakes of oil), in motion-picture production, in television, and in electronic manufacturing. Los Angeles is second in the manufacture of tires, apparel, and furniture, and has more than 500 companies engaged in producing other products.

Another worry is her lack of an adequate public transportation system, which results in the bulk of the population's traveling by automobile. Streets are clogged at peak hours. Freeways are lined bumper to bumper for miles, so that it seems possible that the whole traffic complex will one day come to a grinding halt, drivers and passengers disembarking and seeking their homes on foot, there to wait for more inventive times.

Flipsters have called Los Angeles many things. Such mellifluous and sweetly snide names as "The Old Lady from Dubuque" and "Iowa by the Sea." But of all the names, the one that has real point is "Ten Suburbs in Search of a City." Sprawling into canyons and up watercourses, climbing hills, sending out a tentacle nine miles long and a half mile wide to grasp the fine harbors of San Pedro and Wilmington, Los Angeles has never had a chance to pause long enough to be a city.

Coming of age with the advent of the automobile (unlike San Francisco), she could afford to build out instead of up. But the horizons are closing down; mountains and the sea and other cities block her way and she is beginning to turn back upon herself. An ordinance limiting the height of buildings has been rescinded; the city will soon change directions and build up instead of out—with less sense of impermanence and dispersal. Her citizens, not yet together long enough to be cohesive, will develop unity. When that occurs, the search for the City of the Western World will have ended.

Photo Credits

1. Black Star
2. National Film Board of Canada
3. Galloway
4. National Film Board of Canada
5. National Film Board of Canada
6. National Film Board of Canada
7. Galloway
8. Gilbert A. Milne
9. Canadian National Railways
10. Photographic Survey, N. F. B. of Canada
11. National Film Board of Canada
12. Canadian National Railways
13. British Columbia Government
14. Philip A. Knowlton
15. Black Star
16. H. Armstrong Roberts
17. Black Star
18. Philip A. Knowlton
19. Black Star
20. Black Star
21. Philip A. Knowlton
22. Galloway
23. Galloway
24. H. Armstrong Roberts
25. Black Star
26. Galloway
27. Rockefeller Foundation
28. Monkmeyer
29. Sargent F. Collier
30. Sargent F. Collier
31. Galloway
32. Western Ways
33. Galloway
34. Black Star
35. Western Ways
36. Standard Oil Co. (N. J.)
37. Tulsa Chamber of Commerce
38. Oklahoma Chamber of Commerce
39. Galloway

40. New Mexico Tourist Bureau
41. Richard Schaus
42. Western Ways
43. Tucson News Service
44. Western Ways
45. New Mexico Tourist Bureau
46. Western Ways
47. New Mexico Tourist Bureau
48. Lambert
49. Va. Dept. of Conservation
50. Newport News Shipbuilding Co.
51. Va. Dept. of Conservation
52. Tennessee Chamber of Commerce
53. Florida State News Bureau
54. Florida State News Bureau
55. Arkansas Parks Commission
56. North Carolina Chamber of Commerce
57. Florida State News Bureau
58. Florida State News Bureau
59. Dept. of Public Relations
60. TVA
61. South Carolina Chamber of Commerce
62. New York State Dept. of Commerce
63. Eastman Kodak Company
64. New York State Dept. of Commerce
65. New York State Dept. of Commerce
66. The Port of New York Authority
67. The Port of New York Authority
68. Cornell University News Bureau
69. Triborough Bridge and Tunnel Authority
70. New York Dept. of Commerce
71. H. Armstrong Roberts
72. Buffalo Chamber of Commerce
73. Lambert
74. Maryland Dept. of Information
75. Sargent F. Collier
76. N. J. Dept. of Conservation
77. Dupont Company
78. Galloway
79. Delaware State Development Dept.
80. Johns Hopkins University
81. H. Armstrong Roberts
82. American Bridge Division, USS
83. Pittsburgh Chamber of Commerce
84. Atlantic City Press Bureau
85. Vermont Development Commission
86. Harvard University
87. Smith College News Office
88. Vermont Development Commission
89. H. Armstrong Roberts
90. Quonset Point
91. Galloway
92. Arthur Griffin
93. H. Armstrong Roberts

94. H. Armstrong Roberts
95. H. Armstrong Roberts
96. Dave Lawler
97. Union Pacific Railway
98. S. C. Johnson & Son
99. Wisconsin Dept. of Agriculture
100. University of Wisconsin
101. U. S. Steel Co.
102. Eli Lilly & Co.
103. Firestone
104. Mackinac Bridge Authority
105. Michigan Dept. of Economic Development
106. Cincinnati Chamber of Commerce
107. U. S. Army
108. Cleveland Chamber of Commerce
109. Illinois Departmental Service
110. Missouri Resources Division
111. Div. of Nebraska Resources
112. Missouri Resources Division
113. Missouri Resources Division
114. Div. of Nebraska Resources
115. North Dakota Chamber of Commerce
116. South Dakota Highway Commission
117. Dept. of Business Development, St. Paul
118. Iowa Development Commission
119. Iowa Development Commission
120. Iowa Development Commission
121. U. S. D. A.
122. U. S. D. A.
123. South Dakota Dept. of Highways
124. Northern Pacific Railway
125. Western Ways
126. Great Northern Railway
127. Western Ways
128. Utah Chamber of Commerce
129. Galloway
130. Bureau of Reclamation
131. Publicity Dept. of Colorado
132. Bureau of Reclamation
133. U. S. D. A.
134. Western Ways
135. Union Pacific Railway Co.
136. Boeing Airplane Co.
137. Bureau of Reclamation
138. Oregon Highway Dept.
139. Northern Pacific Railway
140. Portland Chamber of Commerce
141. Oregon Highway Dept.
142. Bureau of Reclamation
143. U. S. D. A.
144. Galloway
145. Kern County Board of Trade
146. Galloway
147. Los Angeles Chamber of Commerce